MARCEL PROUST

This full-scale portrait brings to life one of the greatest of modern writers. A frequenter of the "Great World" — a member of fashionable *salons* and a participant in the glittering society of the 90's — a born writer, so obsessed with his work that his devotion to it literally brought on an early death — a life-long victim of debilitating attacks of asthma, hayfever, crippling allergies — often generous, tender, thoughtful, at other times malicious and calculating — a man of a hundred friends and of multiple feuds — a vigorous supporter of Dreyfus, an acknowledged snob — this was Marcel Proust.

But, beyond this, he was possessed of staggering genius. Born just after the siege of Paris in 1870, he died in 1922, during the aftermath of the first World War. In his lifetime, the fabric of French life was completely transmuted. In his work, Proust celebrated his own experience and shared it with generations of readers. Out of the events of his personal life — the parties, the feuds, the affections, the crises — he forged a new kind of novel, a work in which the new psychological knowledge was for the first time applied to fiction, in which the subconscious plays as large a part as overt experience, in which the very flow of time is captured and, for a moment, held in check.

In drawing his portrait, Dr. Barker has paid close attention to the autobiographical elements in Proust's masterpiece, *Remembrance of Things Past,* and what they reveal of the author's thought. He has also consulted Proust's voluminous correspondence, his notebooks and memoranda. Of special interest is the evidence gathered from the recently published novel *Jean Santeuil,* a "lost" early work of Proust, of which biographers heretofore had no knowledge.

A significant, richly documented study of a man of genius.

Marcel Proust

A BIOGRAPHY

By RICHARD H. BARKER

The Universal Library

GROSSET & DUNLAP, INC.

NEW YORK

Preface

WRITERS, according to Proust, have two lives, quite different from one another. They have a life in the real world when, like other people, they talk too much or dine out too often or neglect their families, and they have a life in the world of the imagination when they write their books. Proust was probably thinking of himself; in any case he certainly had two lives, rather more radically different than those of most writers and also, paradoxically, rather more strikingly similar.

One life, the real one, is revealed in his letters. Many hundreds of these letters have now been published and, taken together, they form a record very much like that of Pepys's diary or Boswell's journal. Comparatively uneventful and necessarily somewhat repetitious, they are remarkably revealing nevertheless. They enable us to follow Proust, sometimes almost day by day, for many years and to see him much as his friends must have seen him. His personality emerges as a very complex and a very neurotic one, not altogether attractive and yet in some ways very attractive, in any case very human and very real. I have tried to portray the Proust of the letters, with, from time to time, considerable help from the letters themselves. If I have not been altogether "objective"—for I have permitted myself to show what I think of Proust—I have at least avoided having theories about him. I have confined myself to what he actually did and I have left to psychiatrists (preferably amateur psychiatrists, who are always so very willing) the task of providing the explanations.

The other life, the one that Proust created for himself when he wrote, I have touched on more briefly. I have had something to say about most of his early pieces and about the various versions of his novel. In these passages I have been inclined to accept Proust's view that the process of artistic creation is an incompletely conscious one and to suppose that this was true in his own case. Hence I have not attached too much importance to his theories, even the ones developed at such length toward the end of *A la Recherche du temps perdu*. It seems to me that involuntary memory, for example, has some of the elements of the literary hoax, and I cannot help regretting that Proust's admirers have given the doctrine such prominence. Proust was not a philosopher and no amount of interpretation will ever turn him into one, but he was a very great novelist and deserves to be represented as such.

Though I have not specified my obligations in footnotes, it will be quite clear, I am sure, that I have relied on many predecessors, among whom I should perhaps single out Feuillerat, Kolb, and Vigneron. Several of my friends, especially Professor Armand Bégué, Professor Jeanne Grosjean, and Dr. Conrad Rosenberg, have given me very valuable help.

Canada Lake, New York.   R. H. BARKER

Acknowledgments

The author is indebted to:

Doubleday & Company, Inc., for permission to use material from Proust's *Pleasures and Days and Other Writings,* Copyright © 1957 by F. W. Dupee and Barbara Dupee, Copyright 1948 by Lear Publishers, Inc. Reprinted by permission of Doubleday & Co., Inc., and Librairie Gallimard. All rights reserved.

Librairie Gallimard for permission to use material from Proust's *Chroniques, Lettres à Reynaldo Hahn,* and *Lettres à la NRF,* from Lucien Daudet's *Autour de soixante lettres de Marcel Proust,* from Louis de Robert's *Comment débuta Marcel Proust,* and from *Hommage à Marcel Proust.* All rights reserved.

Editions Bernard Grasset for permission to use material from Gabriel Astruc's *Le Pavillon des fantômes* and from Robert Dreyfus's *Souvenirs sur Marcel Proust.*

La Guilde du Livre for permission to use material from *Lettres de Marcel Proust à Bibesco.*

Harcourt, Brace and Company, Inc., for permission to use material from Harold Nicolson's *Peacemaking, 1919* and from Clive Bell's *Proust.*

Alfred A. Knopf, Inc., for permission to use material from André Gide's *Journals,* edited by Justin O'Brien.

Librairie Plon for permission to use material from Proust's *Correspondance générale,* volumes 1-6, and *Correspondance avec sa mère,* and from Proust and Jacques Riviere's *Correspondance.*

Random House, Inc., for permission to use material from *Remembrance of Things Past* by Marcel Proust. Copyright 1924, 1925, 1927, 1929, 1930, 1932, and renewed 1951, 1952, 1955, 1956, 1957 by Random House, Inc.

Marie Scheikévitch for permission to use material from her *Time Past*.

Simon and Schuster, Inc., for permission to use material from Proust's *Jean Santeuil*.

La Table Ronde for permission to use material from François Mauriac's *Du Côté de chez Proust* and from Paul Morand's *Journal d'un attaché d'ambassade*.

Contents

MARCEL PROUST

A *Biography*

CHAPTER I

Childhood

I

IN AUGUST, 1870, Prussian armies swept across the French frontier and swiftly inflicted on the French a series of crushing defeats. The Emperor was captured and the Empress escaped to England; the Imperial Government collapsed. While these catastrophic events were in progress, a French physician named Achille-Adrien Proust was making news that might, in less troubled times, have attracted some attention in Paris. In August—it was one of the last acts of the Imperial Government—he was awarded the Legion of Honor; and in September, just as the defeat of Sedan became known, he was married.

Dr. Proust was a tall man, with a strong, handsome face, an impressive black beard, and a pince-nez which he habitually wore, not quite straight, on the end of his nose. He was the son of a shopkeeper in Illiers, a small town not far from Chartres. In records at Illiers his ancestors are mentioned as early as the sixteenth century, sometimes as bailiffs of the town and retainers of the local aristocracy, the lords of Illiers and Méréglise. A young man of considerable promise, Achille-Adrien Proust had been sent first to Chartres and then to Paris for his education. Afterwards he had

practiced medicine in the capital, and begun making a study of
public health, especially the problems involved in cholera epi-
demics. At the age of thirty-five he had been asked by the government to investigate the spread of cholera in southern Russia and
to see what could be done in Persia to stop it. He had traveled
through wild country and interviewed local authorities; he had
been received by the King of Persia in Teheran and by the Grand
Vizir of Turkey in Constantinople. When he returned to Paris he
had brought with him information of considerable value, subsequently published at length in *Le Journal officiel*. It was for this
mission that he was honored, just before his marriage, by the
Empress-Regent Eugénie.

His bride, Jeanne-Clémence Weil, was a member of a Jewish
family, originally from Alsace-Lorraine, now settled in Paris. Her
father, Nathé Weil, was a wealthy stock broker, and her bachelor
uncle, Louis Weil, was also well-to-do; so that she was, if not
exactly an heiress, at least a very good match. An intelligent and
well-educated girl, she played the piano and knew languages—
English and German, even some Latin and Greek. She read a great
deal, and was indeed inclined to be somewhat bookish and shy.
But within the family circle she showed a lively sense of humor
and a great deal of charm. Though no beauty, she had a particularly
sympathetic face and fine large eyes.

The first year of the Prousts' married life was not an easy one.
They endured the siege of Paris and meanwhile worried about
their mothers, especially Dr. Proust's mother, about whom they
had, for a while, no news at all. (Dr. Proust sent out an urgent
inquiry by balloon asking for a reply by carrier pigeon.) Later they
endured the second siege when the Commune was proclaimed and
the forces of the National Assembly attacked the city. Barricades
were thrown up in the quarter where they lived; artillery swept
the streets and snipers fired from housetops. On his way to the
Hôpital de la Charité, Dr. Proust once came very close to losing
his life.

Either during the fighting or shortly after it was over, his wife
went to the home of her uncle in Auteuil, a suburb of Paris; here,
on July 10, 1871, her first son was born. He was named, in the
French fashion, Valentin-Louis-Georges-Eugène-Marcel.

II

The child was delicate, at first so delicate that he was not expected to live. He developed into a sweet, tender, timid, and emotional baby. He clung to his parents even more than other children, he demanded affection from morning till night. Watching him or even looking at him, one might have thought him an unusually pretty little girl. He had a small mouth, a finely modeled nose, large eyes like his mother's, and thick blond hair.

As he grew older and as his affections became fixed, he distinguished sharply between his parents. He respected his father, a tirelessly energetic and efficient man who went from one professional triumph to another. The doctor was indeed indefatigable. He carried on a practice; he wrote books; he attended as technical adviser a series of international conferences; he became Inspector General of Public Health in France and Professor of Public Health at the University of Paris. At the same time he was doing what he could to get a seat in the Academy of Moral and Political Sciences, which he hoped—in vain, as it turned out—to make the crowning triumph of a brilliant career. The child, listening to reports of his father's achievements, felt happy and proud. Yet their relationship was never close and there was often friction between them.

The boy, already a dreamer, inevitably shrank from the man of action and inevitably centered his affection on his mother, whose warmer, more sympathetic nature invited the intimacy that he craved. He never tired of flinging himself into her arms, embracing her, and smothering her with kisses. When he did his lessons he kept her beside him; when he went to bed he made her lie down in his room, so that he could feel the comfort of her presence as long as he was awake. On evenings when she went out he was inconsolable. He wondered what he would do if he ever lost her; he decided that he would kill himself. Once, when she asked him what he wanted for New Year's, he answered, "Your affection." "But my little numskull," she said, "you always have that; I want to know what sort of present you would like." Some years later he once heard about a boy who, finding his mother badly dressed, pretended that she was one of the maids. Marcel, thinking no doubt of his own mother, put his hands over his face and wept.

The Prousts lived near the Champs-Elysées, and in the afternoon the child was often sent to a kind of playground there. He was not in the least athletic, and he showed a distinct preference for girls as companions. The one to whom he was most deeply attached was Marie de Benardaky, daughter of a distinguished Russian. He loved her desperately, hopelessly, without reservation. He followed her about and played the games that she played; he was even ready to die for her sake. Finally, his parents became alarmed at his antics and wisely kept him from the playground when the girl was there. He made scenes. He felt that he would never forget Mademoiselle de Benardaky, and indeed he never did. Years later, when she was the wife of the Prince Michel Radziwill, he still spoke of her as the great love of his youth.

Every spring and summer the Proust family—including a second son, Robert, born two years after Marcel—went away on vacations, sometimes to hotels at watering places and sometimes to the homes of close relatives, the Amiots in Illiers or Louis Weil in Auteuil.

Madame Amiot was Dr. Proust's sister; she seems to have been either an invalid or a hypochondriac. Her husband, a prosperous draper, made a hobby of gardening. He put some effort into the little enclosed plot of ground behind his house in the Rue du Saint Esprit—it had flowers, statuettes, and a palm tree—but he spent most of his time cultivating a park on the outskirts of the town. He called it, after a section of the Bois de Boulogne, the Pré Catelan.

Marcel's routine in the house on the Rue du Saint Esprit in Illiers was quite different from his routine in Paris. On cold mornings he read before the fire in the dining room. He sat facing the mantelpiece, the clock, the calendar, and the painted dishes on the wall. From time to time he could hear the pump in the garden, and through the window he could see the pansies in their beds beside the garden path. As noon approached, the cook set the table, the family gathered, and he was obliged to lay his book aside. After lunch he went upstairs to his own room, a little old-fashioned room with a clock under glass, a *prie-dieu*, and a picture of Prince Eugène. On the backs of the chairs were antimacassars crocheted in rose patterns; on the chest of drawers was a white lace cover on which stood two vases, a figure of the Savior, and a twig of boxwood. A pair of white curtains concealed the bed; no fewer than three pairs of curtains hung before the window, through whose small red panes, however, a scarlet light entered, dyeing the curtains pink and painting strange patterns on the walls. Here, in the afternoons, Marcel went on with his book; here, in the evenings, he waited for his mother to give him his good-night kiss; and here, when she was away or occupied with guests, he experienced the anguish of separation, got up, paced the floor, and counted the chimes of the church clock, so loud that they seemed to be ringing from the roof above his head.

In fine weather Marcel took walks with his family through the town and into the countryside beyond. He saw the market place, where his grandfather had once lived and where his uncle now had his shop. He saw the gray walls and the angular tower of the Church of Saint Jacques, where the Illiers, the patrons of his ancestors, had once worshiped. Inside the church he saw the blue-and-gold Illiers coat of arms, the seats reserved for the family in the Lady Chapel, and the figures of Miles and Florent d'Illiers in stained glass beside those of the Savior and the patron saints of the church, Saint Jacques and Saint Hilaire. On their longer excursions the Prousts saw or heard about places with names that were wonderfully interesting to the boy—Tansonville, Méréglise, Mirougrain, Bailleau-le-Pin, Saint-Loup, Martinville, Vieuxvicq, Rachepelière, Crécy, Chenonville, Montjouvin, and Chantepie. But more often they went only so far as the Pré Catelan, where there were paths and lawns, a small stream that broadened out into an artificial pond, a tiny bridge, and a summer house. Here Marcel played with his brother Robert, or helped his uncle with the gardening, or wandered off by himself to the farther reaches of the park where he had a favorite hornbeam tree. Sometimes, leaving the park altogether, he followed a country lane bordered on one side by hawthorns and on the other by fields where poppies and cornflowers grew.

Illiers was some distance from Paris; Auteuil was so close at hand that the family could stay there and still carry on normal activities—Dr. Proust could go to the Charité or the Hôtel Dieu, and Marcel could go to school by train or bus. The house was larger and more pretentiously furnished than the house of the Amiots. There was a billiard room; in Marcel's room there were curtains of Empire-blue satin and in the dining room there were knife rests—which Marcel found quite fascinating—of prismatic crystal. The family group was larger, too. Marcel's uncle Georges Weil often stayed in the house, and his grandfather and grandmother came at least for the day. The dinners were veritable gatherings of the Weil family, three generations being represented. The eldest, Louis and Nathé, expressed solidly conservative views about business or politics and thus set a good example to the youngest, Marcel and Robert. On warm evenings the conversation went on under the lime trees in the garden.

III

Marcel's health continued to be very uncertain. He had indigestion, and his parents were constantly cautioning him about his diet. He had hay fever during the spring, the pollen season; and when he was nine years old he developed asthma.

His first attack, a very severe one, came on as he was returning from a walk in the Bois de Boulogne. After this he had persistent attacks, and indeed was seldom quite free from them for any length of time. Anxiety or overexertion or a sleepless night might bring one on, as might exposure to dust, dampness, perfume, or smoke, for he had a formidable number of allergies. When he was reasonably well his mother watched over him, and when he was ill she nursed him, so that he became even more dependent upon her. Once at least when he was kept indoors she slept in his room to console him. He was indeed consoled; he began to wish that he might always live so, shut up with his mother, secure in the warmth of her affection.

His indigestion and his asthma were from the beginning accompanied, or complicated, by certain psychological difficulties. More emotional than other children, he was also more completely the plaything of his emotions. He had no sense of proportion; he threw himself too ardently into what he was doing at the moment. He had no stability; he was too easily elated and angered, heartbroken and depressed. When his mother left him for a few days, he wept hysterically. When she refused him what he wanted, he had tantrums during which he was apt to smash things. Perhaps if his parents had been firmer with him he would have learned more self-control. On the other hand, he was a difficult problem for them and they certainly did the best they could. They knew how precarious his health was and they were afraid the discipline appropriate for normal children might in his case prove injurious.

In general, however, his parents had much to be thankful for, since Marcel was obviously a gifted boy, precocious in his intellectual life and correct in his ideas to the point of priggishness. When he was about thirteen, he jotted down some highly characteristic answers in an album belonging to a family friend.[1] He listed his favorite occupations as "reading, daydreaming, verse, history, and the theatre." Under the heading, "Your favorite qualities in man" he put intelligence and moral sense; under "Your favorite qualities in woman," sweetness, freedom from affectation, and intelligence; under "Your pet aversion," people who have no feeling for what is right, who are insensitive to the pleasures of affection. He explained that his idea of happiness was to live near those he loved, close to nature, with a supply of books and musical scores, and not too far from a French theatre; that his idea of misery was to be parted from Mama. "If not yourself, who would you be?" the album asked. Marcel was not sure. "Never having had to consider the question," he wrote, "I prefer not to answer it. Nevertheless, I should very much like to have been Pliny the Younger."

Suggestions of the same priggishness and the same intellectual interests appear in a letter he wrote to his grandmother, Madame Weil, perhaps a year after he annotated the album. He was staying at Salies-de-Béarn with his mother and a very beautiful young friend of his mother's, Madame Anatole Catusse. This lady—afterwards destined to play an important part in Marcel's life—was teasing him by promising to sing him a song if he would describe her in a letter. "That means nothing to you, does it?" Marcel wrote to his grandmother. "But if you had heard yesterday a certain

1. The album was, rather oddly, an English one, but Proust's answers were of course written in French.

voice, deliciously pure and marvelously dramatic, you, who know
how deeply affected I am by singing, you would understand why,
when I am urged to rejoin some friends who are playing croquet,
I sit down . . . to describe Madame C[atusse]." Professing em-
barrassment, swearing affectedly by Artemis the white goddess and
by Pluto the god with fiery eyes, he dashed off a few commonplaces about beautiful black hair, a delicate skin, and a shapely
figure. But the description seemed hopeless; he stopped and addressed his grandmother a little more naturally. "The conversation
of Madame C[atusse]," he wrote, "has reconciled me to my numerous troubles and to the boredom that Salies arouses in one who
hasn't enough 'double muscles,' as Tartarin says, to go out into
the fresh air of the surrounding countryside and seek the grain of
poetry necessary to existence, poetry alas entirely absent on the
terrace, devoted to chatter and tobacco smoke, where we pass our
lives. I bless the immortal gods for bringing here a woman so intelligent, so astonishingly well informed, who studies so many
subjects and who is so remarkably charming, 'mens pulcher [sic]
in corpore pulchro.' "

CHAPTER II

The Lycée Condorcet
and the Army

I

FROM THE AGE of eleven until he was eighteen Proust attended the Lycée Condorcet. He was a good student and he often won honors, but he was apparently kept at home so much by ill health that his progress was somewhat irregular. In 1884, for example, he was behind, and in 1887 he was behind again; but in some way or other he managed to make up lost ground.

His associations at the lycée were at first far from happy. He was ill at ease with the other boys, who seemed to him insensitive and rude, difficult to approach and even more difficult to understand. When he showed his good will by flattering them or writing sonnets on their beauty or promising eternal fidelity, their response was usually disconcerting. One boy, whose hand he seized in a moment of impulsive ardor, shrank away in fear; others drove him off with insults or threatened to give him a thrashing.

He could not be sure why they disliked him; the boys themselves could not be quite sure. But, for one thing, he was too girlish for their taste—too polite, too tender, too effusive, and too

11

insinuating. He even looked like a girl. He was small and frail, with narrow drooping shoulders and delicate limbs, oddly double-jointed. When he walked, he glided, and when he joined a group of boys in the courtyard at school, he seemed to appear mysteriously like a spirit. He had an odd habit of tilting his head diffidently to one side. His hair was now quite dark, and his eyes, dark too, were very large and rather wistful. An adult might well have described him as a boy with a tendency toward inversion, but the other boys at school saw only that he was in some way different from themselves and therefore objectionable. They saw, too, that his fine manners and his delicacy were to some extent deceptive, that actually there was a hard, aggressive element in his nature. He demanded attention and admiration, especially when these were difficult to get; he was outrageously jealous of attention paid to others. When an older boy once gave him a photograph inscribed "To my best friend except X," Proust was heartbroken. He could not bear to be second best and was not satisfied until the boy had considerately canceled the qualifying phrase.

Among the acquaintances Proust made at the lycée were several very talented boys whom he was to see at least casually for the rest of his life. One was Jacques Bizet, son of the composer of *Carmen*; another was Daniel Halévy, son of the author of *L'Abbé Constantin*; and still another—one of the most persistent of Proust's correspondents in later years—was the future journalist, Robert Dreyfus.

If he was not always on the best terms with his schoolmates, Proust found consolation in the society of older women, often rather smart women, whom he was already beginning to prefer. He met them as best he could, through family friends and acquaintances at school; he put in a good deal of effort winning their good will and fishing for invitations. When he was lucky or persistent enough, he was invited to houses he considered really good, once at least to the Princesse de Wagram's. The evening was a triumphant one, or would have been had not his parents behaved so churlishly. They were so indifferent to his success that they refused to let him take out the family carriage and even refused to give him money for a cab. Humiliated and despondent, with the collar of his overcoat turned up over his white shirtfront and only a rose from the garden—a rose without tinfoil!—in his buttonhole, he caught the omnibus that passed by the door and rode like a poor relation to the *hôtel* on the Avenue de l'Alma.

Proust was remarkably precocious about social life, snobbish at an age when other boys were still playing games. He was also precocious about sex. He once went to a brothel in the Latin Quarter, reporting afterwards, somewhat melodramatically, that he had left with the inmates part of his moral being. He made awkward but apparently persistent attempts at seduction. Told by Daniel Halévy about a beautiful dairymaid in Montmartre, Proust insisted on seeing her at once. Together they went to her shop, stood before the door, and stared. "She *is* very beautiful," Proust whispered, "as beautiful as Salammbô." Then, after a pause, he added, "Do you suppose I could sleep with her?" Halévy was startled, for the idea had never even occurred to him. As they walked away he watched Proust, who was obviously thinking hard, trying to decide how the seduction should be carried out. Finally Proust said, "We ought to take her flowers." A few days later they again went to the dairy, carrying with them a bouquet of roses. Halévy waited outside while Proust entered the shop and confronted the woman as beautiful as Salammbô. He offered her the roses: she smiled and shook her head. He insisted: she took a step forward and he took a step back. Deliberately, step by step, she advanced and he retreated, out through the door and into the street again. She was still smiling when he and his companion left.

If the seductions came off badly, Proust was able to satisfy at least part of his curiosity by scraping up acquaintances with famous courtesans—dazzling women, floridly dressed, who appeared in the afternoons on the Allée des Acacias and the Avenue du Bois. They were the darlings of the age, very decorative, very generally admired, and—except perhaps in middle-class circles—very close to being respectable. One of these, and presumably the one he got to know first, was the celebrated Madame Laure Hayman, who was almost an institution in his family. She had apparently once been the mistress of his great-uncle, Louis Weil, and she was now suspiciously well acquainted with his father. Proust admired her because she seemed to him so extremely smart. She dressed magnificently in shimmering gowns, deliciously flounced and embellished with ropes of pearls, in dashing hats, flowered and feathered, set at rakish angles. She was in fact the smartest woman he knew. He admired her, furthermore, because her career seemed to him a romantic one. She had lived hard, she had distributed her favors rather widely and yet with a good deal of discrimination. She had slept with the best people in Europe, not excluding the King of Greece and the Duc d'Orléans. She still received such men at her house in the Rue La Pérouse, and—it was not the least of her attractions—she could introduce them to her young admirer. It is said that she once sent him a copy of Paul Bourget's sketch of her called "Gladys Harvey," the copy being bound in the silk of one of her petticoats. Proust wrote out flattering comments on the piece and had them forwarded to the author, but in this case an introduction could not immediately be arranged. Bourget, though gracious, confined himself to a written acknowledgment.

II

In his last years at the Lycée Condorcet Proust was perhaps a little less unpopular than he had been before. The other boys were growing up; they were better able to appreciate a precocious companion, affected and effeminate no doubt, but undeniably talented. If they still ridiculed him when he described the fine gentlemen he had met at Madame Hayman's, they listened with respect when he talked about books, for they recognized that his insight was superior to their own.

This superiority was apparent in the classroom during his last year but one at the lycée, when he studied under Maxime Gaucher, a popular professor of rhetoric and leading critic on *La Revue bleue*. The themes that Proust wrote for Gaucher scarcely seemed to be the work of a schoolboy. They were mature in judgment, acutely analytical, and—if one may generalize from the single surviving example—completely unparagraphed. Gaucher and many of the boys in the class were delighted, for they felt that they were in the presence of a born writer. Gaucher encouraged Proust to follow his inclinations, even apparently at the expense of the paragraphing. The boys paid him the compliment of attempting to imitate his manner. There were, however, distinct signs of hostility in the class. Some boys scoffed; Cucheval, the other professor of rhetoric, persistently stormed; and the Inspector General from the University, who once heard Proust read his latest theme, was visibly shaken. "Is there not," he asked, "a boy at the bottom of the class who can write French more clearly and more correctly?" But Gaucher defended his protégé's daring, and at the end of the year his opinion prevailed. Proust took the *premier prix des nouveaux* in French composition, as well as *accessits* in Latin and Greek.

In the summer of 1888—the summer following his course under Gaucher—Proust remained at Auteuil while his mother and brother went to Salies-de-Béarn. At the moment of parting he was highly emotional, and he wept for many hours afterwards. His grandparents shook their heads, and his great-uncle Louis announced sententiously that the exhibition was a form of egotism. It was not—Uncle Louis was wrong—but it was not perhaps much more than the violent expression of a temporary mood. The next morning Proust set out for the Bois, intending, not to brood there, but to read Loti. As he walked he felt so exhilarated by the sunshine and the pleasure of moving his limbs that he could not help crying out for joy.

Proust's summer at Auteuil was on the whole a pleasant, and even an exciting one. He visited friends out of town, he exchanged photographs with a famous courtesan, and he carried on a perfunctory love affair with a girl he had met at a dancing school. Through his letters describing these activities runs the strain of affectation to which the boys at the lycée had objected. He was a little too self-conscious, a little too much inclined to dramatize himself as a dashing and abandoned young fellow. In one letter he insisted that fine weather made him feel like giving way to his impulses. He wanted to be detached or passionate or extravagant or lewd. In particular he wanted to shock people by announcing that he was a decadent but, this pleasure being denied him at the moment, he would go for a drive on the Allée des Acacias, where he would find courtesans too elegant and too ravishing for words. Their gowns would be purple or pink like the sky at six o'clock or blue like still water. Their lips would remind him of Luini's or Botticelli's Virgins, their necks of "those amphorae in which the patient Etruscans reflected their ideal of beauty, their consoling dream of grace."

Along with the affectations, the letters display the writer's habit of brooding over his personal difficulties and speculating about their causes. That summer he was disturbed by certain things that had happened at school, specifically by his difficulties with two of the boys whom he admired most—Daniel Halévy and Jacques Bizet. The facts were clear enough: the boys had cut him completely for a month and then had suddenly begun speaking to him again. But the inferences to be drawn from the facts were by no means clear. "I don't believe that a type is a character," Proust remarked in a letter to Robert Dreyfus. "I *do* believe that what we think we know about a person's character is merely the result of an association of ideas." He went on to say that we tend to oversimplify motivation and to forget that the same actions can be explained equally well in several ways. So with the actions of Halévy and Bizet. The two boys might have been really fond of him but perverse enough to tease him and test his affection. On the other hand, they might have found him intolerable but, having put him in his place, been willing to resume formal relations with him. He could scarcely decide which alternative was the more likely, and so he asked his correspondent to tell him what the two boys were in the habit of saying about him. Did they remark "Proust is rather nice" or "Proust is a bore"? Did they, as a matter of fact, talk about him at all? For as he thought the matter over, it seemed to him that there was still a third alternative. They might scarcely be aware of his existence, they might have no feelings about him whatsoever.

The two boys may have behaved oddly toward Proust, but they were quite willing to accept him as an associate in their literary ventures—little journals that they got out at school. In the autumn of 1888 they made him secretary of *La Revue verte*, so primitive that it was limited to a single manuscript copy, and they invited his contributions to a more ambitious journal, *La Revue lilas*.

Once at least they asked him to criticize a manuscript—a poem by Halévy himself. Proust's standards were high and his criticisms necessarily severe. On the margin he jotted down such comments as "Odious," "Formless," "Idiotic," "Naturalistic, ergo stupid," and "Good image unskillfully developed." At the end he gave Halévy a little lecture on taste, advising him to study the classics, from Homer to Anatole France, cautioning him against insincerity, specifically the kind of insincerity that comes from imitating another's style, and recommending simple and unaffected elegance.

The advice was no doubt a reflection of advice that Proust was giving himself, an indication that in the little pieces he wrote he was himself striving for sincerity. If he failed, if in spite of himself he usually echoed such masters as Jules Lemaître and Leconte de Lisle, he at least showed an artistry in the use of words that was quite beyond an amateur like Halévy. One sees it in a prose sketch that he wrote for *La Revue lilas*, an account of his impressions as he sits in his room at night and suddenly feels himself the center of his little universe. One sees it even more distinctly in a poem, inspired by some of Cuyp's pictures in the Louvre, that he dashed off—or so he later said—while he was waiting for a class to begin. He tried to fix, in precious phrases, the quality of Cuyp's landscapes and to describe the cavaliers with pink complexions and pink-feathered hats as they ride by a herd of cattle dreaming in a mist of pale gold. One realizes, as one reads, that Proust was not yet an original writer; but one realizes, too, that he already had a sense of style that was very close to genius.

He was fascinated by style and he was fascinated—it was another aspect of his complex personality—by abstract speculation. In his last year at the lycée he studied philosophy under Professor Darlu—chiefly idealistic philosophy, for the substance of the course was Kant. This most difficult, most technical, and most exciting of German thinkers was bound to make an impression on precocious boys of seventeen or eighteen years of age. If they understood him very imperfectly, for *The Critique of Pure Reason* is not after all directed to adolescents, they at least had a very able guide in Darlu, who invested the subject with wit, with eloquence, and even with a kind of homely charm, as when he used his top hat, conspicuously placed on a chair, to illustrate the external world in his theory of knowledge.

Proust was profoundly impressed, by Darlu as well as by the doctrine, and it is scarcely too much to say that he formed mental habits that were to remain with him for the rest of his life. In any case he acquired a taste for speculating, somewhat in the Kantian manner, about matter and mind, intuition and intelligence, time and space; he may even have begun working out his own curious and somewhat fanciful views on these subjects, ultimately to be embodied in *Le Temps retrouvé*. At the end of the year he took the most coveted of all the prizes, *le prix d'honneur de dissertation française*.

III

Having graduated from the lycée with his name prominent in the prize list, Proust was determined to set out on a literary career. But he realized that to satisfy his parents, who were practical middle-class people, he would have to adopt a profession. This he was quite prepared to do. He would go on studying a little longer, and in the course of time he would drift into some easy and lucrative employment that would not seriously interfere with his writing. Meanwhile, however, he would have to satisfy the army, in which all Frenchmen were required to serve. The period of service was normally five years, but young men willing to pay for their own equipment and able to show proof of exceptional education were permitted to "volunteer" for one year only. On November 15, 1889, Proust volunteered. He was assigned to the 76th Infantry Regiment, stationed at Orleans.

Obviously he was something of a problem for the army. His delicate physique and his uncertain health scarcely fitted him for the field, and his handwriting was so bad that he could not be kept in the administrative offices of the regiment. He was once classified 63rd in an instruction squad of 64 men. But he was fortunate enough to get special consideration from his commanding officer, and he seems to have got through his training reasonably well. He drilled and he shot off 76s; he made attempts at least at such ex-

ercises as swimming and horseback riding. If he was often tired and
depressed, he apparently had no serious indispositions.

His fits of depression seem, however, to have been rather com-
moner than in Paris. In June, 1890, he went through a spell of
grieving for his grandmother, Madame Nathé Weil, who had died
six months before. He could not at first bring himself to write
home because he knew that his mother was despondent enough
already and he could only tell her that he was spending his days
in tears. The following September, on the other hand, he was
feeling unusually cheerful, even though he had just spent a leave at
one of the seaside resorts where he had once spent vacations with
his grandmother. "My health isn't at all bad (except for my
stomach)," he said in a letter to his father, "and I don't even have
that feeling of general depression for which, this year, my absence
from home has been, if not the cause, at least the excuse—hence
the justification. But I find it very hard to concentrate, to read, to
learn things by heart, to remember them." His mother did what
she could to cheer him up. In her letters to Orleans, written, it
seems, almost daily, she teased him, told him how very few months
of exile really remained, reported on the flowers in bloom at
Auteuil, and quoted appropriate passages from Madame de
Sévigné. His father made helpful suggestions about Marcel's indigestion, urging him in particular to cut down on his consumption
of cream cheese.

His isolation was trying, yet it was by no means complete; he
was often able to spend week ends in Paris. On these occasions
he saw a good deal of a new friend, Gaston de Caillavet, and he
went when he could to the Sunday receptions of Gaston's mother,
the celebrated Madame Arman de Caillavet, patron and mistress
of Anatole France. Observers who saw him in the drawing room
on the Avenue Hoche were struck by his ill-fitting uniform, his
quite unmilitary bearing, and his air of weariness. He seemed completely overcome by his week's exertions in the army. He reclined
rather than sat in an armchair; with one hand he supported his
head and with the other he twirled a suggestion of a mustache.
Yet his eyes moved restlessly about the room, missing nothing that
went on, and his conversation was always lively.

His most questionable action at the Avenue Hoche was carrying on a persistent flirtation with Jeanne Pouquet, Gaston's fiancée. She was very good looking and very intelligent, and though Proust was certainly not trying to break up her engagement, there is no doubt that he was genuinely attracted to her. Once he actually went so far as to suggest that she visit him in Orleans and even proposed to rent a country house where she and her mother could stay. Gaston exploded, but good feelings were immediately restored. Proust appeared as before on Sunday afternoons, stayed much too late, lingered over his farewell speeches as Gaston nervously watched the clock, drove at breakneck speed to the station, and arrived just in time to catch the 7:40 train to Orleans.

CHAPTER III

Literature and Society

WHEN HE FINISHED his year of military service, Proust was more than ever determined to become a writer. But meanwhile, to keep his parents happy, he had to go through the motions of studying for a profession, and so, in November, 1890, he entered the university, taking up both law and political science. It was not clear to him to what profession these subjects would lead, whether the practice of law, or the diplomatic service, or something else; nor was he anxious that it should be clear. The main thing was that the final decision should be put off as long as possible. For the time being his parents let him do as he pleased, and he was able to drift along pleasantly enough, attending lectures and even listening to some of them, but devoting himself chiefly to his real interests, literature and society.

I

For Proust, as for many other young men, literature was itself a social pursuit. Sometimes, no doubt, he wanted to be alone in his room so that he could write little sketches and poems like those he had turned out at the Lycée Condorcet; more often he wanted to discuss what he had written or was about to write. He wanted to meet young men with interests similar to his own and to talk with them about form and technique, principles and ideas, movements and schools. He did meet such young men, a great many of them, as many as he possibly could. He saw them too often and he stayed with them too long. He saw them at the Sorbonne in the morning, at the galleries and in the Bois in the afternoon, and at the *salons*, theatres, or concerts in the evening. He was seldom alone during any of his waking hours. Sometimes at midnight he rode home with a friend in a cab, got out before his parents' door and insisted that his companion get out too, sat down on a bench, and talked until dawn.

For the most part these young men liked him, as the boys at the lycée had not. They realized that he was effeminate, but they were tolerant, they accepted the fact. They realized, too, that he flattered them outrageously, and they found themselves obliged to invent a word for the kind of performance he commonly put on. They called it *proustifying*. But even in this they were inclined to see, not so much an attempt at deception, as deliberate virtuosity. He seemed to be playing a game with them, a delightful game that he played supremely well, and one in which there might after all be an element of sincerity. Perhaps he was flattering them because, for the moment at least, he really admired them so very much; perhaps he treated them with such elaborate politeness because he was so very anxious to have them like him. Certainly he did them favors that they would never have expected from other friends. He showed his affection with almost childlike warmth and directness. When he was with them, he skillfully drew them out, explored their interests, and suffered their misfortunes as if they had been his own. He offered to lend them money though he was always short of money himself; he bought them presents far beyond his means. In their circle, in fact, his goodness became almost legendary and they were fond of telling stories to illustrate it—how he had returned borrowed handkerchiefs carefully packed between two sachets, how he left fantastic tips at restaurants, how he had shown consideration to humble people whom he never expected to see again. Once, before a friend's door, he had helped or tried to help an old servant who was struggling with a heavy package of books. Once, at another friend's, he had discovered that the concierge was ill and had immediately taken over the task of answering the doorbell.

But his goodness was not the only quality that impressed his friends. They liked him for his inexhaustible gaiety, his wild outbursts of pure, childlike joy. He told remarkably amusing stories, mimicked people to perfection, and ridiculed affectation delightfully, suffocating with laughter as he did so, giggling like a girl. They liked him for the variety and the intensity of his interests, for he seemed eager to inform himself about every aspect of human experience. He was quite as curious about the social life in remote provinces as about the habits of servants in Paris. In drawing rooms he regretted that he could not take part in every conversation at once; he wanted to pick everyone's brains, to discover precisely what everyone was thinking. Once, while riding on a bus, he noticed that an attractive woman said something to the conductor before she got out. Proust could not contain his curiosity; he left his seat, slipped a coin into the conductor's hand, and asked what the woman had said. His friends liked him, too, for his remarkable powers of observation, in which they seemed most clearly to recognize his genius. He saw more than they saw because he looked harder and longer. Once, while he was walking through the garden of a country house, he stopped to look at a rose bush, and the friend who was with him discreetly walked on. Later, when the friend had finished a tour of the grounds and returned to the garden, he found Proust still standing on the same spot and still looking at the roses. "His head was bent forward, his expression was serious; he screwed up his eyes and wrinkled his brows slightly as if in an effort of passionate concentration; with his left hand he kept pushing the tip of his little black mustache into his mouth and chewing it." He was studying the roses as few people had ever taken the trouble to study roses before.[1]

The young men who recognized Proust's talent and felt the charm of his personality were for the most part talented themselves and devoted to the arts; they were the most promising figures of the younger generation. Proust liked and admired them all indis-

---

1. In the same way Jean Santeuil is left standing before a rose bush, the narrator in Contre Sainte-Beuve before unidentified flowers or trees, and the narrator in A la Recherche du temps perdu before hawthorns.

criminately, liked them as they liked him, liked them at least for
a short time while their experience seemed fresh and their minds
interesting. Afterwards he deserted them quickly, for his affections,
remarkably warm while they lasted, were also remarkably unstable.
It was said of him that everyone he knew had once been his
friend. Yet he felt hopelessly lost if he did not have a friend every
moment, a very special friend from whom he could scarcely bear
to be separated for more than a few hours at a time. He adored
this special friend and experienced in the relationship a wonderful
exhilaration. In the winter the two young men would see each
other constantly—at home, in the classroom, and in society. In
the summer they would travel together, visit the mountains or the
seacoast, and take walks by Alpine lakes or through forests with
an undergrowth of rhododendrons or along cliffs overlooking the
sea. The friendship, nourished by common experiences, would
seem almost too close, and then suddenly another aspect of Proust's
character would reveal itself. Detecting or seeming to detect signs
of coolness in his friend, he would develop the darkest suspicions.
He would reproach his friend, expostulate with him, and pour out
his grievances in petulant letters. It was apparent that he had little
confidence in human nature and, where he himself was concerned,
little understanding of human motives. But if he was easily disturbed, he was also easily reassured. The storm would subside
almost as quickly as it had arisen; the two men were friends again.
They again traveled together, again saw each other daily in town,
again rode home in a cab late at night, got out before his parents'
house in the Boulevard Malesherbes, and talked interminably in
the darkness.

There was certainly a homosexual element in the closest of
these friendships, for Proust was by this time very much concerned
with love—as he showed in annotating another album of confes-
sions—and very much inclined to associate love with handsome
and effeminate young men. In fact, he specified in the album that
what he liked in men was feminine charm and what he wanted
from them—provided of course they were good-looking enough—
was tenderness. He liked women because, when they were somewhat masculine, they made good companions. On the other hand,
he was still devoted to his mother and the memory of his grand-

mother; he could think of no greater misfortune than having had to live his life without them.

II

If Proust's relations with young men were thus undergoing a profound change, it was certainly not a change that he cared to reveal any more than he could help. He still flirted with girls—Mademoiselle Pouquet, for example. He still flirted, or came close to flirting, with several older women who had solid social advantages to offer him. There was certainly a good deal of cynicism in this gallantry, but there were other things—admiration and affection—too. For he was deeply devoted to Madame Straus, Madame de Chevigné, and others like them, and perhaps able to convince himself that he was seriously in love with them.

Madame Straus was indeed a remarkable woman, one of the most cultivated and most intelligent hostesses in Parisian society. She was by birth a Halévy (or Lévy). She had grown up among men for whom Proust had the profoundest respect. Her father, Fromental Halévy, was the composer of *La Juive*; one of her cousins, Ludovic Halévy, was responsible, with Meilhac and Offenbach, for the famous operettas which had captivated Paris under the Second Empire. At the age of nineteen she had married a brilliant pupil of her father's, Georges Bizet, and had shared with him—though without much enthusiasm, it is said—the disappointments of his brief career. She had witnessed the failure of *L'Arlésienne* and the indifferent reception of *Carmen*. In the sixth year of her marriage she had gone through the agony of her husband's sudden and premature death. Now, at the age of forty, she was married to a wealthy lawyer, Emile Straus, an amiable but unprepossessing man with coarse features, a receding hair line, and an affliction of the eyelids that obliged him to keep his eyes half closed.

The Strauses had a large and luxurious apartment on the Boulevard Haussmann, furnished so consistently with period pieces, real or imitation, that even the elevator was Louis XV and made to resemble a Bath chair. In this apartment Madame Straus nursed herself, for she was afflicted with nervous disorders and indeed had nervous tics; here she anxiously guarded herself against draughts and open windows, for she felt able to breathe only in rooms hermetically sealed; and here, to escape the boredom which was the terror of her existence, she entertained a select circle of friends. The most assiduous and most favored were Jewish intellectuals such as Meilhac, now so gouty and fat that he could seldom tie his shoelaces securely, and Arthur Meyer, editor of *Le Gaulois* and an ardent Royalist, a man with a bald head, a pale face, and a disconcerting stare. But there were others who equally enjoyed the hostess's favor—writers like Hervieu, members of the world of finance like the Rothschilds, and members of the aristocracy like the Comte d'Haussonville and the British Ambassador. The chief attraction of the *salon* was not, however, Meilhac or Meyer or even the British Ambassador; it was Madame Straus herself. She was scarcely the beauty she had been in her youth when Delaunay had painted her portrait, but she had great charm and a delightful wit that was constantly sending her admirers into gales of laughter. Her *bons mots* were repeated everywhere. To a young man who had abused her friends but had promised to let her abuse his, she had remarked simply, "You have friends, then?" Of a handsome woman who was growing fat, she had said, "Madame X is more than a statue; she is almost a group." Her wit, in fact, set the tone in her drawing room. There one rarely discussed literature or politics. One played cards, one engaged in airy persiflage, one waited for the sallies of one's hostess, and one listened as Monsieur Straus—his eyes closed but his face beaming with satisfaction—repeated Geneviève's "latest." One behaved, in short, exactly as if one were in aristocratic society, though as a matter of fact one was still at a considerable distance from the La Trémoïlles and the La Rochefoucaulds.

Proust had known Madame Straus for some time—he had apparently met her, while still at school, through her son, Jacques Bizet—and he had been trying to establish himself in the drawing room on the Boulevard Haussmann. He had made it perfectly clear that he adored, that he worshiped his hostess. He had once listened in rapture as she had sung a song for some of her son's schoolmates; he had wanted to kiss her hand, had hesitated for two months, and then perhaps had finally done it; he had begun addressing her, though she was more than twice his age, in a tone of outrageous gallantry. Now, several years later, his tone was still the same. He could not seem to make up his mind whether he was cultivating her as a hostess or courting her as a woman who might grant him heaven knows what favors, who might be persuaded to enter into some kind of rarefied Platonic relationship. Madame Straus was frequently disconcerted. She found that she had to discourage her young admirer's advances and to keep him at a little distance, if only to prevent him from making a fool of himself. On the other hand, it seems clear that she accepted him as a regular member of her circle.

With Madame de Caillavet, another hostess whom he was carefully cultivating, Proust's tone was different, for Madame de Caillavet was an entirely different sort of person. She was formidable—there could be no doubt about that. She owed her success, not so much to charm and wit, as to self-assurance, ruthlessness, immense energy, and an iron will. She had displayed these qualities all her life—even in her childhood, when she had once attempted to throw her brother out a window because he cried too much; she had explained her action quite frankly by saying, "He is a nuisance." She had displayed them in her relations with her husband, a great strapping fellow with a booming voice, a toothless smile, and a wart on the end of his nose. She had been grateful to him for his name, or rather his names, for he had arbitrarily added de Caillavet to his legal name of Arman. She had been quite willing to encourage him in such little hobbies as gambling and writing a yachting column. But she had never permitted him to interfere with her social life or her love affairs, which she had carried on just as if he had never been there. On the whole he had proved quite tolerable, and if he had occasionally rebelled and made scenes—she herself had a horror of scenes—she had usually known how to reduce him to obedience. She had displayed the same qualities in her relations with her son Gaston, whose education she had directed with characteristic firmness and zeal. She had never given the boy a moment's rest, never permitted him to forget his high destiny and his duty to excel. Even when he had been away on vacations, she had read his letters as though they had been exercises in style. Once, for example, she had been able to

tell him that his latest letter was respectable enough—respectable
but not perfect. "The absence of blots lent doubtless a certain
monotony," she had commented, "but I can endure that without
pain. As for style . . . I should like a little more color. We have
plenty of time in later years to simplify our expression and strip
it of ornamentation. Rhetoric is well suited to youth. Try to read
a little Chateaubriand." The boy had survived the formidable
regimen; he had actually learned how to write; he was already turning out plays lively enough to please the audience in his mother's
drawing room.

Strength of character had helped Madame de Caillavet to
achieve the secret ambition of every middle-class hostess—to capture and to keep for her very own a literary lion, none other than
the King of Beasts himself, the incomparable Anatole France. She
had captured him and she had tamed him; she had succeeded in
transforming a timid bohemian into a magnificent presence and
an inexorable literary machine. Instead of a ragged goatee, he now
wore a handsome imperial, surmounted by carefully waxed mustaches. But this was only the most obvious manifestation of a
change that embraced every aspect of his life, for he was now
ruled by a mistress with a purpose and a plan, a mistress who
foresaw and arranged everything, who attended to the smallest
details. She watched his investments and chose his cravats, dragged
him out for walks designed to improve his health, encouraged him
to write on popular subjects, and fixed his hours of work. Regularly,
every day after lunch at the Avenue Hoche, she led him to their
specially furnished study between her bedroom and the linen
closet. She took her seat at a plain school desk, with her little dog
beside her, and either arranged the great man's notes, or corrected
his proofs, or wrote his letters and articles. He sat beyond the fireplace at a Gothic desk, littered with seals, pens, paper weights,
throat lozenges, scissors, a huge pot of paste, and a silver goblet
ornamented with dancing cupids and skeletons. Sometimes he
wrote; sometimes he teased his mistress—fidgeted, played with the
dog, piled up books on his desk, and dozed off to sleep. But somehow the work went forward, the famous novels appeared, his
reputation and consequently hers was enhanced.

After dinner on Sunday afternoons he took a nap while the

company gathered—politicians, journalists, publishers, writers, the intellectual leaders of France. Monsieur de Caillavet, wearing a curious cravat of enormous proportions, moved about the drawing room, thundering out greetings, shaking hands a little too warmly, and smiling his toothless smile. His wife, elaborately dressed, her fingers covered with rings, a white-and-gold lorgnette in one hand, received sitting in a large armchair. She was a brisk little woman with blue eyes, a double chin, rather too much rouge, and henna-dyed hair. At the appropriate moment the great man awoke, descended the stairs, and entered the room. The talk died down, the chairs were respectfully pushed back. He approached Madame de Caillavet, produced a five-franc bunch of violets, flourished it, kissed it, laid it on his heart, and then presented it to her with an odd little bow. "Take your place by the fire," she said, "so that everyone may hear." He did so, leaned against the marble mantelpiece, and began one of his famous monologues, often one which he had rehearsed before Madame de Caillavet earlier in the day. His manner was formal and his voice unctuous. He went on smoothly, tirelessly, relentlessly. As he talked he stroked his beard or made a motion with his left hand as if he were crumbling bread between his fingers; when he was deeply moved he took out his handkerchief and blew his nose. Occasionally the hostess signaled for applause; occasionally she prompted him to keep going. "Tell us that story I enjoyed so much yesterday," she might say. He would take the cue and go on as unctuously as before. When she felt that the audience had had enough, she permitted informal conversation. Released from his duties, the great man chatted with distinguished guests before the mantelpiece or followed pretty women about the room. He dropped his formal manner, ignored Madame de Caillavet's stern glances, and became once more himself—warm, human, sacrilegious, and obscene.

At luncheons and dinners, when the circle was smaller, the monologues were somewhat less formidable. Celebrities and friends of the family like Proust could sit beside the great man and notice imperfections in his manners that his mistress had not yet succeeded in eliminating. They could even ask questions. "Monsieur France," Proust once asked, "how do you manage to know so much?" "It is quite simple, my dear Marcel," the great man replied. "When I was your age I wasn't good-looking like you; I wasn't a social success; instead of going out in society I stayed at home reading, I never stopped reading." Proust yielded to no one in his admiration of France, and in the course of time he received his reward—a dedication in *L'Etui de nacre* and regular reports about the progress of the current work, *Le Lys rouge*. This novel was a project of Madame de Caillavet's, for she had decided that France should now show his knowledge of high society by writing a smart story of adultery. "But I know nothing about society people," he had said. Nevertheless she had insisted, and he had at last agreed to make the attempt if she would help him as much as she could. In the study upstairs and even at meal times she began assembling the material. She singled out people he might use as models; she considered possible settings. One of the principal scenes, she decided, would have to be at the Opera, for she thought a box an excellent place for a declaration of love and music a fitting accompaniment. "But I have never set foot in the Opera," France said. She shrugged her shoulders. "Were you ever in the cenobies in the desert?" she asked. The heroine was perhaps also a problem, but France himself solved it by making her an idealized portrait of Madame de Caillavet, going so far as to give her Madame de Caillavet's gowns and jewels, even the diamond arrow that she wore in her hair. Gradually the story took shape so that, when Proust came for dinner, Madame de Caillavet could always say, "The novel is going forward." After the meal she instructed the great man to read passages aloud and at appropriate intervals she signaled for applause.

Before it was finished, *Le Lys rouge* acquired a connection with another person in whom Proust was deeply interested—Jeanne Pouquet. She and Gaston were married; Proust, pretending a broken heart, refused to attend the ceremony. Afterwards the young couple joined France and Madame de Caillavet on a trip to Italy, where the latter proposed to collect further settings for the novel. Proust later heard the whole story—how Madame de Caillavet, tireless in her sightseeing, had dragged the party from place to place, even forcing the great man to miss meals; how she had taken notes on scraps of paper and stuffed them into her bag; how France, delighted with the company of young Madame Gaston de

Caillavet, had teased her and insisted on calling her Mademoiselle; how together they had stopped before a shoemaker's stall in Florence, where he had promised to put the shoemaker—and her —into the novel. Thus when *Le Lys rouge* finally appeared, Proust found that it awakened memories, not only of France and Madame de Caillavet, but also of a beautiful girl with whom he sometimes liked to think that he was still hopelessly in love.

III

Early in 1892 Proust and several of his friends decided to found a journal in which they could publish their pieces. They called it, after Plato, *Le Banquet*, and they selected for it a cover in blue with the title in purple. Each of them contributed ten francs a month to the enterprise.

The group included Fernand Gregh, Daniel Halévy, Jacques Bizet, Robert Dreyfus, and Louis de La Salle, as well as Proust himself. Several of them were Jews, several were graduates of the Lycée Condorcet, several were related to or protégés of Madame Straus. But they had little else in common, except perhaps for a vague hostility to Symbolism. They were not really interested in starting a movement or founding a school: they merely wanted to get into print. Through Bizet's friend, Henri de Rothschild, they were enabled to use as a meeting place a room over the shop of the bookseller Rouquette in the Passage Choiseul. They selected three of their number—Proust, Halévy, and Dreyfus—as an editorial committee, but the committee did so little work and Gregh so much that he was soon tacitly recognized as the editor. The journal was certainly not a huge success—its circulation was limited to four hundred copies—but in a sense it grew during its short life, for other young men joined the original group. One of them was the future dramatist, Robert de Flers; another was the future author of *Le Feu*, Henri Barbusse; and still another was a future Premier of France, Léon Blum.

Proust's contributions to *Le Banquet* are too short to be very impressive. Nearly all of them seem to be casual jottings—little anecdotes or essays or reviews that the author dashed off merely to provide copy for the paper. Furthermore, they are all written in a

style that is generally just a little too fastidious, as though the
author were giving way for the time being to a congenital weakness.
An extreme example is the sketch of Cydalise, written characteristically after a party, at which Proust had seen one of the famous
beauties of the day, the Comtesse de Mailly-Nesle, subsequently
Madame Jean de Reszké. His Cydalise is ever so slightly disillusioned, so that everything about her, even the dress that she
wears, takes on a weary grace. Nevertheless she is very beautiful.
Her blond hair is like a delicate gold helmet; her eyes seem to
have absorbed "the fresh purity of mornings and of running water
on the first days of spring." "I should have liked to see you,"
Proust says, "with an ancient goblet in your hand, or rather one of
those beakers with so proud and sad a form, that, empty now in
our museums, hold out their drained bowls with a useless grace,
but that were in other times, like you, the fresh delight of Venetian
feasts, and whose last violets and roses seem still to float in the
limpid current of their frothing and cloudy glass."

There is very little character or narrative interest in the pieces,
an indication perhaps that Proust is still very much the disciple of
the philosopher Darlu. He is nearly always the thinker and the
commentator, concerned either with ideas as such or with the
individuals whose behavior serves to illustrate ideas. In one piece
he analyzes a typical society woman who is committed to like
people a little smarter than she is and to hate those who are not
quite so smart. She can be friendly only with her equals or with
people so much her inferiors that her social sense is not called into
play. In another piece the author tells a little anecdote, but only
to exemplify the general statements with which he begins and
ends. "Ambition is more intoxicating than fame," he says; "desire
makes all things flourish, possession withers them; it is better to
dream one's life than to live it. . . . Life is like this little sweet-
heart. We dream of it and we love it in dreaming of it. But we
must not try to live it." In still another piece—"Violante ou la
mondanité," the longest and most ambitious of Proust's contributions to Le Banquet—he contrasts social life with solitude. The one
is frivolous, vapid, and in the long run boring; the other alone is
fruitful and satisfying.

Gregh and other members of the Banquet group presumably

read with approval the story of Violante, in which Proust deplored the sterility of social life. But they were much less enthusiastic about certain other pieces of his, pieces in which he clearly took a different view and in which, or so they thought, he used the journal to advance his social ambitions. In one of them, for example, he described the Comtesse Adhéaume de Chevigné, a hostess whom he had been trying to cultivate in much the same way that he had cultivated Madame Straus. Madame de Chevigné was a beautiful and charming woman who moved in a social world much more exclusive than the one Proust had so far known—the world of aristocratic society. If he could establish himself in her good graces, he might conceivably explore this world and meet some of its more notable figures—perhaps the Duchesse de La Trémoïlle, with whom Madame de Chevigné regularly played whist; perhaps the Prince de Sagan, the most famous dandy of the age, acknowledged arbiter in matters of dress; perhaps even the Comte Aimery de La Rochefoucauld, punctilious and severe, arbiter in matters of deportment, certain just how many minutes early he should arrive when he dined with a prince of the blood and how many minutes late when he dined with a duke whose family had made, a century or two before, a deplorable misalliance. The possibilities were infinitely exciting, but unfortunately Madame de Chevigné was elusive. Proust did what he could to inform himself about her habits and hours, then waited patiently near her house and flung himself in her path if he was fortunate enough to see her when she emerged—dressed in a smart tailored suit and a hat with a tiny veil—for her daily walk in the Champs-Elysées. But the results were much the same whether he met her or failed to meet her: she was always otherwise engaged.

The portrait in *Le Banquet* was apparently another attempt to attract her attention, a deliberate piece of flattery. Like a society painter, like his celebrated contemporary Boldini, Proust undertook to catch and fix his sitter's mysterious charm. He admitted that her beauty was not of the purest type, that her nose was too long and too firmly arched, that her skin was too delicate, and that her upper lip was too thin. But he saw, in the shape of her head, in the firmness of her glance, and even in the line of her nose, a delicate grace unequaled by other society beauties, a grace that seemed to him distinctly birdlike. He sketched her as she sat in her box at the theatre, wearing a filmy white dress and long white gloves, supporting her head on one arm, which rested on the railing of the box, and waving before her her feathered fan like a delicate white wing. He remembered recognizing, in her sons and nephews, the same birdlike features, and it seemed to him that the family must originally have sprung from the union of a goddess and a bird.

If Madame de Chevigné could have foreseen that the piece would appear again, years later, embedded in a famous description of the Duchesse de Guermantes at the opera, she might well have been flattered. But at the moment she received it rather coolly—possibly because she was not anxious to be written up by social climbers in obscure little magazines, possibly because she was unhappy about the reference to her origin. For she was by birth a Sade, a member of a family that had produced, not only Petrarch's Laura, but more recently a deplorable marquis whose sensational career and notorious fondness for unnatural unions perhaps made Proust's remarks seem ambiguous and indelicate. But whatever Madame de Chevigné may have thought, Gregh was clearly annoyed. *Le Banquet* was not a society journal, he was not eager to print articles flattering beautiful women. For the time being he restrained himself, but when Proust wrote another piece open to similar objections Gregh appended a sharp little note disassociating *Le Banquet* from the opinions expressed.

Nevertheless Proust was probably writing or planning other flattering pieces, and—if he had not been afraid of offending her—he would pretty certainly have done a full-length portrait of Madame Straus. He repeatedly sketched her character in letters, always a little querulously to show that he loved her as much as ever. "At first I thought that you liked only beautiful things and that you really understood them," he told her in one of them, "—and then I saw that you didn't care about them at all; then I thought that you liked people, and I see now that you don't care about them either. I am convinced that you like only a certain kind of life which shows off your intelligence less than your wit, your wit less than your tact, and your tact less than your clothes."

"You think one dissipates one's charm by being too friendly," he told her in another, "and I believe you are right. But I am going to tell you what happens to you. . . . If a person talks to you about books, you find him pedantic; if he talks to you about people, you find him indiscreet (if stories are involved) and inquisitive (if he asks questions); if he talks about you, you find him ridiculous. So a hundred times he is on the point of finding you much less charming, when suddenly you grant him a little favor, which seems to show that you like him a little, and he is devoted to you again. But you are not sufficiently aware of this truth (I doubt if you are aware of any truths), that *many concessions must be made in Platonic love*. A person who isn't sentimental at all becomes strangely so when he is reduced to Platonic love. Since I want to follow your charming precepts about bad form, I shall not be specific."

While *Le Banquet* ran, Proust was collaborating on a novel in letter form with three of his fellow contributors, each of whom was responsible for a different character. Gregh was doing a poet, Halévy an abbé, La Salle a man of the world, and Proust himself a young woman. No part of this extraordinary performance has survived.

CHAPTER IV

Montesquiou

I

WHILE HE WAS WRITING for *Le Banquet* and cultivating exciting hostesses, Proust was also leading a more pedestrian life at home, trying to conciliate his parents who had serious misgivings about his social activities, and trying to put up with the hardships imposed by the university. In the summer of 1892, for example, he was faced with one of the worst of such hardships: a series of examinations. He missed a party at Madame Hayman's, and expressed his regret by sending her chrysanthemums with particularly long stems; he was afraid that he would have to miss one of Madame Straus's divine Saturdays. "I have passed so far," he said in his note to Madame Straus, "and I hope to pass again tomorrow so that I can show you how wrong you are in thinking me lazy or preoccupied with social success. Actually I have worked very hard."

His hopes were premature for, though he passed in political science, he seems to have failed in law, to the profound disappointment of his parents. But at least the ordeal was over and he was free to accept attractive invitations, including one from the Princesse Mathilde, the most notable surviving member of Napoleon's family, a hostess of a more heroic age. In August he

visited some friends whose country house, Les Frémonts, overlooked the sea near Trouville. Other members of the *Banquet*
group appeared, and delightful excursions were arranged—walks
along the cliffs or into the countryside, visits to old churches, and
visits to Madame Straus at the Clos des Mûriers, where Proust
sported one of the Liberty cravats he had recently bought and
worried about his nose on which he seemed to notice the suggestion of a hump. Everyone and everything was delightful, the
hump excepted, though he certainly missed seeing the friends
who had gone elsewhere for the summer, in particular a new friend
whose tenderness was exemplary and whose letters were invariably
ten pages long.

During the winter there was the same round of activities in
Paris—parties of all sorts, including dinner parties, large and
small, that the Prousts gave at home. On November 7, for example, they entertained a young professor whom Marcel admired
very much—a relative by marriage, as it happened—a certain
Henri Bergson. The only other guest was Gregh, obviously chosen
because he admired Bergson too. The editors of *Le Banquet* sat
beside the author of the *Essai sur les données immédiates de la
conscience*, drawing him out, listening to him with the profoundest
respect, and indeed treating him exactly as disciples treat a master.

It was all very exciting no doubt, but still Proust could not avoid
occasional fits of depression. He was not accomplishing very much
—he was certainly not writing with any regularity—and meanwhile
he was advancing inexorably in the study of law. The time would
soon come when he would find himself committed to law or some
other equally distasteful profession. Early in 1893 he described
one of his moods to his friend Robert de Billy, from whom he
had recently been separated. (Billy, having finished his studies,
was now connected with the French Embassy in Berlin.) "I think
of you every night when I go to bed," he told Billy, "every morning
when I get up, all the time, every minute of the time. I shouldn't
have thought it possible that I could miss you—so very much."
Fortunately, however, he had already found still another new
friend—"the young, the charming, the intelligent, the good, the
tender Robert de Flers"—and he was in any case often able to
forget his troubles by losing himself in a whirl of social engage-

ments. "You complain that I don't tell you anything," he said
to Billy in another letter. "Actually I don't dare tell you anything
because I am going out much too much to keep your respect if I
told you about it. It would be very nice of you if you would send
me a list of the four examinations I have to pass and of the books
I should read; I lost it! Be sure you don't forget."

II

Among the women whom Proust was now regularly seeing was
Madame Lemaire, a hostess quite different from those he had
known before. Her parties were not so intimate as Madame Straus's
or so formidably intellectual as Madame de Caillavet's. Madame
Lemaire was a professional artist, a smart society painter with a
fashionable clientele. She painted portraits, landscapes, and society scenes, but she preferred to paint flowers. She had created,
it was said, more roses than anyone but the Almighty. With many
friends in artistic circles, she had for some time been giving studio
parties at which musicians such as Massenet and Saint-Saëns,
actresses such as Réjane had displayed, quite spontaneously, their
special talents. Gradually, however, these parties had lost much of
their unrehearsed, bohemian flavor. They had become so famous
that they had attracted society people, even members of the
French aristocracy who, though they perhaps felt that they were
slumming, were still willing to visit the garden studio on the
Rue de Monceau. Madame Lemaire suddenly found herself with
a unique *salon*, as well patronized as any in Paris.

On Thursdays in May, when the lilacs bloomed in her garden,
Madame Lemaire now gave her celebrated soirées. Artists and intellectuals came, and along with them leaders of French society
—the Rohans, the La Tour d'Auvergnes, the La Rochefoucaulds,
and the Luynes. Those who arrived early wandered among the
palms and studied the unfinished canvas on the easel or the
dazzling portrait of Madame Lemaire's daughter on the wall. But
the studio was soon crowded, movement became difficult, the
hostess could no longer find suitable seats for her most distinguished guests. Late arrivals were obliged to wait in the hall or
stroll among the lilacs in the garden. The performance began,

conversation died down, and if anyone still ventured to talk, Madame Lemaire, suddenly formidable, glared at the offender. After the entertainment and the refreshments the more casual guests drifted off, and only a few intimate friends, among whom Proust was one, lingered on in the studio. As the scent of lilacs—unfortunately so very bad for asthma—drifted in through the windows, another piece was played or another poem recited. The hostess, or *la patronne*, as she was sometimes called, complained about bores—presumably the people who had not come to her soirée—and urged the faithful to come particularly early the following week. "I have even more distinguished performers," she said.

In the spring of 1893 the most distinguished performer of all at Madame Lemaire's was a man whom Proust had been particularly anxious to meet, the Comte Robert de Montesquiou-Fezensac. Montesquiou was a poet, the author of *Les Chauves-souris*, published the year before, a volume of precious, intricate, unintelligible verse, displaying, as one critic pointed out, all the disorder without any of the delirium of madness. From this volume or its as yet unpublished successor, *Le Chef des odeurs suaves*, recitations were given at Madame Lemaire's. As a nobleman well connected in aristocratic society, on intimate terms with the Rohans, the Greffulhes, and other notable families, Montesquiou was in a position to offer Proust somewhat the same advantages that Madame de Chevigné had so tantalizingly withheld the previous year. Through him Proust might conceivably enter and explore circles hitherto firmly closed.

Montesquiou's attraction lay not so much in what he was as what he pretended to be. For he was essentially a magnificent, a tremendously successful poseur, with a genius, seldom equaled in literary history, for showmanship and self-advertisement. He posed as the most arrogant of aristocrats, as a *grand seigneur* of a more glorious age; he could do so quite easily because, to affect arrogance, he had only to display his natural ill temper. At the same time he posed as an apostle of beauty, a man so sensitive to art in all its manifestations that he lived by artistic nourishment. His house, a kind of temple of the arts, was furnished with rare and expensive pieces, generally very fine ones—for he had excellent

taste—but oddly assorted and arranged in insanely symbolic patterns. It is said that he lit fires in the summertime to show that
he appreciated fires for their own sake, and that when he wrote,
he dipped his pen in an inkwell preciously concealed in a bowl
filled with rose petals. To his aristocratic friends and, for the
time being at least, to Proust, he seemed a living embodiment of
the rich culture and fierce family pride of an earlier age; to more
discerning observers he was the final and least appetizing product
of the French Decadence.

A less impressive person could never have sustained so outrageous a pose: Montesquiou was remarkably impressive. He
was tall, thin, and somewhat angular; his profile was magnificent.
He had a firm straight nose, deep-set eyes, thick hair brushed back
in waves, and ears so delicately modeled that he could seldom
resist turning his head to show them off. His goatee was unob-
trusive, but his mustaches were large and full, turned up at the
ends and delicately pointed. He dressed with an art that at once
concealed and called attention to itself. His frock coats were
sober and rich; his cravats, as large as scarves, glowed with exactly
the right amount of color. He habitually carried a cane with a
remarkable turquoise on the handle, a cane that had once belonged
to Louis XV. When he took off his gloves he revealed a single
ring, simple and strange. Seated in a drawing room, he talked
easily and elegantly, like a lecturer fully prepared, with delightfully
appropriate and expressive gestures, but when his subject demanded
emotion he could become violently agitated. On these occasions
his body quivered with excitement. He bent and straightened his
legs, clenched and stretched out his fingers, waved his arms in
delicate arabesques, and pointed dramatically toward the ceiling.
His voice was rich and expressive, wonderfully adapted to recita-
tion; it was said of him that even when he pronounced the words
of a title, he seemed to be reading verse. But in moments of petu-
lance or anger the voice rose sharply until it was almost a woman's
scream. It was a voice that was to become famous in literature—the
voice of the Baron de Charlus.

It may well be that, when they met at Madame Lemaire's, Montesquiou and Proust were drawn to each other because they were
both inverts, because—like members of the same club or the same

political group—they discovered that they had certain tastes and attitudes in common. But they were probably not lovers, and they were certainly not friends, for Montesquiou was incapable of friendship; he was never willing to relax for a moment the barriers of formality that separated him from other men. With Proust he was always the master and patron; Proust himself was always the humble disciple. Their relationship endured, not because they became more intimate, but because they contrived to satisfy at a distance each other's deepest needs. Montesquiou craved flattery, perhaps because he was incapable of maintaining his eccentric pose unless he could find enthusiastic admirers who would continually remind him of his genius. Proust supplied the flattery, and in exchange got introductions and invitations—not very many at first but more and more as time went on.

During the early months of their association Proust exercised some reserve, possibly because he was not yet quite sure how far he could go. Thus in acknowledging inscribed copies of *Les Chauves-souris* and *Le Chef des odeurs suaves* he merely compared Montesquiou's work with that of Baudelaire and Corneille, Wagner and da Vinci. He merely pointed out that it had strength, imagination, intellectual power, and incomparable refinement (borrowing, as he did so, one of his purple passages printed in *Le Banquet*). But as he got to know Montesquiou better and was able to gauge more accurately his thirst for praise, Proust began giving way to his natural tendencies and laying on his flattery with a trowel. "One cannot say anything that you have not said better," he remarked in one of his letters. "Every time we meet," he said in another, "I see you a little more clearly, I discover that you are even grander than I had supposed; I am like an astonished traveler who, as he climbs a mountain, gets a better and better view. The vista that opened up the day before yesterday was the most beautiful of all. Am I even now at the top?" When the poet was out of town, Proust became a somewhat metallic Shakespeare, troubled by the anguish of absence, but consoled by the fact that his patron, unlike the patron of the *Sonnets*, had left his image in books. "When you are away," Proust once wrote, "and I miss the electricity of your glance, the tempestuous galvanism of your voice, the stimulation of your profile, which excite me to the most violent intellectual activity, I constantly consult your writings and your remarks, the flame of which I carefully preserve in my memory as an illumination." One can easily imagine the young man as he sat at his desk drafting these lines, as he hesitated before adopting each phrase, wondering if he was going too far, and as he finally decided that Montesquiou was so impervious to shame that he would accept anything.

III

Meanwhile Proust was availing himself of Montesquiou's sponsorship and realizing the rewards of his flattery. He pushed a little when he had to, though always with exemplary tact; he merely hinted that certain introductions interested him especially. Once, for example, he dropped hints about the Princesse de Léon and the Comtesse Greffulhe. The names were scarcely chosen 'at random. The Princesse de Léon was one of the great ladies of French society, the daughter-in-law of the Duc de Rohan, whose historic title she was soon to inherit, if indeed—for Proust was not yet well informed about the aristocracy—she did not bear it already. The Comtesse Greffulhe was an even more dazzling figure—one of the smartest of aristocratic hostesses and one of the most beautiful women of the age. She was married to a man of immense wealth, a gentleman of the old school, who dabbled in politics, hunted with the Prince of Wales, and kept a series of mistresses somewhat less attractive than his wife. The Comte liked old friends and familiar faces; he seldom invited new acquaintances to hunt on his famous preserves at Bois-Boudran unless, like the King of Portugal and the King of Spain, they were men of unusual distinction. The Comtesse, on the other hand, was catholic in her tastes; she liked poets, musicians, doctors, chemists, astronomers— liked everyone, in fact, who provided her with an appreciative audience for one of her celebrated performances.

For the Comtesse Greffulhe was incorrigibly dramatic; she never stopped acting. Her life seemed to fall, quite naturally, into the pattern of a play in which she herself was always the central figure. When she entertained a group of distinguished mathematicians, she insisted on leading the conversation, just to show that she could do so; she talked, to the satisfaction of everyone, about subjects she could not possibly understand. When she showed an interest in music, she became, almost inevitably, the president of the *Société des grandes auditions musicales*. When she took up the cause of reform, as she later did by conducting a campaign to persuade ladies to wear smaller hats at the theatre, she arranged daring little parties at which the *modistes* of Paris met and conferred with the arbiters of fashion. Her presence was so regal, her dress so striking, and her sense of timing so exact that she never entered an exhibit, a concert hall, or a drawing room without creating a sensation. At her brother's marriage in the cathedral at Rheims, she appeared robed in medieval cloth of gold; she rather than the bride was the center of attention. Even among intimate friends she was constantly illustrating her flair for the unexpected. When her cousin Montesquiou admired one of her clocks made in the shape of a lyre with a flower at its base, she promised to leave it to him in her will. But the very next day he received it. "To me it is now insupportable," she told him in a note, "since it reminds me that I must die."

Proust was naturally eager to meet so exciting a person as Madame Greffulhe, and when his first hints were ignored he brought up the subject again, even more tactfully than before. He told Montesquiou that he had seen her at the Princesse de Wagram's and that she had been wearing a coiffure that was almost Polynesian, with mauve orchids in her hair. "She is difficult to judge," he wrote, "no doubt because to judge is to compare, and there is nothing about her that can be seen in any other woman, or indeed anywhere else. But the whole mystery of her beauty seems concentrated in the radiance and especially in the enigma of her eyes. I have never seen so beautiful a woman." He added that he would not be so indiscreet as to ask for an introduction, but that he would like her to know how deeply she had impressed him. "I hope to displease you less," he concluded, "by admiring the woman whom you admire above everything, and I shall henceforth admire after you, according to you, and, as Malebranche says, 'in you.'" Montesquiou can scarcely have ignored so adroit an appeal; the indications are that he arranged, though only after considerable delay, the introduction for which his protégé had been angling. When they met, the great lady perhaps smiled her mysterious smile, perhaps lingered to say a few words, perhaps even suggested another meeting in her own drawing room. In any case, Proust was happy.

IV

During the spring and summer of 1893 Proust was again distracted by his work at the university. He was going through the final stages in the study of law—getting practical experience in a lawyer's office and doing some sort of class work in preparation for the last series of examinations. "I think I shall go to Saint-Moritz for the month of August (if I pass in law)," he wrote Billy. "I am being strongly urged by Robert de Montesquiou and by Madame Howland, both of whom you may perhaps have seen at Saint-Moritz; both are charming. I shall also know many other women there and if I go L. de La Salle will be good enough to go too and stay with me." La Salle was one of the young men with whom he had stayed at Les Frémonts the summer before.

Proust did pass and in fact qualified for his degree in law. He spent a month at Saint-Moritz and Lake Geneva, then went on to Trouville, where his parents began badgering him to make up his mind about a profession once and for all. He tried to, he certainly did his best. He got so far as to eliminate the drearier possibilities and to concentrate on those that were not quite so dreary. "The Cour des Comptes tempts me more and more," he told Billy. "I look at it in this way. If I don't want to go in for a career abroad, I would have just as boring a career at the Foreign Office in Paris as at the Cour des Comptes. Perhaps it would be harder—for me— to prepare for the Cour des Comptes, but wouldn't that be quite offset by the fact that I should have to devote my whole attention to it for a shorter period? The rest of the time I could do what I pleased. Ah, my dear friend, your advice would be more valuable to me than ever here, and I am very unhappy about your absence. Let a good letter make up for it by the all-powerful miracle of communication between minds. Isn't the bench too discredited? What is there left, since I have decided that I am not going to be either a lawyer, or a doctor, or a priest, or. . . ."

When he returned home, Proust wrote his father, who was still away, a long and extremely artful letter. He offered to give in and choose a profession, or rather to let his father choose between two alternatives, both of which involved further study. Thus the worst that could happen to him immediately would be that he would have to go on studying a little longer. At the same time he expressed so much devotion to literature and so much horror of specific professions, particularly law, the only one for which he was qualified, that his father must have felt like a brute in making him choose at all. "I always hoped," Proust wrote, "that in the end you would let me go on with my literary and philosophical studies, for which I feel qualified. But since I see that each year I am subject to an increasingly practical discipline, I prefer to choose immediately one of the practical professions you offer me. I shall work quite seriously to prepare for the examinations in Foreign Affairs or for those at l'École des Chartes, whichever you say.—As to law, I should a thousand times rather go into a stockbroker's office. Anyway I am convinced that I wouldn't stick to law three days! —It isn't that I don't still believe that anything I might do other than literature and philosophy would be a waste of time. But among several evils, there are some that are better and some that are worse. Even in my most desperate moments I can't conceive of anything more odious than becoming a lawyer. If the embassies will help me avoid it, they will seem, not indeed my chosen vocation, but a welcome alternative."

The letter presumably led to further negotiations, and in the end Proust must have induced his parents to make concessions. At least the decision about his profession was indefinitely postponed, with or without their consent. He read for a degree in philosophy and he took lessons with his old teacher Darlu, but there is no evidence that he ever again attempted any sort of professional training.

He was now writing at a somewhat accelerated pace—perhaps to show his parents how serious he was about literature—and contributing to La Revue blanche, which by this time had absorbed Le Banquet. Between August and December, 1893, he published a series of rather interesting pieces, certainly more interesting than those he had published the previous year. Less concerned with ideas, he now concentrates more on narrative and character. In one piece, "Mélancolique villégiature de Madame de Breyves," he studies the growth of love in a woman's mind. In another he follows the thoughts of an aged captain engaged in reviewing his erotic career—follows them and describes them in delightfully precious images. The captain opens his great chest and takes out the records of his conquests: letters, postcards, faded flowers, and photographs that are scarcely recognizable because, like the relics of saints, they have been kissed so often. He weeps because he can no longer experience the same sensuality and because, in any case, he cannot seem to remember distinctly the women who granted him their favors. They are like butterflies—he injures their wings each time he tries to catch them; they are like images in a mirror— he tarnishes the surface as he tries to touch them with his fingers; so that, little by little, they become less charming and even less distinct. Finally he ceases to try, ceases even to care about them at all, and then, like other men, he dies.

In still another piece, "Avant la nuit," the author portrays a heroine with lesbian tendencies. He is interested in her moral struggle and obviously sympathetic. He has her remark: "Because most people see red objects as red, one cannot say that those who see them as purple are wrong."

While he was contributing to *La Revue blanche*, Proust decided to collect all the pieces he had so far written and bring them out as a small volume. He seemed quite confident that he could do so before the end of 1893. It occurred to him that he might dedicate his book to the memory of Edgar Aubert and the Englishman Willie Heath, two young friends who had recently died. But he was inclined to reject the idea because he felt that his pieces were too mediocre and indeed too often improper. Later, however, he reverted to it. "Madame Madeleine Lemaire is going to illustrate my little book," he wrote Billy. "So it will get into the libraries of a good many writers, artists, and important people generally who wouldn't otherwise have known anything about it but will now want it for its illustrations." Proust concluded the letter by hoping that, if Billy was returning to Paris, he would come in time to give further advice about professions.

But the appearance of the book and indeed the decision about the profession Proust was to adopt were both put off. Meanwhile he turned his attention to a new project, a series of critical articles, beginning of course with an article on Montesquiou. "If 'Your Grace' will help me," he told his distinguished friend, "I shall show in it how much you differ from the banal decadent of our time, how strong your will power is and how rich your intelligence, which you inherit from the seventeenth century, in short what I have already taken the liberty of telling you." The poet approved and Proust wrote the article; publishing it was more difficult. His friend Louis Ganderax, now engaged in starting *La Revue de Paris*, refused either to take it himself or to recommend it elsewhere; the editor of *La Revue blanche* took it, postponed its appearance, and afterwards rejected it; the editors of other papers were definitely unreceptive. Finally Proust offered the unfortunate article to Montesquiou, urging him to publish it himself anywhere he could. "If this last door is closed in my face," Proust wrote, "I shall do in the end what I should perhaps have done in the beginning: I shall start a paper of my own." But even starting a paper was not easy. The new project languished and meanwhile no other critical articles were written.

V

If Proust failed in his effort to flatter Montesquiou in print, he was at least able, early in 1894, to produce a new genius of exactly the sort that his patron was fond of sponsoring—the pianist Léon Delafosse. He was an ambitious young man who was trying to establish himself as a concert performer and hence was interested in any publicity he could get. Perhaps as a form of publicity, he had composed musical settings for some of the poems in *Les Chauves-souris*. Proust heard them and recommended them to Montesquiou; subsequently he took Delafosse to call on the poet at his mansion in Versailles. Montesquiou was at first distinctly cool, because he was repelled by the pianist's appearance, but when, in the course of the visit, he heard the young man play, he warmed up immediately. He seemed to recognize an amazing technique and indeed to see the musician himself transformed, as he sat at the piano, into a strikingly attractive figure. There is no reason to be unduly suspicious about the poet's reaction, because, if he was interested in young men, he was also genuinely interested in genius. Furthermore, he was already attached to a young man—a South American named Gabriel d'Yturri—whom he is said to have won, or stolen, from a notorious invert, a certain Baron Doasan.

But whatever the exact nature of the relationship that soon established itself, Montesquiou was wildly excited, convinced that he had discovered an incomparable virtuoso and grateful to Proust who had made the discovery possible. As soon as he could he returned the young man's call, sat by him as he practiced, worked with him, and arranged to introduce him to society at an entertainment of unusual magnificence. The preparations were elaborate and costly; celebrities of every kind were invited. On the afternoon of May 30, 1894, they poured into Versailles, which had not seen in many years so distinguished a gathering. They came by train and by coach; they filled the theatre in the poet's garden, built for the occasion only and therefore appropriately called *Théâtre éphémère*. Proust moved through the crowd, jotting down names and notes about gowns, preparing to write up a full report for *Le Gaulois*. The performance was long and varied. Yann Nibor read his own sea poems; the leading actresses of the Parisian stage—Bernhardt, Bartet, and Reichenberg—read from other poets. Bernhardt did a new masterpiece of the host's, "Le Coucher de la morte." The three actresses—the idea was Yturri's—appeared together on the stage to recite André Chénier's ode to Versailles; Bernhardt, standing in the middle, began the poem and the others took up the verses antiphonally. But for the host the high point of the afternoon was the appearance of the remarkable new genius he was introducing to his friends. Delafosse began with Bach, Chopin, and Rubinstein, went on to accompany a society tenor in the songs from *Les Chauves-souris*, and ended with Liszt. There can be no doubt that, even from the point of view of sheer quantity, the introduction was an entirely adequate one.

Montesquiou's favors were, however, by no means at an end. He sponsored Delafosse in the *salons* and concert halls of the capital; he worked tirelessly advising him and perfecting his style; he celebrated him in verse. The relationship lasted until

Delafosse began showing signs of ingratitude, irrationally attributing his triumphs entirely to his own ability. The poet hesitated and restrained himself as best he could, but at last he decided that he would simply have to "execute" the upstart, to terminate the relationship for ever. When he had done so, he predicted to other admirers that Delafosse, now that he was no longer guided by the hand of genius, would never rise above mediocrity.[1]

Meanwhile Proust himself was in danger, for he too, Montesquiou felt, was showing equally grave signs of ingratitude. He was no longer completely devoted and uncritical, determined to admire and to imitate the mannerisms of the master; he was now mimicking these same mannerisms for the amusement of his friends—waving his arms, tapping with his foot, laughing with his mouth closed as if to conceal his black teeth, and raising his voice in shrill screams as he cashiered imaginary disciples. The performances became so famous that rumors about them ultimately reached Montesquiou, who fulminated, perhaps threatened to "execute" Proust, in any case demanded an explanation. Proust was obliged to prevaricate. While admitting that he had often repeated Montesquiou's remarks and that—since the mind unconsciously influences the body—he had perhaps occasionally adopted the tones of Montesquiou's voice, he denied absolutely that he had ever intended to be unkind. "If your friends have told you more and if they have spoken of caricature," he wrote, "I invoke your maxim: 'A word repeated is never true.' My conscience, which is often troubled about other matters, is quite easy about you, since I have never expressed before others anything but my admiration for you which, thank God, is quite inexhaustible."

The explanation might have been more convincing if other unfortunate incidents had not come up to trouble the relationship. Proust often had giggling fits, especially when he was with friends who shared his sense of humor and who found clichés, for example, irresistibly amusing. He was afraid that he might not always be able to control himself in Montesquiou's presence, and once, when he and a friend expected to meet the poet in

1. Actually Delafosse was a successful concert pianist for over a quarter of a century.

society, he took the precaution of explaining and apologizing in advance. The evening came; the two young men entered the room and approached the poet, only to find him tense and suspicious, fully prepared for a catastrophe of the first magnitude. Nothing more was needed to set the young men off. They exchanged glances, caught the wild light in each other's eyes, lost their composure; then, precipitately retiring to the shelter of the buffet, laughed hysterically as Montesquiou, not quite out of hearing, stormed about the room.

The exhibition was certainly disgraceful, but again Proust escaped the fate of Delafosse, principally because he was afterwards so very apologetic and so determined not to take offense at the poet's insults. He went on seeing his noble friend, flattering him, mimicking him, and studying his eccentricities. He saw him as a typical aristocrat, molded by the traditions of his family and his class, illustrating by the force of atavism both the refinement and the insolence of another age; but he saw him, too, as a typical homosexual, a hopeless neurotic, a man torn by conflicting impulses which he could neither resist nor control. Both types interested him keenly, and in later years he was able to combine them in a remarkable character, in many ways reminiscent of Montesquiou, the Baron de Charlus.

CHAPTER V

Les Plaisirs et les jours

I

AT THE TIME of Montesquiou's party for Delafosse, Proust was a thin, pale young man not quite twenty-three years old. His eyes were heavily circled; his mustaches, already long and full, drooped a little though he could, by twirling them, turn them up at the tips. His expression changed rapidly with his moods. Sometimes he looked like the young man who had giggling fits; more often he looked like quite a different person—one who was habitually introspective and who brooded a great deal, as indeed Proust did. He brooded about many things: about his health, which was gradually getting worse, so that he seemed to be in some danger of becoming a permanent invalid; about his sex life, which was inevitably furtive and hazardous; and about his career, which was not turning out to be a career at all. He was neither earning money nor making a reputation for himself, since he could not even get on with his first book. The obstacles were no doubt within himself, but they were not for that reason any the easier to overcome.

In the autumn of 1893 he had hoped to finish the book by the end of the year, but in the autumn of 1894 he was almost as far from having finished as before. He wrote another story for it, he worked with Madame Lemaire on the illustrations, he drafted the general dedication, and he began singling out friends to whom individual pieces might be dedicated. This in itself was a trying task since Montesquiou was involved; he would of course want a dedication and would certainly make trouble if anyone he disliked—the painter Jacques-Emile Blanche, for example—were so much as mentioned in the volume.

Dissatisfied with his progress, which was indeed exasperatingly slow, Proust again found relief in society, which gave him a sense of activity and achievement and thus helped him to forget for a few hours life's inevitable futility. But he was not the sort of person who is good at forgetting. "Two years ago and last year," he wrote Montesquiou on January 3, 1895, "I gave up hoping for anything from a New Year, either for myself or for others. I had the feeling that if years change people remain the same and that the future, which our desires lead us to dream about, is only an extension of the past, which we should so much like to see changed that we hear only the chimes of the same good and evil bells that we ourselves have before set ringing." He went on to say that he was more hopeful about 1895, but his hope can scarcely have lasted very long.

Society gave him a sense of activity because it released his intelligence, because it provided his mind with material to work on, fresher and more personal than the material in books. He could observe and analyze to his heart's content, thus preparing himself—though he can scarcely yet have suspected that this would ultimately be his task—to become a social historian of his own time. For him a party was successful if, in the course of it, he saw an interesting new face, or established himself in the good graces of a new hostess, or pieced together the facts of a new case history, or discovered a significant new generalization about social behavior. Faces were constantly flashing before him—faces that deeply impressed themselves on his memory and that were one day to reappear, under real or fictitious names, in the various versions of his novel.

Some he saw in drawing rooms he had frequented for years, others in new drawing rooms—Madame Aubernon de Nerville's, for example. Madame Aubernon was the most formidable, the most remorselessly intellectual of all the middle-class hostesses. At her dinners she directed discussions on topics of the utmost seriousness, keeping beside her a bell to silence private conversation. Of the faces he saw at her table, two in particular interested Proust. One was that of Victor Brochard, a brilliant and pathetic man, a professor at the Sorbonne and the author of a notable book on the Greek skeptics. His movements were erratic and jerky; he was nearly blind and his left eye, constantly watering, clouded his spectacles. The other was the face of the Baron Doasan, once reputedly Montesquiou's rival for the affections of Yturri. A decayed pederast who dyed his mustaches and powdered his bloated cheeks, he nevertheless affected virility. In his younger days he is said to have dissipated his fortune in an effort to ingratiate himself with a handsome young Pole. Now he lived on Madame Aubernon's bounty, ogled young men who sat at her table, among them probably Proust himself, and enjoyed the intellectual riches that his hostess spread before him.

In aristocratic society the faces were different, not more intrinsically interesting perhaps, but more interesting to young snobs like Proust, who seemed able to discern in them the continuity of noble families, the reincarnation of features seen in portraits from the past. Such were the faces of Comte d'Haussonville, Comte Louis de Turenne, and Prince Edmond de Polignac; such was eminently the face of Comte Boni de Castellane, who impinged upon Proust's world in the spring of 1895, when he appeared at a ball given by Madame Seminario.

Castellane was the perfect product of a distinguished family, a young man with aristocratic features, a complexion as pink as a girl's, and a bearing at once charmingly gracious and audaciously insolent. Already the most famous dandy of the age, the acknowledged successor of his uncle the Prince de Sagan, he was now preparing further and more notable triumphs, preparing in fact to escape from the vulgarity and the commercialism of the present, which he found so utterly distasteful, and to recreate for himself the beauty and the pageantry of the past. He had just taken the first step—an essential one in his case, since the Castellanes were poor: he had married the heiress of

the fabulously wealthy Jay Gould, who had laid the foundation
for his fortune (or so Boni believed) by patenting a mouse trap.
Anna Gould was not exactly a beauty, but Boni had courted
her as though she had been the most beautiful of women.
He had ridden by her window on horseback, he had sent
her bouquets of lilacs delightfully arranged. When she left
Paris he had dashed off to New York, without even enough
money to pay his cab fare from the pier to the Waldorf-
Astoria, but somehow he had managed to get along. He had put
up with what passed for society in the New World, had eaten
such distasteful dishes as clams and terrapin, had suppressed his
revulsion when he had seen the fantastic decorations of the
Gould mansions—the lamps that looked like tumors, the cement
busts of Gambetta that faced cement angels from Sainte Chapelle.
Finally, he had proposed and been accepted; a preposterous wedding had taken place amid the architectural horrors of the Moorish
Parlor in the mansion on Fifth Avenue. Now the young bride-
groom was back in Paris, on the threshold of his retirement into
the eighteenth century. He was buying up Reynolds portraits and
Boucher tapestries, dressing his footmen in scarlet and powdering
their wigs, planning to build a palace on the Avenue du Bois,
a replica of the Grand Trianon at Versailles. All society was
dazzled, including young Proust, who apparently first met the
exile from the past at Madame Seminario's ball.

Proust did not at the time set down his impressions, but
he certainly recalled them some years later when he was introducing into his novel the aristocratic young Marquis de Saint-
Loup-en-Bray.

II

Meanwhile Proust's work went slowly, almost imperceptibly,
forward, though there was now, every so often, an exciting little
flurry of progress. One such occurred not long after Madame
Seminario's ball when Proust and his most recent friend, Reynaldo
Hahn, had an "evening" at Madame Lemaire's. Hahn was a
young South American musican, not yet out of the Conservatory,
who was already captivating the drawing rooms. His concert

style, obviously designed for *salon* audiences, was a highly artificial one, involving free use of *mezza voce* and falsetto. One of his favorite tricks was to sing conversationally with a cigarette in his mouth, stopping from time to time to sip a glass of port or to take a carnation from a vase that stood on the piano and arrange it in his buttonhole. He composed brilliant songs in the perfumed *salon* style, and he had recently composed musical accompaniments to a set of poems Proust had written on painters, companion pieces to the earlier poem on Cuyp. Proust printed the poems impressively, perhaps at this very time, and apparently sent out some of the invitations for the evening. At least he invited Montesquiou (and urged him to come early, because Risler, the young pianist who was to play the accompaniments, had to leave by eleven o'clock to get back to his regiment in Chartres). The evening was May 28, 1895. Madame Krauss and Fugère sang Hahn songs; Le Bargy recited, presumably to Risler's accompaniment, the poems on painters. In its report on the evening *Le Figaro* praised Hahn but neglected to mention Proust. *Le Gaulois,* however, made amends, not only naming Proust but describing him as a charming poet; the same paper subsequently printed passages from his poems.

For the time being Proust was devoted to Hahn, as to other friends in the past; he was perhaps even more deeply devoted to him, for he once wrote to him, with obvious sincerity: "You [are] really and truly the person that with the exception of Mama I love best in the whole world." [1] The two men had a good many things in common, including a persistent playfulness, a whimsical sense of humor that generally took the form of baby talk, of eccentric pronunciations and spellings, of fanciful and constantly varied names for each other. In their letters Hahn was Genstil or Irnuls or Hibuls or Buninuls or Binchnibuls or Vunchtnibuls—the series could be extended almost indefinitely. Proust was one of the same series, or perhaps the Poney, or Buls or Bincht or Bunnsch or Buncht. They frequented the same

1. Proust's affection can perhaps be measured by the anguish he felt at being separated from Hahn, as on a certain evening when, having missed his friend, he looked for him quite hysterically. The episode may well have suggested the passage in *Du Côté de chez Swann* in which Swann looks for Odette along the boulevards.

hostesses, went to see the same pictures, and read the same books. In music Hahn was naturally the master—and sometimes called Master by Proust—but there were nevertheless differences of opinion between them. Proust was considerably more enthusiastic than his friend about Wagner and Debussy. They agreed, however, in their admiration for Saint-Saëns, and when they were alone together Hahn was fond of playing a transcription of the D Minor Sonata for Piano and Violin, or at least the first movement of it, which was at this time a special favorite of Proust's. Proust was twice inspired to write articles on Saint-Saëns for *Le Gaulois*, and often, when Hahn called at the house in the evening, Proust would ask for his favorite piece. "Come," he would say, "play for me that bit I like, you know, that . . . 'little phrase' by Saint-Saëns."

Proust had by this time taken another degree, his *licence ès lettres* in philosophy, and since the matter of his profession was still undecided, he was again having a good deal of trouble at home. He was still entirely dependent on his parents, specifically his mother, who was nothing if not thrifty. He was always short of money and she was usually unwilling to give him what he asked for unless she was convinced that his expenses were justifiable. Scenes apparently occurred rather regularly. Letters were exchanged within the household—on Proust's side childishly petulant letters. Once, for example, he expressed the hope that he might somehow be able to live away from home, or at least avoid the inevitable disputes at meal times. His mother's nature had its better side, he realized that of course. But how could he be expected to see it when she spent money like water on lessons for him in law, philosophy, and Latin, and then refused to give him anything for trips to London and Rome! At the moment he was feverish, and he could scarcely prevent her from coming to his room and haggling with him and making him more feverish still. But it would certainly be nice if she would not poison his life any more than she had done already—if she would talk to him as a mother to a son and not a creditor to a debtor.

It was all very distressing, no doubt, but the scenes and the letters could scarcely be avoided unless Proust was prepared to earn his own living, as he definitely was not. He did, however, take a curious step, perhaps to show that he was not really averse to work after all: he applied for an unpaid position at the Mazarine Library. The work was apparently pleasant and certainly not arduous; the successful applicant was not expected to put in more than five hours every other day. On June 29, 1895, Proust's application found favor, and he seems to have begun discharging his duties, or occasionally discharging them, when suddenly he was transferred to the Ministry of Public Instruction. The Ministry objected on the ground that Proust's health was delicate; Proust himself objected even more strenuously. He at once applied for a leave of absence or permission to resign, hinting that if the influence of Hanotaux, the Minister of Foreign Affairs, could help him get what he wanted, it could easily be brought to bear. The leave was ultimately granted, whether Hanotaux helped or not, and granted annually for four successive years.

That summer Proust traveled a good deal. He went to Kreuznach in Germany with his mother, and to Dieppe with Hahn. While the two friends were staying with Madame Lemaire in Dieppe, they planned a trip to Brittany and thus infuriated their hostess who could never endure seeing people go elsewhere. Still they kept to their plans, went on to Brittany, and stayed for some weeks at the village of Beg-Meil, where the inn looked like a farm and where one of the other guests, an English painter, served Proust as a model for a character in a new book he was on the point of starting. Later still the two friends stayed with Madame Lemaire again. Clearly Madame Proust's attitude about money was, for the time being at least, somewhat less inflexible.

During the winter of 1895-6 there was rather more than a flurry of progress on the old book; the volume at last definitely took shape. Proust made his final selection of the pieces he wanted to include from *Le Banquet* and *La Revue blanche,* polished up the new pieces, finished negotiating with friends who were to be named in the dedications, and went over the illustrations that Madame Lemaire had prepared. Afterwards he fixed on a title, *Les Plaisirs et les jours,* an allusion to Hesiod's *Work and Days,* an indication of the frivolities with which many of the pieces were to deal. He even fixed on the paper for the printing—heavy, supple, slightly glazed—and the color for the cover, pale green, embellished with Madame Lemaire's irises. Finally, just as the volume was ready for the press, he asked Anatole France for a preface. It is said—though not perhaps on very good authority—that the great man wanted to refuse, that he protested against sponsoring an author whose sentences were interminable and whose structure was deplorably loose. But Madame de Caillavet insisted and in fact wrote the preface herself—a wholly complimentary little piece, dwelling on the exotic hothouse atmosphere of Proust's work, at once breathless and beautiful, ingenuous and sophisticated, calling Proust himself a depraved Bernardin de Saint-Pierre and a naive Petronius. The great man added only a word here and there to make the style more authentic.

The book, thus embellished with another notable name, thus associated with two fashionable hostesses, exhaling the fragrance of violets from the Avenue Hoche and of lilacs from the Rue de Monceau, was at last published in June, 1896, at the outrageously high price of thirteen and a half francs.

III

Les Plaisirs et les jours is the collected work of Proust's youth and should perhaps be read as such. From its pages, dealing recurrently with the same subjects and the same ideas, one gets for the first time distinct impressions of his experience and his thought.

The first impression is that the book is more frequently autobiographical than most works of fiction, that aspects of Proust are repeatedly attributed to the heroes and heroines—in the passages devoted to childhood, for example. In the first story he is Baldassare when Baldassare remembers how his mother used to put him to bed—how she chafed his feet with her hands and stayed with him when he could not sleep. In the last story he is Honoré, who remembers that he could never sleep if his mother was getting dressed for a ball; he insisted that she get dressed before dinner, leave the house early, and wait at a friend's until the ball was ready to begin. In "Violante" he is the child who suffers from lack of will power. In "La Confession d'une jeune fille" he is another child, also lacking in will power, who passionately clings to her mother. She demands a good-night kiss, but her mother is reluctant to give in to her, "because," the young girl says, "it caused me too much pleasure and too much pain, because due to my calling her back to say good night again and again I could never go to sleep, not daring finally to call her any more but feeling more than ever the passionate need, always inventing new excuses, my burning pillow to be turned, my icy feet which her hands alone could warm."

In other passages, Proust intrudes somewhat improbably into his characters. The erotic career described in "La Confession d'une jeune fille" sounds more like his than a young girl's, and the same can be said of Violante's creative instinct and Honoré's nervous asthma. On the other hand, he is never so frankly autobiographical as in his later work. His characters are at least ostensibly imaginary, differing from himself in age, sex, or social position. If he cannot help letting them reflect his experiences, he at least tries to give them a life independent of his own.

The characters fall in love or go out in society—they do very little else. As lovers they are profoundly unhappy. For love is never represented as a normal, healthy passion, leading to permanent attachments; it is invariably furtive and transient, joyless and accompanied by a strong sense of guilt. Proust may well be thinking of his own homosexual experiences. In "La Mort de Baldassare Silvande" the hero toys with adultery; he is conscience-stricken and so is his mistress. As he kisses her he sees that she is weeping and that in her eyes is an expression sadder than tears, "like the torture endured in crucifixion, or at the loss of someone dearly beloved." In "La Confession d'une jeune fille" the heroine begins indulging in sex at the age of sixteen. She suffers appallingly—she even tries to confess to her father—but she still cannot break herself of the habit. She succeeds only—since she cannot now bear to be alone—in acquiring a second vice, that of leading a frivolous social life. "I would go into society," she says, "to calm myself after sinning and then, no sooner calm, would sin again." But she never really frees herself from her sense of guilt. Even in the act of sex she has, "in the depth of [her] heart, an infinite sadness and desolation; it seemed to me that I was causing my mother's soul, the soul of my guardian angel, the soul of God to weep." Finally, after an erotic experience, when her face is still set in a brutally sensual expression, she is aware that her mother is looking at her through a window. The mother falls dead and the girl herself commits suicide.

Proust's lovers invariably suffer, though not always from feelings of guilt. Sometimes they show their affection too plainly and thus alienate a mistress; for only by a display of indifference, Proust says, can a mistress be won. Sometimes, confronted by a mistress, they are obliged to recognize the subjectivity of their passion; the woman before them is clearly not the woman of their dreams. Thus in one of the shorter pieces a little boy is devoted to a little girl, but experiences disillusionment each time he sees her. So appalled is he by the disparity between what he imagines her to be and what he cannot help seeing she really is, that he throws himself out of a window. In a longer and more successful treatment of the same theme, "Mélancolique villégiature," the heroine becomes infatuated with a dull, unprepossessing, rather vulgar young man to whom she has not even been introduced. She has no illusions about him; she recognizes him for what he is. Nevertheless, when love subtly insinuates itself into her mind, she suffers the cruelest anguish. Unable to see him again and scarcely able to endure not seeing him, she pores over a large photograph of Biarritz, where she knows that he is spending the autumn. She plays, in the privacy of her room, a piano transcription of a passage from the *Meistersinger* that she heard the evening she met him— it has become the *leitmotif* of her love. In masterly pages, perhaps the most masterly in the whole volume, Proust traces the course of her suffering as it assumes the proportions of a disease, quite incurable, as he says, because quite irrational.

Jealousy in Proust's stories can be as subjective and as cruel as love: it too becomes a lingering disease. In "La Fin de la jalousie" Honoré and Françoise are devoted to one another. He is faithful to her, except for those purely physical deviations that from time to time Proust's young men permit themselves; he has no reason to suppose that she is ever unfaithful to him. Then one evening his suspicions are aroused by a piece of idle gossip to the effect that she once had another lover, and he loses all peace of mind. He questions her, spies on her, and confesses his own infidelities to induce her to confess hers. He even considers more perverse ways of testing her, such as laying bets on her virtue and thus inciting other young men to attempt her seduction. He discovers nothing; nevertheless he goes on suffering and languishing. He would continue to suffer, Proust says, even if he had proof that she was innocent. "Just as we still tremble in fear of the assassin of our dream even after we know that it was only an illusion, just as men still feel pain in the leg that has been amputated."

If love, whether complicated by jealousy or not, is usually a torment, it fortunately does not last for ever. The time always comes when the lover is completely indifferent to his mistress. Honoré looks forward to this time and prays God to hasten its coming. But in his case it comes only when he is at the point of death; then finally he realizes that Françoise is no more to him than any of his other acquaintances. A lover who is not at the moment suffering feels that he will always be fond of his mistress even when his passion is dead, for he cannot believe that he is devoting his time to a woman who will have no permanent interest for him. But when he ceases to love her, he ceases to see her; she has now no interest for him at all. The eternity of affection that love promises is perhaps the most absurd of all the illusions it creates.

Proust is as skeptical about society as he is about love, but less consistently so. There are at least suggestions of snobbishness in his book. The settings are generally aristocratic and often described with a good deal of unction. The characters are well-born and rich; they enter society as a matter of course, succeed in it brilliantly, and for the most part accept its standards. Sometimes they are scarcely distinguishable from the characters of smart society novelists. On the other hand, when he is explicitly concerned with the subject, Proust's strictures on social life are positively devastating. Snobbishness is represented as the most ridiculous of vices, and all society people are snobs. They are furthermore frivolous, insipid, and dull. Imaginative people should avoid society and other forms of gregariousness, which to them can only be stultifying. If they do not, they soon find that they are good for nothing; they have betrayed themselves. The heroines of "La Confession d'une jeune fille" and "Violante" are examples.

If love and social life are thus profoundly unsatisfactory experiences, what then remains to temper the pessimism of the book?

Where, in Proust's view, does happiness lie? For the girl of "Violante" it seems to lie in solitary communion with nature and art, leading apparently to the exercise of the creative instinct. If she could have used her imagination, if she could have devoted herself to the creation of a work of art, then she would no longer have felt sterile and disillusioned. For other characters in the book the solution is somewhat different. Happiness for them seems to lie, not in creation, but in memory. The present, Proust says, is inevitably disappointing; we have looked forward to it too ardently, we have imagined it to be quite different from what it really is. Only the past, which we invest with charm in the act of remembering it, is ever truly satisfying. But these ideas are suggested rather than completely worked out. Their development belongs to Proust's later years when, identifying art and memory, he placed happiness in the imaginative recreation of the past.

Les Plaisirs et les jours is thus a profoundly thoughtful book; it is not, however, an entirely successful one. Short pieces—both those reprinted from *Le Banquet* and *La Revue blanche* and those written more recently—bulk too large in it. Many of them are scarcely more than fragments, casual jottings, the raw material for a work of art perhaps but certainly not the finished product. Even the longer pieces are generally marred by obvious faults, being either too episodic, too melodramatic, or too intellectual. "Violante," for example, is a story in which an idea is worked out much too abstractly. Parts of it read like a lecture—one, furthermore, that the author is delivering to himself. The fact is that Proust is still something less than a master. He can be wonderfully witty for a few pages, as in "Un Dîner en ville"; he can be wonderfully acute in passages devoted to the anguish of sensitive and rather neurotic people, as in the part about Honoré's suspicions, in "La Fin de la jalousie." But he is seldom consistently good for a long stretch or throughout a whole story, unless it is in "Mélancolique villégiature," the very best of his pieces. He shows great promise as a satirical and psychological writer, but this promise is still incompletely realized.

The shortcomings of the book can be detected in its style— or rather its styles, for it has more than one. Sometimes the author is lucid and simple, rather elegantly simple, as though he were imitating the style of the eighteenth century. At other times he is very much the esthete, the prose poet, who seems to enjoy elaboration for its own sake and who specializes in highly wrought descriptive passages. A typical example of this second style is the episode of the Alpine lake in "Présence réelle":

> One evening the hour was particularly propitious; in a few seconds the setting sun had covered the water with all the colors of the rainbow, our souls with all delights. Suddenly we gave a start; we had just seen a little pink butterfly—then two, then five—leaving the flowers on our shore and fluttering out over the lake. Soon they appeared to us like a rising dust, pink and impalpable. Then they reached the flowers on the opposite shore, started back, and began their adventurous crossing once more, stopping at times, as though tempted, above the lake so preciously tinted at this hour like a great flower that is fading. It was too much for us; our eyes filled with tears. These little butterflies crossing the lake passed and repassed over our souls, taut with emotion before so much beauty, ready to vibrate— passed and repassed like a voluptuous bow.

There is no doubt something of Proust in this precious passage, as there is in the simpler passages of the book. But there is also affectation, something not quite himself, something he has picked up from others. Suggestions at least of this affectation are generally apparent in the book, except perhaps in isolated sentences, usually rather long sentences occurring in passages of intense emotion, where he seems to let himself go and where, in any case, he is neither very simple nor very lucid nor very precious, but merely Proustian.

The different styles might seem even more discordant than they do were it not for the fact that Proust succeeds eminently in one respect: he is able to invest them all with his poetry, he commands the form of magic that reconciles such discords. It is sometimes no doubt poetry rather too liberally perfumed and too much concerned with little pink butterflies and lakes like great fading flowers and voluptuous bows, but it is nevertheless poetry of a sort. The chief element in it is the image, the metaphor. Few prose writers have used imagery more persistently, or more structurally, or more brilliantly, and few have drawn on a wider variety of subjects. Proust draws on common life, religion, medicine, nature, and the arts. If he has a preference, it is perhaps for images of the sea; there are a good many of them and they are often particularly striking. Speaking of the death of love as the ebb of a great tide, for example, he goes on to say that afterwards "we can still gather strange and charming sea shells and, lifting them to our ear, can hear, with a melancholy pleasure and without suffering, the same mighty roar as in the past." But it is after all the variety and the freshness of Proust's imagery that are most impressive. In "La Fin de la jalousie" he uses one striking image after another—the acrobat reaching out for the trapeze, the musical phrase anticipating the chord that resolves it, the woman in love with the mysterious inscription on her bracelet, gods who disguise themselves as men, angels who feel both love and respect for each other, victims of hallucination "whom sometimes one succeeds in curing by having them touch the armchair or the living person occupying the place where they thought they saw a phantom and thus chasing it from the real world, curing them by reality itself, which leaves no room for phantoms." [2]

IV

The book was not and indeed could not have been a popular success. Proust's mood was too somber, his analysis of human experience too devastating, his interest in action and character too slight. The sale was small, too small, it seems, to pay the costs of

2. A characteristically elaborate version of this image appears early in *Sodome et Gomorrhe:* "The famous Huxley (whose grandson occupies an unassailable position in the English literary world of today) relates that one of his patients dared not continue to go into society because often, on the actual chair that was pointed out to her with a courteous gesture, she saw an old gentleman already seated. She could be quite certain that either the gesture of invitation or the old gentleman's presence was a hallucination, for her hostess would not have offered her a chair that was already occupied. And when Huxley, to cure her, forced her to reappear in society, she felt a moment of painful hesitation when she asked herself whether the friendly sign that was being made to her was the real thing, or, in obedience to a non-existent vision, she was about to sit down in public upon the knees of a gentleman in flesh and blood. Her brief uncertainty was agonizing. Less so perhaps than mine." There is a still more elaborate version of the image in *Contre Sainte-Beuve.*

publication. The reviews, even those written by Proust's friends, were either perfunctory or unfavorable. Gregh, in *La Revue de Paris*, sneered at the number of sponsors Proust had called upon —Madame Lemaire, Anatole France, and Hahn. Léon Blum, in *La Revue blanche*, professed the warmest admiration for the author[3] but regretted that the book had not been published two years earlier. He said that he was impatiently waiting for Proust's next book. Only one reviewer was willing to praise Proust without qualification—young Charles Maurras, soon to achieve dubious notoriety as an apologist for French nationalism and a leader in the Action Française. Writing in the *La Revue encyclopédique*, Maurras discussed Proust as an author who had already come close to perfecting his art. He pointed out qualities, certainly apparent in the book, but not everywhere apparent in it—the remarkable combination of intelligence and sensibility, the delicate penetration, the exquisite taste, the simple elegance. Proust might have preferred praise from a different source, but he never ceased to be grateful to Maurras, even during the difficult years of the Dreyfus Case.

3. The admiration was not, or not always, mutual. In 1892 Proust complained to Gregh that *Le Banquet* had accepted a particularly bad piece with particularly offensive passages about money lenders. The author of the piece —whose name Proust pretended to forget—was Léon Blum.

CHAPTER VI

Notebooks and Dinners

I

PERHAPS as much as a year before the appearance of *Les Plaisirs et les jours,* Proust began working on another book, a long novel of some sort. In the early months of 1896 he mentioned it in letters as something that his correspondents were quite familiar with, and in one letter he went on to express the hope, or at least to consider the possibility, that he might finish it and afterwards write other books. During the summer he discussed it repeatedly with his mother and indeed gave her almost daily reports on his progress. "If I can't say that I have yet worked on my novel, in the sense of being absorbed by it and conceiving it as a whole," he once told her in a letter, ". . . still the notebook I bought, which doesn't represent all I have done, because before I worked on loose sheets—that notebook is full, and there are *110 big pages.*" There is good reason to believe that these were the very first pages of Proust's first effort to write what afterwards became, first *Jean Santeuil,* and then in the course of time A *la Recherche du temps perdu.*

The summer of 1896 was not exactly an easy one for Proust. He and his family were in mourning for his great-uncle, Louis Weil, and his grandfather, Nathé Weil, both of whom had recently died. His mother was deeply affected, and Proust himself was for other reasons subject to spells of the blackest melancholy. For one thing, his health was more uncertain than ever. He watched what he ate and how he ate, he dosed himself with bicarbonate of soda and iodide, but even so he had constant attacks of indigestion. He guarded himself against the things to which he knew he was allergic, and he smoked Espic cigarettes or burned Legras powder when he felt his asthma coming on. He avoided fatigue of any sort and slept as much as he could, but his asthma kept him from regular sleep. He usually had at least a mild attack just as he was going to bed, and he was often awakened by attacks during the night. Sometimes his whole existence seemed to resolve itself into a struggle for sleep. He got help from stimulants and rather more from hypnotics like trional. But the hypnotics were habit-forming and tended furthermore to bring on his spells of melancholy, from which he suffered enough already. His struggle for sleep often developed into a struggle to do without the pills that produced sleep. His mother, who could be more objective and who was in any case stronger-minded than he was, always made a point of insisting that he should use trional, or any of his other medicines for that matter, as sparingly as possible.

Both Proust and his mother traveled during the summer, partly at least for reasons of health. In August they were together at Mont-Dore, where however the haying was bad for Proust's asthma and where he caught cold besides. In September his mother went to Dieppe and he stayed, for the time being, in Paris. In their daily letters to each other she asked about his symptoms and he described them in satisfying detail. One night he had to burn powder for a long time before he went to bed, and even so he had to take two capsules of amyl; he was awakened by an attack at 5:30. Another night he got along without anything but Legras powder, tisane, and bicarbonate; he slept well and even managed to go to sleep again after awakening much too soon. On still another night he took amyl and—in the morning, when the painters woke him up—a cachet of trional. In the same letters he told his mother what, if anything, he was doing on his novel. Once he said modestly that he thought he would work on a little episode; once he admitted that he had not done anything the day before but promised that henceforth he would work regularly. At the rate of four hours a day he might perhaps finish by the first of February. On the other hand, he was very much afraid that the manuscript might turn out to be completely worthless.

On October 19 he went to Fontainebleau specifically to work, and a subject for a new episode immediately presented itself. On his arrival at the Hôtel de France et d'Angleterre he missed his mother so much that he simply had to put through a long-distance call to her—or rather to the baker across the street, who had the nearest available telephone. There was a frustrating delay, and when he at last heard her voice, he seemed to realize that he was hearing it as a voice for the very first time. He seemed to notice in particular the grief that had crept into it since the recent deaths in the family. The next day between four and six in the afternoon he had a much more agonizing spell of missing his mother. "I doubt if any of the spells of anguish I have ever had have reached such a pitch of intensity," he told his mother afterwards. That very evening, October 20, he wrote up the two experiences more or less as they had happened except that he reversed their order—made the spell of anguish precede the telephone call—and gave the hotel as the Roches-Noires at Beg-Meil. In sending the manuscript to his mother, he urged her to put it away when she had read it and to remember where she had put it, because, he said, it would go into his novel. It did indeed. Many years later it appeared, in an altered form, as one of the most striking episodes in A la Recherche du temps perdu—the telephone call from Doncières.

At the hotel in Fontainebleau Proust met a friend, who was also there to work on a novel—young Léon Daudet, son of the author of Tartarin de Tarascon. They began eating together and once at least they took a ride together in the forest. But the leaves had not yet turned, the weather was generally bad, and Proust's asthma was troublesome. At first he was upset because the bed in his room was so placed that he had to sleep facing the wall. "All the things I need [at night]," he said in a letter to his mother, "my coffee, my tisane, my candle, my pen, my

matches, etc., etc., are on my right, so that [to reach them] I
always have to turn on my bad side, etc." In a series of four
postscripts to the letter he added that he was having the bed
moved, that he was worried about the bill he was running up
at the hotel, that he was also worried about his nervous laugh,
which might offend Daudet, and wanted to know what he could
do about it, and that he had got through a night without trional.
The next day he was even more worried about the hotel bill
when he discovered that there was a hole in one of his trouser
pockets. After a careful calculation it seemed clear to him that
he had either lost or been robbed of more than thirty francs.
In either case he had been inexcusably careless, and guilty of
a crime against his mother who was supporting him in luxury
at the hotel. He had another spell of anguish, complicated this
time by indigestion. His stay at Fontainebleau was not an altogether happy one.

Not long after his return home, Proust was involved in a
family quarrel that resulted in physical violence of some kind—
glass was broken in at least one of the rooms in the Proust apartment. In a note to his mother Proust apologized, and in her
reply his mother apologized too. "You must know," she said,
"that I never even considered saying anything at all before Jean
[one of the servants] and if I did it was quite inadvertent." She
added that the broken glass would now be, as in the Temple,
"the symbol of indestructible union." The quarrel is pretty clearly
the one written up in the notebooks under the title of "Querelle
de Jean avec ses parents." Proust places it in the school days of
his hero, Jean Santeuil, and attributes it to Madame Santeuil's
quite mistaken suspicions about one of Jean's friends who is
actually a sober and responsible young man. Both she and her
husband reproach Jean before Augustin, one of the servants. As
he leaves the room, Jean slams the door and so breaks its
glass panel. While he is storming about his own room, he inadvertently breaks a piece of Venetian glass that his mother once
gave him. At dinner there is a general reconciliation, during which
Jean confesses that he has broken the Venetian glass, but his
mother merely kisses him and whispers, "It shall be, as in the
Temple, the symbol of an indestructible union."

The two passages in the notebooks—the one about the telephone call from Fontainebleau and "Querelle de Jean avec ses parents"—suggest certain general conclusions about Proust's habits of work. If he was writing what he called a novel, he was not illustrating a theme of any sort or even telling in a completely systematic way the story of his own life. He was often at least doing what he had tended to do since the days of *Le Banquet*—writing up isolated episodes. The units, short and not necessarily related to one another, were fragments of autobiography—moments of what seemed to him intense and significant experience. Sometimes, as in these two cases, the moments described were recent ones; more often, no doubt, they were moments remembered from the past—a vivid impression of a landscape, or intense suffering during a love affair, or intense interest in a new personality. The difficulty was that in this way he could go on writing long after the first of February without ever producing a book. He did go on, the notebooks accumulated, but the novel failed to emerge.

II

In January, 1897—the January following his return from Fontainebleau—Proust again begged off at the Mazarine Library. "The present course of my studies," he said in a letter to the director, "even more than my state of health, has made it necessary for me to ask the Ministry for an extension of my leave." He added that, if he could do so without impropriety, he would like to work at the library. He felt that he would thus facilitate his studies and at the same time renew pleasant contacts with his fellow librarians.

In February and March, while he was presumably working at the Mazarine or elsewhere, he experienced belated and distinctly unpleasant repercussions from *Les Plaisirs et les jours*. The first came, as he might have anticipated, from an old enemy, a persistently scurrilous fellow author named Paul Duval but more generally known under the pseudonym of Jean Lorrain. Lorrain was a man with a remarkably florid personality—an esthete with ulcers, a dandy who reeked of cheap perfume, a sadist who even as a child had plucked feathers from living chickens, an addict of ether and perhaps other drugs, a devotee of sumptuous furniture and exotic jewelry, a collector of frogs and toads in bronze and faience, a believer in goblins and lamias, for he felt sure that his house was haunted and that the persistently lurid dreams from which he suffered were supernaturally inspired. His erotic career had been sensational. He was fond of women and men too—at least there were stories about a certain blond sailor with two missing teeth who reminded him of Botticelli's "Primavera." In a series of decadent novels Lorrain had exploited and indeed exaggerated his vices. In a column, "Pall-Mall Semaine," published in *Le Journal*, he exploited his personality, attacked the Jews, and carried on a campaign against Montesquiou, whose decadence was obviously similar to but more arresting than his own. He detested Proust, who had given Lorrain's mother, Madame Duval, the nickname of "Sycorax." Early in the summer of 1896 he had indulged in persiflage at the expense of both Proust and Montesquiou, whom he had described as "pretty little gentlemen with literary and social aspirations." Now, on February 3, 1897, he devoted a special article to *Les Plaisirs et les jours*, treating it as an insipid society production, precious and indeed pretentious in style. The illustrations, in particular, amused him, and he maintained that Madame Lemaire had once been so hard pressed that she had illustrated a story of friendship with a sketch of two cats playing guitars. The Anatole France preface also amused him, and he predicted that Proust's next preface would come from another eminent novelist, Alphonse Daudet, who was quite incapable of resisting the solicitations of his son—at this time a close friend of Proust's—and of Madame Lemaire.

Taking a somewhat sensational view of the article (though there were precedents for his action in French literary circles), Proust at once challenged Lorrain to a duel. While his seconds— the one an experienced duelist, Gustave de Borda, and the other a society painter, Jean Béraud—were meeting with the seconds of his adversary, Proust was worried that he might have to arise early and fight in the morning. But when he learned that the time had been fixed for the afternoon, he became quite calm, and actually displayed a *sang-froid* that amazed his friends. The antagonists met on a rainy day at the Tour de Villebon and used pistols, necessarily so, since both were invalids and incapable of handling swords. After both had fired twice without touching each other, the seconds decided that the quarrel was ended. Proust, eager to rush forward and shake his adversary's hand, was restrained by his seconds and discreetly escorted from the field of honor.

The episode, prominently reported in the newspapers, can scarcely have been unpleasant in retrospect. The same could scarcely be said of another episode involving *Les Plaisirs et les jours*—persiflage that came, not from Proust's enemies but his friends. They were old friends, from the days of the Lycée Condorcet and *Le Banquet*, who now gathered at Jacques Bizet's apartment on the Quai Bourbon and from time to time gave performances with a magic lantern, somewhat hazardous ones because they had been warned that under certain circumstances the machine might explode and blow up the whole house. On March 18, 19, and 20, they gave an unusually ambitious perform- ance, a kind of revue dealing with their literary activities during the preceding year. They concentrated on first books, not only those of Gregh and Ernest La Jeunesse, but also, inevitably, *Les Plaisirs et les jours*. Bizet and Dreyfus wrote the dialogue, but all the members of the group helped with the production—all, that is, with the exception of Proust, who was busy with literature and society in other quarters of Paris and never came to the Quai Bourbon. In one of the scenes of the revue Proust, whose voice was mimicked by Léon Yeatman, was thus represented as talking with La Jeunesse and Gregh:

PROUST, ADDRESSING ERNEST LA JEUNESSE. Have you read my book?

LA JEUNESSE. No, Monsieur, it costs too much.

PROUST. I'm sorry, that's what everybody tells me. Have you read it, Gregh?

GREGH. Yes, I've cut the pages so I can review it.

PROUST. And are you another one who thinks it costs too much?

GREGH. Not at all, not at all. You get plenty for your money.

PROUST. Of course. A preface by Monsieur Anatole France, four francs. Pictures by Madame Lemaire, four francs. Music by Reynaldo Hahn, four francs. Prose of mine, one franc. A few of my verses, fifty centimes. Total thirteen francs fifty. That's not too much, is it?

LA JEUNESSE. But, Monsieur, there is much more than that in the *Almanach Hachette*, and it costs only twenty-five sous!

PROUST, LAUGHING OUT LOUD. That really is funny! But it's painful for me to laugh like this! You *are* witty, Monsieur La Jeunesse! How amusing it must be to have a wit like yours!

The revue was a huge success and reports of it soon reached Proust, who was perhaps already sensitive about the price of his book. He may well have resolved, even at this time, that he would never again permit himself the luxury of a fine format, illustrations, and a preface by a well-known author. Certainly in later years he never did so. If he was hurt by the persiflage, as he is said to have been, he nevertheless remained on good terms with Bizet and Dreyfus. On the other hand, he was even less inclined than before to join the group on the Quai Bourbon. He persisted in following a separate course, in frequenting the *salons* and in making social conquests that, in this very season, were especially notable.

III

The social season of 1897 was in one respect unusual. Just as it began, the Charity Bazaar in the Rue Jean-Goujon burned to the ground and more than a hundred people, many of them members of high society, lost their lives. All Paris—indeed all Europe—was appalled by the magnitude of the catastrophe and impressed by the eminence of the victims. Messages of condolence were despatched and received; the Prince of Wales and other members of the English Jockey Club considerately wrote the president of the Jockey Club in Paris. The social calendar was completely disrupted, hostesses being obliged to cancel their parties and to arrange other parties appropriate to the occasion. Proust's friend the Comtesse de Beaulaincourt, for example, arranged an elegant little dinner for a certain Princesse Radziwill, who was in Paris to represent the German Empress at the memorial services in Notre Dame.

The Comtesse de Beaulaincourt was one of the most notable

and most obliging of Proust's aristocratic friends. She was the daughter of a distinguished soldier, the Marshal de Castellane; she was related to the Greffulhes and, it might almost be said, to the Molés, for her mother had been for many years the mistress of the Comte de Molé, Prime Minister under Louis Philippe. In her youth Madame de Beaulaincourt had lived a little too ardently and unconventionally. She had boxed men's ears at balls; she had received men—Mérimée, for example—as she lay stretched out on a sofa with her feet bare; she had had rather more than the acceptable number of lovers. Her first husband had suffered severely from her antics. Once he had returned from a long absence in Constantinople to find her with a son, whom he resolutely refused to acknowledge. Her second husband had also suffered, but his martyrdom had been mercifully short—in the fourth month of marriage he had fallen from his horse and impaled himself on the handle of his sword. Now, in her old age, Madame de Beaulaincourt seemed to be expiating these frivolities of other years. She dressed soberly in black silk gowns and she worked hard at making artificial flowers. In her drawing-room she had a special table on which she kept her gum bottles and tubes of paint, the roses and carnations that she used as models. Her most regular guests were members of the Castellane family, including her grand-nephew Boni de Castellane, and old friends such as Emile Ollivier, the Prime Minister who had blundered into the Franco-Prussian War and who had since spent a quarter of a century trying to justify himself.

The dinner in honor of the Princesse Radziwill was an unusual undertaking for Madame de Beaulaincourt, and she obviously chose her guests with the greatest care. There was the Prince Radziwill of course, then the Duchesse de Malakoff, the Marquise de Castellane, the Baron de Saint-Amand, Robert Vallier, and—perhaps as a special favor to a protégé of whom she was fond—Marcel Proust. It is unlikely that Proust had often before appeared in company quite so exclusive. But afterwards he was disconcerted to find that, in reporting the dinner, *Le Figaro* had made a mistake in names and had mentioned Marcel Prévost as the man who was present. Two days elapsed before Proust was able to correct the mistake.

Less than two weeks later, on May 24, 1897, Proust gave a dinner of his own, in its way almost equally notable, a dinner to which he invited his most distinguished literary and artistic friends, several of them, as it happened, members of high society. The guests of honor were Montesquiou and Anatole France, the latter about to leave town and able to accept only at the last moment. Next in order of importance came the Comte Louis de Turenne and the Marquis de Castellane, who could perhaps both by courtesy be described as men of letters. Turenne, a middle-aged clubman with a monocle and reputedly one of the most snobbish men in Parisian society, was interested in women and horses. He had once taken a trip to the United States, where he had eaten roast duck at the best hotels and inspected Jockey Clubs wherever he had been fortunate enough to find them. He had subsequently published his observations in the form of a journal. Castellane was the father of Boni de Castellane and the nephew of Madame de Beaulaincourt. He was a mild man with full mustaches and a lock of hair that curled diagonally across his forehead. In his youth he had gone in for dissipation and politics—royalist politics of course. After the Franco-Prussian War he had sat in the National Assembly, where he earned the distinction of having voted against every clause in the new Constitution. Now he confined himself to literature and society, though he was quite convinced that neither really existed in the modern world. Society seemed to him a hopeless jumble, an appalling parody of society under the Old Regime; he was thankful that he himself had been able to enter the *monde* while there was still a *monde* to enter. And as for literature, what could it possibly be now that education was becoming liberal and secular? Modern writers were obviously deplorable, "obscure in style, weak in phrasing, incapable of rounding off a sentence." Yet he himself did little to correct modern taste, except to write an occasional article for the more conservative journals and to express his nostalgia in an autobiography. Proust's other guests were his seconds, Borda and Béraud, the dramatist Georges de Porto-Riche, the novelist Edouard Rod, and two young friends, Caillavet and Hahn.

It is easy to imagine Proust as, with elaborate and somewhat

artificial politeness, he greeted his guests, as he talked with
them in the drawing room and tried to make them feel at ease
with one another, as he seated them at the great oval table,
and as he signaled for the courses to be brought in, each no
doubt selected by his mother and prepared by the family cook,
presumably one of the models for the admirable Françoise. It
is easy to imagine these things: it is more difficult to imagine
what he talked about or what the guests talked about with each
other, what remarks Anatole France addressed to the Marquis
de Castellane or what Rod and Turenne found in common. Did
they review the afternoon of February 5 when Proust fought
with Lorrain? Or go over the casualty list from the Charity
Bazaar fire? Or deplore the tragic illness of the Prince de Sagan,
on whose account the Marquis de Castellane was obliged to
leave before the evening was over? These things one can never
know. One can only surmise that the conversation was worthy
of the company, that it reflected glory on the host and even
perhaps on the less distinguished guests, and that the dinner was
in fact, as the newspapers later reported, a brilliant success.

CHAPTER VII

The Dreyfus Case

WHILE Proust was working on his novel, a political controversy of almost unprecedented violence broke out in France. The ostensible issue was the guilt or innocence of a certain Captain Dreyfus, convicted three years earlier on a charge of espionage; the real issue, or so Proust felt, was anti-Semitism. In his notebooks Proust was already recording his experiences in the *salons* and his impressions of society. Ultimately—in new notebooks or new versions of the old ones—he began giving these experiences and impressions a special setting, that of the Dreyfus Case itself. He began studying society just at the moment when anti-Semitism was most evident. Thus the politics of the years 1897-1900 became, in the final notebooks at least, an essential element in his novel.

I

Anti-Semitism can scarcely have been new to Proust. He must have encountered it rather generally in society, and at one of the houses he frequented—that of Alphonse Daudet—he had probably met Edouard Drumont, the chief spokesman of the anti-Semitic movement. Drumont was a violent, unscrupulous man with a face like a Hebrew prophet, with a great black

beard and masses of unruly black hair. Some years before he
had written *La France juive,* a book in which he had set forth
at considerable length (in twelve hundred pages, to be exact)
views later to be associated with Hitler and Goebbels. He had
defended Aryan supremacy and deplored the conquest of France
by the Rothschilds and other international Jews. More recently
he had been editing an anti-Semitic newspaper, *La libre Parole.*

Proust may well have·known something of Drumont's activities
during the early stages of the Dreyfus Case, which had, as a
matter of fact, been particularly sinister. For while the government
was still trying to decide whether or not Dreyfus had written a
certain incriminating memorandum, or *bordereau,* Drumont had
freely discussed the case in *La libre Parole.* He had linked Dreyfus
with Joseph Reinach, whom he had identified as the head of a
"Jewish Syndicate" with enormous financial resources trying to
get control of France; he had even charged that the Ministry,
at Reinach's instigation, was deliberately placing Jews in confi-
dential positions. Disturbed by the charges, the Ministry had
acted precipitately—had improvised a case against Dreyfus and
secured a conviction. Proust and other Frenchmen not blinded
by prejudice had certainly regretted the whole episode, but they
had had no reason to believe that Dreyfus was innocent.

Now, however, in the autumn of 1897, it appeared that for
some time a number of men had been quietly sifting the charges
against Captain Dreyfus and accumulating evidence to show that
he was really innocent after all. One of these men was the Captain's brother, Mathieu Dreyfus; another was Auguste Scheurer-
Kestner, an elderly and eminently respectable Alsatian, first vice-
president of the French Senate; another was Colonel Picquart,
head of counter-espionage in the French army until his superiors,
disturbed by his investigations, had sent him to Africa; still
another was Joseph Reinach, now as before the principal object
of Drumont's attacks. Acting independently or together, they
had learned something about the feverish deliberations of the
Ministry, something too about the irregularities of the court-
martial, at which the Minister of War had shown the judges
documents concealed from the defense. But they had learned
something even more important, had learned in fact that the

author of the *bordereau* was not Dreyfus but a certain Comman-
dant Esterhazy, a decayed adventurer with a lurid reputation
and tremendous mustaches.

In November, 1897, *Le Figaro* made the vital disclosures in
the case. It reported the investigations of Scheurer-Kestner, printed
a letter by Mathieu Dreyfus in which Esterhazy was named as
the author of the *bordereau*, and reproduced the *bordereau* in
facsimile beside specimens of Dreyfus's and Esterhazy's hand-
writings. In its comment the newspaper was judicious and dis-
passionate; it confined itself to indisputable facts. Not so the
novelist Zola, who took up the cause of "Revision" when *Le
Figaro*, intimidated by the hostility of subscribers, reluctantly
dropped it, for Zola was incapable of being judicious. His imagination was lively, his taste highly sensational. He saw—he was
determined to see—the case as a national melodrama in which
the villain was an aristocratic officer on the General Staff, a
certain Colonel du Paty de Clam. In an open letter, published
early in 1898 under the sensational headline "J'accuse," Zola
represented himself as a man with "one passion only," a passion
for truth, a man uttering "a burning protest," expressing the agony
of his soul. He represented the unfortunate Paty de Clam, on
the other hand, as a monstrous conspirator who had fabricated
the whole case from the beginning and who had exercised an
almost hypnotic influence over his fellow officers, the generals of
the High Command. He was wrong of course, quite wrong as
far as Paty de Clam was concerned; nevertheless his letter was
remarkably effective. It encouraged the partisans of Dreyfus, even
those who winced when they read its clichés; it infuriated the
partisans of Drumont; it forced people all over France to take
sides for or against Revision.

Unfortunately most people took the wrong side. They were
prepared to believe that the case was a melodrama, as both Zola
and Drumont assured them that it was, but they were generally
inclined to accept Drumont's explanation of the villainy, which
was at least the more plausible of the two. Drumont told them
about the Syndicate, that powerful and sinister organization,
with Reinach at its head, determined ultimately to ruin France
and, at the moment, to undermine the Army. He described men

like Scheurer-Kestner and Picquart as agents or dupes of the
Syndicate, concerned, whether they realized it or not, in an
abominable Semitic conspiracy. Society generally believed in the
Syndicate, particularly aristocratic society, which had always detested the republican point of view that Reinach represented,
and which was in any case committed to defend the Monarchy,
the Army, and the Church. The aristocratic *salons* buzzed with
anti-Semitism, some hostesses, or so Proust later said, going so
far as to lower the tone of their parties by receiving quite unknown
people only because they had refused to buy from Jewish tradesmen
or had printed "Down with the Jews" on their sunshades. The
Bonapartist aristocracy was less violent but no less loyal to the
Army. "I had an uncle who was a soldier," the Princesse Mathilde
said; she considered no other evidence. The middle-class hostesses
were for the most part either anti-Dreyfusard or ambiguously
neutral. Madame Aubernon, for example, refused to decide whether
Dreyfus was guilty or not, preferring, as she put it, to leave the
matter to the courts; Madame Straus made bright remarks about
both sides. Madame Aubernon did heroically announce that she
intended to keep *her* Jews, but she probably lost other luminaries
by so doing, as Madame Straus lost Forain and Meyer. Only
Madame de Caillavet and a few other middle-class hostesses came
out unequivocally for Dreyfus, and indeed made their drawing
rooms centers of Revisionist activity.

Proust himself did not hesitate, though he realized that he
ran the risk of alienating his aristocratic friends: he followed
Reinach whom he knew and admired, he became an ardent
Dreyfusard. Joining a group of young men who met above the
Café des Variétés—some of them the same young men who had
ridiculed *Les Plaisirs et les jours*—he helped to frame the first
Revisionist petition. He himself went, apparently with Gregh
and others, to get the signature of Anatole France, who was ill
at the time but got out of bed to receive them. "Let me see it,"
France said. "I will sign it; I will sign anything; I am shocked."
During the early months of 1898 Proust eagerly followed the
developments in the case—the court-martial and acquittal of
Esterhazy; the trial and conviction of Zola, who afterwards ran
away to England; the persecution of Colonel Picquart, who re-

mained to face his enemies and who became, in the eyes of partisans like Proust, the hero of the Revisionist movement. A professional soldier with a definite feeling against the Jews, Picquart had nevertheless followed the logic of the evidence and refused to accept the conviction of an innocent man, even when he realized that his refusal might lead to his dismissal from the army, as in fact it did. Proust was extremely anxious to meet Picquart and finally succeeded in doing so. Once, when Picquart was in prison, Proust went to a vast amount of trouble to send him a curious present, more valuable in retrospect than it may have seemed at the time, one of the many unsold copies of *Les Plaisirs et les jours.*

Thus Proust did what he could to help and encourage the martyrs in the case, but at the same time he showed a definite reluctance to let his opinions interfere more than necessary with his social life or to quarrel with old friends merely because they hated the Jews. If he had liked Drumont, he would probably have remained on good terms with him. As it was, he remained on excellent terms with Léon Daudet and with Montesquiou, whose views were scarcely distinguishable from Drumont's. Once, when Proust and Montesquiou were together, the poet apparently expressed his anti-Semitism and even appealed to Proust for confirmation. The next day Proust wrote him a letter. "While I am a Catholic like my father and my brother," he said, "my mother, on the other hand, is a Jew. You will understand that this is a sufficiently strong reason for my avoiding discussions of the sort. I thought it more respectful to say this in writing than to say it aloud before another person. But I am very glad that I have this opportunity of telling you what I might perhaps never have thought of telling you. For since our ideas are different, or rather since I am not free to hold ideas that I might perhaps otherwise have held, you could unintentionally have hurt me in a discussion. You will of course understand that I am not speaking of discussions we might have alone, when I shall always be keenly interested in your social and political ideas, if you will explain them, even though a decisive reason prevents me from sharing them."

II

During the dark days of 1898, when the Revisionists were suffering their worst disasters, Proust was working at the apartment of a humble friend in the Passage des Beaux-Arts. So at least he told Madame de Caillavet, when he met her on the street. But she knew that in or near the Passage a broken and bloated acquaintance of Proust's, Oscar Wilde, was living under an assumed name, and she could not help wondering. Was Proust surreptitiously seeing Wilde? Was he paying regular visits to the florid and dingy bedroom at the Hôtel d'Alsace? She was inclined to suspect that he was. But it seems more likely that he was doing exactly what he said—visiting a humble friend and working in surroundings that he found more congenial than those in the Boulevard Malesherbes.

In the notebooks Proust describes several friends at whose apartments he might conceivably have worked. A few of them are women, but they behave, in his account, so little like women that one can scarcely avoid thinking of them as men. One is Madame S., an "independent" young widow of whom Proust's hero is very fond. He visits her regularly, usually between ten and two at night. They read together and plan their days together. Sometimes they are invited out to the same houses, and the hero has reason to hope that, through the courtesy of common friends, they may be able to pass the summer together in the country. Another is Françoise, represented as an accomplished musician. The hero meets her by the lake in the Bois de Boulogne, in Versailles, and on the Terrace at Saint-Germain-en-Laye. But he sees her most often in her apartment, which he visits as regularly as he once visited that of Madame S. Sometimes Françoise sits down at the piano and plays, over and over again, for he never tires of hearing it, a "phrase" from a sonata by Saint-Saëns. Sometimes three friends of hers, all amateur musicians, drop in, and he listens to them as they play together, or chats with them, or writes letters, from time to time surreptitiously pressing Françoise's hand. Both stories end with episodes of jealousy that Proust afterwards worked into the story of Swann and Odette.

It is quite possible that Proust sometimes wrote in the houses of young men with whom he was in love—and indeed described love affairs very similar to those that he was going through at the moment. He also described certain episodes from the Dreyfus Case, though without yet trying to use them as a background for his society scenes. In one of the notebooks his hero attends the sessions of the Zola trial. He arises early, takes along sandwiches and a flask of coffee, drives to the Palais de Justice, and spends the whole day feverishly following the testimony. An expert analyzes the handwriting of the *bordereau* and shows that it is not that of Dreyfus. General de Boisdeffre, the almost legendary Chief of Staff, enters the Palais. A tall man with a stiff leg, a purple complexion, and a nervous tic, he wears, oddly enough, civilian clothes—a shabby overcoat and a top hat. Colonel Picquart, summoned from Mont Valérien, waits for his turn to testify and finally takes the stand.

The scenes are vivid, but the drama is a subjective one, lying not so much in the trial itself as in the mind of the author-hero. Sometimes he is entirely concerned with his own reactions, as when he tries to discover precisely what kind of pleasure he gets from discussing the day's events with a friend in the evening and from reading about them in *Le Figaro* the next morning at breakfast. Sometimes he is concerned with the interplay between his mind and the outside world, between what he imagines reality to be and what in fact it is. He misleads himself and thus invites disappointments, such as the one he experiences when he sees Picquart for the first time. The reality before him is barer and poorer than he expected; the man who saunters about the hall of the Cour d'Assises is not the Picquart of his dreams. This interplay between the subjective and objective worlds, found also in *Les Plaisirs et les jours* and in the definitive version of the novel, is one of Proust's most characteristic themes.

Generally, however, the author-hero is concerned first of all with ideas, often quite abstract ones. It seems natural for him to play the philosopher, to proceed inductively, and to seek the general in the particular. The trial and the workings of his own mind interest him no doubt, but often primarily because they lead him to general reflections and help him to formulate general laws. The testimony of the handwriting expert shows him that truth is the object of science, and that truth really exists. The testimony of Picquart shows him that philosophers can be understood only by philosophers. The mannerisms that Picquart exhibits on the witness stand—his habit of pronouncing *secrets* as though it were *sécrets*, for example—lead to certain conclusions about great men: they are often a little odd; they inspire in us a feeling not so much of respect as of intimacy. "We detect in those who possess grandeur something of our own spiritual essence, what is best and most pleasing in us, and we laugh at them in just the same way that we laugh at ourselves."

The passages on the Dreyfus Case are not perhaps the most brilliant in the notebooks, but they afford a particularly happy illustration of Proust's interest in generalizations. He was still very much what he had been and was to remain until the end of his career—the disciple of his first master, Darlu.

III

In the spring of 1898 Proust was ill and his work interrupted. In the early summer it was interrupted again when his mother went to the hospital for an operation—a routine operation, her doctors thought, but unforeseen difficulties developed. She was on the operating table for three hours and she was not clearly out of danger until the end of the second day. Proust seems to have been constantly with her during the long period of her convalescence.

Just as he began to lead a more normal life again, the Dreyfus Case entered a new phase—took, in fact, a miraculously happy turn, common enough in melodrama but much less common in life. The new developments began in the headquarters of the General Staff, where an officer, checking over the Dreyfus portfolio, suddenly noticed that two of the documents were fabrications—made up of several fragments of manuscript written on paper with various markings. It was clear that a forger had been at work, and equally clear that this forger was none other than Colonel Henry, Picquart's successor in the Intelligence Department. Though committed to the view that Dreyfus was guilty, the new Minister of War acted with exemplary promptness, forcing Henry to confess, arresting him, and sending him to Mont Valérien. The next day Henry was found in his cell with his throat cut and a razor in his hand. The documents that he had forged or touched up were not a vital part of the case against Dreyfus, which still rested chiefly on the *bordereau*, but the damage to the Nationalist cause was irreparable. Nationalist editors modified their policy. Even Drumont was uneasy for a few days, until Charles Maurras, the critic who had so favorably reviewed *Les Plaisirs et les jours*, came forward with an ingenious explanation of Henry's behavior. He had forged for the public good, Maurras argued; he had unselfishly sacrificed himself; he had become a martyr for France. Still it was scarcely to be expected that Frenchmen corrupted by secular education should appreciate the moral and intellectual beauty of his act.

The case was not yet over; Drumont, supported by Maurras, continued to fulminate; difficult days were ahead. But the turning point had clearly been reached and ardent Revisionists like Proust could now feel quite sure that in the end victory would be theirs. At the moment they were trying to do something for Picquart, who was still under arrest and awaiting trial. They felt that a petition might help, especially if they could get the signatures of a few prominent men. At the suggestion of Anatole France, Proust wrote Madame Straus, asking her if she could persuade the Comte d'Haussonville to sign, or, if not Haussonville, then Dufeuille, Ganderax, or even Pozzi. He added that the literary associations of the case were rapidly changing. If before it had been distinctly reminiscent of Balzac, it had become, with the confession and suicide of Henry, positively Shakespearean.

During the winter Proust was probably working again and certainly going out a good deal. He was seeing new hostesses— the Baronne de La Tombelle, the Marquise de Brou, Madame Charles Dettelbach, the Princesse Bibesco, and the Princesse de Brancovan. He was making new friends, notably Prince Antoine

Bibesco, a cultured and entertaining young man in the Rumanian diplomatic service. At their first meeting Bibesco was disturbed by the flabbiness of Proust's handshake—so much so that, when they became better acquainted, he tried to get Proust to cultivate a firmer clasp. Proust followed a demonstration somewhat doubtfully and then remarked, "If I did what you do, people would take me for an invert." But the matter of the handshake was, after all, a minor difference between them. They were both at the moment enthusiastic about Thoreau, and it was soon arranged that they should translate *Walden* together.

Before long Proust was seeing a good deal of Bibesco's cousins, the younger members of the Brancovan family. He liked Prince Constantin de Brancovan, whose interests were literary, and his younger sister, the Princesse de Caraman-Chimay, who was very good-looking. But the member of the family he liked best was the elder sister, the Comtesse Mathieu de Noailles, who was just beginning to publish poems of remarkable freshness and brilliance, who was in fact already recognized in Proust's circle as a writer of unusual promise. She looked even younger than she was, though she was only twenty-two—she might well have been an overdressed little girl with a radiant face and magnificent black eyes. She was so small that she almost disappeared in an armchair. But when she talked it was difficult to ignore her, difficult to avoid ignoring everyone else. For she talked eloquently, poetically, torrentially, talked so fast that she seldom waited for anyone to reply, talked about nature, society, and books, often books that she had opened but had never quite found time to read. At intervals she turned her eyes skyward in a kind of swoon and held up her left hand as though to silence interruptions. Like the other members of the Brancovan family, she shared Proust's views about the Dreyfus Case.

In April, 1899, just as the social season was getting under way, Proust decided to give another grand dinner at which he would honor, not only France and Montesquiou, but also his new friend, Madame de Noailles. Montesquiou was as usual a problem because he was on such bad terms with so many people. He might well insult some of Proust's guests; he might even refuse to come himself if he had to face others. Proust solved the problem by

consulting him in advance and getting him to draw up a black
list, which unfortunately included the Régniers, the Heredias,
the Polignacs, the Blanches, and the Hahns—a substantial number
of the people Proust wanted to entertain. Proust pleaded for one
or two insignificant modifications, but the poet remained inflexible and the black list was allowed to stand. On the appointed
day the acceptable guests gathered, dined, and listened as Mademoiselle Laparcerie of the Odéon Company read poems by each
of the three poets present.

The party, even with the omissions demanded by the black
list, was one of the most brilliant Proust had ever given, but
afterwards something seemed to go quite radically wrong with
the publicity. Le Figaro, not usually obtuse in such matters, was
very obtuse indeed. It violated the rules of social decorum by
ignoring many of the more distinguished guests and by naming
only the Comtesse Potocka, Madame de Brantes, the Marquise
d'Eyragues, Madame Lemaire, Madame Straus, Madame de Caillavet, Cahen d'Anvers, and Léon Bailby. It went on to describe
the other guests as "the notables of the scientific, literary, and
artistic worlds," and to mention only the readings from France
and Madame de Noailles, "in whose honor the reception was
given." Proust's father feared the worst from the notables of the
scientific world, who had not even been invited, and Proust himself knew only too well what to expect from Montesquiou, who
had certainly been one of the more important guests—in his
own eyes obviously the most important of all.

Proust spent a whole day with influential friends arranging
for more satisfactory notices of his party, and he was so far
successful that he got Le Figaro to print a second and eminently
satisfactory notice, quite possibly one that he had drafted himself. This second notice described the party as "literary" and
added that it had been a "real artistic treat." After the poems
by France and Madame de Noailles, the notice said, Mademoiselle
Laparcerie had read "some beautiful new pieces by Montesquiou,
which will be published within a month." The guests named were
the Comtesse de Noailles, the Comtesse de Briey, the Baron
Edmond de Rothschild, the Baronne Deslandes, the Marquis de
Castellane, the Prince Giovanni Borghèse, Madame Léon Fould,

the Comte de Gontaut-Biron, Anatole France, Jean Béraud, Charles Ephrussi, and the Comte de Montesquiou-Fezensac, who —it was specifically said—"enjoyed a double triumph, as an author and as a reader of distinction, for he himself recited, at the insistence of the other guests, some of his own poems." Montesquiou was certainly appeased; one cannot be quite so sure about the scientific friends of Professor Proust.

IV

In the summer of 1899 the Dreyfus Case, still in its Shakespearean phase, passed beyond the catastrophe, to that point in Shakespearean drama at which order is reestablished and comforting speeches made. The villains in the case, the Esterhazys and the Henrys, were now gone; Picquart emerged from prison, Zola returned from his martyrdom in an English hotel. The Ministry was now firmly Revisionist. The Cour de Cassation annulled the old verdict and ordered a second court-martial, for which Dreyfus was brought back from Devil's Island. He was a tragic figure, pathetically listless and prematurely old. To one observer he seemed scarcely human, looking more like a stylized victim in an allegorical painting. On the first day of the court-martial at Rennes he arose uncertainly and protested his innocence in a dry, strangled voice. The witnesses testified, the lawyers wrangled, the battle began again, but this time it was more like a shadow battle, for the evidence was already familiar and the verdict scarcely seemed to be in doubt.

In Paris public attention was even diverted for a time to the last operatic gesture of the Nationalists, made, as it happened, by one of Drumont's followers, Jules Guérin, secretary-general of the Anti-Semitic League and editor of L'Antijuif. Anticipating arrest and eager for martyrdom, Guérin fortified and provisioned his headquarters in the Rue de Chabrol, gathered weapons and dynamite, hung out from the top window a stuffed monkey labeled "Reinach," and with a group of chosen followers defied the Jews and the Dreyfusards to attack him. But, the Ministry having decided that no blood was to be shed, a police officer merely approached the building, delivered through a window the warrant of arrest, and said to Guérin, "You are in a state of rebellion, monsieur." "I know it, monsieur," Guérin answered. The police then quietly blockaded the "Fort Chabrol," as crowds milled about, reporters kept all-night vigils, and the young men of the Anti-Semitic League roamed the streets shouting, "Down with the Jews" and pummeling unsympathetic spectators. One night, to the surprise of everyone, a man cried, "Long live the Jews! Down with the Army!" and fired several shots at the Leaguers, but it later appeared that he was quite a disreputable character, an anarchist in fact. Many influential Nationalists disapproved of Guérin's performance, and some of them, including Drumont and the young Prince de Sagan, entered the Fort Chabrol to expostulate with him. But he still refused to yield, even though he was out of food and obliged to depend on what his Leaguers, riding by on bus tops, could throw in through the windows.

While these events were in progress, Proust was spending a few weeks at a fashionable watering place on the shores of Lake Geneva, Evian-les-Bains. A hotel—even such an expensive hotel as the Splendide—was scarcely the best place for an asthmatic, and there were inevitably certain harrowing incidents. There were nights when Proust was awakened by inconsiderate guests or employees. There was the night when he found himself without any matches except the sinister sulphur matches supplied by the hotel, so that he had to go through strange contortions to light his Legras powder and heat the water for his hot-water bottle. But generally he slept a good deal, if not quite so much as he wanted to, and he got along without too much Legras powder or too much trional or too much of a new medicine he was taking, philogyne. He had acquaintances—or at least his mother, who was with him for a while, had acquaintances—at the hotel, and he was fond of chatting with the servants, among whom he seems to have been popular. In good weather he took walks or went out on the lake or made excursions to such places as Coppet, once the residence of Madame de Staël. He had friends near Thonon, a short train ride away. The train went at a leisurely pace, whistled at stations, waited for late arrivals, and stopped so long at Thonon itself that the passengers could get out and shake hands with acquaintances who were seeing guests off or buying newspapers or merely looking for people they knew. Closer at hand were the Brancovans, whose country residence, the Villa Bassaraba, was at Amphion. The Princesse de Brancovan was dreadfully neurotic, and her daughter, *la petite Noailles*, was, or could be, dreadfully objectionable. One night, when she was questioned about a man who figured in the Dreyfus Case, she said, "I don't know, I've never slept with him"—this in the presence of her husband and her whole family. Still Proust often went to the Villa Bassaraba, where he could discuss with a group of ardent Dreyfusards the siege of the Fort Chabrol and the testimony of the court-martial at Rennes.

On the afternoon of September 9 his mother left for Paris, and a few minutes later Proust saw, posted at the Casino and surrounded by exultant employees, the announcement that Dreyfus had again been convicted of treason. Proust was at the Villa Bassaraba that evening, and as he was preparing to treat his asthma before dinner, he heard Madame de Noailles sobbing and exclaiming; "How could they do it? How could they bear to tell him he was guilty? How could they bear to tell other countries and the world?" Proust's own feelings were not very different. "It is sad for the army, for France, for the judges," he said in a letter to his mother, and in subsequent letters he told her a good deal about unpleasant repercussions at Evian, including cases of overt anti-Semitism. But he urged his mother not to worry, urged his brother not to do anything impulsive that might embarrass the Ministry, urged the family servants with whom he had talked about the case not to think that he had deceived them; for he had no doubt that the new conviction would ultimately be set aside.

After his mother's departure Proust became acutely money conscious. He knew that his mother would call him to account for everything he spent, and so, in his daily letters to her, he tried to overwhelm her with figures and to give her the impression that he was counting every sou. Sometimes he complained: he could not visit his friends because carriage fares were too high and he could not invite them to the hotel because he could not afford to buy them meals. Sometimes he explained away apparent extravagances: the telegraph operator had refused to let him cut out words in his telegrams, and he saw that he could not omit even an indefinite article without running the risk of ambiguity. As often as possible Proust consulted his mother in advance. He asked her what she thought of the laundry bill and exactly how much he should leave in tips for the various members of the hotel staff, tips being a highly controversial matter in the Proust family. Toward the end of his stay he raised the question of further travel, perhaps to the Italian lakes or Rome or Venice, perhaps only to one of the high mountains near by. He promised to do nothing without consulting her, and indeed he could not, because she had left him too short of cash. Meanwhile he was reassuring her about his relationships with men. The most suspicious of the young men in the neighborhood had called at the hotel only once, and she should not suppose that there was anything odd about the local doctor, good heavens, no! It was unfortunate that he had to make such explanations, but he knew how her mind worked. He also urged her to be very discreet when she talked about marrying him off, because he was afraid Anatole France had designs on him for his daughter.

While he was telling her these things, she was reporting to him what he most wanted to hear—the final developments in the Dreyfus Case. The President of the Republic had pardoned Dreyfus, and the combined forces of the police and the fire department, prepared at last to take the Fort Chabrol by assault, had persuaded Guérin that it would be safer for him to finish his martyrdom in jail.

For Proust at least the case was over, becoming in his mind only the memory of a long and bitter struggle against the forces of anti-Semitism, carried to a successful conclusion. In later years he cherished the memory and recalled with keen satisfaction the whole series of events and the final victory. He recalled them in 1906, when Dreyfus was at last exonerated and when, before a large audience in the court of the Ecole Militaire, Dreyfus and Picquart received promotions. He recalled them a little later when, in the final version of his novel, he devoted many brilliant pages to anti-Semitism in high society. He recalled them later still when, through the efforts of Léon Daudet, he received the Goncourt Prize and when, magnifying the part he had played in the now distant past, he wrote to a friend, "I think I was the first Dreyfusard because I was the one who went to ask for the signature of Anatole France." But he recalled them, too, on less important occasions when he encountered the same anti-Semitism that had been so ugly during the years of the case. For though he was himself quite capable of ridiculing the Jews and was fond of telling flagrantly anti-Semitic stories, he now reacted to prejudice —and freedom from prejudice—in a very personal way. He even wrote letters of thanks to people who spoke well of Jews.

CHAPTER VIII

Jean Santeuil

I

PROUST HAD now been working on his novel for at least three years. He had not finished it, and he had no idea when, if ever, he would finish it. Still, he had succeeded in accumulating a large number of notebooks filled with manuscript—perhaps the greater part of the thousand pages recently printed under the title of *Jean Santeuil*.

The notebooks contain what can best be described as a series of autobiographical fragments—studies for what afterwards developed into *A la Recherche du temps perdu*. The story that they tell, in so far as they tell a story at all, is so transparently Proust's own that even he himself was sometimes inclined to doubt whether he could legitimately call it a novel. "It is something less, perhaps," he once says, "and yet much more, the very essence of my life, with nothing extraneous added, as it developed through a long period of wretchedness. This book of mine has not been manufactured: it has been garnered."

The central character, Jean Santeuil, is a self-portrait of the author and intended as such. He even looks like Proust, having black hair, a pale complexion, a somewhat prominent nose, and large eyes with rings under them. While he is in the army, he grows a mustache. Rather careless about his dress, he nevertheless chooses his ties with meticulous care and often wears a flower in his button-hole. He suffers from asthma, rheumatism, and headaches. When he goes to bed, he props himself up on four pillows, obviously so that he can breathe more easily. He is kept awake by human noises, no matter how faint. Having once slid off a horse, he is afraid of horses; he is also afraid of jellyfish. He pretends to study law but never goes to lectures. He wastes his time in society except when he is in love and then he deserts society altogether. Weakness of will and indecision are perhaps his chief faults. He can never resist his impulses, even his impulse to give enormous tips at hotels. When he is forced to choose between alternatives —say, between two invitations for the same evening—he always feels that the alternative he has rejected is the right one.

Jean's family life obviously resembles Proust's. He is generally hostile to his father, who is represented as rude and insensitive. He deplores his mother's middle-class prejudices, which are indeed of the narrowest sort, for she thinks a love match as depraved as adultery, a poet as disreputable as an actor. Money in her view is to be saved; spending of any sort, even from motives of generosity, is a crime. Jean tolerates her solicitude (as when, in her nightly notes to him, she asks him to set down the exact time he comes home) but he often rebels at her discipline—slams doors, breaks convenient glassware, and makes outrageously insulting remarks. In the course of time, however, he has a greater influence on his mother than she has on him. He modifies her prejudices, gives her a taste for scandal, and even persuades her to accept fashionable immorality. Finally—in their morning conversations, when she sits at his bedside—he seems to notice that she judges people exactly as he judges them, and is amused by exactly the same things.

Proust's method is still as casual as it was in the very first notebooks. There is little continuity and no structure other than the chronological one. Once or twice indeed he reviews an earlier episode to show how inaccurate first impressions are. Jean discovers that Monsieur de Lomperolles, who seemed to detest young men, was actually a pederast who liked them only too well. Jean is told, long after the event, that two apparently disreputable women he saw on a train were the Marquise de Lieureux and the wife of the Serbian Minister. But even such passages are not clearly the result of planning. Generally the notebooks read more like an elaborate diary or commonplace book than a novel. Yet somehow, in his desultory way, Proust covers his career—his childhood, his trips, his social life, his love affairs, and his ideas.

II

The story of his childhood begins with an episode already used in *Les Plaisirs et les jours*. Jean's mother always gives him a goodnight kiss to allay the anguish he feels when he goes to bed. But suddenly a new regime starts; he must go to sleep without her kiss. He cannot—his anguish is too intense—and he cannot persuade Augustin, the old family servant, to bring his mother to him. Finally he goes to the window and calls to her in the garden, where she is talking with a guest, Professor Surlande. She yields: she comes to him, she even seems to admit that his anguish is uncontrollable, for she says to Augustin, "Master Jean does not know what is the matter with him, nor what he wants. He is suffering from nerves." The moment, Proust says, is a significant one in Jean's career—he suddenly realizes that he is not responsible for his actions and that he can henceforth think of himself as an invalid, not as a delinquent. It is by no means clear, however, that he is afterwards represented as irresponsible.

Of the episodes that follow, several are concerned with Marie Kossichef, a girl Jean sees in the Champs-Elysées. He is devoted to her exactly as Proust was devoted to Marie de Benardaky. He lives for the moments he spends in her presence, he is inconsolable when bad weather keeps her at home. Once, on a snowy day, he is beside himself with joy when she appears unexpectedly; once, when he is ill, she sends him a letter inviting him to tea. But Jean's mother, convinced that the infatuation is ruining his health, decides to put a stop to the meetings. She tells him that henceforth he is going to take lessons at two o'clock, the hour he habitually leaves for the Champs-Elysées. Jean screams, abuses his mother and his grandfather, seizes a jug of water and smashes it on the floor. The scene is an unpleasant one, perhaps because it is too

close to what actually happened. The reader feels that he is overhearing a nasty family quarrel and witnessing the antics of a
thoroughly spoiled child.

A long section—a hundred printed pages altogether—deals with
Jean's visits to Etreuilles, the Illiers of Proust's childhood. (Indeed
the author sometimes forgets himself and calls it Illiers.) Episodes
still follow one another quite casually. There is something about
a cook named Ernestine, who wrings the necks of geese and tortures the kitchen maid; something about the mornings Jean spends
at his uncle's park; something about lunch and the buzzing of
flies on hot afternoons; something about cold days, the sentences
Jean likes in Gautier, the magic lantern that projects the figures of
Golo and Geneviève de Brabant, the kitchen, the park again, Sun-
days, and Jean's great-aunt, Madame Sureau, who spends her time
looking out of the window. There are descriptions of landscapes,
though not so many as in those sections of the notebooks that deal
with Jean's trips to Beg-Meil and Réveillon. There are descriptions
of flowers, among them lilacs and hawthorns. Proust associates
lilacs with the Orient. Their blood is Persian; they are delicate
Scheherazades, nude and highly perfumed, resting immobile among
their leaves. He associates hawthorns with churches, and when
he describes them his imagery is persistently ecclesiastical. He
thinks of them, furthermore, as the epitome of spring, of past
springs, of the walks at Etreuilles, and of dazzling days when he
came home to read Le Capitaine Fracasse in the afternoon. They
are the flower of the Month of Mary.

III

The society scenes are somewhat ambiguous, like those in Les
Plaisirs et les jours. At times the author seems to admire aristocratic
refinement, and he always represents as a triumph his hero's aristocratic associations. There are a good many passages in the notebooks that can have been written only by a snob. At other times,
he is perfectly well aware that society, whether aristocratic or
middle class, is hopelessly silly. It is the theatre of snobbery where
ridiculous figures, as inhuman as automata, struggle to keep or to
gain social prestige. Jean can play a part on the stage; he can

also, retiring to the audience, appreciate the spectacle as a grotesque but nevertheless engrossing comedy.

Proust is generally more analytical than in *Les Plaisirs et les jours*. He often treats his fine ladies and gentlemen as so many problems to be solved—definitely intellectual problems. He explores their minds at considerable length, scarcely bothering to show them in action at all except by way of illustration. Such is the case in the passage on Bertrand de Réveillon, who walks on the tables at a restaurant in his eagerness to reach Jean; otherwise he does nothing. He is studied as an example of an aristocratic young man who rebels against his heritage, which nevertheless he reflects in every movement he makes. The passage on the Prince de Borodino is a study of the difference between the Napoleonic and the feudal aristocracies. The passage on the Vicomtesse Gaspard de Réveillon is a study of a woman of genius who happens to have a high place in society. Proust is interested in her bad manners or what her aristocratic friends regard as such. The automatism called good manners, he concludes, destroys spontaneity; hence a genius is necessarily rude.

The analytic method does not preclude comedy; quite the contrary, the most amusing passages in the notebooks are often highly analytical. Examples can be found even in the scenes devoted to the most aristocratic of Jean's friends, the Duc and Duchesse de Réveillon, who are generally likable and whose life at their country estate is represented as an eminently satisfactory one. But the Réveillons are after all exclusive and necessarily circumspect with inferiors. Proust studies their attitude and the ridiculous behavior to which it gives rise. Jean's middle-class friends, notably the Marmets, are even more persistently comic. In one of the episodes the Marmets have invited Jean to the opera, but when they discover that the performance is to be a very special one—the first night of *Frédégonde*—they quarrel with him and force him to decline the invitation. The Duchesse de Réveillon, who hears the shabby story, persuades the Marmets' more distinguished friends to decline as well; so that when the performance begins, the Marmets are obliged to appear in their box with only one guest, a disreputable Jew named Shelchtenbourg. Their humiliation reaches the proportions of frenzy when they see Jean in the box

of the Réveillons and beside him no less a personage than the
King of Portugal. In the intermission Jean strolls about with the
King, telling His Majesty the story of the lawsuit between Ruskin
and Whistler. The Marmets are completely crushed, as they deserve
to be; but it is by no means clear that their snobbishness is more
offensive than the author's.

IV

The love stories in the notebooks are not very different from those
in *Les Plaisirs et les jours*, except perhaps that they are even more
clearly based on homosexual experiences. During a trip to Holland,
Jean goes to a convent and looks up a nun, who was once the
mistress of a friend of his. He no sooner sees her than he recognizes
her for what she is; she is glad to be recognized. "For a whole year
I have not slept with a man," she tells him, and she goes on to
indicate that there are only two or three of her kind in the convent.
There can be little doubt that Proust is here thinking of an encounter between inverts. In another passage, a girl named Charlotte appears as a guest in Jean's house. "There is a moment,"
Proust says, "when the woman we love comes to spend two days
beneath the same roof as ourselves, in complete and utter solitude
with us." Jean dines with Charlotte, takes walks with her, leads her
to her room at night, apparently stays there while she undresses, and
then sits at her bedside. But when he tries to kiss her, she resists
and threatens to ring or to leave. The circumstances of her visit
seem preposterous unless one assumes that Charlotte is really a
man.

Love is furtive and transient, as in Proust's first book, but not
now often accompanied by feelings of guilt. While he is visiting
the Réveillons, Jean keeps himself warm at night and satisfies his
physical needs by sleeping with a young woman of the household.
Neither he nor the author is conscience-stricken. One of Jean's
friends, Daltozzi, regularly follows women on the streets at
night, whether they are duchesses or housemaids or prostitutes.
He feels that he is pursuing a dream, seeking a being whose dream
corresponds to his own, and Proust is half inclined to accept this
interpretation of an unsavory sex life.

But if Proust's lovers are now seldom guilty, they are often quite appallingly jealous. Jean is even jealous of Madame S., with whom his relations are entirely platonic. One night when she tells him that she is tired and sends him home early, he wanders back to her street and sees a light in what he takes to be her room. At once convinced that she is entertaining a lover and determined to embarrass her, he knocks on the window. Two old men appear and Jean realizes that the room is not hers after all. In the case of Françoise, with whom he has a more serious love affair, Jean's jealousy takes the form of an almost pathological curiosity about her past. He wants to find out if she has ever slept with anyone else, and when it appears that she has he wants details. His questions seem decidedly odd to anyone unacquainted with homosexual love. He asks if her lover was a young man, an old man, or a woman. The last and most distasteful of the alternatives proves to be the right one; he even wrings from her a name, that of Charlotte.

He smiled, but she saw the blood drain from his face. "So it was Charlotte: how very odd: I'd never have thought it. But not now?—you don't do that now?"—"Oh, Jean! I've told you I don't!"—"How many times—*roughly* how many times, did you do it?"—"Oh, how cruel you are, Jean, how horribly cruel! I've told you—just once . . . perhaps twice . . . I really don't know."

Love cannot survive such persistent cross-examination, especially when it turns on statistics: Françoise and Jean inevitably drift apart. But once more at least, in a particularly brilliant passage, they are together again almost as in happier days. The episode is one of the most illuminating in the whole manuscript since it echoes an episode from *Les Plaisirs et les jours* and anticipates one from *Du Côté de chez Swann*. Jean is sitting across the room from his mistress and brooding, when suddenly she goes to the piano and begins playing part of a sonata by Saint-Saëns—the part that was once the *leitmotif* of their love, as the passage from *Meistersinger* was the *leitmotif* of Madame de Breyves' love for Monsieur de Laléande. Jean is quite overcome with anguish.

Far from her now and all alone, having had this evening not so much as a single kiss, and not daring to ask for one, he listened to the phrase which when they were happy, had seemed to him to greet them with a smile from heaven, but now had lost its power to enchant. In those old days their love had quickly drowned his melancholy, the sense that love was fragile, in the sweetness of the thought that they were keeping it intact. Their separate tenderness had come together then in a shared feeling that though life was all uncertainty, they were never uncertain of each other and that the pain of hearing that all things pass made ever more profound the happiness they felt in the knowledge that their love would last. Hearing this phrase, they knew it for a passing thing but felt its passing as a sweet caress. In the past, when he could join her at the piano and they could play together, sadness had seemed airy by comparison with love. But now it lay so heavy on them that Jean had to lean against a chair to keep from falling, and tense the nerves of his cheeks, like two strong arms, to stop the tears from spilling over into the infinite abysses of his sobs. Yet in that desolating phrase which told how all things pass, the sadness still was light and airy. Not for a moment was the clear and rapid motion of its flight checked in its passage. If once it had seemed to show their fleeting love caught in a pucker of regret, so now it graced with a shy smile the disenchantment, the irremediable despair towards which it was hastening. Everything had changed, all that had made his life was dead, and he too soon would die, or still continue in a life far worse than death. But the lovely little phrase would still with undiminished speed spread its pure sound abroad, intoxication for those whose love had just begun, poison to infect the wound of those who loved no longer.

Such passages help to explain what Proust was trying to accomplish in the years he devoted to *Jean Santeuil*. He was of course accumulating manuscript—turning out what he hoped would be the first draft of a novel—but at the same time he was practicing, sharpening his observation and his style, for the two must have gone together, trying to see more in his experience and to express with greater precision what he saw. As he practiced, he gave up both the preciosity and the elegant simplicity of *Les Plaisirs et les jours*, for both now seemed to him affectations, introducing an alien element into his art. What he wanted—and what in fact he came close to developing—was a style so completely transparent that it would reveal with absolute accuracy the most minute observations.

It was often necessarily a complex style, with many qualifying phrases to mark shades of difference, since what he observed was often complex. In the passage at hand he is chiefly concerned with what, at different times in the course of a love affair, a lover sees in a musical phrase that is both gay and sad, both comforting and disillusioning. The subject is by no means an easy one, and yet Proust brings it off quite effortlessly in wonderfully moving sentences, which are neither very long nor very "hard" nor very involved. They are, furthermore, sentences so perfectly functional that one is scarcely conscious of their "style" as such.

V

Throughout the notebooks, whether the subject is love or society or nature or the childhood of the hero, Proust is as fond as ever of comment and generalization. He turns aside for aphorisms, he even interpolates little essays in his narrative. The fact is that he is still very much under the influence of his philosophical training. He considers himself a thinker as well as a storyteller and a student of character—perhaps a thinker first of all, because his stories and his characters seldom satisfy him unless they help him to establish significant general truths. This intellectual element in his work is nowhere more apparent than in the passages devoted to artists and men of letters. He observes and analyzes C., G., the Vicomtesse Gaspard de Réveillon, Traves, Bastelle, and the painter Bergotte. He is certainly interested in them as individuals, but he is even more interested in fixing, as he studies them, the characteristics of the artistic temperament. The six portraits, along with a few other incidental passages, are really so many fragments of an extended essay on a subject that, obviously for personal reasons, fascinated Proust.

It immediately appears that the artist is a man very much like Proust himself. He is an invalid and a hypochondriac; he suffers from nervousness, insomnia, asthma, and hay fever. He is constantly consulting doctors, who find him difficult to treat; he is easily taken in by quacks. He is lazy, unpunctual, and eccentric. His ideas are never those of other people; he laughs at what they think reasonable and becomes ecstatic about what they regard as trifles. He seems to be an egotist and his life is certainly, by ordinary standards, immoral, but the fact is that he lives for his work. He cultivates the habits that help him to work more easily; he avoids those that do not. He generally avoids society, though for some artists—Bastelle, for example—society is not necessarily a handicap. The artist writes about himself but, paradoxically, his life throws no light on his work. The life is merely the raw material, without interest or value until his imagination has succeeded in transforming it. His conversation throws no light on his work either, for—like Madame Gaspard de Réveillon—he may be frivolous when he talks and profoundly melancholy when he writes. The talk springs from his intellect, the writing from sources deeper in his personality of which he himself is scarcely conscious.

In his study of Madame Gaspard de Réveillon and in several other passages scattered throughout the manuscript, Proust develops his ideas about memory, already suggested in *Les Plaisirs et les jours*. He is now able to formulate them in such a way that they constitute both a theory of happiness and a theory of art. The present is always disappointing; the past as we recall it when we make an effort to do so is also disappointing because it is merely a pallid image of what was once the present. But the past as it comes back to us unexpectedly, in moments of mystic vision, is quite different. It gives us intense pleasure, it seems to free us from the tyranny of time and put us in touch with the eternal. Unfortunately we cannot determine when these moments shall come; we can only wait until something in the present, by its similarity to something in the past, calls up the vision. That something may be quite trivial—the taste of a grape, the sound of wheels in the street, the smell of mouthwash. But the vision itself is never trivial; it is happiness and it is art. Proust once remarks that he himself has never attempted to write about what he has seen or thought or reasoned out or remembered, only about the past as recreated for him by some casual perception. So it is with Madame Gaspard de Réveillon. Her poems commemorate her moments of inspiration, awakened by the scent of tangerines or a certain light in a room; her conversation is not concerned with these things, which are indeed too intimate a part of herself to be the subject of conversation at all.

To the outsider, of course, mystic experiences always seem somewhat dubious, but the experiences Proust describes need not be interpreted as mystical or in any way connected with time and eternity. It is quite possible to believe that Proust himself found an intense satisfaction in recollecting his past when the recollections were suggested to him by something in the present. It is even possible that he wrote parts of his manuscript—those dealing with his childhood, for example—under the inspiration of such recollections. On the other hand, few writers are more intellectual, more analytical, more concerned with abstract truth than he is. He cannot have analyzed the character of Madame Gaspard de Réveillon or worked out his philosophy of love merely by trusting to involuntary memory; his intellect was very actively involved in both cases. His theory of art, possibly applicable to works of a certain type, is quite inapplicable to his own. It can only be taken as an example of how wayward a genius can be. By an elaborate display of reasoning, in a series of highly abstract passages, Proust tries to demonstrate that there is no reasoning in art at all.

Jean Santeuil is a remarkably interesting and intelligent work, but it is not, as it stands, a novel, and it could never have been turned into one without very radical revision. It is not even a coherent autobiography. Some of the difficulty undoubtedly lay in Proust's habit of jotting down episodes more or less as they occurred to him, in the hope that when he had filled several notebooks a structure of some sort would emerge. But by the time he reached the seventieth notebook, he was as far from structure as ever. There was nothing for him to do but to start all over again and begin piecing his separate episodes together in quite a different way. Several years elapsed—apparently as many as six or eight—before he made this fresh start.

CHAPTER IX

Journalism and Translation

It seems clear that Proust never completely abandoned his note-books. He certainly added to them from time to time; he may even have done a certain amount of rewriting. But since he had no immediate prospect of turning out a novel, and since he needed —or his mother felt that he needed—the encouragement of im-mediate publication, he began devoting much of his time to more pedestrian work, chiefly criticism and translation. A year or two earlier his subject would probably have been Thoreau; now, when he was going through a period of enthusiasm for Gothic archi-tecture, it was almost inevitably Ruskin. One is inclined to feel that this more pedestrian work was a mistake since it postponed indefinitely the radical revision that the notebooks needed, yet on considering Proust's career as a whole one can scarcely regret that he undertook it. For it enriched his experience, enriched ultimately the notebooks themselves. If he had not devoted several years to the study of Ruskin and the Gothic, the novel that he finally produced would have lacked many of its most impressive and most characteristic passages.

I

In the autumn of 1899 Proust was reading Ruskin's work as fast as he could—reading it, whenever possible, in translation, for his knowledge of English was far from perfect. If, as he read, the point of view seemed foreign to him and objectionably moralistic, he deliberately shut his eyes to this fact. He tried to be as uncritical as possible because he felt that in this way he could best assimilate Ruskin's thought. The method was successful, the process of assimilation remarkably rapid; soon Proust was ready to write. As early as December, he was working on a study of Ruskin and certain cathedrals. In January, 1900, he was writing or planning other studies, with extensive quotations' from Ruskin; he was also translating something, possibly *The Bible of Amiens*, though he felt that this part of his work must remain unpublished since Ruskin had forbidden translations into French.

While he was still busy with these tasks and while, as it happened, he was rereading the passage in *The Seven Lamps of Architecture* in which, to condemn modern machinery and extol medieval handicraft, Ruskin describes some figures in bas-relief on the north door of Rouen Cathedral, the newspapers reported Ruskin's death, and Proust immediately decided that he must make a memorial pilgrimage, obviously to Rouen. He must see the bas-relief for himself. He went with his friends the Yeatmans, approached the north door, and eagerly scanned the hundreds of figures, looking for the ones immortalized by the master. Finally Madame Yeatman said that she had found them, and there indeed they were—the dragons and the odd little man resting his head on his hand so firmly that his cheek was puffed out under the eye. Few figures on the door can have been more completely insignificant; yet Proust was quite satisfied. Afterwards he questioned the sacristan about Ruskin's visits to Rouen and elicited a certain amount of information which, however, he suspected of being quite wrong.

Meanwhile, since there was a little flurry of interest in Ruskin, Proust hastily prepared two obituary notices, one for *La Chronique des arts et de la curiosité*, a subsidiary of *La Gazette des beaux-arts*, and one for *Le Figaro*. These notices were at least partly designed to announce his studies of Ruskin, which he hoped to publish at once. In writing the notice for *Le Figaro*, he remembered vaguely the story of Shelley's funeral pyre and, wanting to use it in his text, he dispatched one of the family servants to the Yeatmans'. "Mon-

sieur," the servant gravely said, "has sent me to ask what became
of Shelley's heart." The notice, with a reference to the Shelley
story, appeared in *Le Figaro* on February 13, 1900. Unobtrusively,
after a few preliminaries, Proust announced his project. "On
Amiens," he said, "Ruskin wrote a whole book, *The Bible of
Amiens*, which I shall attempt to describe and from which I
shall publish important fragments in a forthcoming issue of *Le
Correspondant*; I shall continue my studies of Ruskin in various
magazines, notably *La Gazette des beaux-arts*. If these lines come
to the attention of any of those favorite friends and disciples of
Ruskin, whom I have often envied when I have read how they
accompanied him on his frequent visits to his old friends, the
cathedrals of France, I cannot tell them how grateful I should
be if they would give me some notion what *The Springs of Eure*
and *Domrémy* were to contain, those works on the Cathedral of
Rouen and the Cathedral of Chartres which Ruskin did not have
time to write, which were to follow *The Bible of Amiens*. If they
could at least tell me some of the things that Ruskin said on those
trips, they would put an end to the questions I am continually
asking myself, questions that the stones of Chartres and of
Bourges have left unanswered."

Whether or not the friends came forward to supply the information that he sought, Proust went on with his articles and
finished them—finished indeed all that he intended to write on
Ruskin. But he apparently found that publishing them was not
quite so easy as he had at first supposed. The first article, on *The
Bible of Amiens*, was presumably rejected by *Le Correspondant*,
as well as by *La Revue de Paris*, whose editor, Ganderax, sadly remarked that he could not take it because he did not have the time
to rewrite it completely; it ultimately appeared in the April issue of
Le Mercure de France. Two other articles, devoted to Ruskin's
work as a whole, were accepted by *La Gazette des beaux-arts*.

The three articles are somewhat acrobatic exercises in sympathetic interpretation, for Proust is still determined to see with the
master's eyes and to offer as little criticism as possible. He summarizes Ruskin's thought, piously and even unctuously; he quotes,
both in the text and in the footnotes, formidably long passages.
His thesis is that Ruskin was in fact what he pretended to be—

a prophet. Now religion is necessarily a prophet's preoccupation, and so it was, Proust says, with Ruskin; he was interested in beauty primarily as a revelation of religious truth. Proust is even able to quote, without too obvious distaste, some of the master's more prophetic pronouncements—as when he said that God made alligators gray because they are dangerous and lizards green because they are not.

But even in articles so deliberately uncritical, Proust cannot help putting in a little of himself, deviating as though involuntarily into personal observations. Thus he permits himself to describe one of his own trips to Amiens and to notice some of the things that Ruskin overlooked. He studies the Virgin of the south porch and tries to define her special charm, which is clearly not that of a work of art. He studies the colors of the carved wood in the choir stalls—the deep purple where the wear has been greatest and where the glowing sap seems to emerge from the heart of the oak, the shadings where the wear has been uneven and where sometimes the color of a leaf differs from that of its stalk. In other passages, not ostensibly so personal, he permits himself to take up aspects of Ruskin's work that he was really committed to admire—its impressionism, for example. He describes the distortion in Ruskin's drawing, "Amiens, le jour des trépassés," and shows that Ruskin reproduced what he saw—what in fact anyone might see from a spot near the slaughterhouse, where the river, the cathedral, and the church of Saint-Leu arrange themselves almost exactly as in the sketch. For in Ruskin, as in the Monet of the cathedral series, Proust finds the significant truth that the human eye distorts its objects. The artist necessarily represents buildings as twisted into fantastic shapes by distance or softened by mist or made irridescent by sunshine, for the artist represents what he sees.

Just as his articles began to appear, and just as he was beginning to be despondent about his health, which seems to have been persistently bad for some months, Proust suddenly decided to make another memorial pilgrimage, this time to the city that Ruskin had consecrated above all others, the Queen of the Adriatic. "I left for Venice," he later explained, "so that I might be able before I died to approach, to touch, to see embodied in palaces, crumbling but still erect and pink, Ruskin's ideas on the domestic architec-

ture of the Middle Ages." His mother went with him; a group of
friends—Madame Hahn, her son, and her niece, Marie Nordlinger
—met him in Venice. At first he was so desperately asthmatic that
he was confined to his room in the Royal Danieli—a luxurious
room with Venetian chandeliers, furniture upholstered in golden
damask, and a window that looked out over the roof of the
Doges' Palace toward the Campanile. Soon, however, he was
better; he put on his heavy overcoat and his grey bowler hat, he
went out in the sunshine. Gliding in a gondola along the Grand
Canal, with a copy of *The Stones of Venice* or *Saint Mark's Rest*
open before him, he studied the palaces—the Palazzo Contarini-
Fasan, for example, which seemed to him especially charming.
Wandering through Saint Mark's, he studied the capitals, the
mosaics, and the tracery. He was happy because, as at Rouen, he
was seeing what Ruskin had seen. When, during a storm, he and
Miss Nordlinger took refuge in Saint Mark's, they read together an
appropriate passage from *The Stones of Venice*. Proust was deeply
moved, but not so much by the mosaics before him as by the
book that described them. When, on an excursion to Padua, he
saw the Giotto frescoes in the Arena Chapel, he perhaps paid
particular attention to the figure that Ruskin had described in
The Bible of Amiens and that he himself had selected as an
illustration for one of his articles—the figure of Charity.

Memories of the trip, the most ambitious that Proust ever made,
inevitably found their way into his notebooks and, in the course
of time, into the definitive version of the novel. The pages devoted
to them are extraordinarily vivid ones, none more vivid perhaps
than the page in which he describes his mother as she watched
for him at one of the windows of the hotel, caught sight of him
in his gondola, and seemed to reach out and try to caress him with
an impassioned smile, framed by the more discreet smile of the
arched window glittering in the sunshine.

II

In the autumn of 1900—a few months after Proust's return from
Venice—his family moved to a house in the Rue de Courcelles,
just at the corner of the Rue de Monceau. It was an impressive

house, an epitome of middle-class grandeur, admirably suited to the needs of a successful physician. In a spacious suite of rooms the Prousts were able to display their mahogany and their plush, their tapestries and their Persian rugs, their family portraits and their bronzes. Proust's own room was comparatively bare, containing only a brass bed, a desk, a couch, a chest of drawers, and a single picture—a reproduction of Whistler's portrait of Carlyle. It was in this room that the principal drama of his domestic life was acted out: his struggle to breathe, to sleep so that he could breathe more easily, and to do without the drugs that produced sleep. In his worst periods he was now inclined to go to bed in the daytime, when his asthma was least troublesome, and treat himself at night. In any case he slept as much as he could and rested when he could not sleep. He was fond, as he lay in bed, of playing a kind of game with himself, distinguishing and interpreting the sounds that reached him from the court outside his windows.

His mother was almost as much of an attendant and nurse for him as she had been in his earliest childhood. When he had visitors in his room late at night, she waited patiently in the dining room to make sure that he was not having an attack when they left. When he slept in the daytime she kept the house quiet and otherwise followed the instructions he left her in notes before he went to bed—querulous and tender notes, sometimes as long as letters. In them he described his symptoms and complained about open windows; he regretted their separation and promised soon, very soon, to change his regime. Once he described a mild attack of asthma which had apparently kept him from digesting his food properly and hence had forced him to stay up until 4:30 in the morning. Another time he described an attack of "incredible violence" which had gone on most of the night; he was still up at 7:30, sweating as if he had run for hours and afraid to stay in his room since he seemed to detect there both dust and a smell, left no doubt by his barber. "My dear Mama," he once wrote, "I can't sleep so I am writing this little note to tell you I am thinking of you. I should much rather get up and have breakfast when you do, and I so much hope I soon can. It would be, it will be so nice for me to feel that our sleeping and waking hours coincide. I went to bed at 1:30 with this in mind, but when I had to get up again I lost my safety pin (the one I use to fasten and take up the slack in my drawers). It goes without saying that my night was ruined."

When his hours were reasonably normal, Proust spent a good deal of his time in the dining room, apparently the most comfortable, and the warmest, room in the apartment. In winter heavy drapes hung across the windows and a fire usually burned in the grate. Proust used an oil lamp because he found its light particularly soft. On the large oval table he spread out his books, notebooks, and papers—papers kept haphazardly in boxes and so hopelessly disarranged that his mother was fond of teasing him about them. "You should tell your friends where you got your filing system," she would say. Sitting at the table near the lamp, he chatted with his mother, or read, or carried on his interminable correspondence, or worked a little, for he was now, perhaps at his mother's insistence, going on with his Ruskin studies. He was translating *The Bible of Amiens* and turning out an occasional article, often connected with Ruskin, for *La Chronique des arts*.

If he was not going out, friends came to see him during the afternoon or evening, generally friends he had made rather recently—fashionable young men of illustrious families who shared his passion for literature and society. The most attentive among them were Prince Antoine Bibesco; Vicomte Bertrand de Salignac-Fénelon, the son of a minister plenipotentiary; and the Marquis d'Albufera, heir to the dukedom created by Napoleon I to honor the victorious Marshal Suchet. But there were others who called at least occasionally. There was Prince Léon Radziwill, one of the wealthiest members of the large Radziwill family, proprietor of a magnificent estate at Ermenonville. There was the Duc de Guiche, heir through his father to the dukedom of Gramont and through his mother to some of the Rothschild millions; he was a sportsman, a collector, a painter, and a physicist, subsequently a member of the Academy of Sciences.

During the afternoon or evening Proust's friends dropped in, singly or in groups. They rang twice to announce their arrival; they appeared in the dining room, where Proust sat with his papers spread out before him; they chatted with his mother, who lingered in the room for a few minutes. When they were alone with Proust, they used a little language peculiar to themselves. Antoine was called Téléphas because he talked with Proust so often on the telephone; anagrams were used for other names—Ocsebib for Bibesco, Nonelef for Fénelon, and Lecram for Marcel. As they talked, Proust sometimes forgot his ill health and his comparative isolation, entered vicariously into their experiences, and lived for a few hours the life of an active young man. He gave them advice—generally rather cynical advice—when they were in love, and tried to reconcile them when they quarreled. Sometimes, however, the very richness of their lives made the poverty of his own seem more intolerable. He pitied himself, complained to those who came about the neglect of those who did not come, and wrote insulting or pathetic notes to the absentees. "If you get back before 12:50," he once wrote Bibesco, "it would be very nice if you would come up for a minute. But if you are tired don't do it. And don't say afterwards, 'I got back at one.' I should much rather know that you got back at 12 and didn't come because you were tired. You would only have to ring twice, as usual."

Proust assured casual acquaintances—usually people he wanted to avoid—that he seldom or never went out, and he certainly compromised his health when he did so, running the risk of getting overtired, or of exposing himself to something, if only fresh air, that would bring on an attack of asthma. Yet he did go out, quite regularly, often every night. He simply had to—he could not endure being shut up for very long; he had to run the risks and take the consequences, no matter how disastrous. Sometimes his mother expostulated with him, for to her it seemed only sensible for him to stay where he could take care of himself and work. She could not understand, he had to point out to her rather sharply, that what he really needed was not work but distraction and frivolity.

Going out no doubt usually involved rather special preparations, like a trip into difficult country. He had to be sure that he was rested and free from asthma, that he was not exposing himself to inclement weather, that in any case he was warmly dressed, with the collar of his overcoat turned up, even on relatively warm nights. If the conditions were right he listened to his mother's parting admonitions, kissed her slowly with childish adoration,

and left. He went to Madame Lemaire's or Madame de Benardaky's [1] or Madame de Ludre's or to one of the fashionable
restaurants. Strangers who saw him for the first time noticed his
unnatural pallor, his large eyes, dilated and heavily ringed, his
drooping shoulders, bent apparently by almost unendurable fatigue.
To them he was a strange figure, remote and mysterious, almost
a visitor from another world from which he had suddenly come
for a few hours and to which he would as suddenly retire. One
observer saw him at the Café Weber, a meeting place of his friends
in the Rue Royale. He came late, ordered a bunch of grapes and a
glass of water, spoke of his ill health, and said that he was going
home immediately. But though the light hurt his eyes and he kept
moving his chair to avoid draughts, he lingered on until most of
the other patrons had left. Another observer saw him at Larue's
coolly insulting a man he thought had slandered him, a man who
had come over to his table and was trying to shake his hand.

III

On his excursions outside Proust still saw something of Montesquiou, but their relationship was not nearly so close as it had
once been. Proust was now too well established in high society to
need further sponsoring and hence was understandably reluctant
to put up with the antics of a man whom he had long recognized
as an ill-tempered esthete. Montesquiou, well aware of his
protégé's defection, was inclined to be even more ill-tempered
than before. Generally his outbursts had some connection with
the parties he was now giving at his new house on the Boulevard
Maillot, preciously called the Pavilion of the Muses. It was lavishly
and on the whole beautifully furnished, with rather less emphasis than might have been expected on the master's favorite
motifs, bats and blue hydrangeas. It had a music room where the

1. The mother of the girl Proust was so fond of in his childhood. He still
saw her—on June 23, 1902, for example, when he went to one of her musical
soirées, at which she herself sang in a duet from Gounod's *Roméo et Juliette*.
Her reputation was as lurid as that of Gilberte's mother in Proust's novel, but
she is said to have lived it down by the simple expedient of excluding from her
drawing room everyone about whom there was a breath of scandal—everyone,
that is, except herself.

emphasis was on roses and a library with shelves of rare volumes and mementoes, including a pair of Becque's spectacles and a lock of Byron's hair. Off the library was a Castiglione Room devoted to mementoes of the famous courtesan of the Second Empire—photographs and paintings of her, some of her jewelry and dresses, her hair-pin box with one hair pin in it, and a plaster cast of her feet. In the garden was still another memento, a basin of pink marble that had once served no fewer than three eminent persons—Louis XIV, Madame de Montespan, and Madame de Pompadour—as a bathtub. It was said that Yturri had found it in a convent at Versailles and had got it by giving the Mother Superior an old slipper of his which he had passed off as the Pope's.

Montesquiou found women's figures distasteful and unnerving especially when they were revealed in evening dress, and so he always gave his parties in the afternoon. But Proust was seldom willing to go out so early in the day and seldom eager to go to Montesquiou's at any time. He was inclined to excuse himself by describing the symptoms of his illnesses, and Montesquiou, who was not for a moment taken in by the symptoms, was inclined to fulminate. He could see in a disciple's persistent absence only the most studied neglect. Proust found it safer to put in at least an occasional appearance at the Pavilion, as on May 30, 1901, when, if he did not actually go himself, he certainly sent his mother. The party was a typical one. Montesquiou—tall, angular, and imperious —stood on the threshold, welcoming the members of society before whom he was prepared to display his riches, and exulting in the discomfiture of those whom he had condemned to remain at home. He shook hands with the men and nodded somewhat curtly to the women, dropping his head so abruptly that it looked as if his spinal cord had been severed. Yturri, now seriously ill with diabetes, pale and emaciated, lingered in the background, arranging everything, seating the guests, and from time to time smoothing tempers ruffled by the host. As the entertainment began, the Comtesse Greffulhe, more dazzling in her forties than she had been in her youth, made one of her dramatic entrances—disrupted the whole assembly as Montesquiou, who was driven to frenzy by the tardiness of others, graciously conducted her to her chair. The program, a kind of rhythmic alternation between verse and music, went forward. Hahn sang, and Madame Bernhardt, back from Brussels for the purpose, recited some poems by Montesquiou and Madame de Noailles to some sort of accompaniment by Thomé. The guests certainly felt that the arts had never before been so smartly and palatably presented. Afterwards Montesquiou, scarcely able to control his elation, strode up and down, waved his arms in arabesques, stretched out and clenched his fingers, reviewed in soliloquy the triumphs of the afternoon, and enumerated the enemies to whom he had denied his favors.

About three weeks later—on June 19, 1901—Proust himself gave a party, a grand dinner at which he entertained friends with quite different political convictions, perhaps in an effort to reconcile them and dissipate the ill will created during the turbulent years of the Dreyfus Case. He asked Anatole France, Léon Daudet, Abel Hermant, and the Comtesse de Noailles from the world of letters; the Prince and Princesse de Polignac, the Princesse de Caraman-Chimay, the Marquis and Marquise d'Eyragues, the Comtesse de Guerne, and the Comte de Briey from high society. He asked also such young friends as the Prince de Brancovan, the Vicomte de Maugny, and the Comte Gabriel de La Rochefoucauld, taking care of course to see that the less distinguished ones—Robert Dreyfus, for example—came only for the reception after dinner. He omitted from his list of guests only one significant name, that of Montesquiou, possibly because he was giving the dinner on a day when he knew Montesquiou would be busy rehearsing a Fauré program at the Pavilion. The party seems to have gone off reasonably well, without even an explosion from Daudet, who was seated next to a Jewish banker's daughter. But of course Proust could not be sure what Montesquiou's reaction would be, and so—after failing to show up for the Fauré program the next day—he took the precaution of writing the poet a tactful little note. He mentioned his dinner, without however dwelling on it unnecessarily; he enclosed his review, published nearly six months earlier, of Montesquiou's *Pays des aromates* and he held out the promise of other and longer studies of the poet's work. In his final sentences he expressed the hope that, since the pollen season was coming to an end, he would soon be able to sit beside the marble basin and enjoy the exquisite pleasure of the poet's company. Montesquiou's reply has not been preserved, but one is tempted—though perhaps on insufficient evidence—to find reflections of it in another of Proust's letters, written to defend himself.

"You are not 'nice,' " Proust complained in this other letter. ". . . You tell me that for some time now I have made you laugh when I don't intend to, because I talk so childishly, I suppose. That in itself is not very nice! Then you tease me by running down the party I gave . . . and finally you tell me . . . that when I write letters I choose my words so unskillfully that, according to you, I only succeed in slandering the people whom I am trying to praise. You have really done well by me. I am, however, keenly aware of the honor you have done me in singling me out as the recipient of such a remarkable specimen of your wit, and I should like to express my deepest gratitude and my profoundest admiration."

IV

In August, 1901, Proust stayed at home when his mother and brother went away for a vacation. He was eating normally at the time—was, in fact, having steaks for dinner every day—but was otherwise not too well. Mosquitoes in his room kept him from sleeping at night, and he had several bad attacks of asthma when he went out. It occurred to him that the steaks might be causing the asthma, and so he asked for the opinion of his brother, who was a medical student. It occurred to him too that he might just possibly have worms—he remembered reading something relevant in a book on asthma—and that he might in fact need a good worming at once. In this case he suggested that his brother telegraph him what to do. Meanwhile, however, he was well enough to take a short trip to Abbeville and indeed to work a little while he was there. The trip was one of many he took to cathedral towns in connection with his study of Ruskin. He often suffered en route; on the other hand, he was often surprisingly robust when he arrived. Once, for example—on a trip to Laon and Coucy—he performed the athletic feat of climbing a high tower, with, it seems, a little help from Fénelon who, as they slowly mounted the steps, hummed the Good Friday Spell from *Parsifal* to encourage him.

In August, 1902, he again stayed at home while his parents went to Evian. In his letters to his mother he complained that he was going through a most "disastrous" period in his life. He was "sad" and "unhappy"; he was suffering from "mental agitation," "worry," and "anguish." He had no particular desire to see his mother or indeed to travel with her later on. The only distraction he wanted, or felt would do him any good, was society, available in Paris if anywhere. The cause is not specified, but the symptoms, and the words used to describe them, point to love, in Proust's case the worst form of anguish. He was fretting himself into an illness, and there were already physical complications—insomnia, palpitations of the heart, and ominous disturbances in the bowels. Having stayed up all one night and finding that he was still too upset to get any sleep the next day, he precipitately called a doctor—first Dr. Bize, who could not see him at once, and then Dr. Vaquez, who could. Vaquez was reassuring. He found nothing wrong with Proust's heart or bowels that persistent anguish would not account for, and he recommended nothing but a fairly regular regime of trional. On the other hand, he could not help remarking that Proust was like all invalids—he was not satisfied with one complaint, he had to develop others by worrying about creatures not worth a moment's notice. Proust recognized the truth of the remark, but what could he do? He could not very well talk himself out of his anguish.

During the rest of the summer, and for a long time afterwards, Proust was irritable and restless. He quarreled with his mother; he went to dinners and gave dinners, including one for Madame de Noailles; he decided that he would have to travel after all. In October, 1902, he seems to have drifted into a trip with Fénelon, and finally toured both Belgium and Holland. It could have been an exciting trip under other circumstances. They glided along wind-swept canals, docked at towns with dark ivy-covered churches, visited galleries and saw Vermeer's *View of Delft* which to Proust seemed the most beautiful picture in the world. But even in these surroundings he could not shake off his depression, and he was sometimes so low that he was afraid of spoiling Fénelon's pleasure. Furthermore, he was robbed and he found the hotels exorbitantly expensive. "I have been staying on almost from day to day," he wrote his mother. "A dozen times I have thought I should see you the day following. I never should have believed I could go for two weeks without kissing you." But the truth of the matter was that he was not especially eager to see his mother, or to be at home, or to be anywhere in particular. He was still thoroughly miserable.

One evening not long after his return he had a curious encounter with Fénelon, who had come to see him with a new acquaintance, Comte Georges de Lauris. Taking offense at something Fénelon said, Proust seemed suddenly to lose all self-control. He flung himself on his friend, seized the new hat he was carrying, tore it, stamped on it, and ripped out the lining. The incident was sufficiently memorable for the notebooks, and eventually found its way into the novel, where Proust blamed the rage on the intolerable behavior of the Baron de Charlus. In real life he blamed it on his mother. She was completely unsympathetic, as he explained to her in a note, and indeed had been for some time. She knew perfectly well that he was spending his nights in tears, and yet she went on trying to make him stay awake in the daytime, even going so far as to punish him by removing necessary furniture from his room and by telling the servants not to answer his rings or to wait on him at meals. That very morning she had begun pounding and shouting as soon as he had taken his trional, and she had kept it up all day long. Hence his irritability and his absurd behavior with Fénelon in the evening. She was entirely responsible. But he was even more disturbed by the fact that she was letting him down in this really desperate period of his life and indeed trying to make him ill again. "This isn't the first time," he added. "I took cold this evening; if it turns into asthma, as it certainly will the way things are going, I don't doubt you will be nice to me again, as soon as I am in the state I was in last year at this time. But it is hard not to have affection and good health simultaneously. If I had both right now I could use them in my fight against an affliction

that, especially since yesterday evening (but I haven't seen you
since), has become so great that I don't think I can go on fighting
against it."

As the winter began, Proust was apparently able to distract
himself a little by working on his Ruskin, but he was still restless and more than half inclined to try another trip. In any case
he felt that, for a reason he was reluctant to reveal, he would
have to leave Paris by the beginning of spring. Suddenly his
course seemed clear to him—he would join Bibesco, whose mother
had recently died in Bucharest, he would in fact settle down in
the wilds of Rumania and offer his friend substantial consolation. But he had no sooner communicated his decision to Bibesco
than fearful complications developed. He caught another cold
and could not leave at once. He was not in any case eager to
leave before the end of the winter because his work was pressing
and his brother was about to get married. He would have to
meet the bride, which would in itself be trying; he would have
to rest up for the ceremony and allow himself afterwards scarcely
less than a week in bed. In the spring it would be different; then
he could cheerfully set out—provided of course that Bibesco
was willing to wait so long for consolation and provided, too,
that there were no spring flowers in Rumania. He was even
willing to negotiate about other meeting places, Egypt or Constantinople or Munich, though in each case the complications
seemed still more formidable. Before any of the complications
could be straightened out, Bibesco returned to Paris.

During the winter Proust's work was indeed pressing. He had
been negotiating with publishers about his translation of *The
Bible of Amiens* and, after at least one disconcerting failure, he
had found a firm that would take it, the Mercure de France.
He had agreed to deliver his manuscript, which was still far
from finished, in February, 1903. He had also agreed to prepare
certain parts of the manuscript for earlier publication in *La
Renaissance latine*, a magazine edited by his friend Brancovan,
and to write for *Le Figaro* a series of articles on the *salons* of
Paris. He worked because he had to. Unfortunately he could
not seem to work quite hard enough; he was tempted, and able,
to go out far too much. He went to dinners, a good many of

them—dinners at Madame Straus's and Madame de Pierrebourg's, at the Princesse de Chimay's and the Comtesse de Noailles's. He went to his brother's wedding, which was even more brutal than he had expected and which left him, or so he afterwards remarked, literally dead for a fortnight. His work inevitably suffered, but still by the end of February he had something to show for his efforts. The fragments were ready for *La Renaissance latine*; the *salon* articles (written under such pseudonyms as Dominique and Horatio) were beginning to appear in *Le Figaro*.

The *salon* articles were obviously the more congenial task for Proust because, as in the notebooks, he was able to draw on memories of his earlier years and to describe the great ladies of society as they had once appeared to him, each gracious and talented in a different way, each the focal point of an intense social life. He described the Princesse Mathilde as she received in the Rue de Berri, seated in her great armchair and surrounded by imperial splendor; the Princesse de Polignac as, in happier days when her husband was alive, she gave musical matinées in her draughty studio; the Comtesse d'Haussonville as she bowed magnificently to her guests, showing her affability by bending her body forward and her reserve by straightening it up precisely to the vertical. The articles must have seemed charmingly gossipy and nostalgic when they appeared in *Le Figaro*, but their charm has since faded. They are a little too snobbish and too sweet. They introduce the names of too many families like the Brancovans and the Albuferas whom Proust was eager to flatter. They lack entirely the tartness of the social scenes in the notebooks, where the mood is not only nostalgic and where, when great ladies bow—the Duchesse de Réveillon, for example—they draw back even beyond the vertical so that the author is able to detect in their retirement arrogance as well as reserve.

The appearance of the Ruskin fragments and the *salon* articles —the very fact that Proust was finishing something—should have helped to reconcile his mother to his strange habits and made his home life more peaceful. But the quarrels went on as before. "You manage to make me hate the days on which [*La Renaissance latine*] comes out," he told his mother in a long note. "And you realize that in my present state of mind I won't get much more pleasure from the second number than, thanks to you, I got from the first. —And since there isn't going to be a third — But I am not looking for pleasure. I gave that up long ago."

The sources of the trouble were much the same as they had been—his extravagance and his eccentric regime. Madame Proust was trying to keep him from spending so much and from sleeping at such unreasonable hours. From time to time she punished him, or at least he thought she did. At the moment she was meting out what he regarded as a punishment, by refusing to entertain certain people he felt under an obligation to, such as the editors of Le Figaro and the Mercure de France. She was even obliging him to give a dinner at a restaurant (a dinner for kept women, she called it) when she knew quite well that he couldn't afford such things on the allowance she gave him. Furthermore, she was not keeping the dining room warm. "You can't, and you aren't taking steps to, do me any positive good," he told her. "But by guarding me against getting chilled too often you could do me a good deal negatively. You would be making less complicated a life that I should prefer, for many reasons, to lead in a separate house." On another occasion, when she gave one of the dinners that he wanted, he had a word of praise for her. At the same time he could not resist pointing out to her afterwards how distasteful to him much of the conversation had been, for something had been said about the huge tips he was in the habit of leaving and more about his methods of treating himself, with the strong implication that he was not nearly so ill as he pretended to be. "Though it is nice for me to have friends at the house, and to see them so pleasantly and so brilliantly entertained," he said in the inevitable note, "I should rather never have them if even the most intimate parties, which should be the most cordial, thus degenerate into squabbles which afterwards profoundly influence Papa and fortify him in his prejudices against which all the evidence in the world would be futile."

Despite the strained relationships, Proust considered joining his parents at Evian that summer as soon as the Splendide Hôtel quieted down, and after some hesitation he finally decided to do so. The trip was both exciting and harrowing, for he undertook to

make stops at Vézelay and Dijon on the way. He was already
so feverish when he left home that he never thought of sleeping.
He spent the night and the early hours of the morning looking
out of the train windows and catching glimpses of villages—for
a time those in the west were still white in the moonlight
while those in the east were already gilded by the dawn. He
was asthmatic at Vézelay, where he went through the historic
Abbey Chuch, and more asthmatic still at Dijon, where he saw
the famous tombs. He reached Evian so completely done in
that he could scarcely walk through the station. A few days'
rest, however, brought him around, and he was soon arising in
the afternoon and discussing finances with his mother. Even
casual acquaintances could not help overhearing their remarks
about the size of tips (as when Proust gave a waiter five francs
for bringing him a paper worth a sou) and the difficulty of
leaving out articles in telegrams. One acquaintance, the future
novelist Maurice Duplay, thought the discussions charming and
described Madame Proust's reproaches as tender. Her son, who
had to listen to them in private as well as in public, was inclined
to describe them differently.

V

Less than three months after the family vacation at Evian, Proust's
father suddenly died. On November 23, 1903, Professor Proust
was apparently in reasonable health and certainly as active as
ever. He took part in the deliberations of the Commission on
Tuberculosis and he visited patients in the hospital. The next
day he looked rather worn but nevertheless set out for the School
of Medicine, where he was scheduled to preside at an examination.
He reached the School, retired to the lavatory, and failed to
emerge. When the door was forced, he was found stretched out
on the floor, unconscious and completely paralyzed. He was
taken to the Rue de Courcelles, where he died, without recovering
consciousness, forty-eight hours later.

The funeral was an impressive one, that of a public figure,
as indeed Professor Proust had been. The President sent a representative; the Prefect of the Seine, the Prefect of Police, and

the President of the Senate attended in person, along with doctors and scientists, literary men and artists, ambassadors and statesmen, friends of the family and friends—many of them aristocratic—of the deceased's elder son.

When the last rites at Père-Lachaise were over, Proust and his mother went home to begin their long period of mourning. They set aside the doctor's study as a kind of shrine, filling it with photographs taken at various periods of his life, but otherwise leaving it exactly as it had been. They suffered together as they talked of the past, and each suffered silently in his own way. Proust suffered quite as much from guilt as from grief. He told himself that he had been the one dark spot in his father's life. He remembered with the keenest regret the squabbles of the last months and a particular one not so long before when, during a political discussion, he had spoken to his father with inexcusable sharpness. But he remembered, too, that their relationship had once been even more distant, that since his ill health had kept him at home so much he had seen more of his father, and that he had to some extent learned to suppress the traits that his father found irritating. He blessed his illness, he looked back on the last few years as the happiest period in his life. His personality, however, was too volatile and the demands of his indisposition were too imperative for any of his moods to last very long. When it was reported to him that Bibesco was expressing doubts about the intensity of his grief, he wrote Bibesco that he never wanted to see him again. But when Bibesco called at the house that night, he talked with him as though nothing had happened and without once mentioning the bereavement.

From time to time Proust worked, not much perhaps, but enough to give his mother the illusion that he was accomplishing something. He turned out more articles for *Le Figaro*, including one a little different from the others, designed to flatter Montesquiou on the eve of his duel with a certain Jean Stern. Written as a parody of Saint-Simon, the article described the parties at the Pavilion of the Muses—described Montesquiou, Yturri, and certain aristocratic guests who were friends of Proust's. It appeared over the signature of Horatio on January 18, 1904, the very day of the duel. Montesquiou acquitted himself well, indeed resisted for some twenty minutes the onslaught of a superior swordsman before he finally collapsed, thrusting his sword through his doctor's trouser leg as he did so. Subsequently he read, with keen satisfaction, the article in the Le Figaro and tried to find out who had written it. When he failed, for the mysterious Horatio refused to come forward, he decided to reprint it at his own expense, with of course a few changes in punctuation. Proust, now terrified by his own success, preserved for some time the secret of his pseudonym.

The articles were apparently easy enough to do; the translation of Ruskin was more difficult, and Proust would gladly have abandoned it if his mother, pleading his father's interest in the project, had not insisted that he go on with it. And so, reluctantly, he saw The Bible of Amiens through the press and worked on another piece he had rashly started, Sesame and Lilies. He got help, as before, from his mother, who sometimes made preliminary translations of the passages he was working on so that he would not have to puzzle over the English text. He got help from other people, too, from Billy, Bibesco, and Humières—from anyone in his circle, in fact, who had a reasonable knowledge of English. On evenings when he was not otherwise engaged he pumped such people, quite shamelessly, for hours on end. At the moment, for example, he was pretty regularly consulting Hahn's English cousin, Marie Nordlinger, who was conveniently employed in Paris. He asked her all sorts of questions about what he had done, and sometimes had her make the preliminary drafts from which he worked; he used in his footnotes parallel passages that she pointed out. Later, when she talked of leaving Paris, he commissioned her to do a bust of his father for the family grave at Père-Lachaise and so kept her near him a little longer. It began to look as if the translation of Sesame would have to be regarded as a joint effort and as if Miss Nordlinger's name would have to go on the title page along with his own. In the end, however, this proved to be unnecessary. He found that he could acknowledge Miss Nordlinger's help quite adequately, and much less conspicuously, in a footnote.

Toward the end of February or the beginning of March, 1904, the translation of The Bible of Amiens finally appeared, with a

dedication to Proust's father, with an introduction (a somewhat
amplified version of Proust's articles in *Le Mercure de France*
and *La Gazette des beaux-arts*), and with notes and parallel
passages. It was an achievement no doubt, but not a very considerable one for three or four years' work. It got notices but not very
many of them, though Proust did what he could to bring it to
the attention of his literary friends. He let it be known that he
would like a substantial review from Léon Daudet, to whom
the preface was dedicated, but Daudet wrote nothing. Through
Madame de Noailles he brought pressure to bear on Abel Hermant,
the distinguished novelist and critic. "If you see Hermant," he
wrote her, "tell him that if, in one of his articles, he could drag
in a few words on my *Bible of Amiens*, he would be doing me
a great favor, because he would be helping to sell copies, a matter
in which I have no financial interest myself, but I shouldn't like
to see the man who has been kind enough to publish my book
lose too much money." But Hermant, like Daudet, ignored the
request. Other friends, however—in particular Bergson and Albert
Sorel—responded more generously. Bergson submitted the book
to the Academy of Moral and Political Sciences, and if the
newspapers had only reported the session adequately, the publicity
might have been very good. Sorel wrote a long and enthusiastic
review in *Le Temps*, describing Proust as an authentic disciple
of Ruskin's, with much of the master's charm, praising in particular
the delicacy, the clarity, and the color of Proust's style, comparing
it with Gallé glass work in which, through a completely transparent
medium, the arabesques of vines are seen.

CHAPTER X

Bereavement

I

WITH THE PUBLICATION of *The Bible of Amiens,* the time had obviously come for Proust to get back to his notebooks and finish the novel he had started so many years before. He himself was well aware of this; he felt the strongest urge to get back. "What I am doing isn't real work," he once wrote Bibesco, "but only documentation, translation, etc. . . . It is enough to awaken my thirst for accomplishment, without of course satisfying it at all." He went on to say that he had thought of a hundred characters and a thousand ideas that he could use in fiction. A hundred characters and a thousand ideas! He might at once have begun incorporating them in the notebooks and thus enriching what would ultimately develop into his novel. But he did not, he could not seem to, begin. The obstacles were the same as ever— his own inertia and his mother's insistence on work that would lead to immediate publication. The odious work on *Sesame and Lilies* was still hanging over him. More years inevitably passed, comparatively idle years, before he could really settle down to creative work.

Proust had, as it happened, less excuse for not working on his novel because, since his father's death, his domestic life had become considerably quieter. He and his mother, drawn together

by their common loss, were less disposed to quarrel. His notes
to her were seldom querulous, and he was apparently never
tempted to fall on his friends and mutilate their new hats. He
made concessions about his hours, or at least still talked of
doing so—he was still promising faithfully that at the very first
opportunity he would get back to sleeping at night. Meanwhile,
however, he slept in the daytime and appeared in the dining
room only as evening began. As before he talked with his mother
and received his friends and read and worked on his translation of
Sesame and Lilies. For a while he lost his manuscript, or part
of it, and when he found it again he decided to rewrite it from
the beginning. He often went out, usually late in the evening,
and invariably suffered some kind of disaster in consequence.

His social life in 1904 was perhaps a shade smarter than it
had been in previous years. His friends were more often drawn
from the circle of aristocratic young men; the invitations that he
accepted were more often the very best. There were exceptions
of course, as when he dined at a house where Montesquiou, who
was by this time distinctly *passé,* was one of the other guests.
Proust found his old friend as long-winded as ever, especially
when he insisted on talking about a recent story of Madame de
Noailles'. "What a genius! what a genius!" he kept exclaiming.
On the way home he suddenly raised his arms above his head
and whispered dramatically, "The color of the sky was indescribable
tonight." Amazed by his antics, people stopped in the street to
stare; Proust caught a dreadful cold.

Another friend who could not claim social distinction was a
young actress, Mademoiselle Louisa de Mornand, who however
was very good looking and was, or had been, the mistress
of one of Proust's really distinguished friends. For some time
Proust went through the motions of flirting with her. He was
constantly seeing her, with or without her lover, at Larue's and
in the dining room on the Rue de Courcelles. He persuaded
friends in the theatre to give her small parts and friends on
newspapers to review her favorably. He tried to advise her when
she was temperamental, as she apparently often was, and when
she seemed to take a perverse delight in awakening her lover's
jealousy. At the moment, however, his task was more difficult.

The lover had announced his engagement and it was necessary to persuade Mademoiselle de Mornand that she was being treated with the utmost consideration. Proust did his best, but she was even more temperamental—quite unreasonable in fact—and he soon had to tell her that he was withdrawing entirely from the affair. Nevertheless he went on seeing her just as frequently.

In July, 1904, Proust gave a dinner for his friend Bertrand de Fénelon, who was now in the diplomatic service and about to return to his post abroad. He also went to several dinners—one given by the Duc de Guiche, one by the Comtesse de Noailles, and one by the Duc and Duchesse de Gramont at which the company was particularly smart. In August he made the daring experiment of joining his friend Billy on a yacht and setting out on a cruise of the Breton coast. The sea was very beautiful and quite calm, but he could not sleep enough on board even with trional. After five days he was back at home, complaining that windows had been left open in his absence and that his room was intolerably damp. Later in the summer he published another article in Le Figaro and did a good deal of publicity—for Humières who was bringing out a new book, for Mademoiselle de Mornand who was appearing in a new part, and for Bibesco who was having a play produced. At the same time he was trying to make up his mind whether he should go to Evian or Dieppe or Trouville, the decision being complicated by the fact that both Albufera and Guiche were getting married soon and he would naturally want to be back for the ceremonies. Suddenly, after a bad night, he decided that he would not go away at all, he would make his hours more reasonable. But this was so very awkward and involved such great sacrifices: to wake up earlier he had to go to bed earlier, and to go to bed earlier he had to dine earlier, in fact much too early for his friends. This meant that he had to decline invitations and, his mother being away, dine alone at home—a dreadfully depressing thing to do. Furthermore, he was not sure how long he could stand waking up in the morning. He found himself trying to treat his asthma or to rest in broad daylight when other people were outdoors enjoying themselves—something that seemed to him really awful. By the end of September he had settled back into his old routine.

"I am very unhappy at the moment," Proust wrote to Bibesco in October. "In every way—morally, physically, intellectually." Perhaps he was worn out by his struggle to change his hours, or depressed by the weddings—it is not always easy to see one's friends married off. Perhaps, on the other hand, his relationships with some of the unmarried men in his circle were at the moment particularly difficult. It is known that at approximately this time he was upset about one friend—a certain M., a young man wealthy enough to have a country house and masculine enough to have a mistress. They were very close to one another, and then quite suddenly Proust seemed to realize that the end had come. "I don't want to see you any more," he wrote M., "I don't think we should write to each other or even know each other any longer. When my friendship for you is dead, I shall —since such friendships never revive—be delighted to meet you if you want. But when? It will depend on what new friendships I can form. I can't tell now." In a letter to another member of his circle Proust explained his position even more clearly. "I am especially anxious that you shouldn't think I am boasting of my inconstancy," he said in this second letter. "I was so much interested in a stable relationship with M. that I have let him treat me like a worm. I wish you could see me. But he seems so rancid to me now that it can't last much longer. And you can imagine how sad I am going to be when I say to myself, 'Another lemon squeezed dry' (Barrès), especially when I was so fond of this one."

Meanwhile the weddings took place and Proust duly delivered his wedding presents, bought for him by his mother. He was very much pleased with them and very anxious that they should be recognized as his when they were on display with other presents that the two couples received. For this reason he felt that he should have new visiting cards on which his name would appear in somewhat larger type. The present for the Duc de Guiche, suggested apparently by Guiche himself, was an odd one—a revolver. It came from the best gunsmith in Paris and its case was decorated with little allegorical scenes of sea-gulls and sailboats, illustrating passages from a volume of poems that the bride, the daughter of the Comte and Comtesse Greffulhe, had published in her childhood. On the proper day the revolver appeared among countless other presents that the Guiches received, presents from everyone in French society, presents from the Queen of Portugal and the King of Sweden.

II

As early as 1904 Proust began to feel that he would have to do something more radical about his asthma than burning Legras powder and guarding himself against fatigue. Accordingly he consulted the celebrated Dr. Merklen, who explained to him that his asthma was, or had become, a nervous habit. He could break himself of it, Merklen said, only by entering a certain institution in Germany and undergoing a treatment somewhat like that given drug addicts. The consultation was a pleasant one and Proust afterwards sent the doctor a copy of *Les Plaisirs et les jours*. But he had no intention of taking the advice, certainly none of going to Germany for treatment.

Perhaps Proust was able to dismiss so cavalierly the eminent doctor's prescription because he was not nearly so ill as he said he was; perhaps the friends who regarded him as a liar or a hypochondriac or both were on the whole right. He certainly was quite capable of telling polite lies. For years he had been exaggerating his symptoms, or even inventing them altogether, so as to avoid distasteful work or dreary social engagements. He was a past master at representing himself as helpless and so persuading his mother, his friends, and even his more distant acquaintances to wait on him. His ill health, as his friend Bibesco afterwards said, was, among other things, "a method of blackmail . . . a means of procuring all the indulgence he found necessary." He was certainly also a hypochondriac, since he often deceived himself, as well as other people, about the seriousness of his complaints. He was always having his pulse taken and his urine analyzed, always brooding about pains he seemed to detect in his back or his wrists or his eyes, it scarcely mattered where. He was not above resorting to eccentric remedies, as when he gave himself a strong dose of cascara to cure a sore throat.

On the other hand, he certainly did have asthma throughout

the year and hay fever in the spring. His asthma seems to have been rather worse than before—always at least inconvenient and often extremely troublesome, even when he was taking care of himself to the best of his ability. It was clearly worth his while to consider new remedies or new forms of treatment that might reduce the frequency of his attacks and thus materially simplify his life.

Toward the end of 1904 and the beginning of 1905 he was again turning over in his mind what Merklen had told him. Perhaps he *should* try a course of treatment, not in Germany, which was pretty far afield, but, say, in Switzerland or even in France. There were two eminent Swiss neurologists he might consult, Dr. Dubois and Dr. Widmer, and at least two in Paris, Dr. Déjerine and Dr. Sollier. He began inquiring about all four of them and trying to decide which one had the most to offer in his case. "From time to time I go to see doctors and they tell me to leave town," he wrote to Madame Straus; "I don't leave, but each visit I make to them costs me whole weeks in bed." In the second half of his sentence he was probably prevaricating, pretending to be bedridden so that he would not have to call on his correspondent. On the other hand, he probably *was* seeing doctors and talking of leaving Paris—there were very few periods in his life when he was not doing both. By February, 1905, he was sure, or fairly sure, that he would try Dr. Dubois' establishment and that he would set out for Switzerland within a week or two. A little later he was not so sure about the time. "Unfortunately I am going to have to enter a kind of sanatorium," he now explained to Madame Straus, "and to spend three or four months there, but I think I am going to put it off until after my hay fever." Later still he was fairly sure about the time—he would set out in the autumn—but not so sure about the doctor. He was considering two, one of whom was Widmer.

In March, while the decision about doctors still hung in the balance, Proust began arranging a grand dinner for some new friends, the Clermont-Tonnerres. The Marquis de Clermont-Tonnerre was an ardent Royalist and a militant anti-Dreyfusard; he was one of the young men who had been arrested at the Auteuil race track some years before when the President of the Republic had been bashed on the head. The Marquise was related to other friends of Proust's; she was the daughter of the Duc de Gramont and the half-sister of the Duc de Guiche. Proust had seen something of her at the Strauses' and at Montesquiou's, where she had counted as one of the faithful. More recently he had dined at her house, and he now felt obligated to entertain her at the Rue de Courcelles.

Arrangements for dinners were difficult now that Madame Proust, who was still in mourning, could not be persuaded to act as hostess. Proust did what he could by himself, but in the end he had to give up the idea of a dinner altogether and compromise on a tea, a small one but very select. The Clermont-Tonnerres were after all not present, but several other notable people were—the Comtesse Aimery de La Rochefoucauld, the Comtesse d'Haussonville, the Duchesse de Gramont, the Duc and Duchesse de Guiche, the Princesse de Brancovan, the Comte and Comtesse Adhéaume de Chevigné, the Comtesse de Briey, the Princesse de Caraman-Chimay, the Comte Ferdinand de Montesquiou, the Baron Théodore de Berckheim. . . . The list of guests was indeed a triumph which any hostess might have envied. While refreshments were served there was conversation, and afterwards there was just the right amount of music—a few songs by Hahn, a Mozart duet by Hahn and the Comtesse de Guerne. Despite his fever, Proust got through the afternoon remarkably well, and when the party broke up he was even able to leave the house for a few minutes, obviously to take his visiting list to the newspapers. The next day Le Figaro was as flattering as he could have wished, describing the tea as one "of great elegance, to which only a score of persons were invited," adding that "after the tea, which was not followed by a reception, the guests of Monsieur Marcel Proust had the pleasure of hearing Monsieur Reynaldo Hahn, who sang at the piano his exquisite melodies."

Retribution, however, was something that Proust could seldom escape, and this time it took at least two forms, a period during which he was asthmatic and a considerably longer period during which he was again bedeviled by Montesquiou. Proust had of course been aware that Montesquiou might make trouble and he had in fact done his best to avert it. In a long letter he had explained that, in giving a tea, he was not so much entertaining as

bidding farewell to society or rather establishing a mental alibi.
"Since I am undoubtedly on the point of making up my mind
to go away for a rest cure," Proust had said, "I don't want people
to say that I have suddenly gone mad and been locked up,
and so I gathered my friends to show them that I was leaving
with a sound mind (if I have ever had one) and by my own
free will (if one ever does anything by free will). But the farewell
would have been more impressive and the alibi more memorable
if the white light in my drawing room had been permitted to
outline the features of the poet of Versailles and of Louis."
Unfortunately, however, the explanation was not quite plausible
enough. Montesquiou, though far away in the Pyrenees, was
under no illusions at all.

When he returned to Paris, the poet was clearly in no mood
to temporize. He invited Proust to a lecture he was giving, and
sent Yturri to the Rue de Courcelles at a highly inopportune
hour to repeat the invitation even more urgently. The overtures
were certainly explicit enough, and when Proust failed to appear
at the lecture, Montesquiou felt quite justified in releasing the
tempest of his wrath. In a stormy letter he insisted that Proust's
asthma was a sham, an excuse for his snobbishness, a convenient
way of avoiding engagements he found distasteful. In another
letter, equally stormy, he ridiculed Proust's handwriting. Proust's
faults were obviously grave; nevertheless the poet was still willing
to be magnanimous. He was willing to admit that his young
friend could not go out; he was willing to give his next lecture
in the privacy of the Rue de Courcelles and, in fact, he insisted
on doing so. Proust was caught. He answered evasively, multiplied
excuses, and tried in every conceivable way to wriggle out, but
the poet went on inexorably making his plans. Finally, on June
2, the lecture—or, more properly, the reading—was given in the
Proust family drawing room.

"Particularly interesting party yesterday at Monsieur Marcel
Proust's," *The New York Herald* afterwards reported, quoting or
summarizing an account sent in by Proust himself, "where the
guests, who were very few in number, unexpectedly heard an
admirable reading by the Comte Robert de Montesquiou-Fezensac,
consisting of fragments from his new book, *Professionnelles beau-*

tés. The presence in the group, which was small, representative, and select, of several persons who are entertainingly and flatteringly described in the poet's beautiful pages made the reading even more piquant. And the guests did not restrain themselves in lavishing their applause and their praise on Comte Robert de Montesquiou, while Monsieur Marcel Proust warmly thanked him for the rare and precious honor he had conferred upon the house."

The poet was again appeased; Proust choked—or so he said— for thirty hours after the reading before he finally found relief.

III

The tea and the reading no doubt retarded Proust's work on *Sesame and Lilies;* nevertheless, with his mother's help, he made quite definite progress. He finished and published in a magazine his translation of the first lecture, the one called "Of Kings' Treasuries." He gathered material for his introduction to the book—singled out certain usable pages from his notebooks and borrowed, or tried to borrow, a guidebook on Holland and an article on Maples furniture. He worked on the introduction, finished it too, and published it—under the title of "Sur la Lecture"—in *La Renaissance latine.*

In this introduction Proust briefly summarizes Ruskin's view that reading is a way of talking with great men, of entering their thoughts and receiving their instructions, of acquiring ideas more profound and more significant than those that we might acquire by our own efforts. He summarizes this view but he rejects it; for to him reading is something quite different, a creative and not a passive experience. It releases our imaginations, stimulates us to think and feel for ourselves, and so helps us to overcome the apathy from which, to some extent, all of us inevitably suffer. Psychiatrists sometimes help neurotics, Proust says, by reawakening their will power and encouraging them to use their faculties, which are, organically, quite sound. In the same way novelists, poets, and painters help us by dissipating our mental torpor and persuading us to see more within ourselves. "Thus Emerson scarcely ever began to write without first reading a few pages of Plato, nor is Dante the only poet whom Virgil piloted to the gates of paradise."

Thus Proust sharply differs with the master whose work he is translating; thus he expounds, in "Sur la Lecture," a doctrine of his own—a highly personal doctrine, one feels, since the reader he describes is quite clearly a man of genius. His illustrations are themselves often personal. He recalls impressions from his immediate and his distant past, impressions of books he once read, *Le Capitaine Fracasse* for example, and impressions of places he once visited, Beaune, Dordrecht, Venice, and Illiers. The passage on Illiers is an especially long and delightful one. It is rather better than the early sections of the notebooks on which, in part at least, it seems to be based; it is almost a "Combray" in miniature. Proust describes both a scene and a group of people. He touches on the dining room where he read in the morning, the park where he went for picnics, and the bedroom where, when his parents had retired, he surreptitiously relit his candle and went on reading until far into the night. He mentions certain relatives—for example, his great-aunt, whom he describes with the most affectionate irony. This great-aunt never ventured to judge books, Proust says, for she was doubtful about the standards of judgment and afraid of giving way to caprice. But she was always prompt and inflexible in judging the way people prepared certain dishes, the way they played the sonatas of Beethoven, and the way they received, for in these things she felt she knew what perfection was and how to achieve it.

Her idea of perfection in each of these three activities was almost the same, and consisted in something that might be called simplicity of means, soberness, and charm. She recoiled in horror from the idea of using spices, except when they were absolutely necessary, from any affectation in piano playing and the abuse of the pedal, from unnatural behavior or overmuch speaking of oneself when one was giving a party. She had only to take a single mouthful, had but to hear one note, had but to look at a card of invitation to claim at once that she could tell whether she had to do with a good cook, a genuine musician, or a well-brought-up woman. "She may have more fingers than I have, but she shows a lack of taste in playing that *andante* with so much emphasis." "She may be very brilliant and have many good qualities, but to talk like that of herself displays a lack of tact." "I've no doubt she knows a great deal about cooking, but she can't manage beefsteak and potatoes." Beefsteak and potatoes were her test dish, difficult because so simple, a sort of *Sonata Pathétique* of the kitchen, the gastronomic equivalent of the visit of a lady come to inquire about a servant, an errand simple enough in itself, but capable of telling all one needed to know about her tact and upbringing.

The preface to *Sesame* is indeed a kind of transitional work. It shows Proust still dealing with Ruskin, though by no means so uncritically as in his first casual articles. At the same time, it shows him turning, as though instinctively, to his own experience—turning, in fact, to his notebooks—reviewing and fixing memories which he had once thought of, and was perhaps now beginning to think of again, as promising material for a novel. The preface is not a masterpiece, nor was it hailed as such when it appeared. But one critic at least—André Beaunier of *Le Figaro*—recognized it as a work of genuine distinction, and described it as "charming, moving, in several places marvelous." Proust suspected that he owed the praise to the fact that Beaunier was a friend of Madame de Noailles, but it was welcome praise nevertheless.

IV

It was Proust's hope that he could finish his translation of *Sesame* by the summer of 1905 so that he would be free to try a course of treatment in the autumn, if by that time treatment still seemed desirable. He worked hard, at least so hard that he constantly complained of eye strain, but the manuscript was not ready on time. At the end of July he consulted still another doctor, a certain Brissaud, who recommended that he see Dr. Sollier, one of the four specialists he had been considering for many months. It does not appear that he took the advice.

In September he went to Evian with his mother, and he may very well have had the idea of going on, after a week or two, to consult Dr. Dubois or Dr. Widmer. But two hours after their arrival in Evian, while he was still acutely asthmatic from the change of air, his mother began having spells of nausea and some sort of difficulty with her speech. The symptoms persisted, yet— in an effort to convince her son that she was really quite all right —she dressed every morning and went down, supported by attendants, to the hotel lounge. After a few days her younger son, Robert, came to Evian and took her back to Paris. But the trip was hard on her, her condition, diagnosed as acute uremia, was aggravated, and she still irrationally resisted treatment. Lingering on, apparently at her insistence, in Evian, Proust anxiously followed reports from home, well aware that the greatest tragedy of his life was at hand. He remembered that he had always wanted to survive his mother so that he might spare her the anguish of another bereavement, but he was not sure now that she was not suffering quite as intensely in a different way. She knew—she must know—that she was dying, and she was perhaps tortured by the thought that she was abandoning him when he needed her as much as ever.

As the crisis of her illness approached, Proust returned to Paris. He found her thinner, for she had eaten little since her illness began, and looking younger. By a strange process she seemed to recover her youth as she wasted away. He stayed near her room, he kept going in to kiss her and talk with her as long as she could still talk. The end came, he kissed her still and smiled at her through his tears.

Since she was not a Christian, there were no church services. The family and friends of the family—including the Noailles, the Albuferas, and the Chevignés—gathered at noon in the Rue de Courcelles, stood in silence as the coffin, laden with flowers, was carried to the hearse, then followed to Père-Lachaise. When he was at last alone again, Proust was inclined to take a rather sensational view of his loss. He felt that without his mother he could scarcely go on living, and that he would never know a moment's happiness again.

His grief, genuine enough, was at the same time curiously self-conscious. While he felt it he was able to stand apart from it, to analyze it, and to describe it in letters to his friends. Sometimes it took the form of guilt, as when he seemed to catch himself forgetting his loss and then recoiled, appalled by his own insensitivity. Often it was connected with specific memories. He thought of going out, but then he remembered that in the past when he had come home his mother had always stood near the door, watching him to see if he was asthmatic and not daring to speak until she was sure that he could answer her without difficulty. He could not go out—he could not bear the idea of returning to an empty house. Once, as he was walking through the apartment, the floor creaked by the door of his mother's room. He remembered that when in the past he had stepped on that spot his mother had always heard him and had insisted that he come in and kiss her. He seemed to be exploring a new avenue of grief; he felt his loss with renewed intensity.

Sometimes, fortunately, his grief took still another form, that of trying to do what his mother would have wanted. It was clear that she would have wanted him to choose a specialist and get on with his course of treatment, and so, early in the winter of 1905, he tried to make a choice. But it was no easier than it had been before, and as always he was feverishly indecisive. For a while he was inclined to prefer either Dr. Dubois in Switzerland or Dr. Sollier in Paris, both interested in what has come to be known as psychosomatic medicine. A man with a bad stomach is no doubt a pessimist, Dubois once said, but one cures one's stomach by changing one's ideas and not the other way around. Proust asked Madame de Noailles to tell him what she could about Dubois and Sollier, but later, acting on other advice, he came to terms with one of the other specialists on his list, Dr. Déjerine. He got so far as to engage, for three months, a room at the Déjerine nursing home in the Rue Blomet. The time for his departure came and he was about to leave the house, when suddenly, relapsing into a frenzy of indecision, he sent an urgent message to Madame Straus asking for further information about Sollier. It now seemed to him that his mother would perhaps have wanted him to be treated at home, that Sollier would perhaps consent to give him such treatment and thus save him the ordeal of a sanatorium. Dr. Sollier came to see him, with the result that he entered, not the Déjerine nursing home in the Rue Blomet, but the Sollier nursing home at Boulogne-Billancourt.

The treatment was a form of pre-Freudian psychoanalysis. The patient was isolated, kept in bed, and encouraged to eat as much as possible. Meanwhile, in daily conversations with his doctor, he talked about his problems and received advice. In Proust's case the advice does not seem to have been very helpful, perhaps in part because he lacked faith in his doctor. He apparently lost what faith he had on the very first day, when Sollier sneered at Bergson. Proust merely smiled; he could scarcely be expected to answer such a sally. Otherwise he apparently followed Sollier's routine—stayed in bed and stuffed himself with food, saw very few visitors and dictated instead of writing his letters, except of course when he particularly wanted to write. But his asthma grew worse rather than better, and before the end of the second month he returned home, quite desperately asthmatic and inclined to take a completely pessimistic view of his case. In letters to his friends he explained, somewhat melodramatically, that he was giving up all thoughts of ever leading a normal life again and was now simply waiting for the inevitable end, which could not be very far off. His one consolation was that his mother had not lived to see him in the final stage of his illness and that she had been able to keep some illusions about his future until the day of her death.

CHAPTER XI

Moving

I

DURING the early months of 1906 Proust's pessimism about his health seemed completely justified. He was either ill or afraid of being ill. He spent the greater part of his time in bed, resting at night and sleeping during the daytime. But by spring he was, if not exactly well again, at least not much worse than he had been for several years before. He went out or talked of going out—he even promised himself that during the following year he would go out every day. He worked a little—reviewed a translation of *The Stones of Venice* and saw his own translation of *Sesame and Lilies* through the press. The publication of *Sesame* pleased him at least partly because he knew that his mother would have been pleased. She had always been interested in the book and always determined that he should persist until he had finished it. Now that it was finished, it seemed quite as much a memorial to her as a mark of his own achievement.

Proust wrote to Calmette, the editor of *Le Figaro*, urging him to give *Sesame* adequate space, and Calmette was unusually gracious. On June 5, 1906, he had André Beaunier do an "instantané" on Proust, a delightfully flattering little note in which

the translator of *Sesame* was described as one of the most polished
and discriminating of contemporary writers, and his preface was
called "original and delicious, moving, droll, tearfully gay, discreetly melancholy." But this was not the end of *Le Figaro's*
favors. In the issue of June 14 Beaunier devoted two columns (on
the front page!) to *Sesame*, quoting extensively and giving the
highest praise to the translation, the notes, and the preface.
Proust's reminiscences of his childhood, Beaunier said, breathe the
perfume of faded flowers. He added that, in their fragile delicacy,
they resemble "those dried flowers that one presses between the
pages of old books, flowers that one dares not touch lest they
crumble, much as one would like to fondle them as in former
days." Beaunier's enthusiasm cooled only when he spoke of
Ruskin, whom he treated as an exasperatingly opinionated author.

The praise was easily the highest that Proust had ever had in
print, and he was naturally eager to get the reaction of his friends.
But to his consternation he seemed to discover that none of them
had noticed either the "instantané" or the review. Hahn, who
called one evening, spoke of an article by Varennes: he had seen
nothing by Beaunier. Albufera, whose whole family subscribed to
Le Figaro, expressed surprise that Calmette had ignored *Sesame*.
When Proust assured him that quite the contrary was true, Albufera
said: "*You must be mistaken*, because my wife reads *Le Figaro*
from one end to the other every morning, and there was absolutely
nothing there about you." Proust was not only dumbfounded, he
was outraged; he reflected darkly on the declining interest in letters.
Our most intelligent contemporaries, he wrote Robert Dreyfus,
"are incapable of *reading* even so much as a *newspaper*." "I don't
read much myself," he added, "but at least I don't read like that.
I assure you (I *swear* to you) that it is not because I myself am
concerned that I am struck by this, that on the contrary it is because I am concerned that I confine myself to these examples and
indeed leave out the most telling of all."

II

If Proust was annoyed with his friends, he was very much encouraged by the praise lavished on his delicate evocations of the

past. It seemed to him that now, with Ruskin out of the way, he might at last get back to his notebooks, give life to the hundred characters and the thousand ideas he felt stirring within him, in fact write a really memorable novel. He might do this, but not at once—the old restlessness overcame him again. He would first have to renew his contact with life by going out regularly, by traveling, and by receiving fresh poetic impressions. Traveling was a particularly inviting possibility because he could now go almost anywhere he wanted to. He was not fabulously rich—he still had to make financial calculations—but at least he could spend as he saw fit the substantial fortune that his parents had left him. One possibility was to join friends near Cabourg; another was to settle down by himself at Trouville; still another was to rent a yacht and perhaps do what he had not been able to do two years before—enjoy the water that he liked so much and visit the ports of Normandy and Brittany. Madame Straus was at Trouville for the summer, and to her, in a series of maddening, incoherent, and indecisive letters, Proust confided his projects and his hopes.

"Do you know," he asked in his first letter, "if the Chalet d'Harcourt—the small cottage of the Crémieux—is for rent, if it is not dangerous to live in so isolated a place, if it is sufficiently well built so that you don't feel the wind and drafts in the rooms? It is also important that the rent shouldn't be more than 1,000 francs for August, because I should in any case have to have a car, etc., and the whole thing would be a great extravagance, which I should gladly put up with to be in Trouville, but I have to set a limit. I have also thought of renting a small boat, just for myself, with which I could tour Normandy and Brittany, starting out at Trouville, spending the night there (on board) and going to see you in the daytime. But I'm afraid that at the price I could pay I could get only yachts that would be too uncomfortable and very dangerous." But, he went on as another idea occurred to him, "if I weren't so much afraid of the noise and the impossibility of warming linen, perhaps the least expensive thing—especially with my meager diet—might be a two-room apartment at the Roches Noires. But it seems to me that the walls are very thin and that every sound can be heard, and the fireplaces probably aren't intended for fires. Normandy is not a very healthy place for me. And even at Trouville the valley fogs in the evening are bad for me, and the sea air is a little disturbing. Still, if I found a house that was well built and neither damp nor dusty, modern in style and bare, not stuck in behind other houses, but either on the beach or on the high ground, and not costing more than 1,000 francs for the month of August, I might perhaps take it. . . . A boat would be very charming, but I'm afraid a sailboat would be very cold and a steamboat, since it would have to be very small, would reek of smoke."

In later letters he pointed out that the illness of an uncle had, among other things, prevented him from deciding what he wanted to do. But since he might decide at any time, even at any hour, it was imperative that he have further information about houses available at Trouville. His top price would now be something like 2,000 francs for August. The house must be "very dry, *away from trees*, high but not overlooking the valley where there is fog (by high I mean not in the town, but the beach would be all right), electricity if possible, construction rather new, neither dusty (the modern style is the sort of thing I need to breathe well—what a style!) nor damp; I only need a room for myself, two rooms for my servants, a dining room, and a kitchen. A bath isn't indispensable though it would be very pleasant. Living room useless. As many toilets as possible." He added that a large house would be quieter and therefore better than a small one. An elevator would be very desirable, but he was not sure that he could expect one in Normandy. "If the trees are rather far away, fairly large, not damp trees or trees with insects and pollen, I shouldn't worry about them." It once occurred to him that the Tour Malakoff might be just the place he was looking for; he seemed to remember that it had once rented for almost nothing. But on second thought this fact seemed to him ominous. Perhaps it was directly behind the Roches Noires in a location he considered intolerable; perhaps there was something unhealthy or dangerous about it that would account for the modest rent. In any case, he was afraid of the stairs. "It is essential that—unless there is an elevator, which seems improbable—I have as few stairs as possible, though I cannot live quite on the ground floor. In whatever place I am, I am anxious that gas shouldn't be indispensable; that if there is gas, I can get along without it, because it makes me ill."

Madame Straus, one imagines, was alternately amused and exasperated by the letters. Proust himself was exhausted. He had consumed so much energy arranging his trip that he had none left to make it, and he so informed his correspondent. "Perhaps I shall take up my project again," he wrote her, "but just now I have to rest from the fatigue of the journey, for a journey that one has planned and is about to begin is quite as exhausting as a journey one has actually made; for three days now I have felt myself en route and everything around me has looked as if it were being left behind." In a subsequent letter he announced that he had gone to Versailles, where he could perhaps get outdoors as well as in Normandy and where he could receive prompt reports from his uncle's sick room.

<h1 style="text-align:center">III</h1>

His sojourn in Versailles was not a very happy one. He could not or did not go out much. Once indeed he went to Paris to see his uncle, but he felt unable to go again, or, after his uncle's death, to attend the funeral. Generally he confined himself to his apartment in the annex of the Hôtel des Réservoirs. It was an expensive and lavishly furnished apartment—it had no fewer than two pianos—but the general impression was one of profound gloom. "It looks like an apartment with a history," Proust said, "one of those places where the guide tells you, 'Here Charles IX died,' and where you cast a quick look around as you hurry to get back to the warm sunlight outside and the reassuring world of today. But when you not only can't get out of it but actually have to make the supreme acceptance of going to bed in it—you are ready to die." Other discomforts, more disturbing to Proust than the gloom, appeared during his stay. The doors and windows closed imperfectly, admitting intolerable drafts; the fireplaces smoked or at least set nearby fireplaces smoking; the meals, carried on trays from the main building, were invariably stone cold.

Still from day to day and from week to week Proust lingered on in the somber annex, dreaming of the gardens he was never able to see, and devoting what little energy he had to practical affairs, which kept forcing themselves on his attention in the most exasperating way. He had to make the most painful decisions, the most complex arrangements. For one thing, he felt that he had to give up the family apartment in the Rue de Courcelles, which was rather too expensive for a single person, and find an apartment of his own. Naturally he could not look himself, and so he did what he had always been disposed to do when he was in difficulty—he relied on other people. Many of his friends must have profoundly regretted the death of Madame Proust, in whose lifetime they had less often been pressed into service. But they helped him now as they had before: they scoured the streets of Paris, as before Madame Straus had scoured the hills and beaches of Trouville, for an apartment suited to his needs. Several possibilities apparently turned up, and Proust considered each in turn, weighed its discomforts and hesitated, worried and thus aggravated his asthma.

Finally, however, it became clear to him that he could not possibly live in a house that his mother had never visited or discussed, that had not in some way formed part of her experience. And so he began considering an apartment in a house that had once belonged to his uncle, Louis Weil, and was now partly his, at 102 Boulevard Haussmann. He remembered dining there with his mother years before, and standing with her in the bedroom on the day his uncle Louis had died. Clearly he would not be leaving her entirely if he moved to such surroundings. He would still be able to sense her presence as he looked about him, though not perhaps quite so definitely as in the Rue de Courcelles.

Unfortunately the apartment was in other respects wholly undesirable. It was too expensive, though for the first year he could get it, by subletting, at a moderate price. It was incredibly ugly—perhaps, he decided, remembering the pinkish walls and gilded mouldings, the ugliest apartment he had ever seen in his life. Furthermore, the location—between a large department store and a church—was really abominable. The dust and noise were alarming to contemplate; the trees growing just outside threatened paroxysms of asthma. Should he be foolish enough to take an apartment where he would obviously be more miserable than before? One night he asked the butler at the hotel to call Madame de Noailles and put the question to her. She thought that he should take it, and he did so. The decision made him unhappy, but it need not be, he told himself, a final one. He could always move again if the rigors of the Boulevard Haussmann proved too much for him. Meanwhile he would get used to living in an apartment that his mother had never actually occupied.

Once the matter of the apartment was settled, Proust began a series of agonizing negotiations—by letter, by telephone, and by messenger—with his brother and his aunt, who were, with himself, joint owners of the building; with the agent; with the tenant from whom he was subletting; with the concierge; with the telephone company; with a firm that sold wallpaper; with electricians, upholsterers, and others. He sent his servants scurrying back and forth between Paris and Versailles. He persuaded an old family friend, Madame Catusse—who can scarcely have realized what she was letting herself in for—to look over his furniture and decide how it could best be placed in the new apartment. In the hope, he told her, of preserving as far as possible the arrangement of the principal rooms at the Rue de Courcelles so as to provide for himself an atmosphere completely familiar, he proposed to transfer the furniture of the large living room, the small living room, and the dining room at the Rue de Courcelles to the corresponding rooms at the Boulevard Haussmann. But there were difficulties—the new rooms were smaller. The furniture would have to be packed in rather tightly; the rugs might even have to be rolled up at the edges. Dust would inevitably accumulate, for Proust, usually obliged to sleep during the daytime, could not permit his servants to clean very regularly. A series of rooms crowded with upholstered pieces might well prove intolerably dusty. Nevertheless he resigned himself to the crowding. He felt that he might soon be moving to a larger apartment where he would need all his furniture, and he was in any case reluctant to banish familiar pieces that seemed to him as precious and as ugly as old friends. Some things, no doubt, would have to be put in storage, some could even be given away. The bronzes, which were especially hideous, might serve as presents for family friends without much taste; odd pieces of furniture to which he was not particularly attached might be divided up among the servants.

The problems connected with the bedroom—a large room facing the Boulevard Haussmann—were even more difficult and more trying. Should he use the blue furniture from his mother's bedroom, even though it would be dusty and would, furthermore, awaken the cruelest memories? If he did use the blue furniture, should he take his mother's bed, as Antoine, the concierge, insisted, or should he keep his own brass bed, as he himself preferred, at the risk of ruining the color scheme? Should he follow Antoine's advice and keep his mother's black wardrobe, or should he take another wardrobe, perhaps the one he had most often seen his mother use? In either case, a thorough cleaning would be in order, for a suggestion of perfume might linger in the wood. He must certainly have rugs; otherwise the tenants downstairs would complain when they heard his servants running errands in the middle of the night. But must the rugs be tacked to the floor? Loose rugs were not nearly so dusty because they were not nearly so hard to clean; on the other hand, they were perhaps a little damp. Should he hang on one of the walls the portrait of his mother done many years ago? He was inclined to think not, since it would remind him too painfully of the way she had looked in her last days, when illness had restored her youth. He could always see the portrait when he wanted to if he hung it in one of the living rooms.

In the course of four months Proust managed to make a little progress without once going to Paris to see the apartment for himself, but other people kept holding him back in the most exasperating way. The agent was dilatory, the tenant was ungracious, the co-owners—his brother and his aunt—were hopelessly inconsiderate. His brother, a practicing physician who should have known better, had been careless enough to visit the apartment while his daughter was ill with diphtheria. A thorough fumigation now seemed necessary, provided of course that it could be carried out without leaving a trace of odor. Finally, about the beginning of November, his brother and his aunt between them hatched up the eccentric idea of renting out the entresol, and renting it to a doctor of all people! Proust could imagine no greater catastrophe.

Though he could scarcely stop them—for he realized that they were only trying to increase their income from the house—he expressed his alarm half a dozen times a day in telegrams and telephone calls. He anticipated a protest, perhaps even a lawsuit from one of the other tenants, and he could look forward to weeks of sheer agony for himself. For the prospective tenant, Dr. Gagey, was preparing to make extensive changes, which would obviously be noisy and go on for some time. What could Proust conceivably do in the interval? If he remained in his draughty room at the Hôtel des Réservoirs he would undoubtedly freeze, and if he moved into the new apartment he would be tortured by Dr. Gagey's workmen tramping and hammering and sawing all day long.

Either prospect was terrifying to Proust, who by this time seems to have literally worried himself sick. But he had to do something and, quite suddenly, on an hour's notice, he moved in at the Boulevard Haussmann. He was able to have the work in Dr. Gagey's apartment stopped, but only for the time being. He faced a really dreary winter.

IV

Proust's first months at the Boulevard Haussmann were certainly very trying. The work in the entresol inevitably began again, and there seems to have been work going on in other apartments as well. Proust could seldom sleep well during the daytime, when his bedroom vibrated with noise, and he could never sleep at night anyway. He was quite wretched and scarcely good for anything. Yet when he found that he had information bearing on a sensational murder case, he was able to write it up for *Le Figaro*.

Proust had twice exchanged letters with a casual acquaintance of his, a certain Henri van Blarenberghe. The first time Proust had written to express regret for the death of van Blarenberghe's father, the Chairman of the Board of Directors of the Chemins de Fer de l'Est. More recently he had written again to inquire about a certain employee of the railroad, possibly one of those effeminate young men of whom he was fond. In the course of a reply to this second letter, van Blarenberghe had expressed regret over the death of Proust's parents and had gone on to speak of himself. "What the year 1907 may have in store for me, I do not know," he had written, "but it is my dearest wish that it may bring some alleviation to you as well as to me and that in the course of the next few months we may be able to meet."

Less than a week after receiving this letter—it was January 25, 1907—Proust picked up *Le Figaro* and read that, in a fit of insanity, van Blarenberghe had killed both his mother and himself. The circumstances of the suicide had been particularly gruesome. The unfortunate young man had ripped open his chest with a knife, and then shot himself through the temple and blown out one of his eyes. As he read, Proust saw the possibility of a timely little article, and after making sure that *Le Figaro* would be interested in it, he rested a few hours and then set to work.

He described van Blarenberghe, copied out his letters, and commented on the sentence that now seemed so tragic, "What the year 1907 may have in store for me I do not know." The year 1907! Not even the first month had elapsed and the writer, after committing a terrible crime, was already dead. He was another Ajax, blinded by Athene, dealing death without knowing what he did—Proust quoted from Sophocles. And yet not so, for Ajax had killed only sheep and shepherds: van Blarenberghe had killed his mother and then blasted out his own left eye. He was another Oedipus, confronting the body of Jocasta and gouging out his eyes so that he could not see the horrors of which he had unwittingly been guilty—Proust quoted from *Oedipus Rex*. He was another Lear, holding the body of Cordelia in his arms and saying, "Never, never, never, never, never"—Proust quoted from Shakespeare. Van Blarenberghe was in fact, Proust decided, a notable figure, comparable to the heroes of Greek tragedy, an enlightened man, an affectionate and devoted son, who had been driven, by an ineluctable fate, to commit and to expiate a crime that deserved to become famous. He had killed his mother—but which of us has not done the same?

> The truth is that, as we grow older, we kill the heart that loves us by reason of the cares we lay on it, by reason of that uneasy tenderness that we inspire and keep forever stretched upon the rack. Could we but see in the beloved body the slow work of destruction that is the product of the painful tenderness which

is the mainspring of its being, could we but see the faded eyes, the hair against whose valiant blackness time had so long been powerless, now sharing in the body's general defeat and suddenly turned white; could we but see the hardened arteries, the congested kidneys, the overworked heart; could we but watch courage failing under the blows of life, the slowing movements, the heavy step, the spirit once so tireless and unconquerable, now conscious of hope gone forever, and that former gaiety, innate and seemingly immortal, so sweet a consort for sad moments, now finally withered—perhaps, seeing all this in a flash of that lucidity now come too late, which even lives spent in a long illusion may sometimes have, as Don Quixote once had his— perhaps, then, like Henri van Blarenberghe when he stabbed his mother to death, we should recoil before the horror of our lives, and seize the nearest gun, and make an end.

Proust worked throughout the night, spinning out his little paradoxes and looking up quotations from the masters. By eight in the morning he had writer's cramp so badly that he was forced to stop. But he could not sleep, for the workmen in the house were already beginning their infernal commotion, and without sleep he felt that he could not possibly write another line; so he sent his article to *Le Figaro* just as it stood. That night, when the proofs arrived, he tried to add a little more, and succeded in turning out a conclusion that he thought rather good; but it was subsequently excised by the managing editor, who apparently felt that the treatment of matricide was already sympathetic enough. The article appeared on February 1, under the appropriately paradoxical title of "Sentiments filiaux d'un parricide."

Encouraged by his success, for the article was warmly praised by several of his friends, Proust arranged to write a second article for *Le Figaro*, this one based on material from his notebooks. He looked forward to a period of quiet, since he was assured that the workmen were almost through with their tasks in the house. But just at this moment another group of workmen began making an even more devastating noise in the house next door. It appeared that another new tenant was starting a program of alterations—in the apartment immediately adjoining Proust's own. The catastrophe was one of the first magnitude, and Proust tried everything he could think of to safeguard his hours of rest. He sent tips to the workmen and urged them to move to the other side of the house. He found out the new tenant's name—Madame Katz—and had one of his friends send her a telegram of expostulation. But neither the tips nor the telegram produced any effect whatsoever; each morning he was kept awake by the same excruciating noise. In his desperation he turned to his old friends, the Strauses, and was encouraged to find that they knew, not Madame Katz, but her son. Proust sent Madame Straus an elaborate statement of his grievances and an equally elaborate set of suggestions to be conveyed to the unspeakable Madame Katz.

"She should know this," Proust wrote: "that the workmen— both those who work for her and those of the landlord—arrive at seven o'clock in the morning, try at once to show their morning good humor by striking terrible blows and by scraping with saws behind my bed, then loaf nearly every half hour, strike more terrible blows so that I can't go to sleep again, then go a little way off at noontime, strike more blows, and after two o'clock there is no more noise. Now if Madame [Katz], by arrangement with her landlord, Monsieur Couvreux, and without waiting for such an arrangement as far as *her own* workmen are concerned, will see that after Thursday they don't come until noon or one o'clock or better still two o'clock (but even noon would be quite satisfactory) and tell them to work until evening, she will save time instead of losing it and even a little money because you can tell her I will pay her anything she wants. I persuaded another tenant to have his work done between 8 o'clock and midnight, and the whole thing was finished very quickly. I don't ask so much of her. If she will really have her work done between noon and 8 o'clock in the evening, her alterations, which are almost done (alas! if I had known I should have asked sooner, but I can't stand it any longer, and my doctor advises me to go away, finding my condition too serious for me to put up with such fatigue) will be finished much more quickly. But suppose (you will have to excuse me!) they are going to put a bowl and a seat in the toilet, which is opposite my room. If they have to pound for only half an hour and they do it at seven in the morning, it will do me as much harm as if it lasted three hours, while she can have it done (or ask Monsieur

Couvreux to have it done) after twelve or one o'clock. The same
for the upholsterer's men who in a few days are going to have to
tack down the carpets and put up the curtains. I hope she is also
willing when she moves in, and she will certainly have things to
nail right away, to have them nailed after noon instead of in the
morning. Finally (I am purposely asking for everything, realizing
that I won't get it all) if for a day I should be too ill and she would
kindly authorize me to stop all work for that one day, she would
be doing me a tremendous service. And if for any reason she has to
have the workmen come in the morning (there are no such reasons
but since she is irresponsible she will find reasons for anything), I
shall ask her to warn me so that at 6 o'clock I don't take a gram
and a half of trional if the workmen are to begin at 7."

The Strauses, who were sympathetic people and who understood Proust's miseries because they had miseries of their own,
undertook to deliver the message as tactfully as possible, by
inviting Monsieur Katz to lunch. But unfortunately their rep-
resentations produced only the most modest results. "That beast
his mother," Proust soon afterwards reported, "has not stopped
building . . . I don't know what! for twelve workmen, pounding
with such frenzy for so many months, must have built something
as majestic as the Pyramid of Cheops, which people who go out
must be astonished to see between Printemps and Saint Augustin.
As for me, I don't see it but I hear it. And when the pounding
of hammers doubles the violence of my attacks, which by themselves are very bad, and I feel that that woman is not only costing
me a year of constant suffering but is cutting off several years
of my life with the attacks I have and the drugs I take, I think
of Sully Prudhomme and the cry of the workman who was building
that same pyramid. . . . Once they had to let the paint dry and
the mother . . . had to stop for several days, even though in the
interval she changed two or three times the seat in her toilet
(too small, I suppose), which I have the honor to be next to
(and always between 7 and 10 in the morning). When she is
installed I shall be a new man, and yet I suppose not, because
a person accustomed to so many luxuries will have countless
pictures to nail up and she will certainly nail them up in the
morning."

CHAPTER XII

Paris and Cabourg

I

IN THE COURSE OF TIME even the terrible Madame Katz desisted. The apartment on the Boulevard Haussmann was quiet again, or at least as quiet as an apartment located on one of the city's main thoroughfares could possibly be. Proust was able to get the rest that he needed, though occasionally he must have had difficult days when, from some unexpected quarter, noise catastrophically burst upon him and he was afraid that the horrors of that first winter were about to return. Once the inside of his fireplace collapsed and he had to put up with workmen who appeared with bricks and mortar at his bedside. Once a valet upstairs began cleaning overzealously in the morning, and another time someone —possibly the same valet—began pounding and tramping about at four in the afternoon. On such occasions Proust had to write the concierge and send urgent messages up or down stairs. But these were only interludes, harrowing enough no doubt while they lasted, in an otherwise peaceful existence. The apartment was generally quite satisfactory. The noise of traffic was not too disturbing, and as time went on the rooms lost their ugliness and their strangeness. They seemed to envelop Proust with their warmth and to protect him from the hostile world outside. They became what the rooms in the Rue de Courcelles had been before, his refuge and his home.

The apartment was no more completely furnished in February, 1907, than it had been a few weeks earlier when Proust had so precipitately moved in. The dining room, for example, piled high with odd furniture, was destined to remain so, for though Proust intended to have the furniture removed and indeed talked of it for perhaps a decade, he never quite got around to making the necessary arrangements. One of the living rooms was however furnished and·usable, in fact rather too generously and floridly furnished. The style was unmistakably that of the Second Empire. The tables were gilded and inlaid and covered with marble. The chairs and the sofas were upholstered in patterns as elaborate as those of the rugs. On the walls were gas bracket-lamps converted to electricity; over the windows hung a green tapestry, representing a hunting scene. There were some dried flowers under glass and a good many pictures—photographs, daguerreotypes, and paintings in heavy gilt frames, including a portrait of Proust's father in a particularly heavy frame, draped in red plush. There were the bronzes (at least those not yet given away to family friends without much taste), including a large and especially hideous piece by Bardedienne. The room was generally dusty, and Proust seldom used it except as a waiting room for visitors. It looked, visitors often thought, like a mausoleum for the Proust family furniture.

Proust's bedroom was furnished somewhat more functionally. In one corner stood a dismal brass bed, apparently his own bed from the Rue de Courcelles and quite possibly the one in which he had slept since his childhood. It was placed so that he could see, as he lay back on the pillows, two doors— the main door through which visitors entered and the service door from which Nicolas or Céline emerged when he rang. Beside the bed was a flimsy bamboo table, littered with medicines and papers. On other tables piles of books, notebooks, letters, and photographs were always so chaotically jumbled together that Proust had difficulty in laying his hands on anything he wanted. There was a fireplace, surmounted by a Regency mantelpiece and a mirror; a chandelier wrapped in cloth; and, in a corner of the room between bookcases, a grand piano. As in the living room, there was generally an accumulation of dust. It was bad for Proust's asthma, but what could he do? Permitting his servants to clean—and to stir up the dust—was obviously worse, and he was inclined to accept its hazards for considerable periods of time.

A person sensitive to his surroundings could never have endured so unattractive an apartment, but Proust was not particular in such matters. His needs were purely sentimental and material: the apartment satisfied both. It preserved his contact with the past, for even its walls had associations for him. When he reached out, he touched old family furniture that he had known all his life; when he rang, old family servants answered his bell. It offered him, furthermore, the isolation and the quiet that he demanded, or at least as much quiet as he could reasonably expect in Paris. He could sleep and work without too much difficulty; he could receive his friends, not well perhaps, but after a fashion; he could listen to music when he had someone to play for him; and from time to time, perhaps once every day or two, he could make one of those trying but nevertheless exhilarating excursions into the outer world that kept him from feeling his isolation too keenly.

The pattern of his life may seem eccentric, yet it was reasonable enough in view of his afflictions. At some time in the afternoon, often around three or four o'clock, he awoke and rang for breakfast. Hot coffee helped him to breathe more easily and he was inclined to drink a good deal of it. If his asthma was at all troublesome, he burned Legras powder and inhaled the fumes— a process that might, under exceptional circumstances, go on for a considerable period of time. He is said to have used as many as fifteen or twenty towels whenever he washed, discarding each as it got damp. When he intended to go out, he had a barber come in to shave him, and apparently had his servants help him dress. His clothes were warmed in advance before the fire or over the stove in the kitchen. Having little sense of time and being incorrigibly dilatory, he was usually late when he went to the theatre or the opera or, in later years, to the Russian ballet.

More than once he called on friends, such as the Strauses and
the Clermont-Tonnerres, just as they were going to bed. He
always apologized profusely and said that he would leave at
once, but inevitably he lingered on, slouched in an armchair,
the collar of his fur coat turned up about his neck, talking interminably while his hosts could scarcely keep from yawning in
his face. He appeared paler and stranger than ever, more remote
and mysterious, more like a visitor from another world or another age. Sometimes he made strange mistakes. Once, when he
was invited to the country in July, he forgot how late the sun
sets in summer. He appeared at seven in evening dress, just as
his hosts were about to go fishing. "Come as you are," they said.

As often as not, however, Proust stayed at home and even
stayed in bed all evening, waiting for his friends to arrive. They
came as they had come to the house in the Rue de Courcelles.
They rang twice; they entered the bedroom. They were appalled,
if they had not seen it for some time, by its hopeless disorder.
They were either stifled by the heat or congealed by the cold,
for Proust had theories about temperature—he kept his room
hot in summer and cold in winter. Before them was the invalid,
under a pile of blankets, wearing a sweater or two over his
nightshirt. His hair was often tousled and his face unshaven.
The sheets on the bed were often far from clean. Reluctant
to have his train of thought interrupted, Proust often began
talking, somewhat abruptly, about subjects that interested him
at the moment. He liked to explore these as completely as he
could and to consider all the associations—even the remote ones—
that they had for him. Hence, as in his writing, his sentences
tended to become elaborately parenthetical and occasionally somewhat tangled. On the other hand, he seldom bored or neglected
his guests. He knew how to draw them out with questions and he
listened eagerly to what they had to say about the outside world.
Albufera told him about society, Billy about politics, Lauris and
Daudet about literature; Hahn sat down at the piano and played
him his favorite pieces, including perhaps the "little phrase"
from Saint-Saëns he had once been so fond of and had more
recently described in *Jean Santeuil.*

Sometimes, however, the visits did not go so well. Friends would arrive only to be told that Proust's asthma was bad, that he was still inhaling, and that he could not see them at once. They would wait in the living room, they would leave, they would return. Finally, hours later if they had so much patience, they would see the invalid for a few minutes—see him without hearing him, for talking at once after an inhalation tended to bring back his asthma and he therefore communicated with them by jotting down notes on scraps of paper. If they left for the night without seeing him at all, they could not help wondering whether the attack was real or not, for they were aware that his asthma was often used as a convenient social excuse. He might be otherwise engaged—he might be deliberately putting them off. Montesquiou knew this trick well. It was certainly no coincidence that, nearly every time he proposed a visit, Proust was either taking unnerving drugs or suffering unspeakable agonies. Once the poet appeared at the door without warning, but he got no farther than the living room. He was dismissed by the servants, who handed him Proust's note of regret. " 'To feel the sky so near and yet not to be able to ascend,' " the note began. And continued: "Dear Sir, it is you! What a dramatic appearance! Emotion, tumult, and then I realize the *physical impossibility* of letting you enter my room, and the physical impossibility of leaving it myself. I will write tomorrow." Montesquiou may have fulminated, but there was nothing he could do, he could not confront the object of his wrath.

Proust's regular or respectable friends—the Hahns, the Billys, and the Montesquious—were not, however, the only ones who came to the apartment on the Boulevard Haussmann. Young men came too, often young men of humble origin—valets or chauffeurs or railroad employees—who had attracted Proust's attention and seemed to him delightfully fresh and alluring. They were summoned and dismissed at Proust's pleasure. In their absence he was not disconsolate, for he was not now—or not always—in love. The worst torments of jealousy at least were reserved for a later period.

II

Life in the bedroom on the Boulevard Haussmann was not really
so bad after all, and Proust was soon working, if not on his
novel, at least on occasional pieces. In March, 1907, he did a
review for *La Chronique des arts* and wrote for *Le Figaro* the
article he had promised to do a month or so before. It was a
curiously discursive piece on telephoning and telephone operators,
reading and the memoirs of the Comtesse de Boigne. It contained, inevitably, flattering references to Madame de Noailles,
who was about to publish a new volume of verse. Proust compared
her work to *Les Feuilles d'automne* and *Les Fleurs du mal*. He had
consulted her in advance, but unfortunately not far enough in
advance so that he could exactly follow her preferences. He
realized too late that he should also have dragged in *Les Amours*
of Ronsard and that he should have substituted *La Légende des
siècles* for *Les Feuilles d'automne*.

In June he made amends for his oversight by devoting a
particularly florid article exclusively to Madame de Noailles' new
volume. But in this case too there were difficulties. The manuscript
he submitted was too long for *Le Figaro*, certainly too long for
the front page, where Proust was determined it should appear.
One night he counted or estimated the total number of letters
in his manuscript: there were 16,900. Then he estimated the
number of letters in four columns of *Le Figaro*: 18,000. This
evidence seemed to him conclusive—the article could appear on
the front page after all. Nevertheless, Calmette, the editor, remained
inflexible. He refused to provide four columns, on the first page or
the last; he insisted on cutting the article and relegating it igno-
miniously to the supplement. In the course of the negotiations
Proust saw Calmette for a few minutes one day and casually
remarked that he would at some time like to invite him to
dinner. Without the slightest hesitation Calmette took out his
memorandum book, looked over his list of free evenings, and
fixed on the first of July. Proust was appalled but—it was scarcely
characteristic of him—he made no attempt to wriggle out of
the invitation. He arranged and actually gave the dinner.

Proust was determined to do the thing right, to overwhelm Calmette by surrounding him with the great ladies of society, but unfortunately the season was far advanced and the great ladies were no longer easy to get. Madame Lemaire, the Comtesse de Noailles, and the Princesse de Caraman-Chimay were out of town; Madame de Brantes and the Marquise d'Eyragues might be otherwise engaged; even Madame Straus was doubtful—she might not be well enough to come for dinner, she might only drop in during the evening. Proust grew more anxious day by day. On June 21 he wrote Madame Straus a particularly urgent letter. "I am sorry to pester you again," he said, "but can you tell now how you will be feeling on Monday the 1st, if you think you can come to dinner or if you won't be able to come until afterwards? I know it is dreadful of me to torment you. But I have six people who have answered just as you have. Now if they leave me in doubt until the final day, I am in danger—if the people I count on don't come—of finding myself almost tête-à-tête with Madame d'Haussonville without her husband and Madame de Clermont-Tonnerre, who are certain to come, which would be very unpleasant for them since I don't know them very well—or if to guard myself against this I invite more people now, if at the last minute the six others come, I am in danger of having women I don't know how to seat or at least that I shall seat very badly. And if you tell me on the 1st of July at seven o'clock that you are coming for dinner, I shall be deliriously happy, but I shall seat you very badly, supposing that the six others come and that I have already invited more. . . . Since it kills me to write, I do the whole thing by telephone, which kills me too even though I don't use the telephone myself—I have my servants do it while I am asleep—with the result that they invite my second choices when my first have already accepted."

Proust went on to say that he had thought of asking Madame Straus's friend Joseph Reinach, but it seemed wiser not to have so prominent a Dreyfusard along with Monsieur de Clermont-Tonnerre, whose Nationalist views were only too pronounced. He had, however, invited Robert Dreyfus, another friend of hers, to drop in during the evening, and he might even extend an invitation of the same sort to his own sister-in-law. In a later

letter he announced that he was giving his dinner in a private
room at the Ritz. He wondered if Madame Straus could help
him with the seating plan. What, in particular, was he to do
with Fauré, Béraud, and Calmette, who were not of noble birth?
"And then, while I am on the subject, do I dare ask you to
make out a menu for a grand dinner and tell me what I ought
to order (nothing but things that you like and that won't disagree
with you too much in case you do happen to come)? Do you
know anything about wines?"

Friends other than Madame Straus were also pressed into
service, and with their help the menu was fixed and the seating
plan finally made out—though not quite satisfactorily, since
Madame de Noailles, who unexpectedly returned to town in time
for the dinner, could not possibly be given a place befitting her
rank. At the last minute there were complications about the
music. Fauré, obviously scheduled to play some of his own works,
was suddenly taken ill, and Proust had to call on Risler, who
had played for him some years before when *Portraits de peintres*
were given at Madame Lemaire's. Risler's fee was high—a thousand
francs. Proust not only had to pay it in full, but had to profess
gratitude that the pianist was willing to come at all on such
short notice. As it happened, another performer who had at
first excused himself came too—the violinist Hayot. His fee, a
mere six hundred francs, was no doubt modest enough, but
still added substantially to the cost of the entertainment.

On the evening of July 1 the guests gathered at the Ritz, in
a room floridly decorated in cerise and gold, blazing with light.
Madame Straus was unfortunately not among them, nor was
the American beauty Miss Gladys Deacon, whom Proust was
even more anxious to have present. Still the number of eminent
hostesses was on the whole very satisfying and Calmette must
indeed have been overwhelmed. Madame d'Haussonville, who
was perhaps the most eminent of all, sported an ostrich plume;
Madame de Noailles and Proust himself—since the heat had
moderated—kept on their fur coats. Dinner was duly served; the
reception and the music began. Hayot played a Fauré sonata;
Risler played whatever came into his head—Chopin, Wagner,
Chabrier, Couperin—after insisting that he knew none of the

pieces that Proust asked for. But Proust was not disturbed by this or anything else; his party seemed to him altogether so perfect, so completely charming. He was not disturbed, that is, until the next day when, resting and nursing the slight cold he had caught, he computed his expenses, which now seemed to him staggering. "[Guiche] chose the dishes and the wines," he wrote to a friend; "unfortunately I paid for them."

III

The dinner was in one respect a revelation to Proust, showing him that he could get through such an ordeal without tiring himself too much, and his thoughts again inevitably turned to travel. A few weeks later he precipitately started on what he hoped would develop into a tour of Normandy and Brittany. He selected the Grand Hôtel in Cabourg as headquarters, presumably because he had once stayed there with his mother and because he felt that it would awaken memories he wished to cherish. A few days after his arrival he wrote a long letter to the eminent archaeologist Emile Mâle, asking for information about places accessible from Cabourg. Where could he find the most interesting old ports, where villages preserved intact from earlier times? Should he go so far afield as Fougères, Vitré, Saint-Malo, and Guérande? Were these towns really first rate? Was the architecture better at Lisieux or Falaise or Vire or Bayeux or Valognes or Coutances or Saint-Lô? If he should return to Paris, was there anything in that neighborhood he might profitably see? If, however, he should remain and should succeed in crossing the peninsula, should he visit Mont Saint-Michel? Was it too much restored or was it really one of the most beautiful things in France?

Without waiting for the eminent archaeologist's reply, Proust rented a taxi—an enclosed red taxi—from a firm in which his old friend Jacques Bizet had a financial interest. The chauffeur regularly assigned to him was a handsome young man, a native of Monte Carlo, named Alfred Agostinelli. Late in the afternoons, Proust and Agostinelli set out on their excursions. They drove in the twilight, with the windows of the car always closed; they studied villages and country houses and churches, at dusk or even after dark. At Caen they were early. They saw, as they approached the town, the spires of Saint-Etienne and Saint-Pierre still gilded by sunlight, and after they had left they saw a little church with a wild-rose bush growing along the porch, the very same rose that appeared in stone on the porch itself. At Bayeux they missed the famous tapestry—the library that housed it was presumably closed when they arrived—but saw the cathedral and admired especially the Romanesque part of the nave. At the château of Balleroy they followed a guide, who supplied them with misinformation about the pictures—hunting scenes by a former proprietor—and the Boucher tapestries. Proust complained a good deal. He said that he felt giddy and feverish, that he was upset by the vibration of the car, that he enjoyed nothing that he did. "I have never been so restless, so sterile, or so unhappy," he wrote to a friend. Nevertheless he went on performing, day after day, the same painful gyrations. At least he was living again, and how could he be sure that he would ever have another chance to live?

On days when he did not travel his activity was scarcely less feverish. He dressed late in the afternoon, descended to the lobby of the hotel, and had his chair carried out to the terrace. About six o'clock he went out, with an umbrella in his hand, to enjoy the view, after lingering for a few minutes in the doorway to make sure that the sun had set. He was fond of remarking that he had once gone out too precipitately when the sun was only behind a cloud, and that he had actually found himself in its light for a moment. The waiters tiptoed about his chair, talked in signs, and tried to avoid making the slightest noise as he sat studying the water and the sky. Later he went to the dining room or the casino, played baccarat by proxy or treated friends to champagne and cigars. The company, however, was not always what it might have been at Cabourg. There were too many undistinguished and rather vulgar people, in particular too many Jews, and Proust often preferred to spend his time at Deauville and Trouville, where high society gathered and where social life was as exciting as in Paris during the spring. In these towns he could hobnob with the Rothschilds, the Marlboroughs, and the Castellanes at concerts and polo matches; he could visit such old friends as the Guiches, the Strauses, and Louisa de Mornand.

Once he got up early enough to have lunch with the Guiches and the Clermont-Tonnerres at the Villa Mon Rêve. After lunch he walked around the garden, braving the sun, admiring the geraniums and the dazzling lights on the sea. Once—or so Gallimard later reported, though the story seems almost incredible—he walked a considerable distance in the daytime to call on Mademoiselle de Mornand and her current lover, Robert Gangnat, to invite them to dinner. He was wearing a battered straw hat, much too small for him, a long overcoat lined with purple velvet, and patent-leather shoes. "An outfit of this sort might have seemed ridiculous on a sunny day, but actually it was not without a kind of pathetic charm. It showed a certain sense of style and at the same time a supreme indifference to all style. . . . He gave us a very amusing account of his walk, without seeming to realize that such a trip on a hot day was a remarkable proof of friendship. Several times he had stopped at different inns to drink coffee and get his strength back. He told the whole story so simply that I was immediately won over. . . . Marcel realized at once that [Louisa and Gangnat] had been having a rather heated argument. But he didn't show that he had noticed it; and I can still see him as he affectionately put his hand on the back of her neck and patted her as if she had been a young colt, at the same time running over, in a teasing and innocently questioning way, the list of her faults, which he was quite familiar with. He scolded her severely in a remarkably mild, a remarkably temperate tone, but with a sense of assurance that took the form of irony and a persistence that surprised me. He didn't repeat his invitation until he was quite sure that good feelings had definitely been restored."

At the dinner, given a few days afterwards at the Grand Hôtel in Cabourg, the most interesting guest was a paralytic old marquis, now completely ruined, abandoned by his family, and constantly ridiculed by the servants at the hotel. Proust helped him, and waited on him, and directed the conversation so that he could shine and appear again, as in former days, a true aristocrat and a wit.

Late in September, when the Grand Hôtel closed, Proust and Agostinelli set out on another trip, perhaps with the idea of visiting cathedral towns close at hand and then going on to Brittany. Their itinerary is not clear, but at some time or other they certainly visited Lisieux. Darkness had already fallen when they stopped before the famous door of the Lisieux cathedral— the door that Ruskin had praised, the one through which, centuries earlier, the marriage procession of Henry II and Eleanor of Aquitaine had probably passed. Proust got out of the car and examined the carved foliage, lit up by the headlights. Curious children watched him; their heads, caught in the beams and apparently projected from the forest of stone, reminded him of angel heads in scenes of the Nativity. The taxi started again, the strange pair hurried on into the night. Sitting bundled up in the front seat, Proust fondly studied his chauffeur, who seemed almost motionless, his hands fixed on the wheel and his beardless face dimly visible under his driver's cap. He looked, now like a nun, now like Saint Cecilia reaching out from time to time to touch the keyboard of an invisible organ, and now like a martyr in stone on the porch of a cathedral, his wheel the symbol of the art in which he excelled.[1]

When they reached Evreux they put up at the Hôtel Moderne, renting two whole floors, it is said, so that they would not be disturbed by neighbors. Though Proust had again begun to suffer from asthma—the first symptoms of which had appeared as he was driving through a foggy little valley outside of town— he went on sightseeing for several days. He saw the abbey-church of Saint Taurin, admiring particularly the stained glass and the curious piscinas. On the evening of a gray day he saw the cathedral and admired the famous windows in the transepts and the Lady Chapel, their panes still glowing, despite the dim light, with azure and purple. He drove out to Conches to see more stained glass. But unfortunately his asthma was becoming more troublesome. When he visited the Clermont-Tonnerres at Glisolles, he had to prepare himself by drinking coffee—seventeen cups of it, he said—and he trembled so much when he arrived that

1. See Proust's article, "Impressions de route en automobile," *Le Figaro*, November 19, 1907.

he had to be helped up the staircase. He liked the house and he liked the roses in the garden, on which he turned the headlights of the car, but he was either too asthmatic or too much pre-occupied with other matters to return the next day for the sight-seeing trip that his hosts had suggested. He had another bad night at the Hôtel Moderne, where, despite his precautions, the noise was deafening. Quite suddenly, the next morning, he returned to Paris.

CHAPTER XIII

The Project

IT SEEMS CLEAR that there was a connection between Proust's trip to Cabourg in the summer of 1907 and the work on his novel that he began doing soon afterwards. The trip may not have been altogether pleasant while it lasted, but its effects were certainly beneficial. It refreshed Proust's memories and added to his experience. Having seen the outer world at close quarters for a considerable period of time, having renewed his contact with average human beings, with the rocks and the sea on the Norman coast, with carved stone and stained glass, he was at last able to take up his novel again. He began working as he had never worked before, immersing himself in work, devoting himself more and more completely to the preparation of the masterpiece which he had projected in his youth. His creative period was at hand.

I

His creative period was at hand but, like everything else in Proust's life, it developed slowly, painfully, and uncertainly. The goal was not at first clear, the line of progression by no means straight, the sense of accomplishment largely or entirely

lacking. His first productions after his trip were not very different
from those of previous years, certainly not much more impressive.

On November 19, 1907, he published in *Le Figaro* an article
called "Impressions de route en automobile," an account of a
drive to Caen and Lisieux, a delightful, a highly imaginative
account, but essentially a trifle. He sent a copy to Agostinelli,
now at his home in Monte Carlo. To Proust the young chauffeur's
letter of acknowledgment seemed particularly charming. On December 26 he wrote a short anonymous sketch of Gustave de
Borda, who had died the week before. He described Borda as
an incomparable fencer, adding: "If our memory is correct, the
last person he served as second on the field of honor was our
contributor, Monsieur Marcel Proust." In January, 1908, he began
writing a series of parodies on the subject of the Lemoine case,
which was then taking up a good deal of space in the newspapers.
Lemoine, an accomplished swindler who specialized in getting
money from wealthy men on the pretense of exploiting discoveries
he had made, had recently claimed that he could make diamonds
synthetically. He had convinced a good many experts, including
Sir Julius Werner, the chairman of De Beers, the largest diamond
corporation in the world. Sir Julius had witnessed ostensibly
scientific experiments and had picked out of the crucibles diamonds
as good as his own—as indeed they were: Lemoine had bought
them from De Beers' South African mines. Subsequently Werner
had advanced nearly two million francs so that Lemoine could
build a synthetic-diamond factory. But there had been too many
unaccountable delays, Werner's suspicions had been aroused, and
finally he had brought the whole matter to the attention of the
courts. Parisians generally wondered whether Lemoine was a
genius or a charlatan: Proust, again kept from sleep by the commotion of workmen, used Lemoine as a pretext for parody (if the
term *pastiche* can be so translated).

In February and March, 1908, he published, in the supplement
of *Le Figaro*, no fewer than seven distinct pieces, parodies of
Balzac, Faguet, Michelet, the Goncourts, Flaubert, Sainte-Beuve,
and Renan. All more or less concern the Lemoine case; two
contain references to Proust himself. In the fourth piece the
Goncourts describe a dinner with Lucien Daudet, in the course

of which Daudet hears that his friend Proust has committed suicide, "à la suite de la baisse des valeurs diamantifères, baisse anéantissant une partie de sa fortune. Un curieux être, assure Lucien, que ce Marcel Proust, un être qui vivrait tout à fait dans l'enthousiasme, dans le *bondieusement* de certains paysages, de certains livres, un être par exemple qui serait complètement enamouré des romans de Léon [Daudet]." In the final piece Renan describes the site of Lemoine's factory and goes on: "Un Anglais qui vivait à cette époque, John Ruskin, que nous ne lisons malheureusement que dans la traduction d'une platitude pitoyable que Marcel Proust nous en a laissée, vante la grâce de ses peupliers, la fraîcheur glacée de ses sources."

Proust's gaiety can perhaps be felt even in single sentences like these. His parodies are the productions of a man in high spirits, a man intoxicated by the pleasure of playing with words and of dashing off at top speed passages in the style of earlier masters. "I didn't make a single correction on the Renan," Proust afterwards said, though he was probably exaggerating his facility. "It came to me so easily that I added and pasted on to the proofs complete pages. . . . I had regulated my inner metronome to Renan's rhythm, and I could have written ten volumes in the same style."

II

Parodies and other occasional pieces for Le Figaro were not, however, what Proust really wanted to write; he was thinking of his novel again. It seemed to him that he might now be able to work over the seventy notebooks of *Jean Santeuil* and such other notebooks as he had accumulated more recently. He might be able to prepare an entirely new version of his story in which he paid particular attention to structure and continuity. He might at last succeed in transforming a series of more or less detached episodes into what could properly be called a novel.

It is scarcely possible, for the present at least, to write a complete history of Proust's revision or even to date the various steps that he took, the decisions he was called upon to make, in the course of his work. Still he did make decisions at one time or another, and it is easy enough to list the more important ones. He decided—it was perhaps the most important one of all—that his book would tell the story of a quest, which can best be described as a quest for knowledge. His hero would always be trying to understand and evaluate his experience. He would be shown learning from the beginning of the book to the end, and indeed learning about many things simultaneously—love, travel, men of letters, friendship, society. . . . The complete list would be a long one. The narrative would be both chronological and, as it were, logical. It would move forward in time as the hero lived and had new experiences and grew older; it would also move forward logically as he learned to understand his experiences better. The book would thus become, from one point of view at least, the odyssey of a thoughtful young man.

To emphasize the logical movement, which was clearly the more important one, Proust worked out, with perhaps some hints from earlier novelists and even from composers (he himself was inclined to speak of *themes* and *leitmotifs*) an ingenious kind of structure. He proposed to have his hero learning all the time about all the aspects of his experience, which would all be present in every chapter or section of the book. Even in the very first chapter, dealing with the hero's childhood, there would be passages about love, society, and inversion; passages too about Gothic architecture, servants, men of letters, nature, travel, the theatre, and the Jews. The hero would learn what, as a child, he could learn about these subjects, and they would then recur in succeeding chapters, occasionally no doubt with a somewhat different emphasis. In one chapter the hero would be principally concerned with love, in another with society, and in still another with inversion, but never only with these subjects. His experience would always be presented as a whole in all its aspects. Each chapter would be a cycle, complete in itself but echoing earlier cycles and anticipating those that were to follow.

Within each chapter the movement of the narrative would also be cyclic, or—to use the word made fashionable by Aldous Huxley—contrapuntal. Several subjects would usually be treated more or less concurrently. Often scenes devoted to love, which would be predominantly serious, would alternate with scenes devoted to society, which would be predominantly comic. But there would be many other sorts of scenes as well; transitions would necessarily be numerous and sometimes abrupt. Successive paragraphs might deal with the hero's grandmother, his visit to a brothel, his fondness for the theatre, and his observations of the Jews. Attention would be constantly shifting, as at dinner parties and receptions, where the observer picks up scraps of a dozen different conversations and forms impressions of a dozen different people. Everywhere there would be variety and multiplicity, which would approximate (as indeed it does in the final version of the novel) the multiplicity of life itself.

To arrange the material of the notebooks into a series of cycles, in each of which the hero understands his experience better, would be to go toward transforming that material into a novel. But to complete the transformation, something more was needed, a central theme. This Proust found in his somewhat Bergsonian ideas about memory and about art. His hero's quest would involve a series of disappointments. He would try love and friendship and travel, only to discover that in the long run none of them are really satisfying. Then, at the end of the book, he would have an experience of involuntary memory. He would realize that the contemplation of the past, recalled by something in the present, is the only happiness that life offers; he would realize too that this contemplation is art, or at least closely related to art. He would be sure of his vocation, he would devote himself to involuntary memory; he would become a novelist, he would tell the story of his own past.

The theme had, as Proust himself must have realized, certain obvious shortcomings. It involved introducing a mystical conception into a book that would otherwise be completely realistic; the passages on involuntary memory were bound to seem somewhat odd. It involved glorifying intuition—for what was involuntary memory but a form of intuition?—and disparaging the intellect when Proust was otherwise committed to being highly intellectual. For many chapters his hero would be shown seeking knowledge, and apparently finding it, with the help of his intellect; but in the last chapter he would have to learn that the intellect is a hopelessly inadequate faculty. The knowledge, laboriously acquired over a long period of time, would inevitably lose much of its value.

On the other hand, there was much in the theme of involuntary memory that made it, from Proust's point of view, indisputably right. It emphasized what had always been central in his thought, a profound faith in art and a profound skepticism about other forms of experience. It explained his conviction that art is not primarily intellectual, or indeed really intellectual at all, but the exercise of quite different mental processes. It explained and justified his own art, which was, and always had been, extremely close to autobiography. For if art and memory are very closely related, he could scarcely avoid drawing on his own experiences, and he was certainly privileged to put in as many of them as he wanted to. He could use all the material in the notebooks and much more besides. He could in fact write an imaginative autobiography that would also be a novel, for it would be an autobiography with a theme. The experiences would be his, but the disappointments they involved and the final illumination to which they led would be universal. What was in origin contingent, would acquire in the context the inevitability of art.

It would scarcely be possible to maintain that the various decisions Proust came to were all wise and consistent with one another or that the structure they provided him with was entirely satisfactory. But at least they gave him a structure of a sort and one that was not too tight or confining. He could do more or less what he wanted, he could digress or be inconsistent with impunity. He was free to make his book richer, if anything, than its structure permitted, truer and more human than its theme. And this is precisely what he did make it. The novel in its final form became the collected work of his maturity, as *Les Plaisirs et les jours* had been the collected work of his youth.

III

To determine general principles of construction was one thing; to write the book itself, or even to begin writing it, was quite another, especially for a person as dilatory and as easily distracted as Proust. He knew that he should begin; he ardently wished to do so. But he kept getting involved in other projects, all of them less promising and, as it turned out, abortive.

In February, 1908, when he was preparing his parodies for *Le Figaro*, Proust wrote to Madame Straus: "I want to get started on a rather long work and, if I do, it will be even more difficult for me to visit you." But apparently he did not get started. In the spring he was still busy with his parodies, trying to find a publisher who would bring them out as a small volume. Either at this time or later he offered them to Fasquelle and the Mercure de France; he considered offering them to Calmann-Lévy as well. Renewing contact with his old friends, the Gaston de Caillavets, who had influence with Monsieur Calmann, he arranged to pay them a visit. He admired the woman he had once been in love with and admired her daughter too; he artfully brought up the subject of publishers. But even with the Caillavets' assistance, the negotiations with Calmann came to nothing.

In May Proust was busy with something else, an article on what was obviously considered a daring subject, possibly inversion. He went so far as to consult a friend about publishing it, but shortly afterwards he abandoned the article, deciding to use the material for a short story. In June he discovered to his horror that a certain Gustave Schlumberger, a man whom he detested, was a candidate for a vacant seat in the Academy. Proust was violently incensed. He at once decided to write, for *Le Figaro*, a damaging article on the man, and he asked Madame Straus, who shared his feelings, to supply him with documentation. Was it true that Schlumberger had not himself written his own works? Had he really been elected to the Academy of Inscriptions (of which he was unfortunately a member) by a kind of fraud? Was he a man of any standing at all? Madame Straus, Proust felt, might get the answers from Reinach. While he was trying to write the article, Proust went one night to the Princesse Murat's, where the first person he encountered was none other than the unspeakable Schlumberger. "It gave me a chance to cut him a dozen times by walking by him to speak to other people," he afterwards reported, "and when someone asked me, 'Don't you know Monsieur S[chlumberger]?' I replied in a loud voice, 'I will speak to him when he speaks to Madame Straus;

she is amused by his antics but I am not amused.' I 'talked' my article to pretty nearly all the guests, so that by now he ought to know my intentions. Madame de Chevigné was sublime and I fell in love with her all over again."

Proust talked and perhaps wrote the article; meanwhile he was still thinking very seriously about his novel. He was apparently planning it, if he was not actually getting anything down on paper. In July he told Montesquiou that he was "floundering about" in it, without however making any progress. Later in the summer he went to Cabourg, partly at least because alterations were again in prospect at the Boulevard Haussmann. His intention was to work while he was away, and he may well have done so— at least he spent very little time sightseeing. On the other hand, he saw people a good deal, including some he was not very anxious to have his older friends meet.

In September he suddenly moved to Versailles so that he could be near his friend, Georges de Lauris, who had been injured in an automobile accident, but actually he visited Lauris only once. Otherwise, when he drove into Paris—for he was again hiring Agostinelli, presumably summoned from Cabourg—he spent his time with some new friends, a woman and a group of young men. Generally, however, his asthma was so bad that he was not inclined to leave his room at the Hôtel des Réservoirs. Hahn came to see him, sometimes bringing along the manuscript of a ballet he was composing, and as he worked on it Proust played dominoes with his valet or Agostinelli.

Proust's asthma seemed to grow worse if anything, and he worried about himself, worried about Lauris, indeed worried about another friend, Billy, who reported from Saint-Jean-de-Luz that his wife had typhoid. "Profoundly moved by your letter," Proust replied in a telegram, "anxiously awaiting news and prognosis. If I could be of any help to you at Saint-Jean-de-Luz, would leave immediately, you have only to tell me. If too ill to make the whole trip at once, will stop over a day on the way." Billy's next report was, however, reassuring, and Proust remained in Versailles, pretty completely bedridden. Twice, so he said, he tried to work, but he was obliged to give up after twenty minutes. "It is discouraging," he wrote Madame Straus, "to have so many ideas and to feel that

the mind where they are imprisoned will soon perish without any-
body's knowing about them. It is true that the ideas are not so
very profound and that other writers will express them better."

Early in November he was driven from Versailles by noise outside his windows, where the Rue des Réservoirs was being torn up.
But there was noise in Paris too, for the alterations in the house
were not yet finished, and the radiator in his bedroom made him
so asthmatic that he was obliged to take the sternest measures—
even open his windows. He promised himself that he would go
away again as soon as he could move, but he made no effort to
go. In his better moments he read and wrote more parodies, and
at least toyed with the idea of doing serious work—not on his
novel, but on another project he had been thinking of for some
time, a magazine article on Sainte-Beuve. One evening he dashed
off a note to Madame de Noailles, telling her that he had considered two quite different plans for his article. He could write a
classical essay in the manner of Taine, or he could imagine himself awakening in the morning and talking with his mother, who
had come to sit by his bed—he could explain to her his interest
in Sainte-Beuve and develop his ideas in the course of their conversation. Each plan had its advantages; could Madame de Noailles
—who was, he felt sure, the greatest living French writer—perhaps help him decide which was the more promising? He wrote a
similar note to Lauris. But though the advice he got was undoubtedly very good, he was not sure whether he ought to take it,
and in any case he was in no condition to work at the moment. As
he went on suffering day after day, he forgot what he had read of
Sainte-Beuve and indeed what he wanted to say. He was profoundly miserable. "I have just gone through," he wrote Lauris,
"what . . . I think have been the worst days of my life, because
for the first time I am completely discouraged, I can't go on
living when my attacks are so persistent."

IV

Proust's discouragement was entirely natural under the circumstances. He was going through a particularly trying period with his
asthma; he was kept from working with any regularity just at the

time when he felt the strongest urge to work. He could scarcely
help being appalled by the disparity between what he might be
doing and what he was actually able to do. Still it seems clear that
he was doing something, rather more perhaps than he cared to
admit, and during the winter he apparently achieved a good deal
more. By the spring of 1909—some six months, that is, after he
consulted Madame de Noailles and Lauris about the form of his
Sainte-Beuve article—he certainly had a substantial accumulation
of manuscript, amounting to some 95 loose sheets—large ones—
and two notebooks.

Most of the loose sheets were devoted to episodes, or fragments
of episodes, obviously intended for the novel and afterwards used
in it. There were six of them altogether: Venice, Balbec (though
not yet so called), the young girls, the goodnight kiss at Combray,
the poetry of names, and the two "ways." The remaining loose
sheets and the two notebooks contained fragments of the Sainte-
Beuve, some in the form that Proust called a classical essay and
some in the form of a conversation between himself and his
mother. Many of these fragments were curiously similar to the
fragments intended for the novel. In one of them he explained
his conception of involuntary memory and illustrated it with the
cup of tea, the uneven flagstones, and the sound of the spoon
striking against the plate. In another he described himself awakening and remembering other beds he had slept in years before. In
still another he reviewed his love affair with a woman of noble
birth, as yet unnamed and identified merely as the Countess.
Clearly he thought of the Sainte-Beuve as something more than
criticism, an essay in which, as in "Sur la Lecture," the criticism
would be introduced by or embedded in long narrative passages.
He could put into it—he was in fact putting into it as it grew—
the material of the novel. There must have been times when he
doubted that he would ever write a novel at all and when he was
half inclined to feel that he could express himself best in a work
essentially critical and philosophical.

In May, 1909, Proust consulted Lauris again, this time about
an attractive name he remembered hearing, the name of Guermantes. It was obviously a family name. But was the Comte or
Marquis de Guermantes related to the Marquis de Pâris? Was the

title now extinct and therefore available to a man of letters? Proust needed names because the characters were beginning to multiply in his manuscript. Specifically he needed a name for his Countess and her family, which by this time seems to have included a Count, a Prince and Princess, and such relatives as a Marquise de Villeparisis. Early in the summer Proust reported to Lauris that he was hard at work on the Sainte-Beuve—beginning it, he said, but he presumably meant that he was beginning a new draft. About midsummer he reported that he had some four or five hundred pages of manuscript altogether, adding that it had already been rejected by the Mercure de France and that it would almost certainly remain unpublished.

The new notebooks, of which there seem to have been five, contained some genuinely critical material—essays on Sainte-Beuve and three of his most illustrious contemporaries, Balzac, Baudelaire, and Gérard de Nerval. But they contained more narrative material, too, some of it so remotely related to Sainte-Beuve that one wonders why Proust ever even considered using it in a critical work. There was a passage about a party given by the Prince and Princesse de Guermantes. The narrator was invited and indeed went, though he suspected, quite without foundation, that he was the victim of a practical joke. At the party he greeted and actually shook hands with the Marquis de Quercy (obviously the Charlus of the novel), who however looked the other way and pretended not to see him. There was a passage about inversion, beginning with a sentence nearly five pages long in which the race of inverts was persistently compared with the Jews. There was a passage about Proust's brother, Robert, who as a child once had to give up a pet goat when he left Combray. Taken together, these passages show how far Proust had strayed from his subject. Starting with the idea of a magazine article on Sainte-Beuve framed in some sort of narrative, he had elaborated the framework out of all proportion to the criticism, which by itself was now long enough for half a dozen articles. He was actually writing at his novel, whether he realized it at the time or not; the whole Sainte-Beuve project, which occupied him for the greater part of a year, must be regarded as a stage, a very important one, in the novel's composition.

Even the critical passages, the essays on Sainte-Beuve and his contemporaries, can be related to the novel, and as one reads them today one is impressed first of all by the fact that they deal with one of the novel's central doctrines, namely that art is something of its own kind, quite unlike other forms of experience. As in so many passages of *Jean Santeuil*, Proust insists on the distinction between the artist and his work, between the man—for there is always a man, often a mediocre and reprehensible one, in every artist—and the genius. Baudelaire was both, and Proust is well aware that he himself has been both too. In the ordinary affairs of life he has been selfish, snobbish, and vain; in his writing he is entirely different, for he draws on a different aspect of his personality, something deep within himself, indeed another self altogether, quite distinct from the first one. At times he is half inclined to feel that this other self is the same for all artists and that there has really been only one poet since the world began. The trouble with Sainte-Beuve was that, despite his reputation as a critic, he failed to distinguish between the two selves. He dealt with the man, the self that was not called into play, when he should have been dealing with the man of genius; he relied on his intelligence, which is scarcely serviceable at all in art, when he should have relied on intuitive penetration.

There are many eloquent and instructive pages of criticism in *Contre Sainte-Beuve*, but the work is chiefly notable for the narrative passages in which it anticipates the novel. These passages are particularly fresh and charming; furthermore, many of them are quite new in Proust's work. For he was not writing with the notebooks of *Jean Santeuil* open before him, or indeed revising at all (though he sometimes went over old material), but making a fresh start. He was trying to set down what he now felt to be significant and useful—sometimes ideas, sometimes sketches of characters and episodes, sometimes impressions. He was also experimenting with a new narrative method, quite different from anything in his earlier work and very close to the one that he adopted, presumably at a later date, for his novel. The movement is not so much linear as spiral. The author progresses only after he has incorporated into his story much more than he can get from the scene at hand. The association of ideas is constantly called into play: the dream of a woman reminds him of his childhood and his first adventures in masturbation; a lilac bush, of walks along the river in the country, and the glass jars used by boys to catch minnows, and the unidentified fisherman on the bridge; the pink sky, of trips when he saw the dawn intermittently from a train window and when, during a stop in a wild mountain gorge, he saw an adorable peasant girl peddling coffee. The method—if one may venture to judge a series of fragments—is not always completely successful, for the transitions sometimes seem unnecessarily abrupt. Still the method is used and the transitions are there. From the technical point of view *Contre Sainte-Beuve* is primarily a study in transitions, and as such it is a work of capital importance.

V

For a while Proust had nothing more to say about his novel, presumably because he was occupied with the Sainte-Beuve and such other matters as, for example, an ulcerated tooth and an opportunity to get married. In the summer of 1909 he hinted to Lauris that, if he left Paris, he might take a wife along. In August he did leave, still single however, for Cabourg. His establishment at the Grand Hôtel was a curious one, chosen so that he would be as far from neighbors as possible. He took a room facing a court on the top floor, a small badly ventilated room, unfortunately rather damp in rainy weather, and he installed his valet in the only room—a palatial one, as it happened—that adjoined his. He seems to have found this valet indispensable, in Normandy as in Paris, partly at least because he was able to help with the notebooks. He proofread manuscript and even took dictation when he had to though, as he told his wife privately, without very much enthusiasm. "Valentin's sentences," he was fond of saying—he irreverently referred to Proust by the first of his given names— "Valentin's sentences are as dull as he is. But you wait and see, when he's dead, he'll be famous."

As soon as he had established himself in his new quarters Proust wrote to his friend Madame Straus, who was in Trouville for the summer. "I have just begun—and finished—the whole of a long book," he told her. "Unfortunately the trip to Cabourg inter-

rupted my work, and I am just about to get down to it again.
Perhaps part of the book will appear serially in Le Figaro, but only
a part because it is too improper and too long to be printed in its
entirety. But I am very anxious to finish it, to get it all done.
Though the whole thing is written, there is still much to revise."
The statement is by no means easy to interpret, but it seems clear
that Proust was at least thinking about his novel again and perhaps
selecting certain passages—he had several suitable for the purpose
—that he could use at the beginning and end. It is very likely that
he was also incorporating in his manuscript some of the Sainte-
Beuve material, including the parts on inversion, which he thought
of as improper.

During the summer he either worked rather hard or saw a
good deal of his disreputable friends or did both, for he was inclined to avoid his usual social engagements. Thus he put off visiting Madame Straus in Trouville, and in a remarkable passage at
once affectionate and adroit, he warned her against visiting him.
"I had rather do that [that is, go to Trouville] than see you at
Cabourg, where the suddenness of your arrival, the fear of your
catching cold, the confusion of the music and the crowd, the
shock of seeing you without the preparation of a pilgrimage during
which I become worthy of you little by little as I think about you
on the way, almost prevent me from realizing that you are here;
I think only of the drafts that may disturb you, of the chocolate
that Monsieur Straus has gone to pay for surreptitiously, and it
is only when your car has left and I am alone again that I say to
myself, 'It was Madame Straus!' and I become sadly aware of
a happiness that I haven't felt." On the other hand, he was quite
willing and able to see people closer at hand, especially people
who could be useful to him. He saw Calmette, talked with him
about the novel, and got him to promise that Le Figaro would
take it; he saw another member of the Figaro staff and talked about
the essay on Sainte-Beuve. He talked so much, in fact, that he
began to be afraid of what might happen when the editors of
Le Figaro met and compared notes.

When the season at Cabourg approached its end, Proust talked
of staying on at the hotel after it had officially closed if he could

persuade the management to postpone certain repairs scheduled for the autumn. He needed a month, he told Lauris, to finish his Sainte-Beuve. He was afraid of the noise and the radiator if he returned to the Boulevard Haussmann, but when the time came he did return. Soon afterwards he read Hahn the beginning of the novel and was very much encouraged by Hahn's reaction—so much so that he decided to drop everything else, including apparently the Sainte-Beuve, and to isolate himself as completely as possible so that he could finish the book. But he was still toying with the idea of marriage, and before his isolation began he felt obliged to entertain some young people from Cabourg, possibly friends of his prospective bride. He arranged a theatre party to which—since he shrank from facing the young people alone—he invited a good many of his own friends, such as Radziwill, Emmanuel Bibesco, Hahn, Lauris, Fénelon, and Mademoiselle de Mornand. In his letter of invitation to Lauris he dropped another hint about his marriage but promised to do nothing rashly. "Georges," he wrote, "I may soon have some news for you, or rather I shall ask your advice. Wouldn't it be a crime to ask a delightful young girl to share my hideous life, even if she herself weren't afraid of it?"

Once the party was over Proust seems to have begun working quite steadily, without however becoming exactly monkish or declining on principle attractive engagements, for after all relaxation was important to him. Still he was more reluctant than ever to take time off merely to fulfill a social duty. He went, or intended to go, to Madame de Caillavet's funeral and to the dress rehearsal of Hahn's ballet, presumably because, in these cases, he felt that he simply had to. But when Madame Gaston de Caillavet threatened him with some sort of engagement, he discouraged her at once. "Alas! it is impossible," he wrote, going on to use one of his standard excuses. "The only person I see at all is Reynaldo, because he is constantly stopping by very late at night, so that once every half dozen times when I am through with my inhalations I can let him in, because he is so used to my affliction that he lets me answer him by writing notes on scraps of paper if I can't talk, etc." His most formidable interruption seems to have occurred in

January and February, 1910, when the Seine overflowed and water
reached the Boulevard Haussmann itself. Many of his neighbors
left their homes in boats. Workmen threw up barricades, pumped
water, tore out rotten flooring in cellars, and built new floors—
making of course a deplorable commotion as they did so. For
Proust the whole experience was a nightmare. To get any sleep at
all he had to drug himself with formidable doses of veronal.

Finally, when the street quieted down, he began working again
and accumulating fresh piles of notebooks on the table by his bed.
He had the notebooks copied; he tore out and added pages in the
copyist's draft. At some time during the winter he sent Lauris at
least two notebooks of the most recent series, swearing his friend
to secrecy as he did so. "What I ask," he wrote, "is that you don't
reveal the subject or the title or in fact anything at all (not that it
would interest anyone) but in any case I don't want to be hurried,
or tormented, or guessed at, or forestalled, or copied, or discussed,
or criticized, or disparaged. When I have finished my work to my
own satisfaction, there will be time enough for the stupidity of
others." He was pleased that Lauris liked the notebooks, pleased
and at the same time rather worried. For if they were as good as
Lauris said they were, was it not a shame that their appearance
should depend on an invalid like himself who might die at any
time? In his next letter to Lauris he said: "I wanted to write you
to ask still another favor. Do you think that if I should die at
this moment without getting farther along with the book, the part
[you have read] could be published as a volume, and if you think it
could, would you be willing, in case I do die, to take charge of it?"

A few months of reflection, however, convinced him that it
would be safer not to rely on Lauris. He would himself publish the
notebooks as soon as he conveniently could; he would remind
Calmette of his promise, made the summer before. Accordingly
Proust took them to *Le Figaro*, where however they were rejected.
"I don't know," Proust wrote Lauris, "who ruined my chances
with Calmette, with whom I was on excellent terms; it hurts me
because I am very fond of him. But for heaven's sake don't say
anything to anyone or I shall be ruined. Incidentally, no one
knows about it and officially I haven't broken with Calmette, I
didn't even express regret when I took back my notebooks."

VI

The rejection was painful, but Proust went on working, during the winter in the bedroom on the Boulevard Haussmann and during the summer at the Grand Hôtel in Cabourg, working feverishly and persistently, as though he were fulfilling a sacred duty. Sometimes he worked on new material, occasionally episodes written in the third person, in which the hero was called Charles Swann. In these episodes Swann carried on somewhat eccentric flirtations with a group of girls in the town of Querqueville (later Balbec), and in Paris a more serious love affair with a girl called Françoise, or Carmen, or Odette. Sometimes Proust worked over old episodes, rearranging and amplifying the material they contained, as when he added, in the episode of the two ways at Combray, something about the character of Aunt Léonie. Sometimes he merely rewrote episodes with slight changes of emphasis, for he did a great deal of rewriting. Thus he apparently prepared several drafts of his general remarks on inverts, in at least one of which he considered cases of curable inversion—men who experience anatomical difficulties in making love to women and men who find the female smell distasteful. But whatever he did, the notebooks multiplied month by month until he had three or four times as many as before.

Still he was not satisfied; he kept working over the manuscript, adding to it and rearranging it, tearing out and pasting in pages, investigating and checking, for however much he might pretend to rely on involuntary memory he still had to do a certain amount of research. He had to be sure about the ramifications of noble families, about the seasons when certain flowers bloom, about the kinds of hats women wore in the now distant past when his story begins. He pored over the *Almanach de Gotha* and studied photographs he kept in his room. Sometimes he sent his servants out to buy reproductions of famous pictures or copies of old fashion magazines; sometimes he turned the pages of books on botany and architecture; sometimes he consulted his friends or experts of one sort or another. His investigations became easier when he got into the habit of hiring a taxi driver, a certain Odilon Albaret, who was willing to run errands at all hours of the night. He could either go out with Albaret on sudden excursions or send Albaret for people he wanted to question. A student of criminal psychology turned up in Paris after extensive study in Italy, and one night Proust sent the taxi to fetch him. He pumped him about scandalous figures in Roman society and persuaded him to copy out some of his case histories, including one of an Italian count who was extremely cultivated, extremely unstable, and extremely fond of young men, whom however he tried to strangle just as they were on the point of getting married. A piece of music ran through Proust's head, a piece by Debussy: he was determined to hear it at once. At three in the morning, or so the story goes, he telephoned the members of a well-known quartet, got them up, and sent Albaret to bring them back in the taxi, so that they could play for him in his bedroom.

During the summer of 1910 this bedroom was in the process of transformation, for Proust was taking steps to guard himself against interruptions in his work, at least from those dreadful spells of insomnia brought on by commotion in the streets or the pounding of inconsiderate neighbors. While he was safely away at Cabourg, he had the bedroom insulated against noise, "soundproofed" in so far as soundproofing was then possible: he had it lined with cork. Thus there came into being the famous insulated room—felt by many people to be the equivalent of an ivory tower—with which Proust's name was afterwards so closely associated. The cork, nailed on in sheets with battens of wood, was of course unsightly, but this failed to disturb Proust in the least— he was never one to be much concerned about appearances. What did disturb him was the fact that the work was expensive and that, unluckily, he had just promised watches to two young girls at Cabourg. Cartier reported that the watches would cost 4,000 francs, and Proust, appalled by what he seemed to have let himself in for, at once wrote to Hahn to see if some saving was not possible. A bargain was the last thing he wanted, but he was inclined to think that he might get two very satisfactory watches elsewhere —say, at the Trois Quartiers—for something like 1,200 francs. In the autumn he had severe attacks of asthma and he was for a while afraid that the cork smell was bringing them on. But in the course of time it became evident that his fears were groundless and that his investment, in cork if not in watches, had been fully justified. The silence in the bedroom was not perhaps absolute, but disagreeable sounds were certainly muted and work on the novel was possible with fewer interruptions than before.

More and more, as time went on, Proust lived for his novel. When he was safely enclosed within his corklined walls, he worked at it or wrote letters about it or questioned people who might supply him with useful information; when he went out he studied faces and mannerisms, storing his mind with impressions that he might later use in one passage or another. He preferred large parties because, where there were many faces, he could select the kind that at the moment interested him most—parties like that given by Madame Edwards on Christmas Eve, 1910. There were many tables and some signs of confusion; there were even people who could not find places. Proust sat beside the hostess, talking steadily in a weary voice and indeed dominating the conversation, surveying the other guests and being himself surveyed. Some observers were surprised to find that he was now wearing a heavy beard, so very black it seemed blue. An Englishman who was present, Arnold Bennett, sized up the bearded man as an aesthete. He was continually twisting himself into strange curves, Bennett noticed; he seemed an ideal figure for Bunthorne in *Patience*.

Sometimes, at such parties, Proust confined his attention to a single person, as at the *Intransigeant* ball in May, 1911, when he fastened on to a talented young woman, the Princesse Bibesco, a relative by marriage of the Bibescos he knew. He placed his chair between her and the dance floor, trying to isolate her and keep her to himself. But she was alarmed by his attentions. She fled, danced continually, and urged her partners not to lead her near the spot where Proust, bearded and pale, with the collar of his overcoat turned up, sat sorrowfully watching her, fixing no doubt an impression that he might later use in his novel. Sometimes, as at the dress rehearsal of D'Annunzio's *Martyre de saint Sébastien*, he circulated more generally, talked with old friends such as Montesquiou, and studied other fashionable people, forming distinct but by no means favorable impressions. "[They] seemed to me much worse," he afterwards reported. "The nicest ones have become intellectuals, but with society people unfortunately, though I don't know how they manage it, intellectual activity only multiplies their silliness until it reaches overwhelming and unprecedented proportions. The only tolerable ones are those who have had the good sense to remain silly."

Once, when he made a radical but unfortunately not very permanent change in his hours, he was able to go out quite early in the afternoon and indeed to visit an exhibition of Chinese pictures. He took an expert along, possibly because he was interested in gathering material for his novel and he wanted to make sure that he had it straight. While he was there he certainly found material, rather more than he had anticipated. He stumbled on an old acquaintance of his, a certain Rodier, who was an inveterate and transparently hypocritical snob—an excellent model for Legrandin. Rodier began by bowing and scraping, then, as his snobbishness was called into play by the presence of Proust's expert, chattered on like a mill wheel. When the name of Cocteau came up, he remarked sagely: "But what I am afraid of in his case is society; he is going out too much; if he keeps on he is lost." The speaker seemed determined not to admit his own snobbishness and indeed dramatized himself as a hermit far above such weaknesses. Proust asked him certain questions about dress. Did he, for example, remember what sort of black hat the courtesan Madame Clomesnil used to wear in the old days? Fortunately Rodier did remember or said he did: it was a hat out of Rembrandt. Proust was delighted because he had another detail which might help him to fill out his description of Odette de Crécy.

In the summer of 1911 Proust wrote to a young friend suggesting that he might care to decipher and copy the notebooks. "Excuse me for asking you a strange question," Proust added, "but I suddenly find that you could do me a great favor. Did you ever happen to have anyone followed for any reason, and if so, have you kept the addresses of detectives or contact with them?" The friend undertook the copying, with the help of the typist at the Grand Hôtel, and Proust went on with his own work as before. He hoped to finish very soon, but actually he never came close to finishing—obstacles of all sorts kept holding him back. He was ill for a while and he was too much preoccupied with gambling in the casino and too much worried about other matters that required the services of private detectives. He was also too prolix and too eager to embody all his experience in his novel. There were always fresh details he might put in, fresh episodes he might conceivably add.

In Paris during the following winter the obstacles became even more formidable. For one thing, Proust took in an ambiguous boarder—none other than Alfred Agostinelli, who had lost his job as a taxi driver. To keep him—or, more probably, to keep him out of mischief—Proust hired him to take over the typing of the novel. But he can scarcely have been an expert typist, and he was otherwise a serious distraction. For another thing, Proust was now gambling, even more heavily, on the stock market. In January, 1912, for example, he was half-heartedly holding on to some two or three thousand shares of mining stock he had bought, stock that was going down at an alarming rate. He sent intricate instructions to his broker and he shopped elsewhere for advice. "Do you, in short, think it desirable for me to keep my Rand Mines and my Crown Mines another month?" he asked Billy in a letter. "Is there a chance they will go up? It seems to me fantastic that mines said to be very good should stay so pitifully low when they pay such a dividend. On the other hand, I have invested so much in them that I don't dare keep them too long." He did not dare, he sold at a loss of 40,000 francs, and the very next day the stocks shot up. But perhaps the loss was after all a blessing, for he was now able to give more attention to his manuscript, even able to detach and send to Le Figaro—where he was apparently still welcomed as a casual contributor—a few of his more striking passages. The first, a passage about hawthorns, was published as "Au Seuil du printemps," a title that outraged Proust, that seemed to him hopelessly idiotic.

The typing might perhaps have gone faster, but by the spring of 1912 Proust was at least ready to solicit advice about publishers. Calmette was in a position to be helpful, and indeed Calmette had so far forgotten his own rejection of the novel that he was now willing to recommend it to Fasquelle, head of a highly repu-

table firm. But other people could also be helpful in other ways—
the editor of *Gil Blas*, René Blum (brother of Proust's old friend
Léon Blum) for example, and the novelist Louis de Robert, with
whom Proust had reestablished contact. For there were many
problems connected with the publication of a novel that was
already unusually long, perhaps as long as twelve or fourteen
hundred pages, who could tell? To emphasize its unity, Proust
wanted to bring it out in a single volume, but he realized that a
publisher might think this impracticable. If he should resign himself to two volumes, he wondered whether he should publish both
together or allow a time interval between them; whether he
should have one title or separate titles; whether he should divide
the manuscript arbitrarily in half or whether he should attempt a
more logical division—by, say, putting the first, second, third, and
fifth chapters in one volume, the fourth, sixth, and subsequent
chapters in the other. He wondered about many things; meanwhile
he supervised the typing of the manuscript or went out with
Albaret to get material for scenes that needed revision.

On a cloudy evening in April he drove to Rueil to see apple
trees in bloom. On the way he developed an attack of asthma, and
returned precipitately to Paris. In May he went to a performance
of the Opéra de Monte-Carlo, at which, oddly enough, the
leading soprano was named Madame Agostinelli. He sat in a box
with two supremely elegant hostesses, Madame Standish and
Madame Greffulhe. It occurred to him that they would make
particularly good models, but when, some time afterwards, he came
to describing them, he floundered so hopelessly that he had to
seek help. "I had the impression that they represented two conceptions of dress and of style," he wrote Madame Gaston de
Caillavet, "quite different, quite opposite conceptions. I don't
suppose you could have seen them that evening because they were
in a box near the stage where it was very dark (nearly two months
ago now), but you may perhaps have seen them separately at
other performances. I shouldn't like either of them to know that
it interests me (otherwise I should quite simply have asked
Madame G[reffulhe] whom I have often seen since), because
the two characters I am going to dress—like two mannequins—
in their clothes have no relation to them, because my novel has no

key, because if I talk with them about it and if afterwards my characters poison someone or commit incest or do anything of the sort, they will think I intend to attribute these actions to them! I had rather not! . . . If I don't feel too tired Thursday, I should love to go to the last soirée of the year (if it is given by people I know) to refresh my mind about faces."

In June he went to a Monet exhibit, apparently to form impressions that he could use in describing the pictures of Elstir. At about the same time he found, somewhere in the apartment, a diary in which his mother had recorded details of illnesses in the family. By following the entries, he could reconstruct the last days of his grandmother, his grandfather, and his father. "It is hard to go on living after reading them," he wrote to Madame de Noailles. But the entries may well have proved useful in helping him fill out his account of the grandmother's death in the novel. Early in the summer he hesitated about going to Cabourg, feeling perhaps that he could scarcely afford it. But on the spur of the moment he went and, as in other years, engaged rooms on the top floor of the hotel. If, as seems probable, Agostinelli went with him, the typing must have gone on as in Paris.

In the casino that summer Proust saw something of a new friend, Madame Scheikévitch, once the wife of Pierre Carolus-Duran. She was well acquainted with the editor of *Le Temps* and therefore perhaps in a position to be helpful about the novel. Sometimes Proust met her as he was wandering about, apparently lost, under the glare of the lights and staggering a little; they sat down to talk. Like other people, Madame Scheikévitch was struck by his black beard, his pale face, and his outfit—for even on warm nights he wore an overcoat with his dinner jacket, and carried in one hand a straw hat. He talked about his novel and about people they both knew, stopping frequently to question servants who came to report on errands they had run or appointments they had made or canceled for him. His tone, Madame Scheikévitch noticed, was often distinctly caustic. "Sometimes he laid traps," she later said, "pretending he had forgotten a fact or a name. His scorn burst out if his interlocutors had erred through boasting. . . . He used to tell stories specially concerned with the ignorance of society people. . . . His eyes, so particularly mobile, flashed with malice; he had great difficulty in veiling his laughter which suddenly burst forth, pitiless, in strident notes." Madame Scheikévitch either did not know or neglected to mention that he was taking a little exercise that summer, dancing in fact every other day.

The dancing may have had something to do with a young man Proust was seeing, one especially fond of dancing and golf. The young man was very nice but unfortunately undependable; he made appointments and then tried to wriggle out of them when he found something better to do. Once, when they were to meet on the beach in the evening, he failed to show up at all, and Proust inevitably brooded for many hours, during dinner in the casino and afterwards in the music hall. The next day he wrote the young man a stern letter in which, while pretending to break off the relationship, he managed to say something about the distinguished company he was used to and the consideration he had a right to expect. One friend — no less a personage than Alphonse Daudet — had written him polite notes at the cost of cruel physical suffering, and another, Anatole France, had been so anxious to have him along on trips to Versailles that he had put off going for days at a time. The young man scarcely moved in such circles, but then the young man was not very promising material and not really interested in self-improvement. If he had been stone, a sculptor — Proust himself of course — might have shaped him into something; actually he was water, "ordinary tap water, elusive, colorless, fluid, eternally insubstantial, and no sooner in than out." This being the case, a reconciliation was pointless, though Proust could scarcely conceal the anguish that he felt at seeing a person he had been so fond of recede into his past.

Whatever happened, whether he saw his young friend again or not, Proust was soon back at the Boulevard Haussmann, at last ready to face the problem of publishers. For by this time he had some seven hundred pages of manuscript typed and corrected—all, it seems, of "Combray," "Un Amour de Swann," and "Noms de pays: le nom," and perhaps two other chapters as well. These chapters could be shown to Fasquelle and could be printed at once. In the meantime, while the printing was in progress, the remaining chapters could be typed and revised.

CHAPTER XIV

The Struggle with Publishers

I

WHEN in the autumn of 1912 Proust set out to find a publisher, his forces were already marshaled; he had only to give his friends the signal that the campaign was about to begin. Two among them, Calmette and Robert, were prepared to recommend the book to the firm of Fasquelle. Calmette, as the editor of *Le Figaro*, was clearly the more influential of the two, and Proust was offering him, perhaps partly as an incentive and partly as a reward, the general dedication. Two other friends had contacts with other publishers: Antoine Bibesco knew at least one of the authors associated with Gide in La Nouvelle Revue Française, which was now bringing out books as well as the magazine; and René Blum knew Grasset. Still other friends could be relied on as needed for specific services. Madame Straus could approach Calmette when Proust did not care to do so himself; Cocteau could persuade the dramatist Edmond Rostand to bring pressure to bear on Fasquelle; Hahn could run errands, report progress, and be generally helpful.

The campaign was difficult, protracted, and involved—so involved, in fact, that one cannot always be sure what Proust was up to at any given time. Still the outlines of his strategy are clear enough. He was fighting for his book in any way he could, against men who would not take the trouble to understand it—he was fighting or at least making his friends fight. He sent these friends out on different missions at the same time, shifted his point of attack from one publishing house to another as the fortunes of the campaign seemed to vary, and involved himself in hazardous tactical situations, only to emerge, in the end, undeniably victorious.

The campaign as a whole was difficult, and even the first step was far from easy. Proust had to wait and brood until Calmette had a chance to see Fasquelle. For as he turned the matter over in his mind during the long nights on the Boulevard Haussmann, it seemed to him that Fasquelle was not perhaps the right publisher after all. If reports were to be believed, Fasquelle went over novels very carefully, demanded changes of various sorts, and had a policy of permitting nothing to impede the movement of plot. Would he be likely to take a lenient view of a novel so slow in its action as Proust's? Would he not rather demand changes altogether outrageous? Proust raised the questions in a letter to Robert and went on to suggest that it might be well to break with Fasquelle and try a publisher not quite so commercial, say the Nouvelle Revue Française. Robert, however, was reassuring—he offered to write Fasquelle and to emphasize Proust's literary stature. Proust therefore decided to wait a little longer and meanwhile to put pressure on Calmette.

"If you see [Calmette]," Proust wrote to Madame Straus, "(and if you don't find it embarrassing to do so, otherwise I can so easily get someone else to remind him) tell him that you have seen me, or that we have corresponded, and that I have asked you to remind him about my book and to tell him that I should be very much obliged if he would speak to Fasquelle as soon as possible, so that the first volume (where unfortunately you won't find your red dress and red shoes, they won't come until the second volume, because the Duchesse de Guermantes appears for only a moment in the first) can appear as promptly as possible. Otherwise I shall be dead long before the third (it would be pointless to tell him so)."

But as he waited impatiently for Madame Straus to report, he could not quite succeed in putting the Nouvelle Revue Française out of his mind. It was certainly undesirable to offer a book to a second publisher when the first one had already accepted it or was about to accept it. A question of good manners, perhaps even of morality was involved. On the other hand, the question would not arise in an acute form until the N. R. F. showed definite interest; preliminary inquiries could at least be made. Accordingly Proust showed his manuscript to Bibesco, communicated, directly or indirectly, with Copeau of the N. R. F. staff, and finally began writing Gallimard, the N. R. F.'s managing editor.

"I already have a publisher for my book," Proust told Gallimard. "I can't withdraw it (though he probably wouldn't be in the least disturbed if I did!) without first consulting my sponsors, who have treated me charmingly and have persuaded him to accept it. . . . To do this, I should have to go out and to go out at a time of day when I could find them. And as yet I haven't been able to." Even so, he felt, Gallimard might be willing to answer certain general questions. Could he publish a volume of 550 pages if Proust paid all the expenses? When could the volume be ready? When could the second volume appear?

Meanwhile Madame Straus reported by forwarding a letter from Calmette. Proust sent one copy of his manuscript to Fasquelle and another to the N. R. F., then pestered both publishers with messages and telephone calls designed to hurry them up. One evening, when he felt unable to endure the suspense any longer, he dragged himself to the offices of *Le Figaro*, ostensibly to thank Calmette. He was told that the editor was not in, but he was not sure that he could believe what he was told. It seemed more likely that something had gone wrong, that Calmette had quarreled with Fasquelle, that the novel was being deliberately sacrificed, and that Calmette was reluctant to tell him the worst. The N. R. F. was perhaps a wiser choice after all. Proust recalled, with considerable satisfaction, the frankness he had shown in his correspondence with Gallimard. He had explained that his book was sometimes indecent, that one of his characters (to be called either Monsieur de Fleurus or de Guray) was a pederast, and that in the second volume the pederast was represented as seducing a concierge and keeping a pianist. Gallimard had not been shocked. Quite the contrary, the negotiations had gone on. The N. R. F. was certainly more discerning than Fasquelle in literary matters and therefore more promising.

Proust could not then know, and did not in fact discover until much later, that at this very time André Gide, the most influential author concerned in the N. R. F., was carelessly turning the pages of the manuscript. Gide was not in the least worried about pederasts; he was worried about frivolity and fine writing, qualities that he expected to find in society authors like Proust. Immediately he singled out an example, a passage in which Aunt Léonie was described as holding out "for me to kiss her sad brow, pale and lifeless . . . through which the vertebrae shone like the points of a crown of thorns or the beads of a rosary." [1] Vertebrae in the forehead: Gide put the manuscript down. The N. R. F. wrote a letter of rejection.

Proust's inclination was to conceal the humiliating development and to assure his friends that he was withdrawing from the N. R. F. because it was not equipped to handle so long a work or because it might find the dedication embarrassing. But he made no secret of the fact that he was returning, with considerably more ardor, to Fasquelle, or that he was now chiefly worried about the changes Fasquelle might ask him to make. Indeed he began pulling wires to see if he could not avoid changes altogether. Through Cocteau he arranged to have Rostand, whom he had never met, write Fasquelle a letter in which it was suggested that the manuscript should be published just as it stood and as promptly as possible.

Meanwhile Proust toyed with the idea of seeing Fasquelle (in the morning if necessary!) and made every effort to see Calmette whenever he could. Thus on December 17 he accepted Madame Straus's invitation to a theatre party that was to include Calmette —accepted even though he was violating the most sacred rule of his personal regimen, never to go out on two successive evenings. "I am going to *Kismet*," he wrote Madame Straus; "I have taken enough medicine to kill me or prepare me to go; and since I am not dead, I am going." He reached the theatre at 11:30, in time to accompany Madame Straus backstage and to witness an unpleasant

1. I have changed Scott Moncrieff's *bones* to *vertebrae*, as corresponding more closely to the French *vertèbres*.

quarrel between Bizet and Comte Hubert de Pierredon, but it does
not appear that he learned anything new about what Fasquelle had
in mind. When he returned home, he discovered that, in dressing
for the theatre, he had made the unpardonable mistake of wearing
his morning coat with the white waistcoat and dark trousers of his
evening suit. "What on earth did you think of me?" he asked
Madame Straus in a letter written that very night. "And naturally
I didn't notice anything and I didn't realize what I had done
until I got home. What on earth did Hervieu and Calmette think,
but especially Jacques?"

Ten days later he received a really crushing blow, a letter of
rejection from Fasquelle. The publisher was considerate and even
flattering, at least in conversation with Hahn, who was immediately despatched to question him. He praised "Combray," regretting that it could not be brought out by itself, but he felt
unable to accept the whole novel, so much longer than other
novels, so different from the novels to which the public was
accustomed. His rejection, though courteous, was definite and
final.

II

Proust was desperate. Three months had passed and he had
made no progress at all. He again considered the idea of publishing
at his own expense, publishing perhaps with a new firm like
Grasset, publishing privately if necessary, but settling the whole
matter at once. In January, 1913, he allowed himself to be dis-
suaded by Robert, who wanted to try the firm of Ollendorff,
but again the manuscript came back. Humblot, Ollendorff's
editor, found it quite unreadable. "My dear friend," he wrote
to Robert, "perhaps I am dense but I just don't understand why
a man should take thirty pages to describe how he rolls about
in bed before he goes to sleep. It made my head swim."

Now, obviously, there was only one course for Proust to take—
to pay off Robert and Calmette, to write René Blum, the
one intermediary on whom he had not yet called, and to arrange
some sort of publication at his own expense. He gave Robert
an engraved sapphire ring and Calmette a black moire cigarette

case with a diamond monogram (costing 400 francs at Tiffany's, but not quite so nice, Proust felt, as one costing 800). He personally delivered the cigarette case. Afterwards he was very unhappy because he remembered having left in the package a slip with figures on it, possibly Tiffany's bill. Meanwhile he drafted a formidable letter to Blum describing exactly what he wanted—two volumes of 650 pages each, the second to appear ten months after the first—and asking for a recommendation to Grasset on terms that would not cost Grasset a single franc.

"Don't tell me, as I know everyone else would," Proust said in the course of the letter: " 'But, my dear friend, Grasset will be delighted to publish you at his own expense and will offer you excellent terms'. . . . I am very ill, I want to be sure [about the book] so that I can set my mind at rest." He failed to mention the rejections by Fasquelle, the N. R. F., and Ollendorff, unless he was thinking of them when he remarked that a well-known publisher had asked for the book and offered unusually flattering terms. He even failed to mention the efforts of his friends, except to say, in the course of the letter, that he had many distinguished friends on whom he could call, Calmette for example. But unfortunately they might try to dissuade him from publishing at his own expense.

Proust sent off the letter, then too late regretted having sent it, perhaps feeling that Blum was not the right intermediary or Grasset the right publisher. Blum replied and sent off the recommendation. Proust wrote to Grasset and duly delivered his manuscript. This time the negotiations went smoothly forward, for though Grasset felt no enthusiasm for the novel, which he could not bring himself to read, he was willing to publish it if Proust was willing to pay.

Only one difference of opinion developed. Grasset wanted to charge 10 francs for the first volume and of this to give Proust 4. But Proust, who remembered how his friends had twitted him about the exorbitant price of Les Plaisirs et les jours, and who was, moreover, determined to reach more than the 10-franc audience, insisted on charging 3.50, of which he would take, not the 1.75 that Grasset offered him, but only 1.50. By this act of generosity Proust hoped to win Grasset's good will, and he seems to have done so. At least there were no unnecessary delays. Proust paid down money for the printing—some 1,730 francs—and the work immediately began. Soon the first proofs arrived.

III

Thus after six months the campaign finally came to an end, and Proust was prepared to feel the elation that accompanies the first moments of victory. But actually he felt no elation at all. He was miserable, as abjectly miserable as he had ever been in the whole course of his life. For something, meanwhile, had gone wrong at home, something that he could not reveal to his friends.

His relations with his secretary, Alfred Agostinelli, had obviously become closer. He now adored Agostinelli, now felt him to be one of the most gifted persons he had ever known. Even in the young man's letters he seemed to detect signs of remarkable talent, sentences that might well have been written by the greatest masters. Unfortunately Agostinelli had a wife—or rather, as it later appeared, a mistress who passed as a wife. Proust thought her a detestable little bitch, ugly, common, and violently jealous. Agostinelli quite clearly lived in the apartment, and the indications are that his wife lived there too. The situation was explosive, and from time to time quite catastrophic explosions undoubtedly occurred. More often there was an atmosphere of tension which Proust, who could not endure tension of any sort, found even more disturbing. There was also, on Proust's part, a sense of frustration. He was trying to win the affections of a man much younger than himself and yet aware—for his vision was quite clear in such matters—that he could never succeed in doing so.

For more than a year Proust had been worried about his household, so much so that he had made unusual requests of his correspondents. "If you write me," he had asked Madame Straus in December, 1912, "could you possibly seal your letter with wax? Otherwise don't allude to my book, because I don't want my servants to know what is going on. —And don't mention it if you see them or talk with them on the telephone." In his first letter to Blum, written in February, 1913, he had made exactly the same request. Apparently he had been posing at home as a successful author and saying that he could publish his novel at any time he chose. Hence he was determined that no one in the household, either Agostinelli or the servants, should learn anything about the three humiliating rejections.

In the spring of 1913 Proust still occasionally cautioned his correspondents, as when he sent fur coats to two girls at Cabourg —coats he had been promising for some time but had not got around to ordering until the hot weather began. He obviously preferred that the girls should not write to thank him. But if they insisted on writing, he had a special request to make: that their father enclose their letters in a single envelope, address it himself, and carefully seal it. Otherwise the letters should be sent to Hahn. But more often, during the spring, Proust complained about the sorrows and vexations he was suffering, distinctly mysterious sorrows because he could never tell his friends exactly what brought them about. He came closest to telling in a letter to Robert, written soon after the contract with Grasset. "My health is *very bad*," he said, "and I am otherwise quite miserable. But perhaps it is better so, because I don't have the strength to face happiness (you understand of course that I am speaking of misery and happiness in love, you wouldn't, I am sure, suppose that I was alluding to my *work*. That has always been a matter of indifference to me, and especially now!)." Misery in love: so much and no more. The door of the Boulevard Haussmann, opened ever so slightly, closed again. Proust recoiled from further revelations.

IV

Despite his sorrows, Proust worked. He had to—there were so many difficult decisions to make, so many questions he had to ask his friends. For one thing, his novel was unusually long. Obviously he should crowd as much as he could on as few pages as possible. Should he not, therefore, have a line around the text, perhaps a red line? Would not this permit somewhat smaller margins and somewhat larger type? He wrote an urgent note to an eminent critic and novelist—Jean-Louis Vaudoyer— asking for an immediate reply. Obviously the novel, no matter how many volumes it filled, should have a title to emphasize its unity. Grasset insisted that the separate volumes should also have titles. Would *Les Intermittences du passé* do as a general title, with *Le Temps perdu* as the title of the first volume and *Le Temps retrouvé* as the title of the second? Proust was inclined to think so: the balance was certainly neat and striking. But he later changed his mind, deciding or half deciding that he needed three volumes instead of two. He substituted *A la Recherche du temps perdu* for *Les Intermittences du passé* and puzzled end- lessly over the titles of the separate volumes.

"Would you have any objection to *Charles Swann* for a first volume in two parts," he once asked a friend, "(if Grasset will consent to a box with two volumes)? But if I have got to have a single volume of 500 pages, I am not in favor of this title, because the final portrait of Swann won't be there, and then my book won't fulfill the promise of the title. How would you like: *Avant que le jour soit levé* (I don't)? I have had to give up: *Les Intermittences du coeur* (original title), *Les Colombes poignardées*, *Le Passé intermittent*, *L'Adoration perpétuelle*, *Le Septième ciel*, *A l'Ombre des jeunes filles en fleur*, which however can be used as titles for chapters in the third volume. I told you, didn't I, that *Du Côté de chez Swann* is an allusion to the two ways or *côtés* at Combray. . . . P.S. —Would you like: *Jardins dans une tasse de thé*, or *L'Age des noms*, as a title for the first? For the second: *L'Age des mots*? For the third: *L'Age des choses*? What I should prefer would be: *Charles Swann*, but with some indication that all of Swann is not there: *Premiers crayons de Charles Swann*." The problem was obviously a very delicate one, and months passed before Proust was able to fix on *Du Côté de chez Swann*, *Le Côté de Guermantes*, and *Le Temps retrouvé*.

The proofs were even more of a problem, involving long hours of hard work as well as speculation. Proust corrected them as they came in, without returning any. He changed sentences he disliked, canceled and added passages, filled the margins with manuscript, pasted more manuscript at the top, the bottom, and the sides. Suddenly, reviewing his work, he exclaimed, "I have written a new book on the proofs," as indeed he had. But was this quite fair to Grasset? Should he not offer his publisher more money? If so, how much? Was it, in any case, a good idea to keep the proofs until the whole set had arrived? Should he not rather return some? How many should he return at one time? Again he consulted Vaudoyer.

The dates for the proofs and the charges for corrections were fixed with or without Vaudoyer's advice. In the course of time Proust began sending duplicate proofs to a few of his friends. He sent a set to Robert, urging him to pick out the dull passages, which could then be excised or, better still, put in as footnotes. But Robert, who read with the greatest enthusiasm, found nothing dull at all. He did, however, suggest that the episode of sadism might be toned down and that the volume might be more unified and more digestible if it stopped with "Combray." Proust could not very well accept either suggestion. He felt that the sadism was necessary preparation for similar episodes later in the novel; he felt that he had to include in his first volume chapters quite different in subject if he was to show the versatility of his talent and keep his book from disintegrating into a series of detached episodes. Still a compromise was possible and he proceeded to work one out. He definitely accepted a division of the novel into three volumes instead of two. By so doing, he was able to cut out something like 200 pages from the first volume (meanwhile adding to it, as a conclusion, a few pages from the middle of the second). Unfortunately it was in some respects a thoroughly bad compromise, as Proust himself, and Robert for that matter, fully realized.

Lucien Daudet, who also read the proofs, was quite as enthusiastic as Robert, his suggestions being confined to matters of detail. He noticed, for example, that some of the flowers in the hawthorn passage grew out of season, and that Françoise served chickens the same day she killed them. "As to the flowers," Proust replied, "I assure you I have many doubts; thus in the first version of the hawthorn passage (which appeared in *Le Figaro*) there were wild roses along the same road. But having found in Bonnier's *Botany* that wild roses don't bloom until later, I corrected the passage so that it reads in the book 'which one could see some weeks later, etc.' As for the verbena and the heliotrope, it is true that Bonnier gives June to October as the blooming season for one, June to August for the other! But since Bonnier is concerned with wild flowers, I thought (and a florist I wrote to assured me I was right) that in a garden (not in a hedge like the haws and the wild roses) they could be made to bloom as early as May when hawthorns are still in flower. Since they can't, what can I substitute? Would mignonette and jasmine be all right or should I put in something else?" In a second letter Proust added: "I have found the passage about the chicken, and you are right, it does say the same day. But I don't know if I can do anything about it, because my illness has now taken the form of making me hesitate for months about words without being able to change them."

The heavy schedule of work inevitably affected Proust both physically and emotionally. He lost weight; he found himself less able to endure the anguish at home. "I told you, I believe, that during the last few months my health has suffered a profound alteration," he wrote to Robert. "And at the same time, just as I am in no condition to bear it, I have been overwhelmed by a great affliction, which is constantly taking new forms." In August he went to Cabourg, with his valet and the cause of his affliction, the two Agostinellis, but—how could it have been otherwise? —his emotional disturbances persisted and he talked daily of going home. Finally he did go, on the spur of the moment. One afternoon, when he was out riding with Agostinelli, he suddenly decided to catch the train at Trouville and to take his secretary along with him. Madame Agostinelli, somewhat disconcerted no doubt, was left to make her way back with the valet. Proust counted on resting in Paris for a few days and then taking another trip, perhaps with Agostinelli alone, but he soon found that he was in no shape to move. He shaved off his beard, perhaps to make himself look younger, and settled down to a winter of anguish.

V

The proofs were almost done but the advance publicity remained. Proust wanted as much of this as possible. In one way or another he arranged for advance notices in several newspapers—little puffs suggesting that an important book was about to appear. The arrangements with *Gil Blas* were typical. Proust went to the editorial offices one night to call on Blum; a few days afterwards he asked for a puff. "It embarrasses me very much to ask you for this," he added. "My dear friend, I have spent my life begging people not to talk about me . . . and now in deference to my publisher I am begging for a 'literary indiscretion'. . . . Naturally I had no idea that I should have to ask you for this when I was at *Gil Blas* the other evening. I didn't see Grasset until two days later." Subsequently he invited Blum to the Boulevard Haussmann, described the novel to him, and even tried to read aloud a few sample pages. When his voice proved unequal to the strain, he had Blum continue. He listened attentively to the serious passages and laughed at the comic ones, his whole body shaking and his face aglow. Blum published the puff and also one of the excerpts that Proust was now sending out to the newspapers—the passage about the soirée at Madame de Saint-Euverte's, which *Le Figaro* had once rejected as too long.

The puffs and the excerpts were, however, only part of the publicity. Through Madame Scheikévitch, Proust arranged for a long interview in *Le Temps*; through other friends he arranged for a series of flattering articles by means of which he perhaps hoped to mold public opinion and assure his book a large audience. Lucien Daudet was to do one for *Le Figaro* (though a message from the Empress Eugénie was required to get it accepted uncut), Cocteau one for *Excelsior*, and Maurice Rostand (son of the dramatist) one for *Comoedia*. The interview in *Le Temps* appeared on November 12, 1913, a few days before the novel's publication. The reporter, Elie Joseph Bois, described his visit to the bedroom on the Boulevard Haussmann, described the pale face and feverish eyes of the author, described *Du Côté de chez Swann*, which he had tried to read at a single sitting.

"Sometimes one is ready to say: 'Enough!' " Bois remarked, "as though one were talking with a surgeon who refuses to pass over a single detail of an operation; but one does not say, 'Enough!' " He went on to the interview proper in which he reproduced Proust's comments. Nearly all of them were unfortunate comments, for Proust chose to dwell on the more abstruse (and least popular) aspects of his work. He talked about his treatment of time and its relation to character, about his strange conception of involuntary memory—talked, in fact, as if he were introducing a book on metaphysics.

Proust himself found fault with the published interview only because it was not quite full enough. As far as it went he was pleased with it, and he wanted to make sure that it was quoted by other newspapers. He wrote Blum; he wrote a particularly urgent letter to Calmette. "I am a little disturbed," he said, ". . . to find that *Le Figaro* is the *only* newspaper partly concerned with literature which has not announced my book. Perhaps, in an echo, it could call attention to the *Temps* interview. You are aware that, when my work is not serious, I am by no means eager to have it discussed. But this book is really important. Is *Le Figaro* serving its best interests by minimizing its contributors and by refusing to give them their full stature (I mean literary stature), which is accorded them elsewhere? If you decide to give me an echo, I hope that the adjectives 'subtle' and 'delicate' won't appear in it and that you won't mention *Les Plaisirs et les jours.*"

Three days later *Du Côté de chez Swann* was released. But Proust, apparently experiencing a new twinge of anguish at home, scarcely had time to think of his book. It occurred to him that he might escape his misery by traveling or by settling down in some isolated spot far away. He remembered hearing that at a place called Caprarola in Italy, though he could not be quite sure of the name, the palace of a Cardinal Farnese was for rent. Perhaps he should take it, perhaps he should leave for Italy at once. He wrote to Vaudoyer for information. "Alas," he said, "even at the very moment my book appears, I am thinking of something quite different."

CHAPTER XV

Du Côté de chez Swann

I

PROUST'S NOVEL is the story of a thoughtful young hero who seeks to understand and evaluate his experience and incidentally to find a vocation. It is the story of a quest that ultimately leads him to involuntary memory. But in Du Côté de chez Swann, which in 1913 comprised approximately a third of the whole, it cannot be said that the hero makes very much progress. He gets started in the opening chapter, called "Combray"; he learns something about his environment and he begins thinking about such matters as love, society, and a literary career. But in the second chapter, "Un Amour de Swann," he does not appear at all, and in the third, "Noms de pays: le nom," his experiences are so disjointed that one cannot be entirely sure what he is up to. Thus when read by itself apart from the rest of the novel, Du Côté de chez Swann is bound to seem more episodic than it actually is. Proust was afraid of this, and hence perhaps dragged in, somewhat prematurely in the first pages, an episode of involuntary memory.

These first pages—which Humblot found so distasteful—are designed as a general introduction to the novel. The narrator-hero—or Marcel, as he is afterwards twice called—sometimes awakens soon after he had gone to sleep and for an instant supposes that he is in one of the other beds he slept in years before in Combray or Balbec or Paris or Doncières or Venice. Generally, when he makes this mistake, he stays awake the greater part of the night recalling experiences connected with that other bedroom—for example, the good-night kiss that his mother gave him, or failed to give him, in the bedroom at Combray. The story of the kiss follows, more or less as in *Jean Santeuil*, except that the family guest is now Swann and the family servant now Françoise. The introduction is so far an entirely adequate and happy one. The reader learns many of the things he needs to know about the principal scenes of the novel and the characters who are to appear first. Before he is well aware of what is happening, he has drifted into the story of the hero's childhood. "Combray" is already under way. But suddenly the reader finds himself back where he started when Proust interrupts the story with a second and, at this point, quite superfluous introduction. The passage, one of the most famous in the novel, is pretty clearly out of place.

Proust begins this second introduction by contrasting intellectual memory, which reveals nothing important about the past, with involuntary memory, which reveals, in a kind of mystic vision, the past as it actually existed. He then gives a long illustration. Many years after the episode of the kiss, Marcel is drinking tea with his mother and dipping in the tea pieces of a cake called a *madeleine*. An image associated with the taste emerges from his subconscious—an image of the madeleine, moistened with tea, that his Aunt Léonie used to give him at Combray when he went to see her on Sunday mornings. In an instant the past— his childhood, his life at Combray—is recreated for him. He sees Aunt Léonie's bedroom and the old grey house and the town and the country roads beyond it. The past, apparently dead for ever, has suddenly come to life again. But, one inevitably asks, if Marcel is dependent on such experiences for his memories, how does it happen that without one, or at least without an experience clearly identified as one, he has already remembered so circumstantially his mother's kiss? How does it happen that he is afterwards able to recreate events in the life of Swann that took place before he himself was born? There can be no really satisfactory answer to these questions. The truth of the matter is that involuntary memory is at best a rather dubious conception and that its appearance at this point in the novel is in any case decidedly arbitrary.

II

Once Proust gets away from theories and back to the story of "Combray," the structure of the novel, or at least part of it, begins to become apparent. He is outlining the world of his hero's childhood, which is also, as it turns out, the world of his maturity. He is adroitly and methodically introducing his hero to the things and people he is to be chiefly concerned with in later years. Thus, though the scene is the country, he has Marcel learn something about snobbery and sadism and men of letters and the theatre and the Jews, about Charlus and Bergotte and Legrandin and 'Bloch. By the time the chapter ends, Marcel has caught at least a glimpse of the kind of life he is destined to lead. His experience, in so far as he can now assimilate it, is already complete.

"Combray," in fact, is the first cycle in a series of cycles, and as such contains all the elements of the chapters that follow it. But even within "Combray" the movement is cyclic; each section of the chapter contains the elements that make up the chapter as a whole. Such characters as Swann, Vinteuil, Odette, and the Duchesse de Guermantes are introduced toward the beginning; afterwards they appear again, alternately, at more or less regular intervals. Each time they reappear the hero learns a little more about them. At first they are not much more than names to him. The Duchesse de Guermantes is scarcely distinguishable from other members of her historic family; Vinteuil is merely a neighbor. But gradually, with successive appearances, they become more distinct. The Duchesse de Guermantes is seen at close range when she attends a wedding in the village church; Vinteuil is seen several times over a period of years—when he modestly refuses to play his own compositions, when he shrinks from his friends because his daughter has formed a lesbian attachment, and when he finally dies of shame. In both cases, however, Marcel's knowledge is still obviously fragmentary. He has not yet even talked with the Duchesse de Guermantes. He has not yet discovered that Vinteuil is the composer of the sonata with the "little phrase" that once captivated Swann; this discovery, like so many others, is reserved for a later cycle of Marcel's experience.

The chief element in the chapter, however, is Combray itself. It is emphasized at the beginning and, in the successive cycles that follow, it is never allowed to drop out of sight for very long. Combray is both a setting and a group of people. It is the Illiers of Proust's childhood or at least a provincial town very much like Illiers—a physical environment in which the chief landmarks are a house, a church, a park, and a river. It is also a group of people native to this environment. The most prominent are Aunt Léonie and Françoise, but there are many others— Eulalie, Madame Goupil, the hero's grandfather, the Curé, the kitchen maid, the grocer's boy. . . . One is tempted to include in the list Madame Sazerat's dog.

The setting is described in a series of passages carefully spaced throughout the chapter. First (inevitably first since it is suggested by the episode of the madeleine) comes a passage on Aunt Léonie's room, in which the hero describes not only the atmosphere, the characteristic conglomeration of smells, but even the lime blossoms used to make Aunt Léonie's *tisane*.

The drying of the stems had twisted them into a fantastic trellis, in whose intervals the pale flowers opened, as though a painter had arranged them there, grouping them in the most decorative poses. The leaves, which had lost or altered their own appearance, assumed those instead of the most incongruous things imaginable, as though the transparent wings of flies or the blank sides of labels or the petals of roses had been collected and pounded, or interwoven as birds weave the material for their nests. A thousand trifling little details—the charming prodigality of the chemist—details which would have been eliminated from an artificial preparation, gave me, like a book in which one is astonished to read the name of a person whom one knows, the pleasure of finding that these were indeed real lime-blossoms, like those I had seen, when coming from the train, in the

Avenue de la Gare, altered, but only because they were not
imitations but the very same blossoms, which had grown old.
And as each new character is merely a metamorphosis from
something older, in these little grey balls I recognized green buds
plucked before their time; but beyond all else the rosy, moony,
tender glow which lit up the blossoms among the frail forest of
stems from which they hung like little golden roses—marking,
as the radiance upon an old wall still marks the place of a
vanished fresco, the difference between those parts of the tree
which had and those which had not been "in bloom"—showed
me that these were petals which, before their flowering-time,
the chemist's package had embalmed on warm evenings of
spring. That rosy candle-light was still their color, but half-
extinguished and deadened in the diminished life which was
now theirs, and which may be called the twilight of a flower.

This may seem pure bravura, and there is certainly such an
element in nearly all the descriptive passages in the novel. We
often feel that Proust has either been carried away by his own
exuberance or has been determined at all costs to introduce a
baroque complexity into his art. He *is* complex, there can be
no doubt about it—wonderfully complex; and he is also precise,
almost microscopic in his observation. He overwhelms us with
profusion and interests us by showing us the little things, the
details overlooked by the casual observer. Thus in the passage on
the lime blossoms, we are invited to see the twisting of the stalks
as they dry, the different textures taken on by the dried leaves,
the gray of the unopened buds, and the faint pink of the blossoms.
It is the same in the later descriptions, where we are often permitted to examine what has never been noticed before and what
indeed without Proust might never have been noticed at all.
In the passage on the church there is the eccentric coloring in
the tapestries—the touch of red on the lips of Esther that has
strayed beyond the outline of the lips—and the eccentric lettering
on the tomb stones in the pavement. In the passage on the
storm near Roussainville there are the rain drops that fall exactly
parallel to one another, and in the passage on the Vivonne there
is the water lily that repeats so exactly its mechanical motions.
　Precise though it is, Proust's observation is never merely factual
or bare, for he records it in metaphor and so clothes it with the

splendor of his poetry. One metaphor follows another until, like the stems of the lime blossoms, they form a fantastic trellis, a tropical forest of imagery. Nearly every one is brilliant and appropriate. The solitary figure in a stained-glass window at the church is a king on a playing-card; the force that rearranges the letters in the Latin inscriptions on the pavement is a tide; the water lily that swings back and forth in the current is a ferryboat mechanically propelled. As often as not—and in this too there is a certain propriety—Proust relies on imagery of a special kind, that drawn from the fine arts. There are examples in the passage on the lime blossoms—the painter arranging flowers, the book that mentions a real person, and the old wall lit up by the radiance of a vanished fresco. Elsewhere in "Combray" the buzzing of the flies is the chamber music of summer, the color of the lilacs is that of Persian miniatures, the shower over Roussainville is the chastisement that strikes a village in the Old Testament. The water lily is at first a ferryboat but then becomes, significantly, one of the wretches in the *Inferno*,

> wretches whose peculiar torments, repeated indefinitely throughout eternity, aroused the curiosity of Dante, who would have inquired of them at greater length and in fuller detail from the victims themselves, had not Virgil, striding on ahead, obliged him to hasten after him at full speed, as I must hasten after my parents.

The effect of such imagery, so persistently used, is to enhance the beauty of what Proust is describing, to give it a special plastic perfection, to associate it with the masterpieces of all ages. "Combray"—and indeed the greater part of the novel—is in fact a masterpiece seen in the light of other masterpieces.

The setting is beautiful and Combray is a beautiful little world, a charming interlude in the more serious and more somber world of the novel. It is not, as one might expect, a stage in the hero's quest, a way of life that seems promising at first but turns out to be disillusioning. On the contrary, it remains beautiful. It is a paradise in the past, charming in itself and inhabited by charming people. They have their comic aspects, these people. They are all somewhat eccentric and hence open to ridicule of a genial sort; but this never for a moment robs them of their charm. Aunt Léonie, for example, is an invalid or hypochondriac, much preoccupied with her pepsin and her prayers, but with a natural craving for excitement. She simply must have it, she must invent it if necesary, and so she is constantly making up the most melodramatic, the most detestable stories about Françoise, her servant, and Eulalie, her most cherished visitor. She is even capable of looking forward with considerable satisfaction to some sort of dramatic catastrophe that will wipe out her whole family. The eccentricity is certainly an odd one, but it is never represented as anything less than amiable. Françoise has similar eccentricities, and yet she is the most admirable, the most indefatigable of servants. No one would think of regretting that she is so set against charity or so outrageously jealous of other servants or so consumed with hatred of both Eulalie and the chickens whose throats she must slit (for dinners now firmly fixed on the following day).

III

In his second chapter Proust turns to a second cycle of his hero's experience, but oddly the hero himself is nowhere directly involved. He is merely the narrator—one can scarcely call him the observer—who tells the story of "Un Amour de Swann" long after the events have taken place. One must assume that he learns something, about both love and society, by recalling these events, as he afterwards learns something by seeing what happens to Saint-Loup and Charlus. But the assumption is not very easy to make, especially at this point in the novel. For many readers the chapter will always seem to be a digression, and there is reason to believe that it is actually a survival from some stage or other in the evolution of Proust's manuscript when he was calling his hero Charles Swann. Thus it may well be, among other things at least, a kind of geological curiosity, a protruding stratum of early work.

Originally, it seems, Swann was another of Proust's self-portraits, and indeed in some respects he still is in "Un Amour de Swann." Like Proust, he is a man of independent wealth who is well received in aristocratic society. He suffers from a chronic complaint, eczema; he takes up, after a period of stagnation, the study of music, as Proust took up the study of architecture; he works in a desultory way on Vermeer, as Proust worked on Ruskin. Swann's habits, furthermore, are strangely nocturnal. Like Jean Santeuil, he rarely sees his mistress until after dark or, for that matter, after dinner. "He went to her only in the evenings," Proust says, "and knew nothing of how she spent her time during the day." Yet he apparently never spends a night at her house. This seems decidedly odd unless one supposes that Proust is really thinking of himself at a time when he slept during the day, dined with his parents, and then saw his friends in the evening.

In other respects, however—as one gathers from a hint in the novel itself and from passages in Proust's correspondence—Swann seems to be an idealized portrait of a man with whom Proust was once distantly acquainted, a certain Charles Haas. At least there is a definite though not a very close resemblance between the character and what is now known about the man. Haas is described as a remarkably successful social climber, a Jew of obscure origin and modest means who wormed his way into aristocratic society. He took advantage of his opportunities, as when, during the confusion caused by the siege of Paris, he got himself elected to the Jockey Club. He groomed himself carefully, affecting gray top hats lined with green leather, exactly like those worn by the Prince de Sagan; he rehearsed before a mirror in the afternoon his evening's repartee. Finally he acquired a manner so perfectly aristocratic that it seemed entirely effortless and casual. His conversation was detached and ironical, even at times rather dry and precise; nothing seemed to interest him less than social prestige. Some, though by no means all of this, appears in the character of Swann.

Since the chapter has more narrative interest than "Combray," its structure is necessarily simpler. There are two main subjects, love and society. They contrast with one another, for love is serious and society is comic. At the same time they supplement one another, for society provides the setting, or part of it, against which the story of love is acted out. The two sets of scenes alternate like fast and slow movements in the works of Baroque composers.

The story of Swann and Odette resembles in a general way the love stories in *Les Plaisirs et les jours* and in *Jean Santeuil*, but there are certain elements in it that are new in Proust's work. For one thing, the lovers now belong to quite different worlds. Swann is represented as socially and intellectually superior to his mistress, for here and elsewhere in the novel Proust associates love with condescension. On the other hand, the lovers have at least this in common, that they have both had quite sensational erotic careers. Swann has spent the greater part of his life pursuing women, often women of the humblest class. He has squandered his social credit in the process and turned, or tried to turn, all his friends into panders. Even during the early days of his association with Odette, he sees a good deal of "a little working girl, as fresh and plump as a rose," who often rides with him in his carriage and holds him in her arms until he reaches his destination. Odette is a prostitute, and it seems curious that so experienced a man as Swann does not immediately recognize her as such. It seems curious, too, that throughout the story she should be a regular member of an artistic *salon* which generally excludes women.

The first stage in the story (distinctly reminiscent of "Mélancolique villégiature") is devoted to the growth of love. Swann is flattered by Odette's attention, but otherwise quite indifferent to her. Her beauty even affects him with something like revulsion. "To give him any pleasure her profile was too sharp, her skin too delicate, her cheek-bones too prominent, her features too tightly drawn. Her eyes were fine, but so large that they seemed to be bending beneath their own weight, strained the rest of her face and always made her appear unwell or in an ill humor." Soon, however, he overcomes his revulsion as he associates her with works of art—first with a fragment of a Vinteuil sonata, different from the rest of the work, "dancing, pastoral, interpolated, episodic, belonging to another world." This fragment, this "little phrase," awakens his affection, as a national anthem awakens a man's love for his country. Later he is struck by her resemblance to the figure of Zipporah in Botticelli's Sistine fresco. He now identifies her with a work he admires, now sees her as a masterpiece "cast for once in a new, a different, an especially charming metal," now admits her to the world of his dreams. But he is not yet in love. It is only when he experiences anguish—when he misses her one evening and searches anxiously in the restaurants on the Boulevards for several hours, afraid that he has lost her—it is only then that love masters him completely. For love, in the novel as in *Les Plaisirs et les jours,* is usually a form of anguish, awakened by the lover's fear of losing a mistress to whom, under other circumstances, he might well be indifferent.

The rest of the story is devoted to Swann's anguish, for his mistress, once assured of his affection, inevitably grows cooler, and his fear of losing her inevitably revives. It is not simple, this anguish, for love and jealousy are never, Proust says, "single, continuous and individual passions."

> They are composed of an infinity of successive loves, of different jealousies, each of which is ephemeral, although by their uninterrupted multitude they give us the impression of continuity, the illusion of unity.

Swann suffers a series of calamities, each member of the series being very much like the others. Odette leaves him to go to the Opéra-Comique for the evening, to Pierrefonds for a few days, to Bayreuth for the season, and to the Near East for a year. She awakens his jealousy at different times and in different ways, for jealousy is the chief form that his anguish takes. Some of the incidents come from the stories of Madame S. and Françoise in *Jean Santeuil,* which may thus be regarded as preliminary sketches for the story of Odette. Like Jean, Swann is sometimes not so much a lover, at least in the accepted sense of the word, as a feverish detective, determined to find out what his mistress does when he is not with her and in fact what she has done in the past. Early in the story he analyzes the evidence he picks up, but without being able to reach a definite conclusion. The evidence is not quite good enough—his mistress may be innocent, or comparatively innocent, after all. As Jean Santeuil reads, through its transparent envelope, a letter Madame S. has given him to mail, so Swann reads a letter of Odette's. He discovers, from its contents, that Odette has lied to him and that she has surreptitiously received a man named Forcheville. The discovery is a painful one, but he cannot be sure that Forcheville is her lover. He can only wait until further evidence turns up.

"To be once in doubt," Othello says, "is once to be resolved." But there is nothing of the Renaissance hero in Swann, whose personality, like that of all Proust's lovers, is essentially a neurotic one. He is never resolved, even when, in the last pages, he gets evidence that is indisputably damaging. He can only go on probing and suffering—probing, in fact, for information that inevitably intensifies his suffering. In the final scenes his anguish is appropriately described in images of physical violence. Odette admits that she has had lesbian experiences "perhaps two or three times," and her words seem to carve "a cross upon the living tissues of his heart." The other admissions that follow are blows or sword wounds, excruciating not only at the time but long afterwards. "He marveled," Proust says, "at the terrible recreative power of his memory. It was only by the weakening of that generative force, whose fecundity diminishes as age creeps over one, that he could hope for a relaxation of his torments. But, as soon as the power that any one of Odette's sentences had to make Swann suffer seemed to be nearly exhausted, lo and behold another, one of those to which he had hitherto paid least attention, almost a new sentence, came to relieve the first, and to strike at him with undiminished force."

The story is a masterly one, magnificent in its psychology, magnificent especially perhaps in the passages Proust himself admired most, those devoted to Swann's final agony. It is, furthermore, a particularly devastating illustration of Proust's view that love is a form of neurosis. The hero is a man with a strange mental quirk, a kind of neurotic compulsion that makes him cling to what he is in danger of losing. Hence the attraction that the elusive Odette has for him; hence his jealousy and his suffering, which are essential elements in his attraction. Naturalists reduce love to sex; Proust reduces it to something altogether different but perhaps, under civilized conditions, equally fundamental. Swann may well be the archetype of the modern lover and neurosis the characteristic modern malady.

The society scenes are as brilliant as the love story they accompany, but quite different in tone. They are pure satiric comedy of a kind not easy to parallel in English literature, except perhaps in the older drama. The characters are perfectly individualized, yet all exhibit—as in, say, the *Volpone* of Ben Jonson— the same basic absurdity, here that of snobbishness. Their gyrations, simple or complex, are always seen to be governed by the immutable law that all men seek social advancement.

Early in the chapter much attention is given to the middle-class *salon* of Madame Verdurin, whose snobbishness takes the form of complacency. She pretends, since there is little else she can pretend, that the members of her circle, her "little nucleus," are the most cultivated and most brilliant people on earth. To laugh at their bad jokes is sometimes difficult, so she invents a symbolic form of laughter. To describe repeatedly the way in which music affects her is also difficult, so she invents for this too a symbolic scene, re-enacted each time her pianist sits down to play.

"No, no, no, not my sonata!" she screamed, "I don't want to be made to cry until I get a cold in the head, and neuralgia all down my face, like last time; thanks very much, I don't intend to repeat that performance; you are all very kind and considerate; it is easy to see that none of you will have to stay in bed for a week."

Madame Verdurin is one of the most brilliant caricatures in fiction, and the members of the "little nucleus"—the Cottards, Brichot, Saniette, and the rest—are often good too. In the later volumes of the novel, where Proust is able to devote more space to them, they become even better, certainly one of the finest group studies in fiction.

The aristocracy appears only once, toward the end of the chapter, when Swann attends a soirée at Madame de Saint-Euverte's. The scene is introduced by one of those particularly florid descriptive passages that, from time to time, the author permits himself. The imagery, still drawn predominantly from the arts, is here riotous, playful, and precious. The footmen in their brilliant liveries are headsmen in certain Renaissance pictures, or saints in niches, or sacristans from Goya, or angels or sentinels

looking out "from the tower of dungeon or cathedral, for the
approach of the enemy or for the hour of Judgment." Even the
monocles of the fine gentlemen suggest odd fancies and delicate
stylistic arabesques. The monocle of General de Froberville is "a
monstrous wound which it might have been glorious to receive
but which it was certainly not decent to expose"; that of the
Marquis de Bréauté is a slide with a specimen prepared for the
microscope; and that of Monsieur de Palancy, whose head resembles a carp's, is a "purely symbolical fragment of the glass wall
of his aquarium, a part intended to suggest the whole which recalled to Swann, a fervent admirer of Giotto's Vices and Virtues at
Padua, that Injustice by whose side a leafy bough evokes the
idea of the forests that enshroud his secret lair."

Once the arabesques are over, it appears that the snobbishness
of the aristocracy is not essentially different from that of the
middle class. Fine ladies whose position is assured confine themselves complacently to their exclusive circle and treat outsiders
with the highest degree of insolence. The example given is the
Princesse des Laumes, the future Duchesse de Guermantes. On
the other hand, ladies not quite so fine are constantly trying to
establish relations with ladies finer than themselves. The best
example here is the Marquise de Gallardon who pursues the
Princesse des Laumes, upsetting all her neighbors in the process.
For the Marquise seeks social advancement, whatever she may
say or think, and is merely illustrating a general law when she
presses her cousin with the most urgent invitation.

IV

In the final chapter, "Noms de pays: le nom," Proust returns to
his narrator-hero, Marcel, and begins what should be easily recognizable as another cycle of Marcel's experience. But since the
chapter is incomplete (some 200 pages having been cut from it
at the last minute) it seems to be not so much a cycle as an account of three different things, at best rather loosely related: a
doctrine, a love story, and some visits to the Bois de Boulogne.
Nowhere else in the volume is the narrative quite so confusing.

The doctrine—that of the vagaries of the imagination—is a

central one in the novel as in all of Proust's work. It is used, here as elsewhere, to explain why the hero too often fails to find what he seeks. He is too imaginative, too much inclined to promise himself more than reality can provide. Thus, when he thinks of traveling, he permits his imagination to play about the places he might visit, such as Balbec, Parma, and Florence. He forms mental pictures, arbitrarily simplified and colored by the names to which they are attached—pictures to which nothing in the real world corresponds. Balbec is not a town like other towns, but a wild fishing settlement on a desolate coast where waves surge "round a church built in the Persian manner." Parma is "compact and glossy, violet-tinted, soft": it owes something to the three consonants in its name and something to memories of Stendhal's *Chartreuse*. Florence is a supernatural city that emerges "from the impregnation by certain vernal scenes of what I supposed to be, in its essentials, the genius of Giotto." Earlier in "Combray" the hero has already formed precisely the same kind of mental picture in dreaming of the Duc and Duchesse de Guermantes.

> I knew that they were real personages who did actually exist, [the hero says,] but whenever I thought about them I pictured them to myself either in tapestry, as was the "Coronation of Esther" which hung in our church, or else in changing, rainbow colors, as was Gilbert the Bad in his window, where he passed from cabbage green, when I was dipping my fingers in the holy water stoup, to plum blue when I had reached our row of chairs, or again altogether impalpable, like the image of Geneviève de Brabant, ancestress of the Guermantes family, which the magic lantern sent wandering over the curtains of my room or flung aloft upon the ceiling—in short, always wrapped in the mystery of the Merovingian age, and bathed, as in a sunset, in the orange light which glowed from the resounding syllable "antes."

There is no episode of travel until later in the story, so that in this one case the hero's disappointment is postponed. But in the present volume he does see the Duchesse de Guermantes long enough at least to realize that she is quite unlike the figure of his dreams. She is not of course bathed in orange light at all; she is just a woman with a red face and a large nose.

The love story in "Noms de pays: le nom" may be described as a more polished and more significant version of the Marie Kossichef story in *Jean Santeuil*. Marcel is now an adolescent Swann, another and somewhat different example of the anguish that love causes and the illusions that it fosters. Marcel must see Gilberte —he is never happy away from her. He must establish a closer intimacy, he must wring from her a confession of love. The most memorable passage is one published earlier in *Le Figaro*—the passage in which Marcel, afraid that rain will keep him from going to the park and seeing Gilberte, anxiously studies the balcony outside his window. Marcel's hopes become as golden as the stone surface when the sun strikes it; but once in the presence of Gilberte, he is as unhappy as before. For the intimacy does not develop, the confession of love is never forthcoming. Sometimes he recognizes that Gilberte is indifferent, but more often, since the illusions of love are strong, he persists in explaining her indifference away. Each new meeting holds out the promise, however vague, that the confession is about to be made.

Before the story of Gilberte is quite finished, the scene shifts to the Bois de Boulogne, where the hero goes to admire Gilberte's mother, the dazzling Madame Swann. Then suddenly years elapse. The hero, by this time approaching old age, goes to the Bois again and searches in vain for the elegance he found there in his youth. The handsome victorias of other days have been replaced by motor cars; the women's hats, once "so low-crowned as to seem no more than garlands," are now immense and ornate, "covered with fruits and flowers and all manner of birds." The passage, undoubtedly the one that Proust wrested from its context in the second volume, is obviously patchwork. But it provides an ending of a sort. It is properly nostalgic, somewhat in the manner of "Combray," and at the same time properly pessimistic, for it illustrates Proust's doctrine of the imagination. The hero fails to find what he seeks in the Bois because it no longer exists and because, in any case, it never completely existed except in his own mind. He begins "to understand how paradoxical it is to seek in reality for the pictures that are stored in one's memory, which must inevitably lose the charm that comes to them from memory itself and from their not being apprehended by the senses."

V

The patchwork ending is merely another of several structural oddities that make *Du Côté de chez Swann* the most episodic of Proust's volumes and hence perhaps the most puzzling to the casual reader. The oddities are a little too glaring. "Combray" is in many ways an admirable introductory chapter, but its tone is not that of the chapters that follow. "Un Amour de Swann" is extremely brilliant, but it interrupts, in a disturbing way, the main story. "Noms de pays: le nom" is a fragment, or more properly a group of fragments: it scarcely stands by itself. Proust wanted in this first volume to illustrate the versatility of his talent and he certainly succeeded in doing so. But the price was a high one (as he was soon to discover when the reviews began to appear).

On the other hand, the separate episodes that make up the volume are among the finest in the whole novel, and show Proust at a particularly happy stage of his development. He is, as he had always been, both an impressionistic and a reflective writer; he is remarkable for both his sensibility and his intelligence. In the volume at hand his sensibility is quite properly dominant. "Un Amour de Swann" is a profoundly significant story, designed to illustrate a theory of love; from the incidental generalizations that are scattered through it, a treatise on love might well be assembled. But the generalizations are never obtrusive and seldom more than a few sentences long. The story is after all a story, a psychological one, concerned with the successive feelings and impressions of a man in love. Even the passage on place names in "Noms de pays: le nom" is not so much an abstract discussion as an account of a stage in the hero's mental life. This emphasis on the immediate and the concrete, this exercise of the sensibility, is indeed to be found in the later volumes, but not so consistently as in *Du Côté de chez Swann*. For in subsequent revisions of his manuscript Proust was inclined to revert to earlier habits, illustrated, for example, in *Jean Santeuil*. He was inclined to amplify the reflective passages, sometimes to the point that he became more of an essayist or philosopher than a novelist.

CHAPTER XVI

The Aftermath

I

PROUST HAD ARRÁNGED for three flattering articles on *Du Côté de chez Swann*—one by Cocteau in *Excelsior* (which appeared on November 23, 1913), one by Lucien Daudet in *Le Figaro* (November 27), and one by Maurice Rostand in *Comoedia* (December 26). The three articles appeared like rockets, splendid, dazzling, and luminous; they contained no suggestion that the novel was anything but an unqualified success. Cocteau called it "a monumental miniature, filled with mirages, with gardens shading into one another, with an interplay of space and time, with fresh sweeping brush strokes in the manner of Manet." Daudet described it as "an extraordinary manifestation of intelligence in the twentieth century," and ranked it with the masterpieces of other ages. Rostand specifically assigned Proust a place beside Shakespeare and Dante. The articles were certainly publicity of a sort; on the other hand, they could scarcely be taken as anything but what they were—extravagant effusions by the author's personal friends.

Meanwhile Proust was angling for one of the annual literary prizes, preferably that offered by the Académie Goncourt. He undoubtedly felt that a prize, if he could get one, would be the best publicity of all. Through Robert he tried to influence two members of the Goncourt committee, but the first reports were not encouraging. At the same time Lucien Daudet was independently trying to influence two other members of the committee, though he neglected to tell Proust what he was up to—a circumstance that Proust, who knew that something was going on, found highly suspicious. When all the prizes, including the Goncourt, went to other books, Proust could not help wondering and brooding. Reluctantly he came to the conclusion that Daudet had deliberately betrayed him. "I was very much hurt," he told Daudet, "when I discovered that you had been to see Messieurs X and Y (whom you never see) just to make sure that they would not under any circumstances give me the Goncourt Prize."

The publicity had not been a howling success; the first important review—that of Paul Souday in *Le Temps* (December 10)—was a distinct disappointment, in view of the fact that Proust seems to have taken steps to intercede with *Le Temps* in advance. Souday was not altogether unfavorable; he was simply obtuse. It can scarcely have occurred to him that the book presented any special difficulties or that, in passing judgment on it, he needed to apply any other standard than that of plain common sense. At the outset the critic remarked that the volume was long, very long, unfortunately long in fact; that the sentences were long too, and therefore hard reading; that the grammar was not always impeccable, particularly where subjunctives were concerned. He duly illustrated. Nevertheless it seemed clear to him that the author had talent—a luxuriant imagination, a delicate sensibility, and a keen sense of observation. He could describe landscapes, a hedge of hawthorns, for example. He could delineate the feelings of his hero—the disillusionment of the child when he sees the Duchesse de Guermantes for the first time, the nostalgia of the grown man when he returns to the Bois de Boulogne. But unfortunately there was too much of everything. There were too many characters (most of them completely insignificant) and too many episodes, including one, "Un Amour de Swann," that took up a good half of the volume. The plain fact of the matter was that the book was too detailed and too long-winded—rather like Ruskin and

Dickens perhaps, certainly more English than French. If it had been ruthlessly cut and given some kind of structure, it might have made a delightful little volume. Souday ended with the hope that in succeeding volumes the style would appear chastened, the narrative more orderly and concise.

Grasset was incensed by the review, and telephoned Proust as though he were announcing a declaration of war. Proust was incensed too, though less by the general strictures on his book than by the remarks about his bad grammar and inadequate command of the subjunctive. He could not help feeling that these remarks, obviously facetious, were based on what the critic must have recognized as misprints. A stiff letter to Souday seemed in order, and Proust promptly drafted one. He took pleasure in pointing out a misprint in the review itself. He showed that Souday, in using a Latin tag, had quoted, not from Horace as he supposed, but from Ovid. "I might add," Proust went on to say, "that the deplorable conditions under which I was obliged to correct the proofs of this book (conditions which do not concern the public, I know, and which it has every right to ignore) have resulted in my publishing a book filled with outrageous mistakes, but the very fact that they are outrageous shows quite clearly that they are not the mistakes of the author." The letter was not printed by *Le Temps*—it was not intended for publication; nevertheless Proust had the satisfaction of feeling that he had successfully scored Souday off.

The other reviewers, though on the whole less captious, did not otherwise react very differently from Souday. Nearly all of them thought of Proust as primarily an impressionist. They admitted that his account of his own sensations was remarkably thorough, but they were by no means sure that such an account was desirable in a novel. It was perhaps a form of egotism and as such rather morbid. In any case, it involved giving too much attention to minute details and thus impeding the flow of the narrative. None of the reviewers realized—or could very well have realized from the first volume—that the book had any structure at all, and few of them failed to point out some of its obvious structural weaknesses. They regarded it as a compilation of impressions—a remarkable compilation perhaps, but scarcely a novel.

Lucien Maury, writing in *La Revue politique et littéraire*

(December 27, 1913), dismissed Proust as an aesthete, a talented one no doubt, but by no means a genius. The critic refused to be impressed by a volume in which, as he said, four or five good, though not unusual, books had been haphazardly thrown together. Rachilde, in *Le Mercure de France* (January 16, 1914), complained that the author was so completely unselective that he had ruined what might have been a masterpiece and made even the most delightful passages seem dull. "I began reading this book with enthusiasm," Rachilde said, "I ended by throwing it down in horror, as a man might refuse to drug himself." Jean de Pierrefeu, in *Opinion* (January 24), tried hard to be fair but could not help pronouncing the book disconcerting and unhealthy. There was clearly something of the Narcissus in an author who devoted so much attention to the inner life. He was not a novelist at all but a "bacteriologist of the soul." André Chaumeix, in *Débats* (January 25), tried to balance Proust's faults against his merits. He was a formless, even a chaotic writer, unnecessarily complex in style and at times even ungrammatical. On the other hand, he was remarkably versatile and remarkably brilliant; individual passages certainly deserved the highest praise. "The reader wanders about," Chaumeix wrote in a sentence afterwards widely paraphrased, "in this strange and charming book as in a tangled and somewhat too magnificent forest, where he loses his way and where indeed there is no way at all, but where the foliage, the forestation, the most ordinary plants, the most fantastic shadows, and the subtle light all contribute to the enchantment."

By the end of January, 1914, Proust must have realized that by itself *Du Côté de chez Swann* was not completely intelligible and that he could answer his critics—or at least those who complained that he had no sense of form—only by publishing the rest of the novel. He was not inclined to write more, or many more, letters of protest, but when he heard privately remarks similar to those in the reviews, he expostulated as best he could. Thus when a fellow author said to him, "You put down everything," he explained at considerable length, at least in a letter to Robert Dreyfus. "Quite the contrary," Proust wrote, "I don't put down anything. He puts things down. Not once does a character of mine close a window, or wash his hands, or put on an overcoat, or introduce someone formally. If indeed there is anything new in the book, it is probably this, though I didn't intend it so; I am just too lazy to write down things that bore me."

On the whole, however, what Proust heard privately was considerably more favorable than what he read in the reviews. Both before and after the major reviews appeared, there were a number of people who were very enthusiastic about *Swann* and convinced that it was a masterpiece. One of them, the poet Francis Jammes, wrote Proust a flattering letter, which he afterwards proudly showed to most of his friends. Another, the producer Gabriel Astruc, also corresponded with Proust, and indeed undertook to be helpful. In a copy of the book he noted misprints, made comments, and identified characters. Proust was grateful for the checking of misprints—about which, by this time, he was rather sensitive—and surprised by the identifications. Yes, it was true, he wrote Astruc, that he had used Haas as his point of departure in drawing the character of Swann, though there were really no portraits in his book. He would like to tell Astruc some charming stories about Haas. He would like, furthermore, to help his new friend write a volume of memoirs, provided of course the whole matter could be kept a dark secret.

More surprising and even more gratifying than the letters from Jammes and Astruc was a letter from André Gide, who had finally and somewhat fortuitously become acquainted with *Swann*. Gide's journal, the N. R. F., had recently reviewed the book. Henri Ghéon, the reviewer, had exploded it on the ground that it was unselective and therefore, by definition, the antithesis of a work of art. Still Ghéon had been sufficiently interested in it to recommend it to another member of the N. R. F. group, Jacques Rivière, who in turn had recommended it to Gide. The man who the year before had been content to turn the pages had now begun actually reading them. He read with mounting enthusiasm, meanwhile searching his conscience. Even before he had finished, he had written Proust a very remarkable letter, at once an apology and a confession. "The rejection of this book will always be the greatest blunder made by the N. R. F.," he had said. Without sparing himself in the least and without attempting to mitigate his enormity, he had gone on to reveal that he had always thought

Proust a snob and a dilettante. In consequence he had scarcely had the decency to thumb through the manuscript that Proust had submitted to him.

Proust replied in a letter equally warm and equally characteristic, but by no means equally candid. He assured Gide that the whole course of events had been providential and that without the rejection by the N. R. F. he would never have experienced the ineffable pleasure of receiving Gide's apology. He had, he said, abandoned his first publisher (presumably Fasquelle) and turned to the N. R. F. partly at least because he had wanted to make sure that his novel would be read by Gide. The beauty of the relationship established in these letters boded ill for Grasset.

II

Under other circumstances it would have been exciting to be alternately attacked and flattered day after day, but Proust was too much preoccupied with his domestic difficulties to feel the excitement very keenly. On the day the letter from Jammes arrived he described himself as almost mad with anxiety. "At this moment," he wrote Astruc in December, 1913, "I am going through the most painful period of my life since the death of my mother. And though you are kind enough to say that my book has helped you, it has not helped me. Its success, if it has any, must inevitably leave me quite cold since I am incapable of feeling any pleasure whatsoever." To cheer himself up, he bought a player piano and sent out for a roll—a piano arrangement—of Beethoven's Fourteenth Quartet. Unfortunately he found that there was no such roll. In ten years, it seems, the company had never had a request for one from any of its fifteen thousand clients.

In January, 1914, Gide wrote again, announcing that the N. R. F. was now eager to publish Proust's novel. The firm wanted to bring out, at its own expense, the second and third volumes; it was willing to take over the first volume as soon as Grasset's edition was sold. "I speak," Gide said, "in the name of eight fervent admirers of your book." Proust had already had, or thought he had had, a somewhat similar offer from Fasquelle. This time he was very much tempted. But he realized that he was indebted to Grasset, who had after all accepted a book that three other publishers had refused to touch. He realized too that, even if he did leave Grasset, he could not without appearing mercenary accept better terms elsewhere. In any case, he needed time to think the matter over and to see if, for example, his contract with Grasset was actually binding for the second and third volumes. For a while he was half inclined to start characteristically devious negotiations with Grasset, through Hahn and another friend, the Princesse de Polignac. But in the end, when the negotiations were direct and when Grasset generously offered to let him leave if he insisted on doing so, Proust decided to remain. He thought that his second volume might be ready by October, though as yet only the pages unused in *Swann* were printed. The rest of the manuscript was not even completely typed.

He settled down to work again, but just at this moment his nerves were completely shattered by a final catastrophe at home. His secretary, his beloved Agostinelli, left him. Proposing to make his fortune in aviation and using as capital money he had earned in Proust's service, the young man entered a flying school on the Riviera. Oddly enough, he adopted the pseudonym of Marcel Swann. Proust, tortured by loneliness, could not persuade him to return, though he tried everything including threats. "If you ever have the misfortune to be involved in an airplane accident," he once wrote Agostinelli, "you can assure your wife that I will not help her, or befriend her, or indeed give her a single sou." But Agostinelli, apparently glad to escape from his prison on the Boulevard Haussmann, remained on the Riviera.

Proust languished and suffered, distracting himself when he could by working on *Le Côté de Guermantes* or arranging further publicity for *Du Côté de chez Swann*. He hired a new typist and tried to revise the clean copy that the typist turned out. He placed an article written by his old friend, Jacques-Emile Blanche, an article answering unfavorable criticism of *Swann*. It was to appear in *L'Echo de Paris*, preferably after the Easter holidays, when it had the best chance of attracting attention. It did appear after Easter. Proust then addressed himself to the task of seeing that other newspapers "echoed" the article. He drafted echoes, praising both himself and Blanche, had Grasset copy them for fear that his own handwriting would be recognized, then sent them to Le Figaro, Gil Blas, Débats, and other papers. He assured his friends that Grasset was paying for the echoes—as indeed he was, but by arrangement Proust invariably reimbursed Grasset.

In May he must have begun sending Grasset his manuscript, for the printing of Le Côté de Guermantes was about to get under way. At the same time he offered the manuscript to the N. R. F. magazine for prior publication, if the magazine was willing to accept so long a work. It was not, and so he singled out for the June and July issues a number of episodes—a hundred pages altogether—as different as possible from anything in Du Côté de chez Swann, for he was still interested in displaying his versatility. While he was working on the proofs he so far forgot his anguish as to cancel and add right and left, to do in fact a very thorough job of revision, the expenses of which he afterwards tried to pay.

Then, just as the June issue of the N. R. F. was ready for release, another, even greater catastrophe occurred. Agostinelli took off from the field in Antibes on his second solo flight, while his wife and his brother watched him from the ground. He soared into the air, daringly left the course prescribed for student pilots, and ventured over the Baie des Anges. Then suddenly, as he started a turn, he seemed to lose control of the machine, which veered over and plunged into the sea about a quarter of a mile from shore. For several minutes the wreck could be seen half floating on the water, and Agostinelli could be heard crying for help; but before boats could reach the spot both the plane and the pilot had sunk. The body was not recovered until eight days later.

It is difficult to know exactly how Proust took the news unless one can suppose that he described his own feelings in the chapter of his novel devoted to his hero's grief for Albertine. The real and the fictitious characters, Agostinelli and Albertine, certainly died in much the same way; Proust and the Marcel of the novel behaved, as far as one can determine, in much the same way too—experiencing a long period of suffering, fighting against it, fighting against ceasing to suffer, and finally feeling the balm of oblivion. The stories are similar, yet the story in the novel is as different from the real story as Proust could possibly make it. It is designed to illustrate general psychological laws; it is the story, not so much of his, but of any man's grief, an attempt to describe a universal human experience. All one can definitely say is that, after Agostinelli's death, Proust suffered anguish as intense and prolonged as the anguish he had suffered while Agostinelli was still with him at the Boulevard Haussmann.

He managed to send out the final excerpts for the N. R. F., but otherwise stopped working; he wanted to think only of his dead friend. When the funeral on the Riviera was held he sent a wreath, a magnificent one costing 400 francs but even so not entirely satisfactory, for the Agostinellis were disturbed to find that it was not made of artificial flowers. Afterwards he watched with horror as the family fought for the money found in the dead man's pockets, some 5000 or 6000 francs that had undoubtedly once been Proust's. He heard that someone, either the father or brother of the dead man, was trying to forestall the widow's claim by telling the Prince de Monaco that she was, after all, only a mistress; he asked Straus, who knew the Prince, to present her case. When she turned up in Paris, he let her stay in the apartment and apparently helped her find employment, without however recommending her very highly to his friends. He was possibly afraid of the scandalous stories she might tell. Later he did what he could to help Agostinelli's father and brother.

Proust spoke of these activities in letters to his friends. He spoke of his grief too, but more guardedly and never in such a way as to show fully what the tragedy had actually meant to him. Thus, in letters to Gide, he remarked that since he was so very unhappy at the moment he must suppose that he had liked Agostinelli better than all his other friends. "He was a boy with a delightful mind," Proust said, "but it was by no means for this that I liked him. I was slow to notice it, not so slow as he was however. I discovered his ability, so wonderfully incompatible with everything he was, discovered it with amazement, but it added nothing to my affection. After I had discovered it, I had only a certain pleasure in pointing it out to him. But he died before he really knew what he was, and even before he had become so completely. The whole thing is involved with circumstances so frightful that, already shattered, I don't know how I am going to endure such grief." He went on to say that he had no idea when, if ever, he could get back to work; the proofs of *Le Côté de Guermantes*, which were now coming in daily, lay unopened in his room. In a letter to Montesquiou, he wrote in much the same vein. "As in the phenomenon of supersaturation, everything that before was fluid and supportable now presses in upon me like an inescapable vise. . . . I have just strength enough to console the widow even though I myself am inconsolable."

Proust was certainly preoccupied with his grief, yet there was one other thing he could scarcely afford to ignore: his investments. All Europe was in turmoil, war was coming, stocks were steadily going down. His losses were already alarming and he was determined to sell what he had at the first rise in the market; but the rise never came. Feeling for the first time in his life that he would have to earn something, he wrote—or so he said later—to Flers, who had succeeded Calmette at *Le Figaro*, asking for any kind of journalistic work. Flers was not encouraging, but he did offer to publish serially a substantial chapter from *Le Côté de Guermantes*, and on July 15 got so far as to announce the chapter under the title of "Odette mariée." But before publication could begin, France was at war. Proust sold some of his stocks, without however being able to lay his hands on the proceeds, and otherwise involved himself in disastrous financial transactions. It seemed clear to him that he was a ruined man, and though his grief for his friend was still as intense as ever, it now necessarily alternated with grief for losses even more material.

CHAPTER XVII

The Early War Years

I

DESPONDENT, ill, still stunned by the death of his friend and the collapse of the stock market, Proust was not at first deeply disturbed by the outbreak of war. After seeing his brother off for the front, he lingered in Paris for a while to look after his sister-in-law and niece, but as soon as they were safely out of the city he began considering his usual summer excursion to Cabourg. He would have preferred to go to Nice, where he could visit the grave of Agostinelli, and he might well have done so if he had not heard that the trip would take thirty hours. As it turned out, however, the trip to Cabourg was almost as arduous, the train on which he traveled being eighteen hours late. He put up as usual at the Grand Hôtel, where he had first known Agostinelli. He suffered constantly as, reminded of his friend by everything he saw, even by the sea itself, he thought back over those happy days; he wished he could die.

Inevitably, however, his attention was diverted toward the present as the German armies moved steadily forward, as public hysteria rose, and as society people, afraid that the fall of Paris was imminent, swarmed into Cabourg. One of them, the Comtesse Greffulhe, called on Proust when he was too ill to receive her.

She was accompanied by a man who failed to leave his name—Montesquiou, as it later appeared. The poet had suffered incredible indignities in escaping from the capital: he had ridden for twenty-four hours in a third-class coach and had even carried his own valise. But the Greffulhes and the Montesquious were not the only new arrivals. The wounded came too, by scores and then by hundreds, invading even the Grand Hôtel itself. When he was well enough to get up, Proust visited them and distributed presents among them, admiring their lean strong bodies as he did so and reflecting ironically that their health was considerably more robust than his own.

As his health improved, Proust emerged from his room more often, for he was desperately lonely. He seems to have stayed with his friends until all hours of the night and then talked with the night watchman in the corridor after his friends had gone to bed. The talk certainly helped him to forget his grief, and indeed when he left for Paris he was obsessed by the fear that oblivion had stolen upon him unawares. On the train he was so asthmatic that he lost the power of speech, and he could not find his medicines, which had obviously been packed in one of his trunks. Finally his valet, who was thoroughly alarmed, elbowed aside the guard who barred the way, entered the luggage van, and brought back the medicines. The invalid reached Paris completely shattered but in one respect happy: he was satisfied that he had not really forgotten his friend and that he could still be as abjectly miserable as before.

As time went on, however, he did begin to forget—his attention was engrossed by the war. He bought a map and plotted the position of the armies. He read regularly several newspapers: read the official communiqués and tried to guess the secrets they failed to reveal; read the military commentators and tried to work out with their help his own characteristically devious notions of strategy; read the articles deploring *Kultur*, condemning Wagner, and describing the Germans as *Boches*. Annoyed by the clichés that were now fashionable and outraged by the stupidity of journalistic patriotism, he often felt that France was deliberately betraying herself, cutting off one of the sources of her inspiration, and thus tarnishing the victories won on the battlefield. "If, instead of being at war with Germany, we had been at war with Russia," he asked, "what would they have said of Tolstoy and Dostoevsky?" Later, when Paul Souday ventured to criticize his journalistic colleagues, Proust immediately wrote him a letter of congratulation, as before, after the strictures on *Swann*, he had written a letter of protest.

But if Proust still liked Wagner and Strauss, if he permitted himself to be annoyed with the men who used the cant of the moment, his patriotism was no less fervent than theirs. "I never knew before how much I love France," he once wrote Madame Straus. "You, who love the roads near Trouville, will understand what the country of Amiens, the country of Rheims, of Laon, where I have been so often, mean to me. . . . But we must love men more than things, and I weep more and have more admiration for the soldiers than for the churches which were only the expression of an heroic gesture, today repeated every moment." Some months after his return from Cabourg, he heard an acquaintance of his, a certain Z., describe a visit to the battlefield of the Marne. Z. kept saying, "You pursued the Germans, you forced them to withdraw." Proust was at first rather embarrassed because he knew that he himself had done nothing at all, but when he realized that Z. was in effect telling him that he too was a Frenchman, he was very deeply moved.

For Proust, however, the war was not only a conflict fought on a far-away battlefield and afterwards described. It directly involved many of his friends and it seemed about to involve him too, for he was, after all, classified as an officer in the army. He rather expected to be called into service as soon as the medical authorities got around to reviewing his case. Scarcely relishing the prospect and half inclined to pull wires that might secure an exemption, he waited anxiously for the appointment that would determine his fate. When it came it was not nearly so formidable as he had anticipated, for the army was not yet taking hopeless invalids. The examination was remarkable in only one respect—the military doctors knew nothing about his family, and even supposed that he himself was an architect. But other examinations might come at any time, the decision was obviously subject to change, and so Proust went on worrying about himself and worrying too about his friends, all of them, wherever they might be. Some, he knew, were at the front; others had simply disappeared—he could not find them though he asked about them everywhere and wrote repeated letters of inquiry.

What reports he got were inevitably alarming, casualties inevitably occurred. In the autumn of 1914 he learned that the hospital where his brother was stationed had been under fire. Shells had fallen on the operating table even as his brother worked over the wounded, and the name of Proust had appeared in an order of the day. In January, 1915, he learned that Fénelon, once his most intimate friend, was missing in action. He gathered what evidence he could about the circumstances and pored over it trying to persuade himself that Fénelon was still alive. A day or two later he learned that another old friend, Gaston de Caillavet, had died, though not in battle. After writing a magnificent letter to the widow but refusing to see her, Proust decided that he must visit her after all. One night about eleven he drove to her house and, finding it dark, waited with the motor of his taxi running. When no light went on and no one appeared at the windows, he left without ringing the bell.

In the spring of 1915, when he had given up hope for Fénelon, other names appeared in the casualty lists, the most disturbing being that of Robert d'Humières. Proust was for a while inconsolable, afraid to open the newspapers for fear of discovering other losses. As he looked back he decided that the death of Agostinelli had set off an uninterrupted series of misfortunes. "You don't know, since our lives have now drifted apart," he wrote to Clément de Maugny, a friend of long standing, "about a friend I lost a year ago, who with my mother and my father was the person I loved best in the world. But since then one death has followed another without interruption." In May he asked Madame Catusse, now living in Nice, to buy a wreath for Agostinelli's grave, preferably a rather ostentatious wreath, but one costing no more than forty francs. "I can't tell you how many friends I have lost," he said in his letter. "For years I haven't seen them. But unfortunately I don't have the gift of oblivion; day and night I shed tears for Fénelon and d'Humières, just as if I had seen them yesterday."

II

In the course of years changes had inevitably taken place in Proust's household. Two of the old family servants, Félicie and Jean, had long since gone; their successors, Céline and Nicolas, were now gone too, the one having been dismissed by Proust and the other having been called up at the outbreak of war. Only one servant seems to have remained in the house, an indication perhaps that Proust was determined to lead a Spartan life in wartime. Her name was Céleste. She was the wife of Proust's taxi driver, Odilon Albaret.

Céleste was already an old friend—Proust had known her ever since her marriage to Albaret in 1913. He had first seen her in his kitchen when she had come to the house on an errand, and he had identified her at once. She was a tall, slender girl with rather coarse features and a complexion so pale that it seemed to him almost the color of lilacs. "Ah, Madame Albaret," he had said, smiling and holding out his hand, "let me introduce Marcel Proust, untidy and uncombed—I must apologize." Later he had employed her as a housekeeper while Céline was ill, and later still, after his quarrel with Céline, he had employed her regularly, from 9 in the morning until 4 or 5 in the afternoon. The first time she entered his bedroom, she had been appalled by the darkness and the strange acrid smell, both associated in her mind with the mines near her native village. Proust had been struck by her speech, in which he seemed to hear the poetry of the peasant, rich in the imagery of nature. He had begun summoning her more frequently and had grown fonder of her day by day. When at the outbreak of the war Odilon had entered the army, Proust had given her a room in the apartment, had taken her with him to Cabourg, and had seen her constantly after his return to Paris. He had made her almost as much a confidante and companion as a servant, so that now, after a year in the house, she occupied somewhat the same place in his life that his mother had occupied a decade before.

He liked Céleste because she introduced him to another world, because, when she entered his room, he seemed to see the mill-house at Auxillac where she had grown up, the convent at La Canourgue where she had spent a year with the nuns, the plateaus and the gorges and the torrents of her native Auvergne. Her moods persistently reminded him of water. For when she teased him, she was impertinent like a brook; when she was angry, she raged like a stream overflowing its banks, furious, destructive, utterly detestable; when she was tired, she seemed quite literally to run dry. "Nothing," as Proust said later, "could then have revived her. Then all of a sudden the circulation was restored in her large body, splendid and light. The water flowed in the opaline transparence of her bluish skin. She smiled at the sun and became bluer still. At such moments she was truly celestial."

Proust learned to recognize her moods and, if not to control them, at least to mitigate their effect upon himself. He took her into his confidence, described his novel, showed her scenes from his manuscript, and made her feel that she had a share in his work. If she rebelled at his demands—which were often outrageous, for he never seemed to realize that she had a life of her own—he explained exactly what he was doing at the moment and persuaded her that her contribution was as important as his own. If in her more violent moods she goaded him to fury, he immediately sent her out of the room. "Céleste," he would say, "I am so angry that I beg you to leave me alone." She was so fond of him that she felt the punishment keenly. Later, when he could control himself, he reproved her, harshly if he felt she had deserved it. But he had other, more effective ways of pointing out her faults and reducing her to obedience. He insinuated criticisms or teased her slyly, much as she teased him. Once, when he complained that his tea was not hot enough, he saw that she was about to explode or weep. "You are quite right, Céleste," he said, "tea should be taken tepid." Once she bought him some handkerchiefs that she thought particularly soft, but he complained that they were not soft enough. She washed them several times to soften them, but still he complained. A day or two later, when she entered his room, she found him cutting the handkerchiefs into strips with a pair of scissors. "Don't you see, Céleste," he said, "this is the only way I can prevent your giving them to me again. . . . My mucous membranes are so sensitive that this rough linen makes me sneeze, and with my asthma this is not prudent."

The daily routine in the bedroom was much the same as it had been for years—the same and yet distinctly different from the very fact that Céleste was there. In the afternoon, when Proust awoke, she appeared in the bedroom, rustling a little in her black taffeta dress, smiling her ineffable smile. She brought him the things that her predecessors, Félicie and Céline, had always brought him: hot coffee, croissants, and Legras powder. But when his inhalations were over, she returned and sat at his bedside as he read his mail. She tried to determine, from his casual comments, what visitors he was willing to receive, what invitations he had decided to accept, and what she herself was expected to do during the night. Later, if visitors came, she ushered them in and out. Often, when they were gone, she mimicked them, apparently without realizing what she was doing —assumed their expressions, adopted their tones of voice, and made up remarks ridiculing their foibles. Proust was convulsed with laughter. Later still she replaced the bottle of Evian water on the bamboo table beside Proust's bed, and made sure that he had enough paper and ink.

Often when Proust was not busy, he persuaded Céleste to linger on in his room throughout the night. Sometimes he read her a story he thought she might like—"Amélie ou une humeur de guerre," for example, a story about a ridiculous maid who closely resembled her. He laughed so much as he read that he was afraid of offending her. But she was not offended, she laughed too, for she recognized, not herself, but the maid upstairs and the cook on the floor below. Sometimes he told her long stories about his early life; sometimes he described parties he had gone to more recently. "Now then, Céleste," he would say, "since you are always alone I must set myself to amuse you, and so I see that I must reconstruct for you all the conversations I have held and heard. I feel the need to tell you everything, to repeat the party." "But, why, Monsieur?" she would ask. "Now, now, don't be naughty, I simply must amuse you a little. Listen to me, it will help you to relax and it will teach you. You shall know everything."

Occasionally, though perhaps more rarely than in previous years, Proust went out at night. In June, 1915, for example, he went to see his old friend Blanche, who, after years of estrangement, had gallantly come forward to defend *Du Côté de chez Swann*. It was an excursion Proust could scarcely avoid. He intended to take Blanche to dinner, but he arrived so late that he found him already in bed. There was nothing to do but to sit down in the living room, to close the window, to borrow an extra overcoat, and to talk. Proust talked on and on, as he talked to Céleste— about the friends he had lost in the war and his regret that he himself could not fight, about the structure of his novel and the homosexual scenes that were to appear in the later volumes. Alarmed by the revelations, Blanche got up and closed the living-room door. At dawn Proust left abruptly as his asthma began to trouble him. The next day he caught a bad cold. As he lay in bed suffering and thinking about the visit, he decided that Blanche had been strangely distant. "You lent me your coat like a good Samaritan, closed the window, and offered me your protection for the coming year," he said in a letter. "But I saw *absolutely nothing* of the affectionate smile that used to make me feel you were glad to see me again (and once not so long ago at *Boris Godounov*). A formal and icy reception. Why?"

Excursions like the one to Blanche's house were no doubt typical, but sometimes, when he felt rested and free from asthma, Proust went to a concert or a brothel. He liked concerts that featured Beethoven symphonies, he liked brothels where the inmates were stalwart young men. It so happened that he had a warm personal interest in a brothel of this sort, one discreetly called Les Bains du Ballon d'Alsace. The proprietor, a certain Albert Le Cuziat, was an old friend, indeed a protégé of his. He had known Le Cuziat as a footman who had freely distributed his favors among members of the nobility, had subsequently encouraged him to set up in business on a somewhat larger scale, and had given him some of the Proust family furniture not in use at the Boulevard Haussmann. The business had prospered, the establishment was now handsomely appointed. In the courtyard by the entrance were shrubs in boxes; in the lobby and in Le Cuziat's own room were the armchairs of the Prousts and the Weils. Le Cuziat usually sat at the cashier's desk, immobile, expressionless, a book on history or genealogy in his hands, for he shared Proust's passion for the aristocracy. Proust came to chat with him, to pump him about sex, and to witness, from a place of concealment, the aberrations of acquaintances. He may also, of course, have revealed aberrations of his own, and indeed there is a story to the effect that he once sent out for a rat and watched as it was stuck to death with hat pins.

But on only one occasion can Proust definitely be placed at an establishment like the Bains du Ballon d'Alsace, and then under comparatively innocuous circumstances. He was sitting at the bar with a group of friends, who were drinking heavily, when another and apparently more intimate friend entered the room. Either from timidity or discretion, Proust scarcely dared to look at him and did not even notice that the man was in evening dress. When the man left Proust felt the anguish of absence. Later in the evening Proust's drunken friends started a fight and Proust characteristically wanted to challenge someone to a duel. Still he was very much preoccupied and as soon as he was home he wrote the man in evening dress, describing the pleasure and the pain he had experienced at their casual encounter and reporting the disturbance. "I go on setting down these trivialities," Proust concluded, "because I am unhappy about leaving you so soon, because as I write I have the illusion that I am with you again, the hope that when the relationship of two men who constantly think of one another (for you have been kind enough to say that you also think of me) has developed into an easy and carefree intimacy, we shall know how to create in Reality a friendship that up to the present time has existed chiefly in our minds and in truth."

III

If for several months after Agostinelli's death Proust had stopped working on his novel, he was certainly now back at it again, going over the proofs of his second volume and the manuscript in the notebooks, correcting, polishing, and amplifying his text. Sometimes he worked from a set of notes in which he had reminded himself of episodes he might put in or expressions his characters might appropriately use or remarks they might make. Thus in one note he had specified certain words that Bloch might use; in another he had told himself to make Charlus complain about the disappearance of men as footmen and waiters and telegraph boys in wartime; in still another—presumably in an effort to clarify for himself the elements of which the character was composed—he had jotted down an equation in which Françoise was made to equal Félicie, a certain Marie, and another old servant at Illiers.

But whether he worked from notes or not, Proust found something to change on almost every page and often a good deal to add. When, for example, the hero's parents give a dinner, he added passages about this same Françoise, who goes to the Halles to buy the best cuts of meat,

> as Michelangelo passed eight months in the mountains of Carrara choosing the most perfect blocks of marble for the monument of Julius II. Françoise expended on these comings and goings so much ardor that Mama, at the sight of her flaming cheeks, was alarmed lest our old servant should make herself ill with overwork, like the sculptor of the Tombs of the Medici in the quarries of Pietrasanta.

When the hero forgets Gilberte, Proust added fifty pages about the break between them and the anguish that the hero suffers. When, in the section on Balbec, the character of Bloch is casually brought in, Proust added thirty pages, singularly brutal ones, about the vulgarity of the Bloch family and about Jews in general, who form a compact colony at seaside resorts, easily distinguishable from other visitors by their strident manners and flashy dress.

As he worked, Proust told Céleste what he was trying to do and what progress he had made. Sometimes he expressed satisfaction, for he felt that he had written a really remarkable passage; sometimes he expressed regret that, by going out, he had wasted valuable time. Sometimes, when he was still at work, he urged Céleste to disturb him as little as possible. "I am doing something which I believe to be extraordinary," he would say. "Don't move. . . . Or, rather, move about in the room without making a noise." She did as she was told: when she moved, only the rustle of her dress could be heard. New passages were often written on the paper with which he lit his Legras powder. As soon as he had finished Céleste pasted the new sheets on to the proofs or into the notebooks, which thus gradually grew in size.

Often, when he needed fresh information, Proust either sent Céleste out to get it or himself interviewed or wrote old friends. Thus, in connection with a passage on the Princesse Mathilde that he was adding to his second volume, he enlisted the help of Lucien Daudet. "Since you saw the Princesse Mathilde when you were very young," he wrote, "you will have to go over (that is, describe for me) one of her outfits, the sort of thing she wore on spring afternoons, a mauve dress rather like crinoline, and perhaps a bonnet with streamers and violets, anyway what you must have seen her wear." Daudet sent the description but Proust found, or so he said, that it differed very little from what he had already written. "Your dress for the Princesse Mathilde won't serve my purpose," he reported in another letter, "but I can show you the mysterious power of our 'pre-established harmony.' It comes close to being a *miracle*. Read the enclosed passage from *Swann*[1] (otherwise stupid) and you will find the whole thing down to your word *saute-en-barque* (I have made a cross by it in the margin) and exactly the same idea about the survival of fashions, etc., etc. If I didn't send you the passage (which you should return), you might think when you read the book that I had borrowed from you (assuming that I keep the passage, which I am not at all satisfied with). Indeed, for the Princesse Mathilde herself, the resemblance is even more striking, because the scene is exactly the same, the Jardin d'Acclimitation! But I don't have the proof sheet at hand, and I am too ill to look things up." Even with the best health in the world Proust could not have found the proof sheet because no such proof sheet existed.[2] He had obviously written his passage on the Princesse Mathilde after receiving Daudet's description.

Once, possibly while he was working over a passage on the

1. Proust usually referred to the whole novel as *Swann*.
2. See Albert Feuillerat, *Comment Marcel Proust a composé son roman* (1934), p. 280.

Duc de Guermantes, Proust made an appointment with a distinguished nobleman he had known for many years, the Comte Greffulhe. Appearing late in the drawing room on the Rue d'Astorg and declining to take off his fur coat, he began by profusely complimenting his host, whom he described as the last great nobleman to keep up the grand style. Gradually, almost imperceptibly, he began to ask questions. He asked about the traditions of the family, about the routine of the household, and about the famous hunting parties at Bois-Boudran. As he listened to the answers, he studied the man before him—blond, massive, deliberate, commanding, the epitome of the *grand seigneur*. Proust half sat, half reclined in an armchair, only his face, a mask mortally pale, visible above his fur coat. To an observer who witnessed the interview, he looked now like a physician conducting an autopsy and now like a cobra hypnotizing a victim. When he felt that he had learned as much as he could, he arose, apologized for coming so late, and left, probably to go home and record his impressions on sheets of paper which Céleste would afterwards paste into the notebooks.

Proust, however, was not only retouching and amplifying the notebooks already filled with manuscript; he was filling new notebooks—drafting new episodes and new chapters, trying to work into the novel, at the risk of making it intolerably long, the more memorable of his recent experiences. The most memorable of all was certainly his experience with Agostinelli. Beginning with a chapter concerned with the hero's flirtations (or so one infers from its title, announced in 1913, "A l'Ombre des jeunes filles en fleurs"), he undertook to describe a long unhappy love affair between his hero and a girl called Albertine. She was, if not an entirely new character, at least one who had played a comparatively minor part in earlier drafts of the novel. Altogether he devoted to Albertine several substantial episodes and three complete chapters—the first two concerned with the hero's jealousy while he lives with her in Paris, the third with his grief after she has left and, a little later, after she has suffered a fatal accident. Though Albertine is scarcely a portrait of Agostinelli and though her story differs in some ways from his, it seems clear that Proust was thinking of his own experiences as he worked, and thinking of them, furthermore—as in certain passages of *Jean Santeuil*—while they were still going on or at least fresh in his memory.

The chapters on Albertine can, in fact, be dated with some degree of accuracy. They were obviously written or sketched out in something like a year and a half after Agostinelli's death, for in November, 1915, Proust was able to summarize them and even to quote from them—in a long passage that he wrote out on the blank leaves of Madame Scheikévitch's copy of *Swann*. Still he was not altogether finished with them, for a month or two later he was considering an addition involving an episode about gowns by the famous designer, Fortuny. What he needed, if he was to write it as he wanted to, was a specific gown adapted from a specific picture, Venetian or Paduan, so that he could make his hero nostalgic about Italy when he saw the gown on Albertine and nostalgic about Albertine when he saw the picture in Italy. Proust consulted society women, as in the novel the hero consults the Duchesse de Guermantes. Madame Straus offered to show him a Fortuny gown, which was no use at all, and Madame Madrazo offered to show him another. Then he discovered that Madame Madrazo could get information from Fortuny himself and so it was to her that he addressed his list of questions. Was there a book on Fortuny? What specific pictures, say by Carpaccio, had he used? Were there examples in his work of the birds symbolizing life and death, so commonly represented on the capitals of St. Mark's? Madame Madrazo presumably did her best, but it is not clear that the answers she supplied were much more useful than those of the duchess in the novel. At least the passages on Fortuny that Proust wrote were not quite so specific as those he had originally had in mind.

During the early months of 1916 Proust was perhaps writing or sketching other new chapters, including one with a scene in a brothel during wartime, apparently suggested by his experiences at the Bains du Ballon d'Alsace. At the same time he was concerned about a more practical aspect of his work, its publication. He saw Gide and Gallimard, who repeated the offer from the N. R. F.; he saw René Blum, who seemed willing to help him break with Grasset if he decided to accept the offer; he did so decide. He felt that, since Grasset's firm was closed for the duration of the war, he had a plausible reason for making the change. He felt, furthermore, that if he handled the negotiations adroitly and if he twisted the facts ever so little, he could avoid the appearance of ingratitude. An indirect approach seemed best, and accordingly he proposed that Blum, who was now at the front, should write a letter to Grasset, who was recovering from typhoid in Switzerland. In the course of the letter Blum should say: "Marcel Proust has lost a large part of his fortune. He can no longer be as indifferent as before to the chance of earning a little money. Your firm is closed, the N. R. F.'s isn't and can publish the book immediately. Because of the war, he wants you to let him take back his promise to give you his other volumes, without your being angry or offended by his action, and consequently he wants you to give up the first volume as well." The case, so stated, was certainly a plausible one. Only the premise was false, for Proust actually had no intention of publishing his book until the end of the war.

Blum wrote the letter as directed. Proust read it but asked Blum to say that he had not read it, so that he would not afterwards be bound by the terms it suggested. He had it sent to a sanatorium but was apparently prepared to pretend that he did not know Grasset was ill. Grasset's reply was prompt and sharp. His letter was passed on to Proust, who wrote back in an even sharper vein. But the publisher afterwards accepted his dismissal so meekly that good feelings were soon restored. Proust began addressing him again as "Dear Friend" instead of "Dear Sir"; the details were arranged, if not quite amicably, at least with a minimum of unpleasantness. Henceforth Proust reserved his ill temper for the N. R. F., which no longer seemed nearly so attractive as in the days of their flirtation.

CHAPTER XVIII

The Return to Society

I

As soon, it seems, as he had finished the most important additions to his novel, Proust began leading a more active social life again. He was able to do so because his asthma was less troublesome than it had been in previous years. He could often receive visitors or go out whenever he wanted to, sometimes quite early in the evening. His chief complaint now was that his eyes bothered him when he read or wrote. He might of course have consulted an oculist, and he often thought of doing so. But it was always easier to postpone the consultation—which might well have involved his arising an hour or two early—and meanwhile to spend as much time as possible in company.

Though many of his closest friends were away, either at the front or in foreign countries, he still saw them from time to time when they came to town, and he saw more regularly the friends who were always available. His relationship with Madame Scheikévitch may be considered typical. One night he suddenly appeared at her apartment and insisted on taking her to Ciro's, where he ordered for her a bottle of excellent champagne, *filets de sole vin blanc, boeuf à la mode*, a small salad, and a *soufflé au chocolat*.

He urged the waiter to see that the *soufflé* was very creamy. For himself he ordered a glass of water, so that he could take his pills, and several cups of particularly strong coffee. In the course of the meal something at a neighboring table seemed to upset him. Suddenly he arose, walked over to the headwaiter, and said in a trembling voice: "Be kind enough to hand my card to one of these gentlemen at the table behind Madame. . . . They behave in the most indecent way, and I will not tolerate it; how dare they!" Madame Scheikévitch had in the meantime recognized the gentlemen as friends of hers, from the Italian Embassy. She introduced them to Proust, who immediately regained his composure. "Ah," he said, "I was fearing . . . you were making a mistake about Madame. . . . I am so glad to know you. I am very fond of Italy and should very much like to see Florence where I have never been." Later, when Madame Scheikévitch was staying in Versailles, Proust paid her another visit, making the trip quite comfortably in the car of an eminent Russian general, commander-in-chief of Russian forces on the Western Front. Before sundown he suggested, and actually took, a walk in the park. Madame Scheikévitch was amazed to see her asthmatic friend bend over the flower beds and ask the names of the flowers, pick up and examine with minute attention leaves and pieces of moss.

Thus Proust went on spending some time with old friends like Madame Scheikévitch, but he was reaching a period in his life when he tended to prefer friends he had made more recently to those he had known in former days. The reasons for this were probably complex. He was interested, as before, in exploring society, perhaps partly for the sake of his work. But society was changing—new names were springing into prominence, new hostesses gathered together the remnants of the *beau monde*. Determined to keep up with the times, to know and to see people who were fashionable at the moment, Proust gradually made new connections and allowed his old ones to lapse. If the process had to some extent gone on all his life, it was definitely accentuated by the war. Furthermore, he himself was changing along with society. He was no longer the elegant dilettante of the pre-war years, a man of considerable promise but negligible accomplishment; he was now a novelist with an established reputation, not widely known perhaps, but in a limited circle admired and even idolized. Eager to be reminded of his reputation and to be treated as the great man he was, he preferred to see less of friends who had known him earlier and more of friends he had made through his work, especially young friends whose enthusiasm, often unrestrained, assured him that he was the master of contemporary letters. This tendency—which afterwards became more pronounced —was already definite and, to some observers, disquieting.

A list of the friends Proust saw most frequently during the last years of the war would include the names of several young men who were just becoming prominent in literature or society or both. But, oddly enough, one of his favorite friends, Walter Berry, was not young—was indeed approaching sixty—though he was in other respects admirably qualified to interest an author with social aspirations. An American born in Paris, a lawyer who had practiced successfully on two continents, Berry was intimate both with the Roosevelts and the Lodges in Washington and with comparable families in Europe. He was well known as a bibliophile and collector; he was known too, in Proust's circle at least, as a lifelong friend and adviser of Edith Wharton's. Now, as president of the American Chamber of Commerce in Paris, he was championing the cause of the Allies and campaigning for American entry into the war.

Berry happened to find, in one of the bookstalls along the Seine, a volume that had once belonged to a member of the Guermantes family, that was indeed stamped with the monogram and crest of a certain Prondre de Guermantes. Remembering Du Côté de chez Swann, which he had recently reread with great pleasure, he bought the book and, at the house of their common friend, Madame Scheikévitch, presented it to Proust. An invitation to the Boulevard Haussmann promptly followed. The two men— the invalid and the elegant bibliophile with pink cheeks and white hair—talked for hours, about the book, about the subsequent history of the Guermantes family in Proust's novel, about life and art. Berry quoted Rémy de Gourmont: "One writes well only about the things one hasn't lived through." "That," exclaimed Proust, rising dramatically from his chair, "that is my whole work!" At the moment he perhaps felt that he had never found, in the whole course of his life, a more understanding friend. Other meetings inevitably followed, at the Boulevard Haussmann, at Berry's house in the Rue Guillaume, and at the houses of fashionable hostesses. Berry proved a delightful companion, cultured and worldly. He was, furthermore, quite smart enough to be included in the dinner parties that Proust was beginning to give at Ciro's, Larue's, and the Crillon.

Another new friend, and an even closer one than Berry, was the Princesse Soutzo, whose connections were extremely good, not only in the diplomatic and literary worlds, but in European society generally. Her list of acquaintances included even a few specimens of royalty such as the Queen of Rumania and the King of Montenegro. In other respects she was the sort of woman Proust often found himself attracted to—she was good-looking, intelligent, and witty. She once said (though *bons mots* of this sort seldom stand the test of time) that pretty women are the easiest to seduce because their defenses have been weakened by repeated solicitation. Generally her views seem to have been less cosmopolitan than Berry's, and indeed she once remarked that the French were contributing everything to the war and getting nothing while the English were taking care of themselves but obviously losing to the Americans.

Proust's first meeting with the Princesse Soutzo occurred on March 4, 1917, while he was dining alone at Larue's, somewhat disconcerted by the fact that Céleste had given him a threadbare waistcoat to wear with his dinner jacket and a shirt covered with soap spots. At another table—the only other table that was occupied, as it happened—he saw his friend Paul Morand, a young man in the diplomatic service who was just on the threshold of a successful literary career. With Morand was the Princesse Soutzo. Proust joined them, met the Princess, apologized for his soapy shirt and ordered some pastry. Afterwards he drank several cups of coffee, then finished his meal with a salad, which he ate with his gloves on. The conversation at first turned, perhaps inevitably, on *Du Côté de chez Swann*. Later Proust offered to summon the Poulet Quartet for a private performance of César Franck in the apartment of the Princess at the Ritz. He actually went off in a taxi and awakened Poulet, only to discover that one member of the quartet, the cellist, was at the moment in the hospital. Toward midnight Proust appeared at the Ritz, reported his failure, and lingered on to discuss Flaubert and repeat society gossip of an earlier generation.

As with Berry, other meetings inevitably followed, first of all, it seems, on March 16, when at the last minute—at 7:30 in the evening—Proust invited the Princess to dinner at Ciro's. His other guests were Morand and Prince Antoine Bibesco. He attracted a good deal of attention in the restaurant—the ladies of easy virtue could not help staring at a man who drank champagne with his gloves on—but he was quite at ease and indeed in excellent form. He told story after story about the immediate or the distant past: about Maurice Rostand, whose perfumes had penetrated several partitions at the Boulevard Haussmann and given him an attack of asthma; about Bibesco, who had telegraphed him at the outbreak of war, "I hope you are going to be put into the shock troops"; about his unfortunate speculations in 1913, when he had lost, he said, 700,000 francs. As the party broke up, Proust left enormous tips, and Bibesco lingered behind with the waiters to find out exactly how much money was involved. "He is explaining to them that I made a mistake, so that I won't get any credit for it," Proust said. Morand was puzzled by his host's fondness, which almost amounted to an obsession, for anti-Semitic stories. Bibesco, however, explained to him privately (the explanation seemed quite adequate) that Proust's mother's maiden name had been Weil.

Two weeks later the Princesse Soutzo gave a dinner at the Ritz, inviting, along with Proust and several of his friends, a Rumanian, General Iliesco. Proust arrived late, wearing a white tie with his dinner jacket. The general studied him curiously. Proust studied the general, who, he felt, might be—who indeed seemed to be—a notorious traitor about whom he had recently been told. The conversation touched on a persistent practical joke that some one was playing on Proust. Regularly every evening a dinner was brought to the door of the Boulevard Haussmann, sometimes from one restaurant and sometimes from another, but always including ravioli and always unpaid for. Afterwards, usually about ten, a waiter appeared to ask if Proust had had enough ravioli. "Since

I have no enemies," Proust explained, "I am obliged to suspect all
my friends. It is quite dreadful!" He added that he was half inclined to accuse Bibesco, in whose presence he remembered remarking, "I can very well dine at home. All I have to do is to order
a cold dinner or some ravioli." On the other hand, Bibesco was
not at the moment in Paris.

At the same time Proust was also seeing a good deal of a young
man of letters, Emmanuel Berl, who was particularly interesting
because he had romantic tendencies. Proust eagerly lectured him
on the illusions of love and the inevitable disappointments they
lead to, every so often putting in a good word for inversion. If he
was not actually making an impression on his young friend, he was
at least easing his own conscience by giving wholesome advice.
But then suddenly one evening Berl announced what he thought
of as his engagement. Proust remained ominously silent as the
story was told, then began his little lecture all over again. The
young man had obviously been "infected" by his mistress. He
was laying himself open to the cruelest disappointments, and indeed if his mistress had died he would have had much more reason
to be happy. Berl restrained himself as long as he could and then
tartly remarked that in his friend's view love was obviously no more
than a form of masturbation. The invalid's pale face became even
paler. He arose and went into his dressing room, pouring out insults all the time and growing angrier by the minute. Finally even
the semblance of good manners deserted him. "Get out!" he cried.
"Get out!" Berl did get out, and so Proust illustrated another
of the ideas he had been fond of expounding to the young man,
that friendship was as valueless as love.

II

As the weeks passed, Proust found himself making appointments
more and more regularly. The habit became a fixed one—not for
years had he been nearly so adventurous. Several times a week he
either dined out at restaurants or invited one of his young
friends—Morand perhaps—to the Boulevard Haussmann for cider
and fried potatoes. The appointments were usually made by
Céleste. "Monsieur Marcel Proust would be glad to dine with

Monsieur Morand this evening," she once said on the telephone,
using the starched idioms she had picked up from her master.
"Monsieur Morand may invite anyone he pleases if it would bore
him to dine alone with Monsieur Marcel Proust, but since Monsieur Marcel Proust is not shaved, Monsieur Marcel Proust begs
Monsieur Morand not to embarrass him with strange ladies."
Sometimes, as they ate the meatless wartime meals at Larue's,
confining themselves abstemiously to lobster, Proust described
the hardships of his social life. Sometimes he discussed people he
had known in the past; sometimes *Swann* and the characters who
were to appear in subsequent volumes, especially Saint-Loup and
Charlus; sometimes inversion. He liked to speak of inverts as the
normal ones, since they were now so numerous. Of a man who
preferred women he would say, "I can answer for him. He is
completely abnormal." Once, when the conversation turned on a
man of doubtful reputation who had distinguished himself at the
front, Proust remarked, "His fondness for men led him to virility,
and his virility to glory."

A social life perhaps needs a focal point, and this in the course
of time the Princesse Soutzo provided for Proust. She became for
him indeed very much what Madame Straus and Madame
Lemaire had been a generation before. Treating her exactly as he
had treated them, flattering her, praising her gowns, and affecting
jealousy when she deserted him, he kept up the pretense that he
was in love with her, though not perhaps very seriously. But quite
apart from any tender feelings he may have had, he was well
aware that she had solid advantages to offer him. She had an
apartment at the Ritz, where he was always welcome, where he
could meet important and interesting people, where he could
come at all hours without bothering to let her know in advance,
where he could bring his own friends and even invite them to
dinner parties—where, in short, he was completely at home. The
apartment was a matter of considerable importance in wartime,
when restaurants put their lights out at 9:30, just as Proust's social
life was about to begin.

And so it was that, deserting other restaurants, he confined
himself to the Ritz, which, strange at first, became in the course
of time almost a second home to him, as familiar and as friendly

as the bedroom on the Boulevard Haussmann. He knew it all—the lounge, the dining room, the kitchen, the Princesse Soutzo's apartment upstairs—all, that is, except the grill room, which for some reason he had managed to avoid. He knew the managers, the waiters, and the lift boys, who were quite as much his friends as the Princess. He talked with them for hours, exploring their experiences, tipped them magnificently, helped them when they got into trouble, and received from them, on New Year's Day, touching letters of gratitude. They, for their part, saw to his comforts—kept him out of drafts, served his guests the creamiest *soufflés*, and escorted him to a private room whenever he wanted to interview an attractive boy from the kitchen or to correct some of the proofs that soon began reaching him from the N. R. F.

On evenings when he went to the Ritz, Céleste summoned a barber (if one was available) to shave him and do his hair. Afterwards she helped him wash and dress, for he was always late and always feverishly trying to save time. At the last minute she handed him his hat, his fur coat, his gloves, and his cane. When he reached the hotel, often with his tie scarcely tied and his hat tilted a little too far back on his head, he lingered near the door to chat with acquaintances. Then, if he was himself entertaining, he followed the manager to the spot where his guests were sitting expectantly, or, if he was not, he took the lift to the Princesse Soutzo's apartment. In meeting people he showed a curious diffidence. "He advanced with a kind of embarrassed hesitation," one of his guests later said, "a kind of intimidated stupefaction—or rather he did not advance toward you: he appeared." He was heavier than he had been, especially in the chest which, as often in asthmatics, had developed out of proportion to the rest of his body. But he was otherwise much the same. He still affected the full haircuts—especially full at the nape of the neck —the high collars, and the fitted coats of his youth, so that he seemed more than ever a survivor from another age.

With his friends he was at first rather querulous and inclined to enumerate his troubles, which did seem quite endless. But he became, when he got away from himself, remarkably charming and gay. When he laughed he exploded quite suddenly, showing magnificent teeth, then immediately covered his mouth with his hand, like an urchin caught in a prank. To one observer at least he seemed a strangely baffling personality—sometimes impressively forceful and sometimes utterly feminine, sometimes fulsomely polite and sometimes completely unrestrained. He was at once, the observer decided, a very old mandarin and a child. Even on evenings when he ate in the dining room he finished the evening upstairs, usually because the dining-room lights were being turned out. "Put them on again for a moment," he instructed the waiters. "I am quite willing to leave but I don't want to feel that I am being ejected." Sitting by the Louis XVI fireplace in the drawing room of the Princess, he talked on and on, until finally, preparing to leave, he took off his fur coat—a gesture designed, he said, to establish a momentary equilibrium between the temperature in the room and the temperature outside. But when he put the coat on again, he forgot that he was going and kept on talking interminably.

The pace of his social life was now positively giddy. Dinners, often at the Princesse Soutzo's, followed one another in rapid, in bewildering succession. On or about April 21, 1917, for example, he dined in her apartment with Morand, Cocteau, and two of his older friends, the Marquise de Ludre and the Comtesse Adhéaume de Chevigné. He was apparently getting on well with the woman he had pursued in his youth, when someone inadvertently remarked that Proust was in the habit of coming upstairs unannounced to see the Princess. He was appalled by the revelation, for he remembered assuring Madame de Chevigné that he never went out. On July 14 he entertained the Princess, Morand, and the Etienne de Beaumonts, who combined the advantages of being particularly smart people and admirers of *Swann*. The Comte de Beaumont obligingly told stories about society figures of the past, especially about two of Proust's favorites, Madame Standish and Robert de Montesquiou. Proust himself described his meeting, some months before, with the Catholic poet, Francis Jammes, whom he had always imagined as poor and devout. Actually, however, he found Jammes particularly worldly, proud of his social connections and determined to talk about oil stocks and hunting. In the course of the evening Proust privately assured Morand that he was planning a grand party, with some forty guests, at which some of Morand's poems would be recited by a well-known actress.

Before the grand party could be arranged, Proust, Morand, and the Beaumonts again dined together, this time at the Princesse Soutzo's. Other guests were Reinach, Cocteau, and the Princesse Murat. Beaumont discussed hypnotism and finally summoned a professional hypnotist, who put the guests to sleep one after the other. While the demonstration was still in progress, there was an air-raid alert. Sirens sounded, searchlights played, and French fighter planes appeared in the sky. Proust, perfectly calm, went on talking for some time about the subject at hand. "People who are put to sleep," he said, "want to be told about their futures so that they won't have to own up to their pasts." Later, however, he stepped out onto the balcony and studied the apocalyptic scene in the sky—the planes that soared upwards and gathered together to form constellations, then fell and burst asunder. As he contrasted it with the scene inside the hotel, where women in nightgowns, clutching pearl necklaces, scurried through corridors, he was reminded of El Greco's painting, *The Burial of Count Orgaz*, in which two levels of action are shown, one in heaven and one on the earth below. His observations subsequently contributed to a passage in *Le Temps retrouvé*, where the women in nightgowns are identified as American Jewesses "clasping to their scrawny bosoms the pearl necklaces that are going to make it possible for them to marry penniless dukes."

III

Proust not only paid for his own dinner parties but made contributions, presumably substantial, to those given by the Princesse Soutzo. In normal times the expense could scarcely have bothered him, but during the war, when the income on his investments was curtailed, he was, he said, frequently hard pressed for cash. He began looking about for ways of raising extra money and finally hit on the idea of doing what certain other affluent Parisians had been doing for some time: selling some of his furniture. Much of it, indeed almost all of it, was quite useless to him. He had in mind specifically some Louis XVI armchairs and a sofa that were in danger of being eaten by moths, some tapestries, some dining-room chairs, some rugs that had been in storage for ten years, a wardrobe, a hideous clock that disfigured the living-room mantelpiece, and the family silver. He talked—in strict confidence of course—to three of his friends, Berry, Madame Catusse, and Straus. Berry gave him an estimate on a few of the pieces, but was not otherwise helpful. Madame Catusse gave him another estimate and sent to the house two prospective customers, ladies interested in antiques. To Proust's horror, they arrived at two in the afternoon, an hour at which no one had ever before called at the Boulevard Haussmann. Céleste, however, received them and even opened the living-room shutters. They examined the furniture, complaining as they did so—complaining that the green tapestries were too green and that the armchairs had been mended. Proust, meanwhile, feeling the cold from the unshuttered windows, shivered in bed. He was annoyed with the two ladies and annoyed with Madame Catusse, for when he entertained her at the Ritz she insisted on talking about his financial problems. It occurred to him that if she had been overheard, as she apparently had been, he might be asked to pay in advance next time he dined at the Ritz.

Monsieur Straus, the third friend whom Proust consulted, was more considerate and more helpful. He sent for some of the pieces, had them appraised, interviewed dealers and other prospective purchasers, and finally effected a sale. Before the end of the year he delivered to Céleste some 14,000 francs—4,000 for two tapestries (a detestable price, Proust thought) and 10,000 for a sofa and four armchairs (a price that could scarcely have been better). Proust talked of sending out other pieces and did send the rugs from storage, but suddenly lost interest in further sales.

Meanwhile the dinners continued, though adjusted to the exigencies of the moment—the departure of old friends, the arrival of proofs from the N. R. F., and the sudden lapses in health to which both Proust and the Princesse Soutzo were occasionally subject. On November 15, 1917, he took her to the Crillon for a change and noticed with alarm that she ate scarcely anything. The next day Céleste was instructed to ask how she was, to advise her not to go out for a while, and to assure her that Proust had walked so far in the fog that he himself was ill. On December 1 he went, somewhat reluctantly, to one of her dinners. He was nostalgic with Morand, who was on the point of being transferred to Italy but, suddenly feeling an attack of asthma coming on, he abruptly excused himself. Downstairs he waited so long for a taxi that he saw most of the other guests leave, and when he finally got home he was so depressed that he was half inclined to go back. But as he discussed the matter with Céleste, the minutes passed, the hour grew later and later. Finally it was too late—he could only write the Princess. A few days afterwards he wrote her again. "Instead of correcting my proofs," he began, "still so full of the memory of intolerable moments when I have seen you without really being near you, I can at least write you a letter before I begin to work. . . ." He advised her to have her appendix out at once.

Toward the end of December she acted on his advice, and he wrote her even more frequently, received reports from her bedside and telegraphed them on to Morand, saw her regularly as soon as she had recovered a little. But difficulties inevitably occur when one invalid visits another. The hours were unreasonable and the visits were tiring; the weather was bad; the time of year—around New Year's Day—was in itself depressing. Unhappy and completely worn out, suffering from heart attacks and even experiencing symptoms of bronchitis, Proust had to force himself to go on with the dreary excursions to the Ritz. Occasionally he faltered—one night, for example, he gave up going when he saw fog outside and found that his florist was closed. More often he asked himself whether in wartime the Ritz was not, after all, just a little bit too elegant for a man pronounced unfit for military service.

IV

The year 1918 began; the war approached its climax; soldiers of the Allied nations—French, British, and American—poured into Paris. Isolated though he was, alternating between the bedroom on the Boulevard Haussmann and the drawing room on the Place Vendôme, Proust felt their presence. One night he discovered that the storeroom in his house had been rented to Canadians. He supposed that they were hoarding sugar and other necessities, of which they obviously had enough already—hoarding them while the French starved. Another night, when he rashly went out for a walk on the icy pavement, he encountered two American soldiers looking for a hotel he had never heard of, the Hotel Bedford. Since he could not speak to them in English and could scarcely understand their French, he set out silently with them to search for the hotel, which they found just around the corner. On still another night, when he was dining alone at the Ritz, he saw at the next table a group of Englishmen among whom was a distinguished descendant of the Duke of Marlborough, Winston Churchill.

At the end of January the Gothas began attacking Paris at night, and civilians were urged to take refuge in cellars. Céleste scrambled down to the cellar in the Boulevard Haussmann, though the house was scarcely high enough to afford the best protection. She was terrified, and Proust was terrified for fear she would leave him. Proust himself remained quietly in bed during raids, when indeed he was not outside. Once the sirens sounded just as he was leaving Gabriel de La Rochefoucauld's, where he had gone to hear Borodin's Second Quartet. His taxi, driven by a deaf old man, would not start for half an hour and afterwards stalled for another half hour in the Avenue de Messine. Getting out and standing beside the car, Proust studied the sky and tried to follow the progress of the raid. When he reached his house, he offered the driver a bed for the night, but the old man was obviously unaware that a raid had begun. "It's a false alarm," he said. "No planes have reached the city." Just at that moment a bomb exploded a few streets away.

During another alert Proust deliberately emerged from his apartment, determined at once to see his friend Ramon Fernandez. He found Fernandez' house but not the concierge, who had taken refuge in the cellar. When a mobile gun at the corner was not firing, Proust called his friend's name in the courtyard. Fernandez, who was in bed, heard the call through the open window, and the concierge heard it too. The visitor was directed upstairs. "I want to ask a favor, a highly inopportune favor," Proust began, "but it will perhaps explain, if it doesn't justify, the trouble I am causing you, which I suppose you will always hold against me. Since you know Italian, could you tell me how to pronounce the Italian equivalent of *sans rigueur?*" Fernandez pronounced the words *senza rigore* as distinctly as he could. "Would it be too much if I asked you to do it again?" Proust continued. "A foreign word that I don't know how to pronounce affects me with a kind of anguish. I can't feel it, possess it, I can't make it part of myself." He explained that he had been foolish enough to use *senza rigore* in his manuscript and that he was feeling very unhappy about it. Fernandez again pronounced the words and Proust listened with his eyes closed. Afterwards he profusely thanked his friend and disappeared into the flaming streets.

Proust was stoical about bombs and shrapnel, but quite the opposite about his personal vexations, which at the moment were as numerous as ever, those with the N. R. F. being particularly disturbing. He was reading proofs on his second volume, now given the title once reserved for a chapter, A *l'Ombre des jeunes filles en fleurs.* The task was an arduous one, since his eyes were bothering him, and unfortunately he could not count on getting the proofs with any regularity. The printer seemed quite irresponsible. He was careless with the manuscript and once indeed lost a whole notebook. For a while he stopped sending proofs altogether, maintaining that no workmen were available. But was a printer, after all, to be trusted? Proust was occasionally inclined to regret that he had ever made terms with the N. R. F.

Then in March, just as the great German offensive opened and the long-range gun began shelling Paris, Proust's health suddenly took a disquieting turn. His new symptoms involved spells of dizziness and spells during which his power of muscular coordination, especially in his vocal organs, was somewhat uncertain. He could not always speak as rapidly and as distinctly as before. The symptoms were not perhaps by themselves very serious, yet they reminded him uncomfortably of his mother's last illness and hence suggested several alarming possibilities, one of which was a cerebral condition. He was inclined to feel that, at the very least, he was developing an impediment in his speech and that he was well on the way to complete aphasia. Perhaps he should isolate himself, perhaps he should undergo, as a last desperate measure, a brain operation. But his doctors refused to operate or even to take a very serious view of his case. This in itself was alarming because it seemed to indicate that they were afraid to tell him the truth. One of the great crises of his life was obviously at hand. The symptoms persisted, at least intermittently; but for one reason or another the crisis was indefinitely postponed.

Meanwhile Proust had rashly involved himself in other tasks —collecting his articles and parodies for a volume to be called *Pastiches et mélanges* and writing a preface for Jacques-Emile Blanche's book, *De David à Degas*. The preface, in particular, caused an inordinate amount of trouble. Blanche seemed dissatisfied with it, or so Proust was led to believe by stories he heard. Furthermore, Blanche, though sworn to secrecy, was talking to everyone and apparently saying, among other things, that the preface described a ball for fairies at the Salle Wagram! Proust tried as hard as he could to let the whole thing drop. "Wouldn't it be better," he wrote Blanche, "now that I have had the pleasure of receiving your charming request and of writing as I wished, that [the preface] should remain unpublished, known only to the two of us?"

During the spring and summer, while the decisive battles of the war were being fought, Proust worried about his preface, about his proofs, about his approaching aphasia, and also, it seems, about a new secretary he had taken on. The secretary was a not particularly literate boy from the Ritz who showed, Proust felt, considerable promise as a painter. Sometimes, when they were not working, Proust took him out to look at pictures—one night, for example, they went to Blanche's just to study a still life by Fantin-Latour. Sometimes, when there were guests at the Boulevard Haussmann and the boy was inclined to sit silently in a corner, Proust tried to encourage him by getting him to display some of his canvases. But despite its artistic flavor—and despite the help that Proust got with his manuscript—the relationship does not seem to have been altogether happy, probably because the secretary was too young and the employer too infirm.

Early in October, when the Germans were retreating across France, Proust learned that his brother had narrowly escaped death at the front. His car had collided with another car, his head had been badly cut, and he had been carried, bleeding profusely, to a country house nearby. Soon afterwards he appeared in Paris but, despite Proust's entreaties, insisted on returning to the front. Proust caught cold going out to see him and deserted the Ritz for a week. Soon, however, he was back again, dining with various friends but not, it seems, with the Princesse Soutzo, with whom he was having a tiff. "Shall I see you again?" he asked her in a letter, "or is it really this time, 'Goodbye, Princess'? . . . I again see the comic aspect of the situation when I reflect that you are going to invent some new grievance against me, as you always do. You use these tactics as persistently as the Germans use encirclement. But the defense is easy." Later that month he was having a good deal of trouble with a new parody he had written for *Pastiches et mélanges,* or rather an old parody which he had revised and enlarged, taking the opportunity to mention such friends as the Duc de Guiche, Prince Antoine Bibesco, and Madame Straus. But Madame Straus did not like to be mentioned in print, and Proust was obliged to write her repeatedly, to show her the proofs, to tone down the passage, and to promise her other proofs. Before the matter was quite straightened out, the Armistice came.

That night Proust wrote Madame Straus still another letter. "You and I have talked so much about the war," he began, "that it seems only right we should exchange affectionate notes on the night of Victory, happy that it has been won and sad that so many of our friends have not lived to see it. What a marvelous *allegro presto* in the *finale* after the infinite tedium of the beginning and all the rest! What a magnificent dramatist Destiny is, or man who has been its instrument! I would have written you on the night of the Armistice even if I hadn't had any favors to ask you." But, as it happened, he did have favors to ask, several in fact. He was again short of money and again interested in selling more of his furniture. He wanted his rugs to be auctioned off at once; he wanted a van to come for the odd pieces in his dining room and perhaps for his silver; he wanted these things too to be sold at auction as soon as possible. Thus for Proust the war, which had begun with disasters on the stock market, ended with arrangements for a sale at the Hôtel des Ventes.

CHAPTER XIX

Moving Again

To FRANCE the Armistice brought victory, Wilson, the Peace Conference, the triumphs and disasters of the postwar world. To Proust it brought the publication of his novel with all that this involved—the Goncourt Prize, the Legion of Honor, an international reputation, recognition such as he had never even dreamed of when, years before, he had begun sketching scenes in his notebooks. It brought these things but not immediately, even though A l'Ombre des jeunes filles en fleurs was almost through the press. He had to wait for many months, to endure colds and financial disappointments, to move, not once but twice, and to settle down at last in an unpleasant furnished apartment on the Rue Hamelin before his triumphs could finally begin. In his case the first months of the peace were not very different from the last months of the war.

I

On Christmas Eve, 1918, Proust dined at the Princesse Lucien Murat's and went on to a supper at the house of an Italian officer stationed in Paris. On the following Saturday he dined with the Princesse Soutzo—with whom he was on good terms again—but made the mistake of taking off his fur coat. He drank a cup of tepid coffee in the drawing room, felt a chill coming on, and called for his fur coat again just a little too late. When he got home he had a fever and a severe case of laryngitis. By the end of January, 1919, he was well enough to attend a dinner for Lord Derby, the British Ambassador, who was afterwards heard to remark that he had never before eaten beside a man in a fur coat. But the laryngitis was still occasionally troublesome, and one night when Prince Antoine Bibesco called at the Boulevard Haussmann (bringing with him his fiancée, Miss Asquith, daughter of a former British Prime Minister) Proust felt unable to get out of bed. He received them very reluctantly since he was obliged to violate a sacred rule that women, except of course Céleste, should never be admitted to his bedroom.

Meanwhile he was trying to finish up the proofs of *Pastiches et mélanges*—to straighten out once and for all the passage on Madame Straus, to draft a dedication acceptable to Berry, and to insert a flattering allusion to the Princesse Soutzo. He was also trying to raise money in any way he could. Somehow the proofs got done, but the money was somewhat elusive. He succeeded only in selling off the rugs at the Straus's; he could not seem to make much progress with his other furniture, some of which Berry was now storing at the American Chamber of Commerce. Unfortunately his needs at the moment were particularly pressing. The house on the Boulevard Haussmann had just been sold, and it seemed likely that the new landlord would immediately demand some 25,000 francs in back rent, a staggering sum for a man already in financial straits. A disaster of the first magnitude seemed about to overwhelm him.

Proust was passively awaiting his fate when he suddenly received, from his old friend Albufera, a clipping to the effect that evicted tenants were now entitled to substantial compensation. The tenants at the Boulevard Haussmann were perhaps on the point of being evicted since the man who had bought the building was planning to remodel it and turn it into a bank. Proust therefore communicated with another old friend, the Duc de Guiche, talked with him, briefed him, and sent him off to see what could be done with the new landlord. The results of the interview were gratifying almost beyond belief. For when accounts were balanced, the compensation against the back rent, it appeared that Proust owed the landlord nothing and was in fact entitled to a little money himself. Proust remembered with some satisfaction that he had included, on the proofs of *Pastiches et mélanges*, a flattering allusion to the Duc de Guiche.

When his laryngitis cleared up, Proust was free to worry about his other complaints, which still led him to fear something like complete facial paralysis. "I have an impediment in my speech," he wrote Berry, "which, since I am not syphilitic, is probably the result of a serious cerebral disorder. In any case, this difficulty in pronouncing words is extremely disturbing. My only hope is that it is entirely due to intoxication brought on by my abuse of veronal. But I am afraid that there is very little chance of this being the real cause." It was certainly disturbing; on the other hand, it was not serious enough to keep him at home or to prevent him from enjoying himself when the company was right at the Ritz or elsewhere.

One evening at the Princesse Soutzo's—it was March 2, 1919— he had a particularly interesting conversation with a British delegate to the Peace Conference, Harold Nicolson. Looking rather grubby, for he had not been able to shave, and wisely keeping his fur coat on, at least when coffee was served, Proust plied his new friend with questions about the way the committees worked. "Well," Nicolson said, "we generally meet at ten, there are secretaries behind. . . ." "But wait a minute, wait a minute," Proust interrupted, "you are going too fast. Begin all over again. You take the official car. You get out at the Quai d'Orsay. You go upstairs. You enter the room. And what happens then? Tell me everything, my dear friend, everything." So Nicolson began again and described the handshakes, the maps, the papers, and the tea and macaroons served in an adjoining room, as Proust listened fascinated, only interrupting to say, "But tell me everything, my dear friend, don't go too fast." On another evening, when the two men met in the dining room at the Ritz, Proust asked more questions and went on to discuss the subject of inversion. "It is a matter of habit," he said. Nicolson protested. "No—that was silly of me—", Proust continued, "what I meant was that it was a matter of delicacy."

When a new friend, Madame Hennessy, proposed a dinner in his honor, Proust was inclined to accept, provided the conditions were right. "If your house is warm," he wrote her, "and if all the windows are closed in the dining room, but more particularly in the room where you go afterwards, I shall do my best to come to dinner. . . . I am not on any special diet, I eat everything and I drink everything, I think I don't like red wines but I like all sorts of white wines, as well as beer and cider. My only peculiarity will be that, with your permission, I shall bring a bottle of Contrexéville or Evian water, and drink a little of it in a separate glass." He added that he was not especially concerned about the temperature of the dining room because he found that he warmed up as he ate. In a postscript he added further that about the middle of the meal the dining-room doors might well be opened —might better be opened, in fact, so that he would not afterwards feel so keenly the chill in the drawing room.

Presumably Madame Hennessy paid particular attention to the temperature in her house, but on the appointed evening Proust could not come to dinner. He did, however, drop in during the evening, in time to have one of his disquieting encounters, unfortunately too common these days, with the Princesse Soutzo. When he told her about his latest symptoms, she seemed completely indifferent, and when he proposed to take her home, she went off with the Beaumonts. Feeling that the whole matter had to be thrashed out, he wrote her a long letter. "I still remember," he told her, "the slight shock I had [on another occasion] when (after supposing all evening that there would be no difficulty) I said, 'Princess, I am going to take you home,' and you answered, 'No, I am going with the Beaumonts.' Really in a case of this sort, when you know the anguish you are going to cause, you should say at the start: 'I warn you that I can't go home with you.' Then one has a chance to get used to it, one doesn't lose at the same moment the person one is fond of and the hope of seeing her in the moments that follow."

In the course of his letter Proust declined an invitation to a dinner Madame Soutzo was giving for the Queen of Rumania, a grand dinner at which Foch and Briand, Prime Ministers and Ambassadors, were to be present. The next day he declined again though perhaps a little less firmly. He would not appear for dinner and probably not for the reception afterwards since he would have to arrive too late. "Either the Queen would have left, or you would no longer be talking to her. But it is not absolutely impossible that I may go all the same, but I am afraid the old ceremonies, the torchlight procession, the men with their hats on, etc., are no longer observed."

II

Though the problems connected with the sale of Proust's house were no longer financial, they were quite as difficult as before. For one thing at least clearly emerged from the negotiations: Proust would have to move at a time when his ill health made rest imperative. He was inevitably committed to a period of anguish and turmoil. But where on earth could he go? Most neighborhoods in Paris were noisy and his walls of cork were scarcely transportable. His future seemed almost too painful to contemplate. Still the time came when he simply had to contemplate it, and to begin going over the map of Paris to find possible locations. The Rue de Rivoli was not perhaps so bad. It was noisy, no doubt, but he could always try ear-stoppers (he decided to investigate their use). If he got an apartment on the top floor, he could at least avoid what he found most disturbing, the noise of other people in the house. Suddenly, however, another possibility occurred to him. He remembered being offered a house between Nice and Monte Carlo, a kind of tower in fact, high up on a cliff overlooking the sea, almost certainly isolated, and probably an idyllic spot for an invalid. Since it belonged to his friend Madame Catusse, he immediately wrote her a letter.

"Is the Tower rented or not?" he asked. "If it isn't, despite the dangers my doctors forsee for me in a trip to Nice (what I am suffering from is not in any way contagious), I should there have the advantage (since I presume that the Tower is not near any other building) of having a house entirely to myself, where, not hearing a suggestion of noise, I could try cutting down on my sleeping pills, though I am afraid the benefits anticipated from this will prove somewhat elusory. If then the Tower is free, I might arrive about the middle of May, or even toward the beginning of May (in case I decide to attempt the trip at all), and when winter sets in (*si fate* . . .) I might visit some cities in Italy, Pisa, Siena, Perugia, where I might perhaps settle down. . . . Is the Tower right on the sea (and above it)? Is it in excellent condition? Or is it back among the trees, shaded by foliage, infested with mosquitoes, etc.? Is it built of stone, without woodwork, so that I wouldn't hear Céleste going up and down stairs (because I count on occupying the top floor where at least I won't hear footsteps)? Finally would you be kind enough to tell me the rent from May 15 to November 15; also, in case I get used to the location, the rent for a longer period, which might be as much as a year?"

The answers to his questions were apparently satisfactory, but meanwhile he found an apartment on the Rue de Rivoli considerably less expensive than the tower at Nice. As he wavered between the alternatives, he worried about a new love affair, now approaching a critical stage, and about his three books—*A l'Ombre des jeunes filles en fleurs*, *Pastiches et mélanges*, and a reissue of *Swann*—which seemed fated never to appear. The publication date was constantly being put off, for one reason or another, or for no reason at all. The editors of the N. R. F. were incorrigibly dilatory and often obtuse as well. Though they employed incompetent printers, they complained about the number of errors on the proofs; though they knew that Proust habitually revised while a book was in press, they complained about the revisions. "Let us assume for a moment that all the mistakes are mine," he wrote Gallimard, "the proofreaders should do something. You say that you have gone from printer to printer, and I am grateful to you, I am overwhelmed by your consideration, but then you have done this only to go back to the same old one, because it is the same name as the one you mentioned in December, when we left [the printing establishment of] La Semeuse. Otherwise perhaps he has many virtues, but I should like to ask you to keep a copy of the pages he took out of *A l'Ombre des jeunes filles en fleurs* for *La Nouvelle Revue*

Française. Some evening we will read them together at the Ritz or here, and you will see what a master he is. Do me this favor, and I promise you that you will be really amazed. My dear friend and publisher, you seem to be reproaching me for my system of revision, and I am aware that it involves many complications (though certainly not in the piece for the *Revue*). But when you asked me to leave Grasset and come over to you, you knew about it, because you were here when Copeau saw the revised Grasset proofs and exclaimed: 'But it's a new book!' " Proust was still on good terms with his publishers, but he could no longer regard them as reasonable men.

As yet he could not make up his mind about the crucial matter of moving. On May 1 he was inclined to take the tower at Nice, if only because it was immediately available and belonged to a person he knew; on May 8 he was completely at sea again, faced, he felt, with hopeless difficulties; on May 11 he was negotiating for the apartment on the Rue de Rivoli. A few days later, however, he seems to have rejected both alternatives, for he began sorting over and packing his possessions without any idea where he was going. Céleste worked steadily, night and day, scarcely stopping to sleep; Proust watched and occasionally helped. He found strange things in closets and trunks, precious and painful things, awakening memories of happier days. He found, for example, his mother's dresses, including one she had bought for his brother's wedding and had worn only on that day. Reflecting that the fashions of 1900 were being revived and that the dresses could now be worn again, Proust sent them to friends and relatives, feeling as he did so that he was severing still another bond with the past. Once, when Céleste was burning old photographs and manuscripts, he suddenly recognized a photograph that had been one of the treasures of his childhood. "No, not that," he cried as he rescued it from the flames. It was a photograph of Abel Desjardins, inscribed "To Marcel Proust, my best friend except X," with the words "except X" crossed out.

On May 29, 1919, just before he was obliged to move, a furnished apartment providentially turned up in the house of the actress, Madame Réjane, on the Rue Laurent-Pichat. Proust took it at once. Two days later the storage men appeared at the

Boulevard Haussmann, creating an intolerable turmoil and driving Proust almost to frenzy. He was three-quarters dead, he felt, when he left the house; he was quite ready to expire after a day at Madame Réjane's, for it appeared that providence had not been nearly so kind as he had at first supposed. The new apartment was so incredibly noisy that he could scarcely sleep at all—the walls and floors were apparently too thin. People could be heard talking, opening windows, taking baths; drafts could be felt from every quarter. Proust's first impulse was to move out at once, but since he had nowhere to go he stayed on and suffered. He was obliged to drug himself so that he could write essential letters, in particular letters to the N. R. F., which was still postponing the appearance of his three books.

The editors of the N. R. F. had announced publication for the first week in June and now they were vaguely talking of the second or third week. But Proust's spies—presumably Odilon (now back from the army) and Céleste, who were sent out to inquire surreptitiously—could get no definite information. Proust was particularly worried because the season was nearly over and society people were beginning to leave Paris. He pleaded for an early and definite date, say June 15. But again there were infuriating delays, and when finally, about June 23, the books were ready, he got only second or third printings of the *Jeunes filles*, the first printing having mysteriously disappeared, obviously through the incompetence of the N. R. F. Agitated by the perfidy of his publishers, maddened by weeks of insomnia, asthmatic and otherwise miserable, Proust awaited the first reviews.

CHAPTER XX

A l'Ombre des jeunes filles en fleurs

I

A l'Ombre des jeunes filles en fleurs takes up the story of the hero, abruptly dropped at the end of *Du Côté de chez Swann.* Chronology is more strictly observed than in the earlier volume, yet the structure is quite as complex. The narrative still moves in cycles and epicycles; the characters—with a few notable exceptions, characters already more or less familiar—appear in each chapter and even in each section of each chapter. Several of them are nearly always before the reader. Thus in the first eighty pages, devoted to the events of a single day, Marcel sees his parents, his grandmother, Françoise, and Norpois; furthermore, he thinks about or discusses Swann, Odette, Cottard, Gilberte, and Bergotte. It would be difficult to say which are the main characters, for all are important. The effect is that of a particularly large circus where something is going on in all the rings, and even outside the rings, at the same time.

The narrative is so complicated as to resist summary, but it is perhaps possible to pick out a few strands from the closely woven fabric. In the first chapter, "Autour de Madame Swann," considerable space is devoted to certain characters who seem, more definitely than the others, to represent groups or professions. Thus Norpois is always felt to be the Diplomat, La Berma the Actress, and Bergotte the Man of Letters, as elsewhere in the novel Vinteuil is the Composer and Bloch the Jew. Though generically similar, these figures are treated quite differently. Norpois, for example, is a caricature—a pompous ass who always uses journalistic clichés and always talks discreet nonsense. It is he who now gives the hero fatuous advice about a literary career, thus inheriting the role assigned, in *Jean Santeuil*, to Duroc, and, in subsequent notebooks, to Monsieur de Guray. Bergotte is also for a few pages a caricature, when the hero first sees him and experiences disappointment similar to that he felt when he first saw the Duchesse de Guermantes. But Bergotte soon changes and becomes an entirely serious study of a man of letters, similar to several such studies in *Jean Santeuil* in which Proust tries to determine the relationship between the writer and his work. Proust's conclusion here—almost exactly the opposite of that in *Jean Santeuil* and in *Contre Sainte-Beuve*—is that the two are recognizably the same. The man is the style: Bergotte talks as he writes. On the other hand, the morality of the man is not necessarily the same as that exemplified in his books. Bergotte permits himself moments of weakness which his heroes, almost painfully scrupulous, would never give way to.

> It is the vices (or merely the weaknesses and follies) of the circle in which they live, the meaningless conversation, the frivolous or shocking lives of their daughters, the infidelity of their wives, or their own misdeeds that writers have most often castigated in their books, without, however, thinking it necessary to alter their domestic economy or to improve the tone of their households.

While he is observing and speculating about the Diplomat and the Man of Letters, Proust's hero succeeds in making some progress in his love for Gilberte. At least the complexion of the story is different from what it was in *Du Côté de chez Swann*. Gilberte is now apparently complaisant and certainly accessible enough. She permits Marcel to have in her presence—and one might almost say with her—an experience of sex; she even invites him to her tea parties. But suddenly, for reasons that are not entirely clear, she becomes difficult, and Marcel ceases to see her. He suffers for many pages until his love, deprived of its object, gradually dies. The passages devoted to his suffering were written during the war years and were obviously favorites of Proust's, for he chose them— or permitted Rivière to choose them—for separate publication in the N. R. F. magazine. They are certainly a brilliant, though a rather formidable, example of his talent for analysis. The feelings of a disappointed lover have perhaps never been so exhaustively or so dispassionately studied. Proust might well be considering the decline of plant life in the first Ice Age.

The story of Gilberte repeatedly drifts off into the story of Swann, which is also quite different from what it was in the first volume. Swann himself has changed, as so many other characters afterwards change in the course of the novel. In his interview with Bois, published in 1913, Proust explained these changes as an attempt to represent the passage of time in the narrative. As there is a plane and a solid geometry, he said, so there is a plane psychology and one involving the dimension of time. A passenger on a train who sees the same village now on his right and now on his left realizes that his position is changing; the reader of a novel who gets different impressions of the same characters realizes that time is going by. One might add, as Proust did not, that readers often come to this realization, for characters in novels are seldom entirely static. What is peculiar to Proust's novel is that the successive impressions are sometimes so different that the characters no longer seem to be the same. They are apparently quite distinct figures who have arbitrarily been given the same names. More often than not one suspects that Proust has either changed his mind about them or used different models for them in different parts of his work.

The change in Swann is indeed radical: he now appears as the husband of Odette. Long after he ceased to love her, it seems, he permitted himself to be bullied and blackmailed into marriage. This development, so little in keeping with what is so far known about the characters of Swann and Odette, is hard to swallow, but Proust offers many ingenious explanations. He suggests that after all Swann and Odette did have something in common. Odette understood her lover's character and even, to a limited extent, his work; she was able to give him shrewd literary advice. In any case, Swann was not likely to be deterred from an impossible marriage by his fear of what society would say about it, because he had long since withdrawn from society. Perhaps he actually liked the idea of such a marriage; perhaps

the artistic, if not the perverse side of Swann's nature would in any event have derived a certain amount of pleasure from coupling with himself, in one of those crossings of species such as Mendelians practise and mythology records, a creature of a different race, archduchess or prostitute, from contracting a royal alliance or from marrying beneath him.

Or perhaps he merely hoped that, when he was married, he could take Odette—and their daughter too—to call on the Duchesse de Guermantes, whose opinion alone he valued. Proust's speculations are so interesting that in the end one scarcely cares whether Swann is the same person or not.

Odette has changed too, even more radically. She is no longer the disturbing phantom with sensational vices who so persistently eluded her lover; she is now a relatively respectable married woman, intent on forming a *salon*. But even the new Odette is not always the same. In many passages her social success is described as extremely modest; she lures to her drawing room only the wives of Assistant Under Secretaries and such members of the Jockey Club as she knew in her unregenerate days. Yet in other passages she is seen to be on good terms with the Princesse Mathilde and the Duchesse de Vendôme. Furthermore, she arouses the envy of Madame Verdurin, whose protégée she once was, for—in certain passages at least—she already has a notable *salon*, of which the chief ornament is Bergotte. The different passages are scarcely consistent, and it is hard to avoid the conclusion that Proust is using more than one model for Odette. Sometimes he remembers ex-courtesans with social aspirations, perhaps chiefly Madame Hayman, and sometimes (especially when he identifies Gilberte with Jeanne Pouquet and Bergotte with Anatole France) he remembers established hostesses, of whom one was certainly Madame Arman de Caillavet.

In the chapter as a whole the Madame Hayman strain can perhaps be called the dominant one, for Odette emerges as, first of all, a dazzling figure, a woman of great beauty and great elegance, who completely captivates a youthful admirer. Analysis of motives, so persistent when Proust is trying to account for Odette's social position, gives way to description as florid and nostalgic as in "Combray." The hero is recalling an entirely happy association as he fixes impressions that Odette has made on him in different places and at different seasons of the year. Sometimes his attention is caught by the room in which she receives him—as by the drawing room with the great bay window. The afternoon light is a "sparkling tide of gold out of which the bluish crags of sofas and vaporous carpet beaches emerged like enchanted islands." Sometimes he sees her reflected in her favorite flowers.

> There was always beside her chair an immense bowl of crystal filled to the brim with Parma violets or with long white daisy-petals scattered upon the water, which seemed to be testifying, in the eyes of the arriving guest, to some favorite and interrupted occupation, such as the cup of tea which Madame Swann would, for her own amusement, have been drinking there by herself; an occupation more intimate still and more mysterious, so much so that one felt oneself impelled to apologize on seeing the flowers exposed there by her side, as one would have apologized for looking at the title of the still open book which would have revealed to one what had just been read by—and so, perhaps, what was still in the mind of Odette.

But always her dress is the main thing, for Odette is now essentially a woman who dresses superbly. In the house she wears one of a marvelous and bewildering assortment of wrappers made of "*crêpe-de-Chine* or silk, old rose, cherry-colored, Tiepolo pink, white, mauve, green, red or yellow, plain or patterned." There is always, in these wrappers and in the more sumptuous gowns she wears outdoors, a suggestion of archaism, a passing allusion to older fashions that Odette has not yet quite forgotten.

> As in a fine literary style which overlays with its different forms and so strengthens a tradition which lies concealed among them, so in Madame Swann's attire those half-hinted memories of

waistcoats or of ringlets, sometimes a tendency, at once repressed, towards the "all aboard," or even a distant and vague allusion to the "chase me" kept alive beneath the concrete form the unfinished likeness of other, older forms which you would not have succeeded, now, in making a tailor or a dressmaker reproduce, but about which your thoughts incessantly hovered, and enwrapped Madame Swann in a cloak of nobility—perhaps because the sheer uselessness of these fripperies made them seem meant to serve some more than utilitarian purpose, perhaps because of the traces they preserved of vanished years, or else because there was a sort of personality permeating this lady's wardrobe, which gave to the most dissimilar of her costumes a distinct family likeness. One felt that she did not dress simply for the comfort or the adornment of her body; she was surrounded by her garments as by the delicate and spiritualized machinery of a whole form of civilization.

Finally, in a supremely florid and supremely beautiful passage, Marcel describes her as she appears on the Avenue du Bois, where she takes her morning walk. She is now full sail, like another Millamant, with her parasol up, her streamers out, and a shoal of fine gentlemen for tenders. Bows are made and acknowledged, and the Prince de Sagan, wheeling his horse around, doffs "his hat with a sweeping theatrical and, so to speak, allegorical flourish in which he displayed all the chivalrous courtesy of a great noble bowing in token of his respect for Woman."

II

In the second chapter, "Noms de pays: le pays," the scene shifts to Balbec. This is not unexpected: from the beginning of the novel the hero has looked forward to visiting Normandy and seeing the celebrated Balbec church, so curious an example of the Norman style that it seems almost Persian. He has imagined it as standing by the sea, on a reef of wild rocks around which the sea birds wheel. The reality is of course quite different and as usual disappointing. The church is not at Balbec at all, but at Balbec-en-Terre, miles away from the sea. It actually stands on a square from which two tram lines emerge, opposite a café marked, in gold letters, with the word "Billiards."

But the disappointment is only momentary, for Balbec proper
—the seaside resort where Marcel and his grandmother stay—is
a new and exciting world, as individual and as different from
Paris as Combray. The center of this world is the Grand Hôtel,
a palatial establishment with a large staff of employees and an
odd assortment of guests. Marcel observes and studies them all.
He observes the hotel itself—his own room, the elevator, the
dining room—and beyond the hotel the sea, dazzling and moun-
tainous, but seldom the same on successive days, changing with
the light and the tide. Balbec, in fact, has an interest of its own
and is on the whole quite as charming as Combray. But it is
also the scene on which several characters, hitherto mentioned
quite casually, assume importance in the narrative. They drift
in at intervals. Three of them—the Marquise de Villeparisis, the
Marquis de Saint-Loup-en-Bray, and the Baron de Charlus—are
members of the highest aristocracy and in fact close relatives of
the Duchesse de Guermantes. For the first time Marcel is able
to study the effects of an aristocratic heritage.

The Marquise de Villeparisis is a rich old lady who affects
old-fashioned bonnets and shows a number of other eccentricities.
She moves into the hotel with a whole staff of servants and even
brings her own curtains and screens. She is particularly friendly
with Marcel and his grandmother; she is constantly taking them
for rides in her carriage or sending them presents. Yet, as the
acquaintanceship develops, it appears that Madame de Villeparisis
is essentially a snob, though of a kind Marcel has not encountered
before. She is, however much she may try to conceal the fact,
a typical product of her class. When she talks about architecture,
she inevitably mentions the house where she grew up, one of
the finest examples of the Renaissance style. When she talks
about the writers of an earlier generation, she judges them as
they were judged by Sainte-Beuve (at least the Sainte-Beuve
described by Proust) or by the fine gentlemen who frequented
her father's drawing-room. Even her friendliness is finally seen
to be a class product, a reversion "to her early training, to the
aristocratic manner in which a great lady is supposed to show
common people that she is glad to see them, that she is not at all
stiff."

In Madame de Villeparisis's nephew, Saint-Loup, the class heritage appears so differently at different times that he can almost be described as two or three distinct characters. At first he is a typical dandy, an epitome of aristocratic insolence. He wears daring clothes and a monocle, which keeps falling off and darting before him like a butterfly. When he is introduced to Marcel, not a muscle of his face moves:

> his eyes, in which there shone not the faintest gleam of human sympathy, showed merely in the insensibility, in the inanity of their gaze an exaggeration failing which there would have been nothing to distinguish them from lifeless mirrors. Then fastening on me those hard eyes, as though he wished to make sure of me before returning my salute, by an abrupt release which seemed to be due rather to a reflex action of his muscles than to an exercise of his will, keeping between himself and me the greatest possible interval, he stretched his arm out to its full extension and, at the end of it, offered me his hand. I supposed that it must mean, at the very least, a duel when, next day, he sent me his card.

Later, when Marcel gets to know him, he reveals himself as a rebel against his class, a somewhat too ardent intellectual with a quixotic passion for equality. He is now warm, kind, impulsive, and supremely natural. His heritage is still aristocratic but less obviously so. (The passage is based on the one about Bertrand de Réveillon in *Jean Santeuil*.) Later still, when his love affair is described, he is a typically barbaric young aristocrat civilized by a woman. His mistress has "opened his mind to the invisible" and brought "delicacy into his heart." She has taught him, among other things, to be attentive to his friends. Despite transitional passages, the different Saint-Loups remain different. The portrait is apparently pieced together from Proust's memories of several young men, perhaps chiefly Castellane, Fénelon, and Albufera. Yet these memories add so much to the chapter that one would scarcely sacrifice any of them merely for the sake of consistency, which is after all not the only virtue in fiction.

The third character, the Baron de Charlus, is the most obviously aristocratic of all. His manner is habitually insolent; his views, refined no doubt by his culture, are still patently those of his class. Since he attaches the highest importance to birth and social position, he prefers to associate with certain great ladies "whose ancestresses, two centuries earlier, had shared in all the glory and grace of the old order." But Charlus is an invert as well as an aristocrat, and though Proust preserves the somewhat unsatisfactory fiction that his hero does not recognize the fact, the evidence rapidly accumulates. This evidence is so detailed and so striking that Charlus at once emerges as the most successful of all Proust's characters.

The hero's first impression of Charlus is a particularly significant one. As he is walking by the Casino one day, he has the sensation of being watched. "I turned my head," he says,

> and saw a man of about forty, very tall and rather stout, with a very dark moustache, who, nervously slapping the leg of his trousers with a switch, kept fastened upon me a pair of eyes dilated with observation. Every now and then those eyes were shot through by a look of intense activity such as the sight of a person whom they do not know excites only in men to whom, for whatever reason, it suggests thoughts that would not occur to anyone else—madmen, for instance, or spies. He trained upon me a supreme stare at once bold, prudent, rapid and profound.

The principal element in the impression is the eyes, or, more specifically, the intense, furtive glance that emanates from the eyes. Afterwards, when he gets to know Charlus, the hero mentions it repeatedly, and indeed describes it, significantly, in images drawn from the underworld. Charlus is a hotel crook caught in the act of spying; a detective on special duty who ignores his friends and concentrates on strangers; and a peddler with illicit wares who keeps a sharp lookout, though without turning his head, "on the different points of the horizon from any of which may appear, suddenly, the police."

Charlus's glance of course betrays him as an invert, but other things betray him too. His voice tends to be shrill and feminine; when he is expressing certain delicate sentiments, it rises to a higher register, takes on "an unexpected sweetness," and seems "to be embodying choirs of betrothed maidens, of sisters, who poured out the treasures of their love." His dress is somewhat too deliberately sober. Once, when he notices that his embroidered handkerchief is protruding from his pocket, he quickly stuffs it back out of sight "with the scandalized air of a prudish but far from innocent lady concealing attractions which, by an excess of scrupulosity, she regards as indecent." He is constantly making discreet advances to Marcel and then, to cover himself, relapsing into insolence. The most revealing passage is one in which, meeting Marcel on the way down to bathe, he is irresistibly impelled to reach out and give the young man's neck a pinch.

III

The seacoast, for Proust, is the place where classes mingle most freely and where a young man of the middle class can most easily meet members of the aristocracy. It is also the place where the sexes mingle, where girls are most numerous and most approachable. Marcel sees and admires a good many girls; finally he succeeds in meeting a whole group of them, a compact "little band," *les jeunes filles en fleurs* who give the book its title. In this part of his story, the reader is repeatedly struck by the fact that the girls behave so very much like young men.

Marcel first sees the members of the little band as they file along the walk before the hotel in a kind of Bacchic procession. They are as different from the other people at Balbec as "a flight of gulls which performed with measured steps upon the sands—the dawdlers using their wings to overtake the rest—a movement the purpose of which seems as obscure to the human bathers, whom they do not appear to see, as it is clearly determined in their own birdish minds." Marcel is sure that they are particularly athletic girls, for they push bicycles or carry golf clubs. He is sure, too, that they are by nature "bold, frivolous, and hard," that they carry to the point of cruelty their contempt for the rest of the human race. Indeed he imagines that if he could get to know them, he would be penetrating—"like a cultivated pagan or a meticulous Christian going among barbarians—into a rejuvenating society in which reigned health, unconsciousness of others, sensual pleasures, cruelty, unintellectuality and joy."

When he makes their acquaintance, Marcel finds that they

are by no means so barbaric as he supposed. They come from quite respectable—in fact very prosperous—middle-class families and they have thoroughly conventional ideas. They distinguish sharply between good and bad form; they hate the Government and the Jews. On the other hand, they seem strange to the reader if not to the hero in that they are so completely free from restraint or supervision of any kind. They frequent golf courses and race tracks. At the Casino they make themselves objectionable by playing tricks on the dancing master, sliding on the floors, and smashing chairs; the manager is constantly admonishing them. They seem strange, too, in that, though they show very little interest in men, they admit Marcel as a regular member of their little band and are quite as sensible of his attraction as he is of theirs.

Marcel is in love with them all, successively and even simultaneously, for a kind of collective charm seems to pervade the whole group. They all have the freshness of roses, the plastic beauty of "statues exposed to the sunlight upon a Grecian shore." Yet even from the beginning one girl, Albertine Simonet, detaches herself from the others as especially interesting to him. Though he sees her more often than the others and learns more about her, it would be difficult to say that he ever gets to know her. She exists for him, and indeed for the reader, only in the series of quite different impressions she makes on him. This is a matter of principle with Proust, who here explains it by saying that in life mistresses are never distinct personalities and should not therefore be distinct in fiction.

We understand the characters of people who do not interest us; how can we ever grasp that of a person who is an intimate part of our existence, whom after a little we no longer distinguish in any way from ourselves, whose motives provide us with an inexhaustible supply of anxious hypotheses which we perpetually reconstruct. Springing from somewhere beyond our understanding, our curiosity as to the woman whom we love overleaps the bounds of that woman's character, which we might if we chose but probably will not choose to stop and examine.

So it is with Marcel's curiosity about Albertine. Each time he sees her she seems to be a different personality—first "the bacchante with the bicycle, the frenzied muse of the golf course," then the respectably bred and rather frightened young woman, then the hoyden using slang and speaking in a nasal drawl, "into the composition of which there entered perhaps a provincial descent, a juvenile affectation of British phlegm, the teaching of a foreign governess and a congestive hypertrophy of the mucus of the nose." Even her appearance seems to be in a state of constant flux, as Gilberte's once was when the hero saw her in the Champs-Elysées. Albertine has a temple that is unpleasantly flushed, at first but not afterwards. She has a mole that wanders about her face, appearing now on her cheek and now on her chin, but finally coming to rest on her upper lip. She has the complexion of a chameleon, sometimes gray, sometimes pink, and sometimes even purplish.

Interspersed with the story of Albertine are episodes devoted to a painter named Elstir, whose theories are expounded at considerable length. He distinguishes sharply between the sensibility, which offers material to the artist, and the intelligence, which does not. When he paints, he tries to put on the canvas what he sees, not what his intelligence tells him that he sees, and he makes a deliberate effort to "strip himself . . . of every intellectual concept." In such passages Proust is obviously thinking of himself and expounding in a general way the principles that he himself hoped to follow in writing his novel. Yet, oddly enough, he abandons these principles just at the moment he expounds them, for he is no longer content to rely entirely on his sensibility. There are no doubt many passages in *A l'Ombre des jeunes filles en fleurs* in which his sensibility only is called into play, passages concerned with the hero's impressions of Odette and Balbec and Saint-Loup and the young girls of the little band. But these passages are almost invariably followed by other highly intellectual ones, in which the impressions are interpreted or supplemented. Saint-Loup is a dandified young man with a monocle that dances before him like a butterfly, then an example of an aristocratic heritage: the portrait is both impressionistic and analytical. Gilberte and Albertine are characters in a story as well as convenient illustrations of a philosophy of love: the author's method is alternately narrative and expository. It is as though Stendhal, in describing the love affair of Julien and Madame de Rênal, had introduced into it appropriate passages from *De l'Amour*.

A l'Ombre des jeunes filles en fleurs is, in short, a more intellectual volume than its predecessor, *Du Côté de chez Swann*. It can perhaps be described as a reversion to the manner of Proust's early work, the first part of his novel in which the versatility of his genius—which he thought he was illustrating in *Swann*—is really apparent. In certain passages, notably those devoted to Odette, it has the fresh poetic quality, the rich impressionism of "Combray." Elsewhere it is more thoughtful, more analytical, and more concerned with motives and psychological laws. One is aware, as one is not in "Combray," that the author's aim is truth.

CHAPTER XXI

The Goncourt Prize

I

THE FIRST ARTICLE on A *l'Ombre des jeunes filles en fleurs*, and the other books published with it, appeared in *Le Figaro* on July 7, 1919. It was written by Proust's friend Robert Dreyfus, using the pseudonym of Bartholo; it was in fact written at Proust's request. He had asked for something better, a leading article by a really distinguished friend, say Gide or Léon Blum. The Dreyfus article was the best he could get.

The remarks were necessarily somewhat general, since Dreyfus had not yet read the *Jeunes filles* and had not recently reread either *Swann* or the pieces in *Pastiches et mélanges*. Still a number of kind things were said. There was something about Proust's martyrdom and enforced isolation, something about the poetry and meticulous analysis in his novel, and something about the dexterity of the parodies in *Pastiches et mélanges*. The three books were described as "witty, strange, incomparable," "superior and charming." Proust, however, was far from satisfied. In a letter to Dreyfus he complained that the references to his ill health were in poor taste, that the use of a pseudonym was unfortunate, that the type used in the article was too small, and that his novel was quite unlike the description, since it was not really meticulous at all. Nevertheless he thanked Dreyfus and Flers, the editor of *Le Figaro*. The article was after all publicity of a sort, though far inferior to the publicity that had announced *Du Côté de chez Swann*.

Other articles and reviews were less flattering, though by no means definitely unfavorable. Vandérem, the critic of *La Revue de Paris* (July 15), complained that both *Swann* and the *Jeunes filles* positively bristled with faults—they were too long, too detailed, too difficult stylistically, and too completely destitute of action. Nevertheless they were the most absorbing and the most important of contemporary novels. If they violated all the rules by lacking unity, selection, and restraint, they still revealed a remarkably interesting mind, a new sensibility, a fresh and active intelligence. The writing was never mediocre; the characters were worthy of Tolstoy. The only profoundly disturbing fault that Vandérem noticed was the author's dated and somewhat stuffy attitude, of which his snobbishness was a prime example. André Billy, the critic of *L'Oeuvre* (August 26), worked out a similar balance between virtues and faults, though with rather more emphasis on the snobbishness of the author, the length of the volumes, and the number of digressions. Proust was pitiless, he decided, though certainly a man of remarkable sensibility, subtle and acute to the point of being morbid.

While these first reviews were coming out, Proust was gradually accustoming himself to the hardships at Madame Réjane's. The noise began to seem more remote, probably because he was becoming more expert in the use of ear-stoppers. The wall paper —a flaming red with black-and-white flower patterns—began to seem positively cheerful, and indeed Proust was inspired to describe it as such in a passage added to the proofs of *Le Côté de Guermantes*. Soon he was dining out again or receiving company at home. And when no other company was available he could always rap three times on the floor and summon Madame Réjane's son, Jacques Porel, who lived conveniently in the apartment below. Once during the summer when Blanche called at the house, he was admitted by Céleste and conducted to a sepulchral room, where Proust was resting in bed. He complained a good deal—he said that he was at the point of death at least three times a day—but he looked surprisingly healthy. At the moment he was considering a trip to Cabourg. After getting Céleste to provide refreshments, he talked gaily and tirelessly —Blanche had seldom seen him in better form. Some days later the invalid dined at Berry's, drank rather too much of the excellent champagne that was served, and afterwards drove through the Bois to sober up. He was a little tired by morning and it seemed wiser to give up the trip to Cabourg.

The apartment at Madame Réjane's was clearly not so bad after all, but Proust decided not to take it permanently because the rent was too high and the central heating might turn out to be bad for his asthma. He still hoped for something on the Rue de Rivoli, preferably at the corner of the Rue Castiglione, just a few doors away from the Ritz. Nothing, however, was available there, and little anywhere else. Once he consulted Dreyfus about an apartment on the Boulevard Malesherbes, and once the Princesse Soutzo about a hotel suite at the Ritz or the Majestic or even at the hotel in Hendaye where she was then staying. In the end, however, he gave up the idea of a suite and took what apparently was the only thing he could get—a furnished apartment on the Rue Hamelin. It seemed in every respect undesirable. It was hideous and dingy, twice as expensive as it should have been, and about half as large—there was scarcely room for his secretary. Proust could only describe it as a rat hole.

While he was preparing to move or suffering attacks of asthma after he had taken the decisive step, he read further reviews of A l'Ombre des jeunes filles en fleurs. They were on the whole more favorable than the first ones, at least sufficiently favorable to suggest that the book was gaining in popularity. The critic of Le Crapouillot (September 1) described the cult for Swann and announced that he himself was now completely won over; he accepted Proust as the most original of contemporary writers. Blanche, again assuming the role of champion and again echoing ideas he had picked up from the author, praised the book in Le Figaro (September 22). He defended even its form, which, he said, would become clearer as the later volumes appeared; he answered the strictures of earlier critics, in particular those of Billy.

Comoedia (October 5) described Proust as "un grand poète douloureux"; *Le Gaulois* (October 25) said that the book was one in which "the soul confronts itself"; *La Revue du mois* (November 10) wrote that it enriched French literature. By December Proust was satisfied that his novel was at least modestly successful, certainly far more successful than *Swann* had been in 1913. He hoped to make money but feared that, as usual, the N. R. F. was bungling its job. It was obviously bungling the printings. It had issued a sixth in June and now, five months later, it was still sending out the third. But what else could be expected from men so completely irresponsible?

II

Better known than he had ever been before, hovering on the verge of fame, Proust felt that if he could get a prize for his book, in particular the Goncourt Prize, he would become a really popular author. Discreet inquiries revealed that at least two members of the Goncourt Academy would certainly vote for him—Léon Daudet, a friend of long standing, and the elder Rosny, a more distant friend, who had voted for *Swann* in 1913. But further inquiries suggested that there was no obvious way of bringing pressure to bear on the other eight members, and Proust half decided not to submit his book. In the end, however, he did submit it.

The Goncourt Academy met on December 10, 1919. There was strong sentiment for *A l'Ombre des jeunes filles en fleurs* and almost equally strong sentiment for *Les Croix de bois* by Dorgelès. But on the third ballot, when the less popular contenders were eliminated, Proust got a bare majority of six votes out of ten. That afternoon triumphant callers appeared at the rat hole on the Rue Hamelin to announce the award—Léon Daudet from the Goncourt Academy, and Gallimard, Tronche, and Rivière from the N. R. F. Proust accepted their congratulations and at once began preparing a flattering article about himself and his work, designed for publication in *L'Eclair*. Later in the day reporters appeared, eager for interviews, but all were somewhat injudiciously turned away at the door, obviously because Proust was unwilling to have either his rat hole or his infirmities described in the press.

To Proust the award was a triumph—both a final justification of a long career passed in obscurity and an assurance of future success. To the newspapers, or to most of them, it was a hideous mistake, as scandalous as it was unexpected. For they knew Dorgelès, who was a war veteran and an author with a popular following; they had scarcely heard of Proust. Critics who before had ignored his book now tried to review it on the spur of the moment, but they found it extraordinarily hard skimming. One critic gave up in disgust, another decided to wait until larger type was used, and still another remarked that it was bad manners on the part of the author to publish so long a work. Critics and reporters generally suspected a plot, perhaps a political plot engineered by Daudet, an ardent Royalist and editor of *L'Action française*. Only he, they felt, could have awarded a prize intended for a young man to a decrepit invalid of indeterminate age. *L'Humanité* ran the headline, "Place aux vieux!"; *Paris-midi* complained that the Goncourt Academy was controlled by the Right; *Le Journal du peuple* described Proust as a reactionary without talent; *Entente* accused Daudet of betraying the youth of France, whom before he had so persistently courted. The publishers of Proust's rival, encouraged by the outcry, seemed half to believe that their man had won the award. Their advertisement ran: "Goncourt Prize: Roland Dorgelès. *Les Croix de bois*," though they added in small letters, "4 votes out of 10."

Proust himself was certainly disconcerted. The fame that he had waited for so long had come in a form scarcely distinguishable from notoriety. Having achieved the ambition of a lifetime, he suddenly found himself a national scandal, a social climber, a reactionary, and a valetudinarian. "It seems that you come to see me all the time," he wrote Blanche, "if one can believe the Socialist papers when they say: 'Monsieur Proust receives only his favorite painter, Monsieur Jacques-Emile Blanche.' These papers are fantastic. They add a year to one's life every day. Just before the award (the date of which I didn't know) they said (I didn't discover it until afterwards from a 'clipping') that I shouldn't get it because I was forty-seven. The next day I shouldn't have had it because I was fifty. Now they have got me up to fifty-eight, and I am resigned to being shortly a hundred." (Actually he was forty-eight.)

Proust was disconcerted but he was nevertheless not inclined to take too serious a view of the newspaper campaign. For one thing, he realized that publicity, even unfavorable publicity, was a good thing for his book. He now hoped to sell as many as fifteen or twenty printings, though when he remembered the incompetence of his publishers, he realized that the figure would be much more modest. For another thing, he knew, as the public did not, that he had many distinguished admirers. He was getting letters of congratulation, not only from friends, but from other authors and Academicians—letters that gave him every reason to believe that the best people were on his side. The men who had voted for him, he once assured Gallimard, were the most talented members of the Goncourt Academy. But the others were not completely devoid of talent, for they now wrote to say that they would have voted for him had the circumstances been different. Members of the French Academy wrote too—no fewer than a score of them, Proust boasted. They were disturbed that the Goncourt Academy had anticipated them, for they had intended to give him their own prize, the *Grand Prix de Littérature*.

In the course of time this more enlightened opinion made itself manifest in the newspapers. Champions came forward to defend Proust's work, as Blanche had defended it earlier—champions as influential as Proust himself could have wished. One was Jacques Boulenger, editor of *Opinion*. He defended the award of the Goncourt Academy, answered the attacks of the critic in *Débats*, and praised Proust's work, though with many reservations. Proust twice invited him to dinner along with members of the nobility. Boulenger could not come either time, but the grateful author, determined to be friendly, went on writing him assiduously. "I can't possibly correct all the errors about myself in the press," he once said. "But I hope that at least you won't think me a snob. If you read *Swann* and my other books attentively, you will see that I always give my family and myself the most modest social position and that I am neither dazzled nor angered by dukes. You can ask Guiche, who knows me well." (Guiche could certainly qualify as an authority in the matter since he was a duke himself.)

Another champion was, oddly enough, the critic who had irritated Proust in 1913, Paul Souday. Writing in *Le Temps* of

January 1, 1920, Souday gave a favorable account of the *Jeunes filles* and went out of his way to justify the Goncourt Academy. If he again touched on the faults in Proust's style, he now did so only to emphasize its virtues. "The reader notices," he said, "not only the somewhat long-winded and involved construction in the sentences of Monsieur Marcel Proust, but also their almost uniform originality in thought or feeling, and in verbal expression." He praised the characterization—the admirable portraits of Norpois, Charlus, Saint-Loup, and Madame de Villeparisis. He ended with an eloquent passage on Proust's treatment of love. "It is unfortunately only too true," he said, "that this principle of relativity manifests itself not only in the motion of masses but also, so to speak, in the mechanics of morality, that it makes all human happiness precarious, all love imperfect. Few novelists have expressed, more forcefully or more bitterly, the feeling of change and incessant instability that makes human life an uninterrupted series of partial deaths. Hence the book is somber like most great books concerned with human destiny."

Highly elated by the review and determined, if possible, to win another friend in the critical world, Proust at once wrote Souday a long letter, in the course of which he suggested a dinner appointment. "The last lines on love are superb," he said. "I shall return to them in a minute. In your first lines, where you take my side in the controversy about the Goncourt Prize, I detect not only justice but good will, which I should very much like, when we see each other, to try transforming into friendship." Before the end of his letter, however, Proust felt obliged to express some dissatisfaction. The review was badly timed, it should not have appeared at New Year's, when few people are disposed to read criticism. The remarks about long sentences were unfortunate and the remarks about the characters not always very discerning. "I am a little frightened," Proust said in a postscript, "when I realize that Monsieur de Charlus seems only a nobleman with the prejudices of his class. This is indeed the impression that he first makes and will for some time continue to make on the 'narrator,' whose personality you have so discerningly distinguished from mine, but actually Monsieur de Charlus (and this explains his misanthropy and his eccentric behavior with 'me') is an old auntie (I can use the word because it is in Balzac)."

The controversy was by no means over, hostile articles continued to appear, but by February, 1920, *Le Figaro* was at least able to report that public sentiment was definitely changing. There was less inclination to judge Proust by his income or his social standing or his eccentricities, the newspaper said. He was at last accepted as a writer, and indeed widely praised by competent judges as one of the most original writers of the day. "The chief complaint against him has been his age: he was twenty somewhere around 1895. But what difference does that make? If his work is new, is he not young?"

III

The statement in *Le Figaro* was a fair one and its list of competent judges impressive. Proust could scarcely have hoped for more, unless perhaps—the thought must certainly have occurred to him— two other names might have been added to the list, the names of men whose disciple he had once been and whose approbation now, at the moment of his triumph, would have been particularly gratifying: Montesquiou and Anatole France. But unfortunately neither had come forward to defend A *l'Ombre des jeunes filles en fleurs.*

The silence of France was certainly excusable. He was now a man of seventy-five, living in retirement at La Béchellerie, not very much concerned with recent developments in the world of letters, and not very clear in his mind about young authors he had known a generation before. Proust had dropped out of France's sight, and, according to reports that reached La Béchellerie, he had become a hopeless neurotic with a passion for staying in bed behind closed shutters with the electric lights on. Still the old master considerately examined the work of his former disciple, without however making anything out of it at all. "The fault is not [Proust's], it is mine," he afterwards remarked. "We understand only our own generation." What more was there to be said?

The silence of Montesquiou was excusable too, though for different and more complex reasons. He was younger than France, but he had long outlived his reputation. The world had changed but he had not. He now appeared as a somewhat distasteful survival from another era, a decayed dandy whose pose was no longer arresting, whose poems no one read, and whose parties few people were willing to attend. Consequently he hated the world and especially those former disciples who had deserted him as his star had set. Proust, who had once been more assiduous than the others, could only seem to him a particularly flagrant case of desertion. He was in fact no longer able even to see Proust, for having once been admitted for a brief call at Proust's apartment and having injudiciously stayed on for many hours, he was never admitted again. Proust made it perfectly clear that he was willing to follow, but only at a safe distance, the disappointments of the poet's career.

The publication of the *Jeunes filles* and the Goncourt award thus created a particularly difficult problem for Montesquiou, who was already incensed by the shabby treatment he had received. He wanted to seem pleased, and he went so far as to write Proust a long and by no means unfavorable letter about the novel. But there could be no doubt that he keenly resented his former disciple's success, which could not help reminding him how completely he himself had fallen into neglect. "I too should like a little glory," he was once heard to say. "To get it, I have only to call myself Montesproust." In private he consoled himself by adding, to the already interminable manuscript of his memoirs, a venomous note in which he attributed Proust's triumph entirely to skillful publicity. But Montesquiou was not only jealous, he was also alarmed. For he seemed to find himself caricatured in the novel as the ambiguous invert Charlus, and he could not help suspecting that he would be dealt with more fully in the later volumes, where, it was rumored, the subject of inversion would become central. The suspicions must have been particularly disturbing to a man who had already been caricatured by Huysmans and Rostand.[1]

One afternoon Montesquiou was talking with Henri Bardac and outlining his grievances against Proust and other men of let-

1. As Des Esseintes in *A Rebours (Against the Grain)* and as the Peacock in *Chantecler*.

ters. Suddenly, just as he seemed to have exhausted the subject, he leaned forward, seized Bardac's arm, and blurted out the question: "Who is that astonishing, that preposterous creature who makes his appearance on the beach at Balbec?" Bardac said that he did not know. On the evening of the same day Bardac called on Proust and told him about the conversation. Proust merely laughed, holding his hands clasped beneath his chin—laughed and quoted a few lines from La Fontaine about the vengeance from on high that ultimately overtakes the arrogant. He was perhaps suggesting that there was an element of malice in his novel and that through Charlus he was settling an old score, paying off Montesquiou for indignities once patiently suffered.

CHAPTER XXII

Le Côté de Guermantes and Sodome et Gomorrhe

ON THE FLOOR and on the mantelpiece of Proust's bedroom in the Rue Hamelin lay piles of notebooks containing the manuscript of his novel. There was an almost incredible amount of manuscript, enough to fill some five more volumes, each about as long as the volumes that had already been published. None of it apparently was in finished form, not even the manuscript of the volume scheduled to appear next, *Le Côté de Guermantes I*, for Proust still revised as he read proofs. He still felt that he could not give his work the final polish until he saw it in print. Nevertheless the story was there in the notebooks, substantially as it was to appear in the published volumes.

I

The structure has not changed, the story still moves in cycles, and *Le Côté de Guermantes* can best be described as a single cycle of considerable length. It deals with the whole of the hero's experience at one period of his career. Whether the scene is the opera or Doncières or the drawing room of Madame de Villeparisis, Proust is nearly always concerned, in alternate passages, with a large number of subjects and characters, most of which have appeared in the novel before. But, as in such earlier cycles as

"Combray," one subject dominates the others, here aristocratic society. It is announced in the title; it is touched on at the beginning and the end; it is treated at length in the two longest scenes, comprising nearly half the whole work, the afternoon at Madame de Villeparisis' and the dinner at the Guermantes'.

Society in Proust is always the theatre of snobbishness, and aristocratic society is no exception. The characters in *Le Côté de Guermantes* are all snobs—hypocritical snobs, in fact, since they pretend to respect, not social distinction, but intelligence. The nobleman with the scarcely credible name, the Comte Hannibal de Bréauté-Consalvi, is a typical specimen. He has intellectual pretensions himself—he is the author of an essay on the Mormons, published by *La Revue des deux mondes*. He affects a loathing of society and a hatred of snobs; yet he is careful to frequent only the most aristocratic circles. "His hatred of snobs," Proust says, "was a derivative of his snobbishness, but made the simpletons (in other words, everyone) believe that he was immune from snobbishness."

There are, however, certain differences within the aristocracy. Snobs who are still climbing measure their success by the number of people they know; snobs at the top measure theirs by the number they refuse to know. Thus Charlus, whose social preeminence is beyond question, will have nothing whatsoever to do with the Napoleonic families, the Iénas, for example. "There is perhaps an aristocracy among the Tahitians," he remarks, "but I must confess that I know nothing about it." Monsieur de Bréauté, who is also at the top, would not normally care to know Marcel, but he realizes that the circumstances are exceptional, that in certain *salons* one is occasionally expected to meet celebrities who have come into prominence by experimenting with a serum to cure cancer or writing a curtain-raiser for the Théâtre Français.

The account of aristocratic society and of the Duchesse de Guermantes, who is the central figure in it, begins with one of those passages, at once subjective and analytical, of which Proust is particularly fond. He reviews the transformations that the name *Guermantes* had undergone in his hero's mind. At Combray, in Marcel's childhood, it suggested certain scenes, first of all "a dungeon keep without mass, no more indeed than a band of orange light from the summit of which the lord and his lady dealt out life and death to their vassals." Now, in later years, it suggests a remote and mysterious social life, carried on, paradoxically, right next door—exclusive family parties in the Hôtel de Guermantes, at which twelve refulgent figures gather "around the dazzling napery and plate . . . like the golden statues of the Apostles in the Sainte-Chapelle, symbolic, consecrative pillars before the Holy Table."

Once, in the celebrated scene at the Opéra or the Opéra-Comique (both are mentioned in the text) Marcel catches a glimpse of this life. The description is impressionistic, florid, and somewhat confused since the law of gravity seems to be violated. The orchestra is the shore, the abode of mortals; the boxes are grottoes under the sea, inhabited by water nymphs, bearded tritons, and aquatic demi-gods—the mysterious aristocrats whom Marcel so much longs to meet. One of them is the somewhat fishlike Marquis de Palancy, already mentioned in *Du Côté de chez Swann*. "Now and again," Proust says, "he paused, a venerable, wheezing monument, and the audience could not have told whether he was in pain, asleep, swimming, about to spawn, or merely taking breath." Another, the Princesse de Guermantes-Bavière, sits on a sofa, "red as a reef of coral," and wears in her hair what appears to be a great white flower that, like "certain subaqueous growths," is both plume and blossom. Still another, the Duchesse de Guermantes herself, reveals her incomparable elegance where it can be seen by the appreciative Marcel. After this exciting marine vision, Marcel half falls in love with the Duchess and repeatedly tries to attract her attention as she goes out for her morning walks. Proust is here drawing on memories of his passion for the Comtesse Adhéaume de Chevigné, as elsewhere on memories of the Comtesse Greffulhe, Madame Straus, the Comtesse Aimery de La Rochefoucauld, and perhaps other hostesses he once knew.

When Marcel finally enters aristocratic society and begins to experience the inevitable disillusionment, the subjective element in the narrative tends to disappear. Marcel is not now often concerned with his own feelings; he is for the most part a detached and ironical observer, who records fatuities and analyzes shams. His first observations are made in the *salon* of Madame de Villeparisis, which is by no means first rate, for it appears that the hostess has alienated her fine friends, perhaps by leading too scandalous a life and certainly by showing her intelligence too plainly. She is now reduced to receiving mixed company— a few diplomats, a few smart relatives (mostly Guermantes), and a good many members of the middle class.

The scene is incredibly long and incredibly brilliant. A dozen characters appear in the drawing room together and reveal, in alternating passages, their individual absurdities. The contrasts are sharp. At one extreme is Bloch, a hideous caricature of a Jew, an epitome of bad manners; at the other is the Duchesse de Guermantes, the social arbiter of the Faubourg Saint-Germain. Somewhere in between is the German diplomat with the name that rivals Bréauté's—the Prince von Faffenheim-Munsterburg-Weinigen. Inevitably the conversation turns on the Dreyfus Case. Norpois is characteristically evasive and Madame de Guermantes characteristically perverse, but the other members of the aristocracy quite openly display their anti-Semitism. The young Duc de Châtellerault insolently refuses to discuss the case with a Jew. Charlus, following Barrès, maintains that Dreyfus cannot very well be convicted of treason, since a Jew can never be a Frenchman; he should rather be convicted of violating the laws of hospitality. Finally it becomes apparent that Madame de Villeparisis will have to declare herself by dismissing Bloch, the one Jew present in the room, and she has

> no difficulty in finding, among her social repertory, the scene by which a great lady shows anyone her door, a scene which does not in any way involve the raised finger and blazing eyes that people imagine. As Bloch came up to her to say good-bye, buried in her deep armchair, she seemed only half awakened from a vague somnolence. Her sunken eyes gleamed with only the feeble though charming light of a pair of pearls. Bloch's farewell, barely pencilling on the Marquise's face a languid smile, drew from her not a word, nor did she offer him her hand.

After an interval the scene shifts to the Hôtel de Guermantes, where a dinner party is in progress—one of those exclusive dinners about which, not long before, Marcel's imagination played. Here the company scarcely admits of admixture. Except for Marcel himself, only persons of the highest rank are present, including, naturally, a lady of royal birth, Son Altesse la Princesse de Parme. The scene is even longer than its predecessor, partly because it includes toward the beginning much incidental analysis of the Guermantes family and even of a rival (though closely related) family, the Courvoisiers.

Much is made of the fundamental hypocrisy of the Guermantes, their persistent attempt to disguise their snobbishness as respect for intelligence. Ostensibly the Duchess dotes on clever people; yet the necessary coefficient of cleverness declines as the rank of her friends increases, approaching zero where the Crowned Heads of Europe are concerned. On the other hand, it rises sharply for friends of humble birth, who in any case are never admitted to her *salon* in a ratio exceeding one per cent. But even more attention is paid to the "wit" of the Guermantes, which in the Duchess takes the form of a neurotic perversity—an irresistible impulse to say or to do things that will seem daring to members of her class. Society is always agog, repeating and discussing Oriane's "latest." She is either snubbing the Greek Minister, or admiring the Prince of Bulgaria's bracelets, or starting on a cruise just as the "season" gets under way, or dashing off some malicious witticism or outrageous critical judgment.

At the dinner the most appreciative member of the Duchess's audience is the Princesse de Parme, a rather dull, conventional woman, who has come in the expectation of being pleasantly shocked by the display of wit. She is not disappointed. When the realism of Zola is mentioned, the Duchess promptly says: "But Zola is not a realist, Ma'am, he's a poet!" The remark, not too obviously secondhand, is completely devastating.

Agreeably buffeted hitherto, in the course of this bath of wit, a bath stirred for herself, which she was taking this evening and which, she considered, must be particularly good for her health, letting herself be swept away by the waves of paradox which curled and broke one after another, before this, the most enormous of them all, the Princesse de Parme jumped for fear of being knocked over. And it was in a choking voice, as though she were quite out of breath, that she now gasped: "Zola a poet!"

But the perversity of the Duchess, so exhilarating to her royal guest, is not confined to literature: she specializes in blasting the reputations of her friends. As names come up in the conversation, she has something outrageously spiteful to say about each. Madame d'Heudicourt is half-witted and niggardly; Monsieur de Bornier stinks ("I was obliged to stop my nose as best I could, all through dinner; until the gruyère came round I didn't dare to breathe"); Madame de Villeparisis is middle-class and commonplace ("she was once the mistress of a great painter, though he was never able to make her understand what a picture was"); the Queen of Naples is delighted by her sister's death. In fact, one soon forms the impression that, for all her culture and her intelligence, the Duchess is essentially a backbiter, and that the whole scene of the dinner is not very different, except in scale, from a scene in *The School for Scandal*.

The analysis and the illustrations of the Duchess's wit form the climax of the book; yet it is not her wit but Proust's that is memorable. For in *Le Côté de Guermantes*—as often elsewhere in the novel—he seems particularly close to the English tradition of Congreve and Sheridan. He is a supremely witty man exercising his wit at the expense of shallow, snobbish, and malicious people; his most characteristic scenes are pure comedy of manners.

The book is thus essentially a comic masterpiece—but it is not altogether comic, for it admits passages like the one on the death of Marcel's grandmother and even, at the very end, a passage about the Guermantes in which the comedy becomes pretty grim. Proust seems afraid of letting his fine lady and his fine gentleman off too easily. He has made them silly; now, in a final scene, he must make them callous as well—callous about the deaths of friends and relatives, which in Proust comes close to being the worst form of depravity. And so he has the Duke and Duchess preparing to leave for a gala evening, which includes a dinner party, a reception, and a costume ball, just as a relative lies dying and just as a close friend—Swann himself—confesses to them that he has only a few weeks to live. The Duke, frantic at the prospect of missing his pleasures, refuses to understand messages from the relative's bedside; the Duchess refuses to understand Swann. The carriage is summoned quite punctually, as the noble pair complain about their own ailments and tell Swann how hungry they are.

II

With *Sodome et Gomorrhe* the element of inversion—announced early in *Du Côté de chez Swann* and developed unobtrusively in *A l'Ombre des jeunes filles en fleurs*—finally becomes explicit. Marcel witnesses a casual encounter between Charlus and an ex-tailor named Jupien: witnesses it standing on a ladder and looking through a ventilator, so that there can now be no conceivable doubt in his mind as to what inversion is. Immediately afterwards he gives a long, learned, and—to the uninitiated reader at least—somewhat puzzling account of various kinds of inverts.

What seems central in the passage, and indeed in the book as a whole, is the thesis that inversion is not a vice, but a malady, a kind of nervous complaint that turns men into women. For inverts *are* women. Like other members of their sex, they are invariably attracted to men—quite manly men, boxers for example. But except when they are able to hire their lovers, they are forced, somewhat unhappily, to confine themselves to their own kind. Solitary inverts, who perhaps live in the country with their wives, find solace in silent encounters with compliant neighbors on the grass at night. Their more sophisticated congeners in cities gather in groups, like collectors of old snuff-boxes or Japanese prints. Most members of such groups are discreet, but not all of them—some daringly flaunt their femininity by using cosmetics or wearing bracelets and necklaces.

The tastes of inverts are, however, by no means always the same. Some are attracted only by men considerably older than themselves. Thus Jupien yields to Charlus when presumably he would not have yielded to a man of his own age. Others are attracted, not only by men, but by women who love other women. In such cases, it seems—though the relationship is a little difficult for the normal person to understand—the men play the parts of women, and the women the parts of men. Still others are attracted to men in such a way that they can experience satisfaction without physical contact.

Once the preliminary explanations are over, Proust describes another large party, this time at the Princesse de Guermantes-Bavière's. The comedy of social life is the same as before, and yet not quite the same either, for the author is now free to point out the part that inversion plays in it. The Duc de Châtellerault is announced by the footman whose favors he has enjoyed in the Champs-Elysées. The Minister to the Court of King Theodosius, the Marquis de Vaugoubert, casts timidly lascivious glances at the members of the Legation staffs—staffs carefully chosen, made up entirely of effeminate young men. Vaugoubert is surprised and delighted, but since he has long lived a life of enforced chastity, he cannot be entirely sure that the young men before him are inverts, and so he turns, with a smiling glance at once "fatuously interrogative and concupiscent," to the better informed Charlus. "Why, of course they are," Charlus says. Here and elsewhere the comedy of manners shades off into a kind of Walpurgisnacht of inversion.

As early as the scene of the Princesse de Guermantes' party, Charlus begins to emerge as a central figure in the novel, almost as important as Marcel himself. His position in society, now more specifically defined, turns out to resemble very closely that of Montesquiou in 1900. The Baron is a favored guest in several smart *salons*, including that of the Princesse de Guermantes. He censors her visiting list much as Montesquiou once censored Proust's. But since he is constantly fulminating against people he dislikes or imagines to be his enemies (there is an appalling example in his tirade before Madame de Saint-Euverte) and since he quarrels sooner or later with almost everyone, the Princess and other members of the Guermantes family are beginning to pay less attention to his censorship. Charlus realizes this. He is shrewd enough to see that, if he goes on trying to exclude people from society, he himself will finally be excluded.

But if Charlus is now more clearly a prominent and difficult member of the Guermantes set, he is also more clearly an invert. His tastes have affected his appearance; by thinking too fondly of men, he has gradually transformed himself into a woman. He is stouter and his behind protrudes almost symbolically; he powders his nose and paints his lips. When he enters a drawing room he flutters archly and seems to be wearing an invisible skirt. Between outbursts of insolence, he constantly pursues handsome young men, either the two sons of Madame de Surgis-le-Duc or the footman of Madame de Chevregny. He makes an assignation with the footman, who however turns out to be insufficiently virile. "But I have not taken a vow that I will know only Madame de Chevregny's men," Charlus says to him. "Surely there are plenty of fellows in one house or another here or in Paris, since you are leaving soon, that you could introduce to me?"

At Balbec, where most of the action takes place, Charlus forms a more permanent attachment with young Charles Morel, a talented violinist and a complete cad. The story is not very different from other love stories in the novel, except perhaps that the author takes it less seriously. He sees both its pathetic and its comic aspects; he represents Charlus as both a victim and a fool. In a scene in which he is deserted by Morel early in the afternoon, Charlus is heart-broken and his tears, running down his cheeks, ruin his make-up. But when, by pretending that he is about to fight a duel, he persuades his friend to return, he becomes quite preposterously quixotic—convinced, it would seem, that he is actually going to the field of battle like his illustrious ancestor, the Constable de Guermantes.

"I am sure it will be a fine sight," he said to us in all sincerity, dwelling upon each word. "To see Sarah Bernhardt in *L'Aiglon*, what is that but tripe? Mounet-Sully in *Oedipus*, tripe! At the most it assumes a certain pallid transfiguration when it is performed in the Arena of Nîmes. But what is it compared to that unimaginable spectacle, the lineal descendant of the Constable engaged in battle." And at the mere thought of such a thing, M. de Charlus, unable to contain himself for joy, began to make passes in the air which recalled Molière, made us take the precaution of drawing our glasses closer, and fear that, when the swords crossed, the combatants, doctor and seconds would at once be wounded. "What a tempting spectacle it would be for a painter. You who know Monsieur Elstir," he said to me, "you ought to bring him."

Here the model is certainly Montesquiou who, when he fought with Régnier, took at least three fashionable painters along with him, and it seems probable that the whole episode of Charlus and Morel was suggested by Montesquiou's passionate sponsorship of talented young men.

Charlus is another example of a man who loves beneath himself, for Proust still associates love with social inequality. And as Swann and Saint-Loup were led by their mistresses to frequent inferior social circles, so Charlus is now led to the *salon* of the Verdurins—the very *salon* in fact where Swann and Odette met before. The situation—that of a man of the highest social distinction appearing unrecognized for what he is among complacent middle-class people—is a favorite one with Proust. In the very first pages of the novel he shows Swann, a member of the Jockey Club and a companion of the Prince of Wales, being received by Marcel's parents merely as a family friend. So now he shows Charlus being received by the Verdurins as a nondescript nobleman with an obviously second-rate title. But Charlus is no Swann, and if he generally restrains himself in the interests of his love, he cannot help occasional outbursts of insolence. Thus when Monsieur Verdurin apologizes for giving him an inferior place at dinner, Charlus remarks: "Why! That is not of the slightest importance, *here*." "But, don't you see," Verdurin explains, "since we happened to have Monsieur de Cambremer here, and he is a Marquis, while you are only a Baron. . . . " "Pardon me," Charlus replies with an arrogant air to the astonished Verdurin, "I am also Duc de Brabant, Damoiseau de Montargis, Prince d'Oloron, de Carency, de Viareggio and des Dunes." The exchange passes off pleasantly enough; but soon there is another, this time with Madame Verdurin. It is ominous because hostesses in Proust determine the course of love affairs. Madame Verdurin, who once separated Swann and Odette, now has it in her power to separate Charlus and Morel. "By the way, Charlus," she remarks, "you don't know of any ruined old nobleman in your Faubourg who would come to me as porter?" "Why, yes . . . why, yes," Charlus replies with a genial smile, "but I don't advise it." "Why not?" "I should be afraid for your sake, that your smart visitors would call at the lodge and go no farther."

The Verdurins are foils for Charlus, but not only that. In the present cycle of the novel they again play a prominent and indeed a very interesting part. There are long passages about the trips the "faithful" take on the little railroad called the Transatlantic, and an even longer passage about a dinner party at their rented summer home, La Raspelière. Cottard, now an eminent physician, is still as silly and as vulgar as ever; Brichot is still as learned and as pedantically jocular—he now discusses the etymologies of place names for pages on end. Madame Verdurin is often as amusing as in *Du Côté de chez Swann*, especially when she presses invitations on her guests and tries to dissuade them from accepting invitations elsewhere. But she is not always amusing, or meant to be, for there is now an element of cruelty in her character comparable to that revealed by the Guermantes when they discover that Swann is dying. She is cruel to Brichot, whom she finds too docile a follower; she breaks up his love affairs, sneers at him behind his back, and sometimes even ridicules him in public. She is positively sadistic with Saniette, whom she never tires of torturing. Both she and her husband, Proust says, need a whipping post for every day in the year, and Saniette provides it, "thanks to his shuddering sensibility, his timorous and quickly aroused shyness."

Meanwhile another love affair is developing, that between Marcel and Albertine, the girl he met during his first visit to Balbec. Their relationship is not quite what it was. She has been to his apartment in Paris and has become, in some sense at least, his mistress. But he is not in love with her yet, though it is made clear that under certain circumstances he might easily fall in love with her. The story, as it unfolds in *Sodome* and the subsequent volumes, is the longest, the most curious, and in many ways the most improbable of all the love stories in the novel.

Albertine is quite as baffling a character as she was in *A l'Ombre des jeunes filles en fleurs*. Despite her poverty—for unlike the other members of the little band she is poor—she is represented as a girl whom Marcel might marry, but she never acts like a

marriage prospect. She is not chaste, as Marcel has the best reason
to know, and she may well be promiscuous. Her habits are
otherwise most unladylike. She wanders mysteriously about Balbec
(and indeed about Europe) without any regard for propriety.
She appears in Marcel's room at all hours of the night; once she
even stays at the hotel and goes to his room before dawn. Her
social position, though never entirely clear, seems to resemble
that of a servant or a kept woman. Marcel can buy her clothes;
he can summon or dismiss her at will; and he can, when the
mood strikes him, insult her outrageously without fear that she
will take offense. The truth seems to be that Proust is not
thinking of a marriageable girl at all, but of a young man very
much his hero's social inferior. The chief model for Albertine
was almost certainly Alfred Agostinelli. Proust has again tried
to transform his own homosexual experiences into a story of
heterosexual love, and has again failed to make the transformation
complete. The story, as he tells it, is not always entirely intelligible.

Soon after he meets Albertine at Balbec again, Marcel begins
to suspect that she has lesbian tendencies. He sees her dancing
in a close embrace with Andrée, and he hears Cottard remark
that she is keenly aroused. Marcel's eyes are opened to Gomorrah
as well as Sodom; he now realizes that inversion among women
is as common as among men. Balbec, in fact, is a hotbed of
lesbianism. Everywhere notorious women are staring at each
other, or rubbing legs under tables, or even embracing in public.
Albertine, if she has such tendencies, is constantly exposed to
temptation. Marcel's jealousy, now thoroughly aroused, takes the
form of horror, and it is difficult to see why. He has given on
the whole a sympathetic account of homosexuality, and he has
himself acted as the confidant of Charlus and Morel. Why then
should he be horrified by the corresponding propensity in women?
Can it be that Proust is actually of two minds about inversion
and that he sometimes feels obliged to condemn what at other
times he excuses? Or can it be that he is really thinking of a
specific vice that is recognized as such by both homosexual and
heterosexual lovers—the union of masculine women and effeminate men? Is he illustrating by his attitude a remark, made
in the first chapter of *Sodome*, that "for the invert vice begins,

not when he forms relations (for there are all sorts of reasons that may enjoin these), but when he takes his pleasure with women"? No definite answer can be given to these questions, but the fact remains that in Proust extreme jealousy is nearly always aroused by some form of inversion. So it is with Jean Santeuil and Swann, who discover that their mistresses have had lesbian relationships, and so it is, later on, with Charlus, who discovers that Morel has a particularly perverse relationship with a woman. The story of Albertine merely gives greater emphasis to what is elsewhere apparent in Proust's work.

For a time Marcel's suspicions are allayed; he decides that he will not marry Albertine and in fact that he will break with her at once. But suddenly his suspicions revive in a much more acute form when she tells him that she has long been intimate with a woman he knows to be a lesbian—the very woman whose sadistic orgy with Vinteuil's daughter he witnessed at Combray many years before. The effect of this revelation is to transform Marcel into a man with a single purpose. He must keep Albertine from meeting this woman or any other lesbian again; he must indeed lock up her in his house in Paris and perhaps marry her after all. And so with Marcel, as with Swann, love is born of jealousy, but with this difference, that whereas Swann experiences only a vague sense of loss, Marcel deliberately sets out to keep his mistress from others. Swann's love is difficult to understand, Marcel's seems scarcely distinguishable from insanity.

Thus the subject of inversion, announced at the beginning of *Sodome,* recurs at the end. It is a subject which will perhaps always have a definite fascination for some readers, and it is certainly one on which Proust is able to write with rare authority. Yet quite apart from inversion, the book is a particularly interesting one. It has so many other subjects and so many fine scenes incidental to the careers of Charlus and Marcel—scenes in Paris and on the sea coast, scenes in aristocratic and in middle-class drawing rooms—that it can perhaps be described as the best-balanced of all the books that make up the novel. Certainly no other book in the series gives a more comprehensive and more entertaining picture of the whole world Proust was trying to represent.

CHAPTER XXIII

La Prisonnière, Albertine disparue, and
Le Temps retrouvé

I

La Prisonnière and *Albertine disparue,* which immediately follow *Sodome et Gomorrhe* in the series, are so closely related that they can best be considered together. The most obviously autobiographical of Proust's volumes, they show the hero leading a kind of life that is almost indistinguishable from Proust's own, and going through the final stages of a love affair that can only be based on that of Proust and Agostinelli. Nowhere else in the novel is the difference between author and narrator, between truth and fiction, so tenuous.

The principal scene, and indeed almost the only one, is Marcel's apartment in Paris, from which he now rarely emerges. It seems to be an ugly apartment, since Marcel, like his creator, is too lazy to take pains with it and is in any case indifferent to the things he sees every day. The bedroom, where the greater part of the action takes place, has a wardrobe, a sofa, armchairs upholstered in blue satin, and, in a corner between bookcases, a player piano. It also has a telephone, on which, in the interests of quiet, a rattle has been substituted for the bell. Somewhere in the room is a hideous bronze by Barbedienne, obviously identical with the one Proust inherited from his parents. The rules of the apartment are strict. No doors are to be left open, for Marcel lives in a perpetual fear of drafts, and no windows are to be opened at night. If Marcel's hours are not eccentric, he at least shows a persistent familiarity with the dawn, the white light of which he notices above his curtains. It seems clear that he has trouble sleeping and that he habitually uses soporifics; he is never, under any circumstances, to be awakened until he rings. His bell hangs from one of the rods at the head of his bed, and once he is described as fumbling for it in vain. Sounds from the street filter into the bedroom—the horn of the tramcar, the bell of the neighboring convent, the rattle of iron shutters being raised at the baker's and the dairy—and Marcel, skilled by long practice, can determine from the sounds exactly what the weather is like outside. "As soon as I heard the rumble of the first tramcar," he says, "I could tell whether it was sodden with rain or setting forth into the blue." The cries of the street vendors have a particular fascination for him. They are the bird songs of the invalid confined to the city, and yet not quite songs either. They are more like "the psalmody of a priest chanting his office" or "the declamation—barely colored by imperceptible modulations—of *Boris Godounov* and *Pelléas*." The vegetable woman uses the Gregorian division for her litany; the vendor of snails intones the words *"On les vend six sous la douzaine"* with "the vague melancholy of Maeterlinck, transposed into music by Debussy . . . in one of those pathetic finales in which the composer of *Pelléas* shows his kinship with Rameau."

Albertine now lives with Marcel in this apartment. When she goes out, he tries to see that she has someone along who can keep an eye on her, and that she at all times avoids certain dangerous places. She must not go to large shops, where she would be perpetually rubbing against other women and perhaps tempted to escape through one of the many doors. She must not go to see Elstir's pictures at the Luxembourg, for the nude female figures might awaken her desires. She must not, in general, go anywhere she really wants to. But Marcel lies about what he is doing to restrict her freedom, and when she returns from her excursions, she lies about what she has done. Otherwise there is very little action. The drama is a static—or, more properly perhaps, an intellectual—one, for most of it unfolds in the mind of the hero. It has certain resemblances to the drama in the modern detective novel.

Albertine is still as baffling as she was in A *l'Ombre des jeunes filles en fleurs*. She is not so much a character as an object of suspicion, constantly changing as the evidence, accumulated by the hero-detective, points now to her guilt and now to her innocence. The hero's attitude toward her changes at the same time. When his suspicions are darkest, he loves or hates her; it scarcely matters which, for in either case he suffers and insists on keeping her under the closest surveillance. When his suspicions are allayed, he finds her dull and regrets the other mistresses he might have had or the trips he might have made. Once he points out that she seemed to him good looking only in the early days at Balbec, but he goes on to say that certain memories, in which jealousy plays a prominent part, can bring that beauty back. The relationship satisfies him only when he finds his mistress asleep, a mere breathing vegetable and hence no longer elusive. At such times, he says,

> her personality did not escape at every moment, as when we were talking, by the channels of her unacknowledged thoughts and of her gaze. She had called back into herself everything of her that lay outside, had taken refuge, enclosed, reabsorbed, in her body. In keeping her before my eyes, in my hands, I had that impression of possessing her altogether, which I never had when she was awake. Her life was submitted to me, exhaled towards me its gentle breath.

The entire passage, published separately in the N. R. F. as "La Regarder dormir," is a particularly brilliant one.

The part of the story told in *La Prisonnière* is remarkable in that rather more than half of it takes place in a single day. Albertine proposes to call on the Verdurins, and Marcel characteristically decides that she must under no circumstances pay such a call. So she goes to the Trocadéro instead. Subsequently he discovers that notorious lesbians were expected in both places —Mademoiselle Vinteuil at the Verdurins and the actress Léa at the Trocadéro. The discovery leads to one of those scenes of cross-examination which are perhaps inevitable, sooner or later, in Proust's love stories. There are examples in *Jean Santeuil* and in "Un Amour de Swann." The lover, heretofore a detective, becomes a prosecuting attorney; love assumes, as Proust says, the form of a criminal trial. But unfortunately it is a trial in which the prosecutor suffers with every admission he wrings from the accused. Marcel suffers because Albertine's admissions always take him by surprise and suggest that she is even more of a sex maniac than he has suspected. Thus when he casually mentions her three-day trip to Balbec, she at once interrupts him to remark: "You mean to say that I never went to Balbec at all? Of course I didn't!" She goes on to tell him that she spent the three days with a friend in Auteuil and indeed appeared on the streets dressed as a man! Finally—still facing her in the bedroom and still with his fur coat on, for he has been out during the evening— Marcel pretends that he must get rid of her, and suffers acutely in the process. Some time after the scene of cross-examination he decides that he must really send her away—since she is obviously restless and will leave him anyway—and that, in doing so, he must choose exactly the moment when he will suffer least. But that moment never comes, for she anticipates him by leaving of her own accord.

Her flight and her death in an accident shortly afterwards reawaken Marcel's love, and in a long passage at the beginning of *Albertine disparue* he describes his grief—describes it without however exactly expressing it. He analyzes it, breaks it down into its elements, and repeatedly turns aside to point out the psychological laws that it illustrates. In an earlier passage the hero has represented himself as playing a piece of music over and over again until his intellect has penetrated its structure, cleared up its mysteries, and extracted from it "some profitable reflection." He treats his grief in the same way, by permitting his intellect to work on it until no mystery remains and profitable reflections can be made. At one stage, for example, he notices that, though he keeps repeating her name, he never remembers what Albertine was like. The inevitable reflection follows:

Perhaps there is something symbolical and true in the minute place occupied in our anxiety by the person who is its cause. The fact is that the person counts for little or nothing; what

is almost everything is the series of emotions, of agonies which
similar mishaps have made us feel in the past in connection with
her and which habit has attached to her.

At another stage, he notices that Albertine is as much alive as
ever in his fragmentary memories of her, and he feels that she
must die many times within himself if he is finally to forget
her.

In order to enter into us, another person must first have assumed
the form, have entered into the surroundings of the moment;
appearing to us only in a succession of momentary flashes, he
has never been able to furnish us with more than one aspect of
himself at a time, to present us with more than a single photograph of himself. A great weakness, no doubt, for a person to
consist merely in a collection of moments; a great strength
also: it is dependent upon memory, and our memory of a
moment is not informed of everything that has happened since;
this moment which it has registered endures still, lives still,
and with it the person whose form is outlined in it. And moreover, this disintegration does not only make the dead man live,
it multiplies him. To find consolation, it was not one, it was
innumerable Albertines that I must first forget.

The whole passage is a triumph of analysis, and indeed rather
like a long case history in a treatise on the pathology of grief.
Jealousy is an element in it, since Marcel still thinks of Albertine
as she was when she was alive. He is almost as much of a detective
as he was before. Remembering that she once blushed when her
bath wrap was mentioned, he hires a head waiter of his acquaintance to investigate the bathing establishment at Balbec. Subsequently he has the same head waiter conduct investigations in
Touraine, and he himself spends hours questioning Albertine's
friend, Andrée. The result is a formidable body of evidence
indicating that Albertine went in for lesbian orgies of the most
sensational sort. But almost immediately evidence—rather too pat
to the purpose—turns up on the other side. The hero still cannot
reach a definite conclusion about her guilt (or at least Proust,
obviously writing to a thesis at this point, will not let him).
Emotionally, however, the hero seems to have little trouble accepting the worst, and indeed he soon begins to feel an attraction

for the women to whom he supposes that Albertine was attracted before. "The thought that a woman had perhaps had relations with Albertine," he says, "no longer provoked in me anything save the desire to have relations myself also with that woman." He becomes, in fact, what he tried so hard to prevent Albertine from becoming, obsessed with sex, showing a preference for women of the working class because Albertine preferred them and because they remind him of her. In the final stage, however, when he quite ceases to grieve, he reverts to an earlier habit—he keeps another girl in his apartment. "As other people need the aroma of forests or the ripple of a lake," he says, "so I needed her to sleep near at hand during the night and by day to have her always by my side in the carriage. For even if one love passes into oblivion, it may determine the form of the love that is to follow it."

The cyclic movement of the narrative is not quite so apparent in *La Prisonnière* and *Albertine disparue* as in the earlier volumes, but there are passages and chapters not concerned with Albertine. There is a chapter on the hero's trip to Venice, another on Gilberte (now Mademoiselle de Forcheville), and still another on Saint-Loup. The last two anticipate *Le Temps retrouvé* by showing the confusion that is beginning to appear in society. Jupien's niece, adopted by Charlus and given one of the Guermantes titles, marries into the Cambremer family. Gilberte, offspring of a Jew and a harlot, becomes the Marquise de Saint-Loup. The Duchesse de Guermantes thus finds herself obliged to call on the distasteful Marquise de Cambremer and to accept as a relative Odette's daughter, whom in Swann's lifetime she resolutely refused to meet. But the confusion is not only social, it appears in the world of sex as well. The most surprising people turn out to have tendencies toward inversion. Young Cambremer has them, Legrandin develops them, and even Gilberte is not above suspicion. But the oddest case of all is that of Saint-Loup, once apparently the most masculine of men and now the counterpart of his uncle, Charlus. He makes an elaborate pretence of infidelities with women while actually he picks up waiters in restaurants and even shows (as his uncle does not) a perverse fondness for lesbians. Once he gets his former mistress, Rachel, to

dress as a man, in the hope that, so transformed, she will arouse
his desire. Saint-Loup keeps Morel, who in turn has formed a
perverse attachment to the actress Léa. In a letter to Morel, she
addresses him in the feminine gender and uses such expressions
as "Go on, you bad woman!" and "Of course you are so, my
pretty, you know you are." Léa herself is kept by an officer.

These confusions, like those of the lovers in A *Midsummer
Night's Dream,* border on the fantastic and add little to the novel.
The episode in the chapter called "Les Verdurin se brouillent
avec Monsieur de Charlus" does, however, add a great deal. It is
the most dramatic and in many ways the most moving of all
Proust's episodes, pitting against each other powerful adversaries
—the Verdurins, who have a genius for quarreling with their
friends, and Charlus, who has a genius for insolence. The outcome
determines the fate of Charlus's love affair with Morel.

II

After a little more about the domestic difficulties of the Saint-
Loups, Proust goes on, in *Le Temps retrouvé,* to a chapter on
the war years. Life in Paris, even social life, has changed. Upstarts
—young ladies in high cylindrical turbans—appear everywhere.
In the afternoon they go to bridge-teas for the benefit of refugees
or war cripples; in the evening they join the crowds of slackers
at fashionable restaurants while soldiers on leave disconsolately
look in through the windows. Promptly at half-past nine restaurant
lights go off, and the crowds pour out on their way to cinemas.
The streets are dark, like roads in the country. One stumbles
against ash cans; one jostles soldiers in strange uniforms, perhaps
Africans or Hindus; one makes love, if one is so minded, immediately and without any preliminaries. "The hands," Proust says
specifically, "the hands, the lips, the bodies can come into play
right from the start. And, if one is rebuffed, there is always the
excuse of the darkness and the mistakes it gives rise to." The siren
opens up "like the shrieking call of a Valkyrie—the only German
music heard since the beginning of the war." Searchlights sweep
back and forth; squadrons of friendly airplanes shoot up into the
sky; bombs fall. In private houses and hotels, fine ladies and

gentlemen, dressed in nightgowns and bathrobes, scurry down to cellars. The narrator-observer, like Proust himself in 1917, is reminded of the parallel planes in El Greco's picture, *The Burial of Count Orgaz.*

In this setting the chief characters appear as in a sequel or a series of notes at the end of a volume telling what happens to them in later years. Bloch, the Jew, is rabidly patriotic until, despite his nearsightedness, he is accepted for military service; then he shows himself to be a detestable coward. Saint-Loup, scion of an aristocratic family, is so reticent in his patriotism that he still refers to the Kaiser as "Emperor William," still admires Wagner, and still sings Schumann songs in German. But Saint-Loup reënlists, demands active service, and dies a hero's death on the battlefield. Madame Verdurin gives her *salon* a political complexion and moves it to a hotel (apparently the Majestic) where light and heat are available. Her invitations are now extended to duchesses, who are eager for the "inside" information about strategy that she alone can provide; as such invitations become more numerous, those to the faithful become rarer. On the whole indeed the war is a blessing for Madame Verdurin, but it does confront her with a difficult problem — how to get croissants to relieve her headaches.

Permanently estranged from Charlus, Madame Verdurin now condemns him as an extinguished luminary, a too hopelessly "pre-war" figure. There is some truth in the charge, for his reputation has declined exactly like that of Proust's friend Montesquiou. Charlus was once, Proust says, the poet of high society;

> it was he who had been able to discover in the gay world about him a sort of poetry containing elements of history, beauty, picturesqueness, humor, light-hearted elegance. But society folk, unable to understand this poetry and seeing none in their own lives, looked for it elsewhere and esteemed far above Monsieur de Charlus men who were far inferior to him but who affected scorn for society and, instead, preached advanced social and economic theories.

Charlus consoles himself by cultivating the rabble. "I detest half-way types," he says. "Middle-class comedy is stilted. I must have either the princesses of classic tragedy or the broad farce of

the common people. *Phèdre* or the clowns—nothing in between."
His opinions sometimes shock his new associates, for if he is not,
as Madame Verdurin says, a spy, he is certainly a Germanophile
and something of a defeatist. Proust analyzes and illustrates these
opinions at great length.

Much space is also devoted to the Baron's sex life, for the
action in the chapter is in this respect, too, similar to *The Burial
of Count Orgaz*, in that it takes place on parallel planes.
Passages on sex alternate with passages on politics and society.
Charlus is for a time hard pressed by the dearth of young men,
so much so that he has to acquire a taste for boys. But soon he
sets up Jupien as proprietor of a brothel for inverts, where the
possibilities are almost unlimited. Jupien boasts that his patrons—
among whom are a deputy from the *Action libérale*, a priest, and
the Prince de Foix—are "among the finest, most sensitive and
likable men in their professions." Their tastes, however, are eccentric. One asks for a colored chauffeur, another for a choir boy,
and still another—an old man who has satisfied most of his
curiosities—for a mutilated soldier. A good many ask for Scotch-
men in kilts, who are apparently at a premium in establishments
of this sort. Charlus always asks for a ruffian, an *apache*, if possible a murderer, for Charlus now goes in for masochism. But his
request is difficult to satisfy, and Jupien usually has to pass off as
a ruffian a quite innocuous young man who has come to the brothel
merely to earn an honest penny. Charlus is chained to a bed and
beaten with a whip studded with nails until he is covered with
blood and welts. The aberration seems appallingly ugly, yet to the
victim, Proust says, it is not so. Charlus is realizing an essentially
poetic dream—a dream of virility proved by brutal tests if need
be, a dream associated in his imagination with a "rich store of
medieval scenes, crucifixions and feudal tortures." One is reminded of a moving, equally humane passage in Proust's early
work, *Jean Santeuil*, in which he describes sympathetically a con-
sumptive young man who pursues strange women on the streets at
night.

Once the war years are over, the novel enters its final phase.
Marcel gets another view of the characters, or at least those who
survive, when they are assembled at the Princesse de Guermantes',

and he dedicates himself to the task of writing a book. The dedication comes first and is associated with further experiences of involuntary memory, somewhat more intelligible than those that have occurred earlier in the novel. As he enters the court of the Guermantes residence, Marcel steps on two uneven flagstones, and immediately a scene from his past comes back to him, a scene in the baptistry of Saint Mark's. The experience is repeated a second, a third, and even a fourth time. It is essentially an artistic experience, but not only that. It represents a triumph over Time, for the past becomes the present, and it brings with it the only happiness that can be known in this life. All this is of course more than a little disconcerting after what has gone before in the novel. One can scarcely help thinking of those mental patients mentioned by Proust in *La Prisonnière* who, after carrying on a perfectly sane conversation, suddenly point at an old gentleman and say, "That's Joan of Arc."

The account of involuntary memory develops into an account of the novel Marcel proposes to write—the very novel, it seems, that the reader is just finishing. Thus, as later in *Les Faux-monnayeurs* and *Point Counter Point*, the author discusses his own work. The discussion is long-winded and repetitious but revealing in several ways. It suggests that memory, whether involuntary or otherwise, is not after all of primary importance in fiction. The novelist certainly remembers his past, particularly his moments of suffering, which are the most signficant part of it. But moments are only moments: they can never be completely recaptured. The novelist must fill out fragmentary memories of one moment with memories of others. He must piece together and fuse bits of his experience to portray the emotions of his hero and the characters with whom his hero comes into contact. Thus there can be no definite originals for his characters, and studies that seek to discover such originals are invariably worthless. But even if the novelist could remember his experiences exactly as they happened, he could scarcely reproduce them in his work. Memory deals with the particular, and fiction with the universal. Before it has been interpreted by the intellect, the material that memory offers has neither interest nor value.

The intellect has a curious history in Proust's novel. Generally in the earlier volumes, and even in *Le Temps retrouvé*, it is represented as an inferior function of the mind, one that falsifies and distorts. It is almost invariably contrasted with sensibility, which alone reveals the real world. But now, in discussing his novel, Proust suddenly remarks that the intellect is not after all contemptible. The truths that it draws from reality may at least supplement, may, as it were, "enchase in a grosser substance," the impressions of sensibility or memory. But as he goes on, Proust indicates that these truths of the intellect are far more than a supplement: they are the very substance of a work of art. For the novelist is a man who instinctively, from his earliest years, has trained himself to see the general in the particular and to ignore everything that is not general. He observes what appear to be childish trifles—"the tone in which a sentence had been spoken, the facial expression and movement of the shoulders of someone about whom perhaps he knows nothing else"—but always because such trifles help him to formulate psychological laws. "He retains in his memory," Proust says, "only what is of a general character." There is no suggestion, at this point, that his memory is arbitrary or mystical, or that its exercise is always accompanied by unearthly happiness. In fact, the sense of relief that the novelist feels comes from his intellect, which enables him to understand his suffering, to represent it in its most general form, and thus, in some measure at least, to escape its strangling grip.

The importance that Proust now attaches to the intellect suggests that his ideas about art have undergone a profound change. The conception of involuntary memory, with which he started, was never a very promising one. But in the early drafts of the novel, of which *Du Côté de chez Swann* is a specimen, it seemed adequate because he chose to rely as little as possible on his intelligence and to give free rein to his sensibility. In the later drafts, however, first represented by *A l'Ombre des jeunes filles en fleurs*, his sensibility became less evident and his intelligence much more so. No theory of intuitive perception could account for *Sodome et Gomorrhe* or *La Prisonnière* or *Albertine disparue*. Certainly no theory minimizing the part played by the intellect in art could account for the final chapter in *Le Temps retrouvé*. For this chapter is quite definitely written to a thesis; it is made up very largely of rather too pat examples designed to illustrate an abstract idea.

The idea is an old one, the Triumph of Time, one of the commonplaces of Renaissance poetry. Time is inexorable; everything changes and decays, including human beings. The scene is the drawing room of the Princesse de Guermantes, but it might well be the country of the Struldbrugs visited by Gulliver. The guests, people whom Marcel (who has long been in a sanatorium) has not seen for years, have suddenly become so old that they are often unrecognizable. Their beards are white; their cheeks are puffy and covered with red blotches; their expressions, once haughty, are now fixed in a perpetual smirk. Very ugly women have resisted old age best, for age is after all a human thing. "They were monsters and did not seem to have changed any more than whales." Beautiful women sometimes seem to have resisted it too, but when Marcel approaches them he finds that they look quite different,

> as happens with the outer surface of a vegetable or a drop of water or blood when placed under the microscope. Then I discerned a multitude of fatty splotches under the skin that I had thought so smooth, but which now sickened me. Nor did the lines of the face withstand this enlargement any better. When viewed at close range, the line of the nose was interrupted and weakened and the same oily spots were here as on the rest of the face, while the eyes were seen to be sunken behind pouches that destroyed the likeness which I thought I had discovered between this face and the one of former days.

The inspiration here seems more obviously Swift—a passage in "A Voyage to Brobdingnag."

But the changes that Time brings are not only physical: society itself has changed. The old distinctions are no longer observed or even remembered; the aristocracy now mingles with the middle class. The social climbers have risen and the socially prominent have gone down. The Duchesse de Guermantes is one of the latter, having lost both her wit and her exclusiveness; she now runs after actresses, in particular the actress Rachel, her *bête noire* of other days. Charlus now bows obsequiously to Madame de Saint-Euverte—perhaps, however, without recognizing her, for

he has had a stroke. His faculties have been impaired—or rather
some of them, for he is still able, when left unguarded, to seduce
a child of ten. Odette has risen considerably and is already in
the process of descending. At a ripe age (calculations based on the
novel seem to show that she must be at least seventy or eighty)
she has become the mistress of the Duc de Guermantes. A kept
woman in her youth, she is now a kept woman again. Such unlikely characters as Legrandin and Bloch have risen persistently.
The latter, having changed his name and become famous, is
received everywhere. An even more striking example is Madame
Verdurin, once the epitome of the middle class. Since the death
of her husband she has been remarrying to advantage. She was
for a while the Duchesse de Duras, and she is now—this is perhaps
Proust's ultimate surprise—the Princesse de Guermantes.

Proust's interest in Time is certainly not new. Since the beginning of the novel, he has been concerned with the social fluctu-
ations that it brings; he has explored the rise of Odette and the
decline of Madame de Villeparisis. But as he represents them,
changes in social position often involve changes in character. The
elegant aristocratic Swann of the first volume is the complacent
middle-class Swann of the second. Despite all the elaborate explanations that are given, one sometimes doubts that he is really
the same man. So it is here with the Duchesse de Guermantes and
Madame Verdurin. The Duchess who dotes on Rachel can
scarcely be identified with the elegant and malicious hostess of
the earlier volumes; the Madame Verdurin who has neither a
little nucleus to entertain nor a Saniette to torture is just no one
at all. In Madame Verdurin's case, Proust's failure is particularly
obvious since, in the course of a whole chapter devoted to a reception at her house, he gives her only a single remark. "That's it!"
she says, with a metallic rattle in her voice, caused by her false
teeth. "We'll get up a little clan! How I like these intelligent
young people who take part in everything! Ah, what a muzhishian
you are!" But even in this remark she is not the Madame Verdurin
of old. One can scarcely help feeling that on the whole Proust's
interest in Time is too self-conscious, and that the sacrifices it
involves are too great.

The chief weakness in Le Temps retrouvé is not, however, the transformations in character that occur at the end; it is the fact that the intellectual element in Proust's art has become somewhat too prominent. It has been present, no doubt, since the beginning of the novel, and with each succeeding volume its importance has grown. *A l'Ombre des jeunes filles en fleurs* is more intellectual than *Du Côté de chez Swann*; *La Prisonnière* and *Albertine disparue* are more intellectual than *Le Côté de Guermantes* and *Sodome et Gomorrhe*. Yet in none of these volumes, even in the last of them, is the balance between sensibility and intellect quite upset. In *Le Temps retrouvé* it is. The starting point—as in some of Proust's earliest pieces—is an abstract idea, a favorite theory of the author's; the narrative, or what narrative remains, becomes little more than a convenient illustration. No one has condemned abstract ideas more strongly than Proust. "A book in which there are theories," he says, "is like an article from which the price mark has not been removed." Yet it would be difficult to deny that he himself has here written such a book. In *Le Temps retrouvé* the price mark is Time.

CHAPTER XXIV

Publication:

Le Côté de Guermantes I

THE NOTEBOOKS of the novel lay at Proust's side in the bedroom on the Rue Hamelin, but a vast amount of work remained to be done before they could be transformed into salable volumes. The manuscript had to be prepared for the printer and proofs had to be read, each in itself a long process involving a great deal of correction and amplification. When the publication dates had been fixed, publicity had to be arranged. Critics had to be dined or otherwise cultivated; the N. R. F. had to be cajoled or quarreled with. Finally, when the volumes were out, favorable comment had to be echoed as widely as possible; unfavorable comment had to be promptly answered and exploded. The task would have been a formidable one even if Proust had devoted himself to it entirely and given up his social life. But his social life was now more important to him than ever, since it permitted him to see his fame reflected in the eyes of others. Even an evening at the Ritz was more exciting than it had been before. When he entered the dining room, he could not help noticing that there was a slight stir of interest and that even quite distant acquaintances got up to greet him and shake his hand.

I

Thus the success of A *l'Ombre des jeunes filles en fleurs* and the Goncourt Prize led to no radical changes in the routine of Proust's life. He still worked, hard and steadily, in his dingy bedroom; he still suffered from asthma and heart attacks and dizzy spells; he still went out from time to time, when his health permitted and attractive engagements presented themselves. He was apparently the same man he had always been, the same in appearance at least, though perhaps a little heavier and a little fuller in the face. On his evening excursions he wore the same old-fashioned dinner jacket, the same white gloves, often rather soiled, and the same crumpled opera hat. But the discerning observer could detect in his manner a slight shade of difference, a suggestion of assurance that had certainly never been there before. He seemed just a little less like himself and a little more like the famous man he had become. He was inclined to be difficult and distant with friends he felt he had outgrown, when indeed he did not avoid them altogether. It almost seemed as if, having won the Goncourt Prize, he were deliberately confining himself to friends worthy of a celebrity.

The problems of his social life were the same as ever, and we inevitably find him accepting and declining invitations, appearing and failing to appear in public, satisfying and disappointing his admirers. Thus in February, 1920, he refused a theatre invitation from the Princesse Soutzo, for the performance was not an especially interesting one and he was not, in any case, nearly so fond of the Princess as he had once been. Like much older friends— Lucien Daudet, for example—she tended to drop out of his life, though in her case he felt a vague sense of regret. "There was a time," he told her in his letter of refusal, "when my greatest happiness was to be alone with you, in your drawing room, while Morand was with us or rather while I was with you two, and those delightful dinners you gave were for me above all a different background and lighting for your appearances which were always new. I paid you compliments on your dress and you said, 'I am glad you like it,' with a smiling assurance that in another would have

seemed naive but in you touched me so deeply because it never
even occurred to you that I was trying to pay you an ordinary
compliment and that I didn't really 'like your dress as much as
all that.' "

He permitted himself to be nostalgic, but for the time being
at least he made no effort to renew the association. In May he
accepted a theatre invitation from another hostess. It was the
sort of performance he had come to like best, a gala at the Opéra,
arranged by his friend the Princesse Murat and attended by society
people generally, including such notables as the Guiches, the
Haussonvilles, the Beaumonts, Montesquiou, the Comtesse de
Chevigné, and the Princesse de Polignac. Arriving at ten, just
before a dreadful performance of *Scheherazade,* Proust paid particular attention to the audience. One of the figures in the
orchestra interested him especially—that of the aged Comte
d'Haussonville, whose head, still magnificently erect, seemed more
majestic than ever. (The majestic head afterwards served for a line
in *Le Temps retrouvé.*) Either that night or some other night in
May, Proust went to a supper party at which Stravinsky and Clive
Bell were among the guests. He seems to have antagonized Stravinsky, whom he was trying to compliment, and he certainly made
an unfavorable impression on Bell. "[He was] too sleek and dank
and plastered," the Englishman later said; "his eyes were glorious
however."

In June, when the season was at its height and invitations
came thick and fast, Proust accepted several from the Princesse
Soutzo, for the moment in his good graces again. Once, possibly
after a dinner party, she spent an hour at his apartment, and he
kept away from her as far as possible because he suspected that
there was alcohol on his breath. When she complained about the
heat, for he had a fire going, he heroically opened a window.
Once he accompanied her to another gala at the Opéra, a performance of *Antony and Cleopatra* in the Gide translation,
costumed in the style of Veronese, with Ida Rubinstein as the
Egyptian Queen. He sat well back in his box, talked persistently
with his neighbors, and apparently ignored the play. Then,
hearing that Madame Réjane had just died, he abruptly left the
theatre and drove straight to the Rue Laurent-Pichat, where he

had recently been a tenant. Madame Réjane's son, Jacques Porel, was in a highly emotional state, and Proust did what he could to console him. "He looked like a man who has been thunderstruck," Porel said later. He was very pale and he seemed so completely petrified by his young friend's grief that he scarcely moved. The interview was remarkable for the fact that, in the course of it, Proust spoke not so much as a single word.

II

Le Côté de Guermantes was so long that it was to be published in two installments, with an interval between them. In the summer of 1920 Proust finished the proofs of the first installment, printed under the title of *Le Côté de Guermantes I*. The dedication went, almost inevitably, to Léon Daudet, the most serviceable of Proust's friends, since it was he who had been chiefly responsible for the Goncourt award. Meanwhile Proust solicited subscriptions to another volume now ready for publication, an expensive *de luxe* edition of *A l'Ombre des jeunes filles en fleurs*, limited to fifty copies and interleaved with pages of his manuscript.

If at the moment Proust's relations with his publishers were a little easier, his friendship with Jacques Rivière, the editor of the N. R. F. magazine, was perhaps partly responsible. Rivière had long been one of the warmest and most articulate admirers of *A la Recherche du temps perdu*. In his letters to Proust he praised each new installment as it appeared, sometimes in language not very different from that used by Proust himself some years before in letters to Montesquiou. But no doubt Rivière's language *was* different; he really meant what he said. He really believed that the novel was not only a very good one but a "deliverance" to him, that the author was not only another Saint-Simon but another Racine, another Stendhal. In print he was one of the most dependable and most valuable of Proust's champions, performing services almost comparable to those of Léon Daudet. During the Goncourt controversy he had entered the lists no fewer than three times. In the last and most impressive of his sallies he had maintained that the author of *Swann* and the *Jeunes filles* was not only a genius but a literary force as well.

He was reviving the French classical tradition, broken during the nineteenth century, and encouraging French writers to concentrate on the study of human nature. He was thus profoundly changing the course of French literary history.

The relationship between Proust and Rivière was more literary than personal. They had no social life together. There is no evidence that Proust ever went to Rivière's home (which he no doubt suspected of being uncomfortably bourgeois), or that he ever very seriously considered inviting Rivière to select dinners at the Ritz. Still, within certain limits, he was very fond of his young champion—as indeed everyone else was, for Rivière was a man of almost exemplary character—and deeply grateful for the persistent praise in the N. R. F. magazine. He did what he could to show his gratitude—he lent Rivière money and gave him advice, found him a doctor and surreptitiously paid the doctor's fee, even read one of his manuscripts and made occasional comments on it. He wanted to do (and he was soon afterwards able to do) considerably more. Meanwhile, however, he felt no scruples about making Rivière toe the mark and calling him to account when anything even vaguely critical of the novel crept into the magazine's pages.

In 1920 Proust's grievances centered about Roger Allard, one of the N. R. F.'s most persistent contributors and, in Proust's view, one of the most obviously wrong-headed. It was no doubt a pity that the N. R. F. permitted Allard to write in its columns at all. Once, in the course of a review, he sneered—or seemed to sneer—at the *Jeunes filles*, and Proust, suddenly transformed into another Montesquiou, began hurling thunderbolts at the head of the unfortunate Rivière. He blasted, he condemned as completely worthless, a succeeding issue of the magazine in which Allard bulked larger than ever, in which he had an article and three reviews. Later, in the issue of July, 1920, Allard had the bad taste to praise a book by Pierrefeu, one of the critics who had shown the least enthusiasm for Proust's novel. This, in Proust's opinion, was almost the last straw. Here was the N. R. F. showering favors on one of his worst enemies—obviously for personal reasons, for who could tolerate praise of Pierrefeu otherwise?—and meanwhile neglecting its obligations, failing to give proper attention to such books as *Pastiches et mélanges* and *Le Côté de Guermantes*. Proust blasted Rivière again, and this time Rivière replied in kind. "My dear Marcel," he said, "you will have to let me be violent for a minute; you are shockingly unfair." But before too much ill feeling could be generated, the two men suddenly found themselves obliged to join forces in face of the common enemy—a certain Pierre Lasserre who, writing in *La Revue universelle*, was considerably harsher about Proust's novel than Allard and Pierrefeu put together. Proust was at first inclined to write an answer himself, surreptitiously of course. He would have his manuscript copied so that no one, not even members of the N. R. F. staff, would suspect his authorship. In the end, however, after a good deal of negotiation, Rivière wrote the answer, a deliberately flippant one, in which everything that Lasserre had said was shown to be the exact opposite of the truth.

Just as the answer appeared in the magazine, Proust discovered that, with a little wire pulling, he could get the Legion of Honor, an award not only intrinsically desirable but promising additional publicity for his books. His friends pulled the wires: Flers saw the Minister of Public Instruction; Léon Blum, Hahn, Morand, and others helped. But when the official announcement was made, Proust was somewhat disconcerted to find that he was not the only one so honored and that in fact the company was not very good. "I see in *Débats* that I have been decorated," he wrote to Flers, now editor of *Le Gaulois*. "Unfortunately I am grouped with people whose literary merit is slight. Could you possibly publish a little note mentioning me apart from the others, along with such really distinguished authors as Madame de Noailles or Monsieur Fabre (I am not quite sure who was decorated, because I am suffering from an earache and I saw the paper for only a moment before it was taken away)?"

The Legion of Honor was not perhaps, after all, worth his while. What he really wanted was a seat in the Academy, and so one night he suddenly called on Barrès, whom he had not seen for many years. He had not been able to shave before he left home, and he arrived late, just as the Academician was going to bed. Feeling that the subject required tactful introduc-

tion, Proust began by wondering whether he could afford any
longer to ignore the summons that the Academy was sending
out. But Barrès, amazed that anyone could have so exaggerated
a sense of his own importance, refused to take the hint or to say
anything really helpful. Subsequently Proust brought up the
matter in a letter to Barrès, but without making any progress.

On September 30 Proust went out again, this time in broad
daylight, to do another, a more substantial favor for Rivière by
getting him the Blumenthal Prize. He was late for the meeting
and completely exhausted since he had not been to bed the
night before; his fellow committeemen of the Blumenthal Foundation—Bergson, Boylesve, Régnier, and others—could not help
regarding him as a very curious figure. Boylesve, getting up to
shake hands with him, noticed that his gloves were dirty, that
his tie was frayed, and that his collar had been worn for at
least a week. From the front, Boylesve decided, he looked rather
like a fortuneteller; in profile, like an elderly Jewish woman
who had once been pretty. His face bulged in the most unexpected places, as if it had once been deflated and then blown
up again, quite haphazardly. "Young, old, invalid, woman—
altogether a strange personage," Boylesve later remarked. Proust
wore his overcoat thoughout the meeting, and got the prize for
Rivière. Afterwards he seems to have talked with Bergson about
sleeping pills and to have picked up information about the
philosopher's views which he was subsequently able to incorporate
in *Sodome et Gomorrhe*.

The daylight excursion seemed to revive some of Proust's
old complaints—his speech difficulty, for example—and certainly
his earaches were no better. He could not decide whether they
were just earaches or some sort of inflammation caused by
fragments of car-stoppers he had been unable to remove from
his ears. Nevertheless, since the publication date of *Guermantes I*
was approaching, he worked as much as he could. One of his
tasks was to send out presentation copies of the book, either
inscribed or accompanied by letters. "If this week," he wrote in
Vaudoyer's copy, "I have the Fourteenth Quartet played at my
bedside for two or three Beethovians (people quite out of date
because it seems he is the poorest of composers) would you come?"

The most interesting of the inscriptions and letters were those addressed to two women, Madame Straus and the Comtesse de Chevigné, whom Proust had used as models for the Duchesse de Guermantes. "A fever of 40 degrees (*not contagious*) doesn't make it easy for me to write," he told Madame Straus. "But I want to send you my book before it appears. . . . *Everything* witty in it is yours." He was assuring her, as indeed he assured other people, that she had been his model for the Duchess's conversation. Some time before, he had told Madame de Chevigné that she was his principal model. "I don't write you," he had said, "*but I write only about you. All my next volume is about you.*" He now said the same thing again: "In my next book (which is coming out in a week) there are persistent appearances of a woman who wears a cornflower hat when she goes calling, and is smartly dressed at other times too. If she appeals to you half as much as she does to the narrator (who is mad about her in the book) I shall feel repaid."

Still another woman seems to have appeared in *Guermantes I,* the actress Mademoiselle de Mornand. At least the evidence suggests that in certain scenes she was used as a model for the character of Rachel. Proust considered writing her too and perhaps trying to conciliate her in advance, but he got only so far as to ask his publishers for her address. Mademoiselle de Mornand was left to recognize or refuse to recognize herself, as she chose. There were no preliminary explanations.

III

An advance notice of *Le Côté de Guermantes I* appeared in *L'Action française* of October 8, 1920. It was written by Léon Daudet, to whom the volume was dedicated. In the dedication Proust was expressing his gratitude for an earlier favor, and now Daudet was either expressing *his* gratitude or acceding to Proust's request for a little more publicity. In any case the notice was entirely flattering. Daudet described *Guermantes I* as better than the earlier volumes in the series.

Toward the end of October Proust began sending his taxi for important critics, hoping that a dinner at the Ritz and a little conversation would improve their reviews, but two of them at least, Souday and Boulenger, could not be found when he sent. *Guermantes I* was released and the reviews began coming out. Some were entirely favorable like that of Henry Bidou in *Annales politiques et littéraires* of November 21; some contained disturbing reservations like that of Pierrefeu in *Débats* of November 24. While gracefully admitting that at his best Proust was incomparable, rich in characterization, in thought, and in poetry, Pierrefeu still refused to consider him a novelist. *Guermantes I* seemed clearly another fragment of the author's life, as completely structureless as its predecessors had been, almost indeed a daily diary. Anyone could have accomplished as much—any neurotic, that is, afflicted with insomnia and gifted with infinite patience.

Proust protested in a letter to Pierrefeu, but meanwhile he was even more deeply distressed by Souday, whose review in *Le Temps* also appeared in November. For Souday chose to dwell on the snobbishness of the book. He detested, not only the Duchesse de Guermantes, but the young hero who permits himself to worship so odious a snob. "Monsieur Marcel Proust resembles and even surpasses Saint-Simon," Souday said, "in his passionate preoccupation with, his fixation on, genealogies, rank, and precedence. He is literally obsessed with the subject." Souday added that the comparison, often made, between Proust and Saint-Simon was not entirely inappropriate, though Proust was "primarily a nervous aesthete, a little morbid, almost feminine."

In a letter acknowledging the review, Proust tried to show that he was not hurt and that he could put up with even tarter criticism from a man whom he so genuinely admired. But he could not refrain from questioning one unfortunate adjective. "At the moment when I am about to publish *Sodome et Gomorrhe*," he said, "and when, since I am going to talk about Sodome, no one will have the courage to defend me, you pave the way (though without malice, I am sure) for all sorts of malicious people by describing me as 'feminine.' From feminine to effeminate is only a step. My seconds in duels can tell you whether I behave with the weakness of effeminate men." A few days later he entertained Souday at the Ritz and apparently spent the meal assuring his friend that he was not hurt. Afterwards, however, he again brought up the matter of the unfortunate adjective. " 'Feminine,' applied to me, has made headway, as I feared it would," he said in a letter, "I have learned this from clippings, notably from *Le Figaro*, and the road to *Sodome* is also becoming a *leitmotif*. They have not yet taken away my cross of the Legion of Honor (but this may happen)."

Jacques Boulenger, Proust's other friend in the world of criticism, was also inconsiderate, though in a somewhat different way. Some time before he got around to reviewing *Guermantes I*, he printed or allowed to be printed in *Opinion* a sentence to the effect that Proust had been very much interested in getting the Goncourt Prize. Proust felt that the idea was preposterous. He had certainly never been interested in it at all: the prize had literally been thrust upon him. Twice he overwhelmed Boulenger with long letters of expostulation and with evidence, though never quite the evidence that proved the point. In the course of the correspondence Boulenger once jocularly remarked that a duel was in order. Proust was horrified. "My dear friend," he wrote, "how could you possibly think that anything I may have said about a duel could concern you, who have always been so good to me? I should rather put a pistol to my own head. What an idea!" In another letter Boulenger said parenthetically that he had no time to write. Proust was puzzled. After rereading the sentence several times and brooding about it, he was half inclined to believe that Boulenger was hard up and was in fact asking for money. "I said to myself," Proust now wrote, " 'Could it by any chance be financial difficulties that oblige him to do other things than writing?' Once again, I have certainly misunderstood, and you are probably much richer than I. But even though there is only one chance in a hundred that I am right, I should certainly not like to take that chance since it would mean leaving you in your difficulties."

The problem of the sentence in *Opinion* seemed to straighten itself out, but meanwhile another problem arose. Proust had published, in *La Revue de Paris*, a preface he had written for Morand's *Tendres Stocks*, and he was afraid that he had not been paid enough. Was it possible, he asked Boulenger, that the owners of the magazine were insulting him by sending a paltry two hundred francs? If so, should he not fling the money in their faces? Boulenger assured him that he should not.

In his next letter—since Boulenger's review of *Guermantes I* was about to appear—Proust again suggested a dinner at the Ritz, perhaps with Souday and Guiche or Castellane (not both because they would be too hard to seat), perhaps with a woman, say Madame Antoine Bibesco or Madame Hennessy or Madame de Ludre, perhaps with the novelist and critic Edmond Jaloux, or with Blanche or Boylesve. But before the dinner could be arranged, the review appeared. It contained strictures as harsh as those of Pierrefeu and Souday, exactly the same strictures in fact, for the book was described as structureless and snobbish; yet the tone was gratifyingly favorable. Proust paid off at once by sending Boulenger a copy of the expensive *de luxe* edition of *A l'Ombre des jeunes filles en fleurs*.

He got a box of chocolates from Souday and soon afterwards sent *him* a copy of the *de luxe* edition. But Céleste—if these were indeed the chocolates of which she afterwards spoke—Céleste was promptly instructed to throw them into the fire. "It is better, Céleste," Proust said. "The man who sent them is capable of any thing."

CHAPTER XXV

Publication:

Le Côté de Guermantes II and
Sodome et Gomorrhe I

I

THE SECOND PART of *Le Côté de Guermantes*, along with the first pages of *Sodome et Gomorrhe*, were scheduled for prompt publication, but during the winter of 1920-1921 Proust was apparently slow getting through the proofs. His eyes were bothering him again, and though he got glasses he promptly broke them. He went through a long siege of bronchitis and completely lost his voice. The appearance of the new volume was thus inevitably postponed.

There can be no doubt that Proust was deeply disturbed by the charge of snobbishness, repeatedly leveled against him. In January, 1921, it cropped up again in a particularly exasperating form. The source of it was no other than his old friend Blanche who, obviously feeling neglected, now complained in print that he could never approach the celebrated author of *A l'Ombre des jeunes filles en fleurs* and *Le Côté de Guermantes*. Ill as he was, Proust at once wrote a letter of expostulation, rather more remarkable for its good will than its candor. "For the time being I have to nurse my bronchitis," he told Blanche, "and I can't

possibly get out of bed or talk. But I hope I shall soon be
better and then I can talk with you and show you that I have
never 'entertained' without asking you to be the most distinguished of my guests. *Never.* . . . Before my bronchitis I gave,
about half past nine, a few unpretentious dinners at the Ritz,
but I always had my servants telephone you first. I know they
didn't call much in advance. But ask my guests (Madame de
Noailles who was asked the very day I gave a dinner and still
came)."

In February Proust was well enough to begin thinking about
advance publicity for *Sodome et Gomorrhe*—obviously a matter
to which he attached considerable importance, for even the
first pages of the book might arouse a storm of criticism. His
first step was to make use of an article in *La Revue hebdomadaire*
of February 26, an article so pat to his purpose that he might
have inspired it and indeed he afterwards seems to have thought
that he had. The author was François Mauriac. In the course
of the article he defended Proust much as Blanche had defended him in previous years, but more sweepingly and with
somewhat more transparent casuistry. He denied that the novel
was snobbish or structureless or undisciplined in style or, for
that matter, immoral. For was not the study of the human mind
basic in all morality, and who had more searchingly studied the
mind than Proust?

The passage about morality was the perfect justification for
his preoccupation in *Sodome*, and Proust naturally arranged to
have it echoed—by Léon Bailby in the *Intransigeant* and by
Boulenger in *Opinion*. The Boulenger echo turned out particularly
well and Proust was in so expansive a mood that he considered
inviting his friend to dinner that very night. Céleste exploded.
"Monsieur doesn't seem to realize that it's Saturday," she said.
"All the shops are shut up tight. Of course I can get chicken.
But lobster is out of the question. And Monsieur doesn't seem
to remember that Monsieur Boulenger would be dining here
for the first time. What would he think? It would be more to
the point if Monsieur were to call Dr. Bize and get an adrenalin
injection."

Proust acquiesced. Later, however, he was able to invite Mauriac;

Céleste herself delivered the invitation. "Monsieur Marcel Proust would like to know," she said over the telephone, "if, during the meal, Monsieur François Mauriac would like to hear the Capet Quartet or if he would prefer to dine with the Comte and Comtesse de X." Mauriac, somewhat disconcerted, decided that he would prefer no company at all. At ten o'clock on the appointed evening he ate at Proust's bedside, even more disconcerted by his surroundings—the bare walls and battered woodwork, the piles of notebooks, the dirty bed sheets. The face of his host, unshaved and obviously Semitic, seemed as lifeless as a mask of wax. As he studied it, the young Catholic decided that it was the face of a Jew who had reverted to something like his ancestral squalor. They were alone except for Proust's young secretary.

During the spring Proust was ill again (for a while at least with rheumatic fever) and he may not have been able to read the final proofs of *Guermantes II* and of *Sodome I*. Indeed he afterwards maintained that he had not read any proofs at all. Still with the help of Rivière and other friends at the N. R. F. he managed to get the book through the press, and by the end of April he was ready for more advance publicity of the sort supplied by Mauriac. This time the task fell, appropriately, to André Gide, who was himself a homosexual and therefore not likely to be frightened by the theme of *Sodome*. Writing in the N. R. F. of May 1, Gide described Proust's novel as the most important one written in recent years. It exemplified a new kind of observation, more accurate and more subtle than that of other novelists. It was written in a style absolutely faultless, and indeed without a dominant quality, because in appropriate places all admirable qualities were brought into play. To those who found the sentences difficult, Gide said: "Read them aloud and see how quickly the structure becomes clear, how each word falls exactly into place." The novel was an enchanted forest, Gide wrote in what was easily his most striking passage, a forest in which the reader immediately lost himself and was quite happy to do so, in which he knew neither where he had entered or where he would come out, in which he sometimes seemed to walk without advancing and sometimes to advance without walking, but always with the same result—the enchantment was omnipresent, delightful, and compelling. The passage was almost a paraphrase of what Chaumeix had written about *Swann* in 1914.

Gide's article obviously demanded recompense of some sort, and Proust began sending out his taxi, night after night, to find his new champion. At last, on May 13, Gide appeared at the Rue Hamelin, though rather inopportunely as it happened, for Proust was getting ready to go out. As she opened the door, Céleste regretted that the interview had been so long postponed. "Monsieur begs Monsieur Gide," she said, "to have no doubt that he is thinking constantly of him." Gide entered the drawing room and met his host, who seemed fat, or puffy, and who looked a little like the man with whom he had once fought a duel, Jean Lorrain. The room was very hot but Proust was shivering.

Gide had with him a copy of *Corydon*, his most daring book, still unacknowledged, a determined and ingenious defense of inversion. He offered the book to Proust, swearing him to secrecy as he did so. Proust talked pathetically about his sufferings and politely about the Gospels, in which, with Gide's help, of course, he hoped to find consolation. But his chief subject of conversation, suggested no doubt by *Corydon*, was homosexuality. He freely confessed his own inclinations, but defended his practice of not confessing in his novel. "You can tell anything," he remarked; "but on condition that you never say: *I*." Gide, who always said *I* and would have felt dishonest if he had said anything else, was profoundly shocked. "Far from denying or hiding his homosexuality," Gide afterwards noted in his journal, "he exhibits it, and I could almost say boasts of it. He claims never to have loved women save spiritually and never to have known love except with men. His conversation, ceaselessly cut by parenthetical clauses, runs on without continuity. He tells me his conviction that Baudelaire was homosexual: 'The way he speaks of Lesbos, and the mere need of speaking of it, would be enough to convince me,' and when I protest: 'In any case, if he was homosexual, it was almost without his knowing it; and you don't believe that he ever practiced. . . . ' 'What!' he exclaims. 'I am sure of the contrary; how can you doubt that he practiced? He, Baudelaire!'

And in the tone of his voice it is implied that by doubting I am insulting Baudelaire."

Proust was aware that the interview had not gone very well. "You know that I have offended a good many homosexuals by my last chapter," he wrote to Boulenger; the remark was general but he was apparently thinking of Gide. "I feel very much upset about it." And when, a few days later, he sent for Gide again, he went on with the conversation in a quite different vein. He now condemned in *Sodome* the very things that before he had justified. Gide apparently sat, this time, in the bedroom. He noticed that Proust kept rubbing his nose with the side of one of his hands. The fingers were oddly stiff and separated so that the hand seemed quite dead. The gesture was that of an animal or a madman. "We scarcely talked, this evening again," Gide wrote in his journal, "of anything but homosexuality. He says he blames himself for that 'indecision' which made him, in order to fill out the heterosexual part of his book, transpose A *l'Ombre des jeunes filles* all the attractive, affectionate, and charming elements contained in his homosexual recollections, so that for *Sodome* he is left nothing but the grotesque and the abject. But he shows himself to be very much concerned when I tell him that he seems to have wanted to stigmatize homosexuality; he protests; and eventually I understand that what we consider vile, an object of laughter or disgust, does not seem so repulsive to him. When I ask him if he will ever present that Eros in a young and beautiful guise, he replies that, to begin with, what attracts him is almost never beauty and that he considers it to have very little to do with desire—and that, as for youth, this was what he could most easily transpose (what lent itself best to a transposition)."

II

Meanwhile *Guermantes II, Sodome I* was released. There was nothing like the outburst of criticism that Proust seems to have feared, and indeed there scarcely could have been because the specimen of *Sodome* was too short. On the other hand, the reviews were neither very numerous nor very favorable. Souday's review, in *Le Temps* of May 12, was positively nasty. He began by ridiculing what Gide had said about reading long sentences aloud; he went on to explode Proust's ideas about style and genius; and he ended by alluding with obvious distaste to the subject of *Sodome*. After a month's delay Proust replied, point by point, but rather perfunctorily. He had almost given up Souday as a champion of the novel.

Boulenger, hitherto fairly dependable, did not even mention the book, but there was perhaps a reason for this—an absurd misunderstanding for which Proust was not really responsible. Boulenger had recently published a volume of his criticism under the title *Mais l'art est difficile*, and Proust had somewhat officiously promised to see that it got proper attention in the N. R. F. He had certainly done his best. He had repeatedly discussed reviewers with the editor of the magazine, and he had considered tacking on to the review, once it was written, a paragraph of his own to the effect that Boulenger was the greatest living critic. But throughout the negotiations the N. R. F. had been reassuring, and Proust had had every reason to believe that, even without the additional paragraph, the review would be entirely satisfactory. It was not, unfortunately, satisfactory at all, for it was not entirely favorable and it contained a deplorable, a deliberately insulting, sentence in which Boulenger was accused of venally praising an Academician. Proust was at once humiliated and incensed. He apologized and encouraged Boulenger to write a public reply; he demanded an explanation from the N. R. F. Boulenger did reply, sharply and effectively, in a public letter; Proust praised the letter but wondered if a reply had been desirable after all. The N. R. F. replied to Boulenger. Meanwhile *Guermantes II, Sodome I* was ignored by *Opinion*.

Proust was still agitated by the review when he inadvertently fell foul of Boulenger again, in circumstances that were particularly involved. Proust had continued to correspond with his old friend Montesquiou. Indeed as *Guermantes II, Sodome I* appeared, the correspondence had become, on Proust's side, a little fuller and a little warmer, for at the moment he was feeling guilty. He knew that Montesquiou would now certainly recognize himself in

Charlus, and so he took particular pains to assure his old friend that he had seldom or never used models for his characters. It was no doubt true that he had used Madame de Beaulaincourt for Madame de Villeparisis; also Fénelon for Saint-Loup and the Baron Doasan for Charlus in single scenes. But otherwise his characters, in particular Charlus, were entirely imaginary.

The correspondence was not, however, confined to explanations. Proust now proposed to rescue his former master from neglect by recommending him to editors as the best art critic of his generation. Boulenger was a convenient editor. It was no doubt true that he already had in Vaudoyer a distinguished art critic and one, furthermore, with whom Proust was on very good terms. Nevertheless Proust made the recommendation.

"I started writing [Montesquiou] again, even more friendly letters," Proust explained to Boulenger, "because people have been absurd enough to say that I have portrayed him in Charlus. This is particularly malicious because, though I have known an enormous number of inverts whom no one suspected, I have never in all the years I have known Montesquiou seen him either at home or in company or anywhere else give the slightest indication of it. In spite of that, I think (?) he imagines that I had him in mind. But since he is infinitely intelligent, instead of showing he believes it, he has been the first to write me particularly warm letters about *Guermantes* and *Sodome*. But I am sure he thinks so all the same. So the nice things he says in his letters make me feel dreadful. Especially since I should be offering him the greatest insult if I even appeared to suspect what people are saying and tried to apologize. . . . Burn this letter because there are things in it that would mortally offend this count for whom I am so very anxious to do something."

Boulenger, still nettled by the fiasco of the N. R. F. review, replied rather coolly. He was taking over a new journal, *La Revue de la semaine*, which might well offer Montesquiou space in its pages, but he showed very little enthusiasm for the idea. Proust forwarded the letter to Montesquiou and half suggested a meeting with Boulenger—not of course at the Rue Hamelin, for Proust was afraid that his old friend would get into the habit of calling, and not at Montesquiou's, but on neutral ground. Quite suddenly, before the meeting could be arranged, Montesquiou erupted as he had so often done in the past. In a letter to Proust he blasted Boulenger and his journals—specifically, someone on the staff of *Opinion*—and refused to have anything to do with the favors that were being, somewhat patronizingly, offered him. Proust was appalled. Seeing himself the victim of a second misunderstanding with Boulenger and afraid that he would lose, through no fault of his own, a most valuable champion, he felt obliged to clear himself by betraying Montesquiou's confidence. And so somewhat diffidently, with many apologies, he turned over to his new friend Montesquiou's angry outburst.

"I had just written you a very long letter," Proust told Boulenger, "when I received this one, which I am sending you *confidentially*. If it had been anyone else, I shouldn't feel right about passing it on. But I suspect that despite its madness (the contingent reason for which I don't know, you should recognize the man by whom he thinks he is hated) you will find it well written and rather picturesque. It lacks common sense. But, since I know it won't offend you, it may well amuse you a great deal. For this reason I don't think that, in sending it, I am betraying the author, whose insane genius you will be in a better position to appreciate. I could do it only because you and he are involved. It seems to me that I should be keeping a good joke from you if I didn't send it, and on the other hand, it will give you a better idea of this angry Saint-Simon."

III

During the period of his rheumatic fever Proust was generally bedridden, but in May he seems to have gone out occasionally and once at least in the daytime, when he felt an overpowering desire to see the Vermeer and Ingres exhibitions that were now on. His preparations were the same as for most of his other daylight excursions: he stayed up all night so that he would be able to leave the first thing in the morning. He persuaded his friend Vaudoyer, whose recent articles on Vermeer he had very much admired, to act as his guide. As the two men left the apartment on the Rue Hamelin there was a moment of uncertainty. Proust was so dizzy on the stairway that he was not sure he could go on. But he persevered, and saw both exhibitions. "I treasure the luminous memory of the only morning I have seen in years," he afterwards wrote Vaudoyer, "when you affectionately guided me, as I staggered, toward that Vermeer in which the gables of the houses 'are like priceless specimens of Chinese art.' Since then I have been able to get a Belgian book with a great many reproductions, and by studying them with your article beside me, I have been able to identify the same objects in different pictures."

The daylight excursion, the criticism of Vaudoyer in *Opinion*, and perhaps the Belgian book on Vermeer suggested to Proust a new episode for his novel. He imagined Bergotte, in his last illness, reading about an exhibition of Dutch painting, reading in particular a critic who said that the little patch of yellow wall in Vermeer's *View of Delft* was so perfectly done that it resembled a priceless specimen of Chinese art.

Bergotte ate a few potatoes, left the house, and went to the exhibition. At the first few steps that he had to climb he was overcome by giddiness. He passed in front of several pictures and was struck by the stiffness and futility of so artificial a school, nothing of which equalled the fresh air and sunshine of a Venetian palazzo, or of an ordinary house by the sea. At last he came to the Vermeer which he remembered as more striking, more different from anything else that he knew, but in which, thanks to the critic's article, he remarked for the first time some small figures in blue, that the ground was pink, and finally the precious substance of the tiny patch of yellow wall. His giddiness increased; he fixed his eyes, like a child upon a yellow butterfly which it is trying to catch, upon the precious little patch of wall. "That is how I ought to have written," he said. "My last books are too dry, I ought to have gone over them with several coats of paint, made my language exquisite in itself, like this little patch of yellow wall". . . . He repeated to himself: "Little patch of yellow wall, with a sloping roof, little patch of yellow wall." While doing so he sank down upon a circular divan . . . [and] rolled from the divan to the floor, as visitors and attendants came hurrying to his assistance. He was dead.

In June Proust still complained about his health, but he was

well enough to have another little fling at social life. At least he
was on hand for the most important social event of the month,
the dinner given by Madame Hennessy for the engagement of
the Duke of Marlborough and Gladys Deacon. The company
was good, and the guests of honor may well have had a special
interest for Proust because both had somewhat vulnerable reputations. The Deacons, a well-publicized American family, had suffered from scandal, and Miss Deacon herself had not escaped it
—quite recently she had sued the *Daily Graphic* for libel. The
Duke of Marlborough had been so recently divorced that he
could not at once find a clergyman willing to marry him again.
The newspapers, both in Europe and America, were publicizing
his search, and he was a little sensitive about it. He was also
sensitive about the valuable presents he was giving his bride,
at a time when there was starvation in the English coal fields.
"One should not mention these things now, especially in the
English press," he said in an interview. "What will the miners
think, reading about wedding presents, jewelry costing £50,000?
It makes them dissatisfied."

It is a pity that the conversation between eminent personages
at grand dinners is so often lost to posterity. In this case, for
example, only two or three remarks out of a whole evening's
conversation have transpired. Proust talked about his illness and
was pleased to find that the Duke of Marlborough was sympathetic and even helpful. A man can feel well, the Duke suggested,
if only he can think that he is well. There was also talk about
Le Côté de Guermantes, which society people were apparently
reading. Someone, either Madame Hennessy or the Duc de Guiche,
maintained that the Duchesse de Guermantes was a portrait of
Madame Greffulhe. At first Proust protested, but in the end
he admitted that the character did indeed resemble the celebrated
hostess for a few moments in the scene at the opera.

Not long after the dinner, Proust pursued the discussion of
the Duchesse de Guermantes in a letter to the Duc de Guiche.
The character, he said, was really much closer to someone else,
whom however he refused to name (obviously Madame de
Chevigné). "Except that she is virtuous, the Duchesse de Guermantes is a little like the tough old hen I once took for a bird of

paradise, who could only keep repeating like a parrot, 'Fitz-James is waiting for me,' when I wanted to capture her under the trees on the Avenue Gabriel. In making her a mighty vulture, I have at least prevented people from taking her for an old magpie. This abuse however is entirely verbal because I still suffer as keenly as I suffered in the past the first time she cut me." Proust sent off the letter, then, appalled by his own slanders, considered writing Madame de Chevigné a letter of apology and explanation. Finally he did so. He could not bring himself, he told her, to repeat his offensive remarks as perhaps he should, but at least he could discuss the cause of his bitterness. She alone of all his old friends —she who was uniquely concerned in *Le Côté de Guermantes*— had not taken the trouble to write him about the book. Her silence was one of the few great tragedies he was able to feel in his declining years.

It was a tragedy but not apparently quite so great as another that he suffered at almost exactly the same time—the loss of his secretary, the boy who had been his companion for more than two years and who, not so many weeks before, had dined with Mauriac in the bedroom at the Rue Hamelin. The trouble seems to have been that the boy was bored, so much so that from time to time he ran away or threatened to. To distract him, Proust proposed to marry him off to the daughter of a concierge, but the boy refused to go through with the marriage. This may have suggested the episode in the novel in which Morel, so bored that he has to kill time studying algebra, toys with the idea of marrying Jupien's niece. Morel's patron, Charlus, is very much in favor of it, but suddenly—for no very good reason, other than that he is a highly neurotic young man—Morel breaks with the girl and decides that he has "to 'b—— off' to an unknown destination."

Proust's secretary left for America, where he had found a job or Proust had found one for him. Afterwards Proust wrote a letter to Mauriac in which he wistfully referred to the evening they had spent together "with my only H.," now on his way to a distant country.

CHAPTER XXVI

Publication:

Sodome et Gomorrhe II

I

DURING the last six months of 1921 Proust's health was even worse than it had been during the spring. Sometimes he could not seem to keep warm, and even during heat waves he had a fire in his grate, blankets piled high on his bed, and as many as three hot-water bottles beside him. Sometimes his power of coordination seemed about to desert him completely. He had all his old trouble articulating words and he had trouble walking besides—he was apt to stumble or fall even in going from one room to another. His doctor told him not to stay in bed too much, and so whenever he felt able to he dragged himself out to the Ritz. Generally he avoided the dining room, which was drafty, and ate in a private room, where he was not obliged to wear his dinner jacket. But even informal meals in the private room were prostrating, and he apparently returned as soon as possible to his hot-water bottles and his blankets.

The irony of his situation could not help impressing that master of irony. He was scarcely able to appreciate the fame he had sought so long; he was losing all sense of happiness just as happiness seemed to lie within his reach. "If I were capable of pleasure, I should feel it now," he wrote to a friend, "because people are giving courses on me in all important universities. Men of the caliber of Bergson are studying my books. Eminent men in America, in Germany, etc. write me more than enthusiastically (I suppose that Elles and Rey [the managers of the Ritz], who are generally very nice, know nothing about this, otherwise they would be more careful about drafts, but another hotel would be better). But I suffer too much to be capable of pleasure."

As he suffered he worked, principally on extracts from his novel for the N. R. F. and other journals. For years he had been selling extracts; now he was selling them wholesale—detaching from his notebooks and publishing, in one journal or another, every episode that seemed able to stand by itself. He did so to make money and also perhaps to advertise his work, for he apparently felt that by anticipating the contents of future volumes he was whetting the curiosity of his readers. In September, 1921, he sold to *Oeuvres libres* a particularly long extract, subsequently published under the title of "Jalousie," and got for it a particularly good price. The editors of the N. R. F. were furious. They accused Proust of violating the spirit of his contract and made him promise that he would never publish with *Oeuvres libres* again. Meanwhile, however, they were getting plenty of extracts themselves. In the last months of 1921 they got both "Les Intermittences du coeur" and "En Tram jusqu'à la Raspelière," and they could have had a third if they had not been so timid. Rivière was afraid of long extracts and, for the time being at least, afraid of anything that might be considered improper. Specifically he wanted as little as possible about Charlus. Proust's reaction to his friend's timidity was a strong one.

Once the extracts were out of the way, Proust set to work on *Sodome et Gomorrhe II* itself. In September he spoke of adding new passages, thereby improving it enormously; he was pushing himself to the utmost, he said, in the hope that he could deliver the whole manuscript within a month and a half. In November, when he was apparently reading proofs, he saw a friend who tried to alarm him by reporting that the N. R. F. was about to be boycotted by the papers. The friend also ventured the opinion that, if *A l'Ombre des jeunes filles en fleurs* had been published by any other firm, it would now be in its hundredth thousand. Proust told the N. R. F. that he did not exactly believe this, but at the same time he could not help pointing out that another Goncourt Prize book, published since the *Jeunes filles* and scarcely so distinguished, was being advertised as in its seventy-fifth thousand. The explanations of the N. R. F. seem, however, to have been reassuring, and meanwhile Proust went on with his proofs. By December he was so far along that he was ready to begin thinking about his next volume, still untitled except for the designation *Sodome III*. As a first step, he proposed to have it typed, for he was half inclined to believe that, if he had a clean copy to work with, he could make most of his changes on the manuscript. The typing could best be done under his immediate supervision at the Rue Hamelin, and so he needed a new secretary to replace the one who had left, or at least a typist. At the moment his physical resources were indeed strained —even dictating a letter was uncertain. "I am writing the end myself," he said in the course of a letter to the N. R. F., "because the groaning woman who has been taking my dictation sounds so much as if she were going through labor pains that I am afraid to keep her in my room for fear I shall soon be confronted with two beings instead of one."

As he worked, Proust occasionally thought of stopping, as he had in the past, to write articles of one sort or another. He felt the strongest obligation to write an article on Léon Daudet, whose favors never ceased. He had repeatedly praised the two parts of *Le Côté de Guermantes* and he had recently dedicated to Proust a volume of his own. But Daudet was unpopular and somewhat disreputable. The N. R. F. would not publish the kind of article on him that Proust proposed to write, and might not even, in view of the fracas about *Oeuvres libres*, permit it to be published elsewhere. Nevertheless Proust went on with his plans, arranging to market his article, if he should ever get around to writing it, in one of Boulenger's journals.

Meanwhile he thought of doing an article on Montesquiou, who had recently died, perhaps an article for one of the American journals, which were reported to pay so handsomely. But in this case he was a little afraid. He could not be sure that the funeral had not been a gigantic hoax and that the showman of other days would not reappear fulminating at the proper moment to confront his posthumous critics. Finally Proust wrote to Madame de Clermont-Tonnerre, who had attended the funeral. "I am quite convinced that he isn't dead," Proust confessed, "and that . . . his coffin was empty." Proust's fears may have persisted since he gave up writing the article. Now worried about Montesquiou's memoirs, which contained, as he suspected, unpleasant passages about himself, he talked of suing someone, the executors or the publishers—talked, that is, until he received tentative assurances that the memoirs would not be published without proper excisions.

On New Year's Eve Proust went to a ball at the Beaumonts' and on February 7, 1922, to another ball at the Princesse Soutzo's. Afterwards, in a letter of thanks to the Princess, he was able to report further praise from abroad—an article on his novel by the eminent Professor Curtius of Munich. Unfortunately he could not understand the article, which was in German. He could be sure only of the quotations, which were given in the original French, and of certain proper names, such as Molière and Racine, to whom perhaps he was being compared.

II

Despite interruptions the work on the novel went forward, and by spring the second part of *Sodome et Gomorrhe*, filling no fewer than three volumes, was ready for release. Presentation copies arrived at the Rue Hamelin for Proust to inscribe and send off. Before inscribing them, he made his usual gesture of friendship toward Souday—he took the critic to dinner—though this time he was himself inclined to feel that the gesture was a little too obvious. Afterwards he assured Souday that the dinner had no connection whatsoever with the appearance of his book, which, as a matter of fact, had come to him as a complete surprise. It is not clear whether he expected Souday to believe this or not.

Early in May, 1922, there were difficulties with the mail at the Rue Hamelin. The concierge's daughter had measles or whooping cough or both, and Proust refused to touch letters that the concierge delivered until they had been soaked for two hours in a solution of formaldehyde. But the letters were not always entirely legible at the end of the two hours, and awkward confusions developed. One night, for example, Proust waited in vain at the Ritz for two English friends who had just arrived in Paris; when he got home and looked at their letter again he discovered that they were waiting for him at Foyot's. A second appointment was arranged, but this time, just before he left the house, Proust fortified himself with what proved to be undiluted adrenalin. Immediately seized with violent abdominal pains, he writhed and groaned for several hours before he was able to go out. That night he returned home completely shattered. Feverish, unable to eat anything but ices, and quite convinced that his stomach was ulcerated, he remained for some days under the care of his doctor. Meanwhile the presentation copies of *Sodome II* could neither be inscribed nor sent out.

Reviews of the book began to appear, Souday's on May 12 being one of the first. Though not nearly so damning as the year before, Souday was perhaps even more irritating. He managed to complain about the length of the volumes, the grammatical— or typographical—errors, and the occasional vulgarities of the Baron de Charlus, and he managed to touch on the theme of inversion without either naming it or showing the slightest enthusiasm. "It is very daring," he said, "and basically without much interest, but pointless rather than really shocking." Proust, who had after all recently fed the critic and who might therefore have expected a little more consideration, was definitely annoyed. He wrote out a long parody of the review, concerned chiefly with the remarks on grammar, and sent it to Souday. The two men do not seem to have communicated again.

Proust was equally annoyed with Boulenger, who ignored the book as he had ignored its predecessor, this time at least because he was afraid to mention, even in a review, the subject of inversion. After pointing out, in an otherwise friendly letter, that *Opinion* might at least have avoided saying, as it once did say, that all his characters were tainted with shameful vices, Proust apparently wrote off Boulenger as he had written off Souday.

Henceforth he communicated with the editor of *Opinion* only when he had to and then indirectly, through another friend on the paper.

The reaction of Souday and Boulenger was, however, exceptional. Few other critics were intimidated by the theme of inversion, and at least three of them, writing in perfectly respectable journals—Patin in *Le Figaro*, Vandérem in *La Revue de France*, and Bidou in *La Revue de Paris*—gave the book the very highest praise. Patin touched on its morality, Vandérem on its remarkable analysis of inverts, at once playful and tender, and Bidou on the wonderful realism of the characters and the narrative. Society people were equally enthusiastic, or so Proust apparently discovered on one of his excursions into the outside world. The response of the women impressed him as particularly gratifying. "Either they don't understand what they read," he once remarked, "or perhaps they have looked about and assured themselves that the proportion of people tainted with 'shameful vices' is just a little bit greater in society than in my books."

Of the letters of congratulation that Proust received, the most moving was perhaps one from his old friend Madame Straus. She was obviously fascinated by the homosexual passages, and indeed she was reading *Sodome* even more eagerly than she had read the *Jeunes filles* and *Guermantes*. "I take up the book," she reported, "I cut the pages and I tell myself: I am going to read for a quarter of an hour, and at the end of that time . . . I am still reading . . . I keep on reading. The servant tells me that dinner is ready, I say: 'I am coming' . . . and I read on. The servant comes timidly back and stays . . . so, disturbed by his presence, I go downstairs. After dinner we go up again, and quite unobtrusively, with an air of innocence, I pick up the precious book. . . . Marcel, my dear Marcel," she added, "how I should like to see you! It seems to me that we should have so much to say to each other! but it would be both too amusing . . . and too sad, and I am afraid it will never happen again. *Never*." Madame Straus was right, the end was approaching both for herself and her protégé of other years. They were destined never to meet again.

The letter Proust received from Madame Hayman, another old friend though long since estranged, was quite different from

Madame Straus's. For Madame Hayman now seemed to discover, either by herself or by talking with more discerning readers, that she was in the book and had in fact played a prominent part in the earlier volumes under the name of Odette de Crécy. Her letter was an angry one. Replying as he had replied to Montesquiou, but more directly since the issue was more directly raised, and more irritably, Proust specifically said that he had never used living models for his characters except in matters of detail. As far as Odette was concerned, he had used, for her *salon*, the favorite flowers of a certain aristocratic hostess, and for her appearance in the Bois, the dress and walk of a courtesan named Closmenil. But he had never used anything connected with Madame Hayman.

"Odette de Crécy not only isn't you," he said, "but is exactly the opposite of you. It seems to me that every time she speaks, this is perfectly apparent. . . . You tell me . . . that your 'cage' is like Odette's. I am very much surprised by this. You have exquisite and daring taste! If I wanted to find out the name of a piece of furniture or a kind of material I should much rather ask you than any artist I could think of. Now, very unskillfully perhaps, but to the best of my ability, I have tried to show that Odette, unlike you, had no more taste in furniture than in anything else, and that she was always (except in dress) a generation behind the times. I wouldn't know how to describe your apartment on the Avenue du Trocadéro, or your house on the Rue La Pérouse, but I remember them as just the opposite of Odette's house[1]. . . . Society people have no idea what a literary work is, unless they happen to be exceptional. But I remember you as being really exceptional. Your letter has completely disillusioned me."

Despite this little encounter with Madame Hayman, and the earlier ones with Souday and Boulenger, Proust had got through successfully what he had feared would be a difficult stage in the publication of his novel. He had treated the subject of inversion

1. In this particular Proust may have been telling the truth. The principal model for Odette's house is said to have been "les Talus," at No. 9 Boulevard Lannes, a house built by an American dentist named Evans for his mistress, Méry Laurent.

without losing either his reputation or his public. The book was selling remarkably well, and he was inclined to feel that if it could be pushed a little, it might sell even better. Noticing in the newspaper *Eve* that his friend Morand's *Ouvert la nuit* was advertised as "Not to be read by young girls," Proust immediately instructed the N. R. F. to arrange a similar advertisement. This time his publishers actually took the necessary steps, and in the course of time the advertisement duly appeared: "Not to be read by young girls: *Sodome et Gomorrhe*."

CHAPTER XXVII

The End

I

.FIVE PARTS of the novel were now out of the way, but three very substantial parts remained. For the time being Proust could not work very much because he was still suffering from his experience with undiluted adrenalin and still living on beer and ices, fetched by Odilon from the Ritz. The diet was not especially nourishing and had other disadvantages; it was expensive and so chilling that it tended to give Proust sore throats. But by the beginning of June, 1922, he got around to more solid meals again and got back to work on his manuscript. He was revising the next two parts— *La Prisonnière*, already typed, and its successor, tentatively called *La Fugitive*. One of his first additions, presumably, was a passage on ices, concerned in particular with the kind served at the Ritz.

During the two or three years that he had lived at the Rue Hamelin, Proust's habits had changed ever so slightly. His health had become a little more brittle and his treatments correspondingly more resolute. He took rather more sleeping pills and had adrenalin injections rather more often. His sensitivity to chills was greater and his apartment, or at least his bedroom, was hotter, so that he himself was now inclined to describe it as a Turkish bath. Since his secretary had left, he spent rather more time with Céleste and Odilon, talking with them when he felt the need for companionship late at night and even giving them little lessons in French history. But work still formed a substantial part of his routine. Sometimes he felt that he could afford to work at a leisurely pace, since his public, still digesting the three formidable volumes of *Sodome II*, would not immediately be ready to continue the story. At other times, acutely aware of imperfections in his current draft, he felt harried and pressed. There was, after all, so much to do and he could scarcely believe that he had very much time left. When he finished *La Prisonnière*, he began going over it again from the beginning and puzzling over his own manuscript changes, which were not always entirely legible.

Periodically, as in other years, the routine was broken by visits from friends and excursions outside and heated controversies with his publishers, who from time to time were still guilty of intolerable derelictions. The friends Proust received as before: willingly and warmly if they still interested him, coolly if he was now inclined to feel that they were not quite worthy of an eminent man of letters. Thus he was very glad to receive the Prince Antoine Bibesco, who was returning from a diplomatic post in America and who brought news about the reception of the novel on another continent. The news was in one particular disquieting, for it seems that a certain Pierre de Lanux, once secretary of the N. R. F., had been so injudicious as to mention in print the N. R. F.'s original rejection of *Du Côté de chez Swann*. Proust complained to his publishers about this and other matters—complained until Gide was forced to tell him that he was shockingly ungrateful.

Glad to see Bibesco, Proust was by no means so glad to see Lucien Daudet, for he was now bored by this friend of other years. His manner betrayed his feelings, and indeed he warmed up only once during the visit, when he was reminded of a little ivory box he had given Daudet many years before. "My God!" he exclaimed. "You mean to say you still have the box! It must be terribly ugly. Isn't there something nicer here I can give you?" For the moment he seemed almost affectionate, but he immediately froze again and began talking about one of his new friends, a man whom Daudet could not endure. "Likes and dislikes can't be transmitted," Proust remarked impersonally; "that is the great tragedy of friendships and relationships generally." As he got up to go, Daudet leaned over the bed and tried to kiss his friend on the cheek. "I haven't shaved," Proust said, drawing back. Daudet seized one of the hands lying limp on the covers and kissed it. He left with tears in his eyes.

Proust's excursions outside were generally confined to the Ritz, but twice at least he went farther afield—on June 12 to a soirée at Madame Hennessy's and on July 15 to a fashionable new restaurant, the Boeuf sur le Toit. The soirée attracted him because it offered him another chance to see crowds of people, and indeed he saw many fashionable, or once fashionable, friends like Boni de Castellane. But on the whole he was somewhat disappointed because he could not help noticing that the gathering was by no means one of Madame Hennessy's best. Nevertheless he thanked her, by writing out and sending her a fragment of conversation he had overheard in the course of the evening—the silly chatter of two society women who were curious about him but under the impression that his name was Marcel Prévost.

The excursion to the Boeuf sur le Toit turned out to be more sensational, if not perhaps quite so instructive. Proust went with two friends who had been or could be useful—Paul Brach, editor of a small magazine, and Edmond Jaloux, novelist and critic, who had not yet reviewed *Sodome II*. While they were eating dinner, a man almost dead drunk staggered up to the table and made jocular remarks about Proust who, even in midsummer, was inevitably wearing his fur coat. Proust wanted to appoint seconds at once and did not apparently give up the idea until the next day, when he received a satisfactory letter of apology. "I was hopeful," he replied to his prospective antagonist, alluding to the moment when the altercation had taken place, "I was hopeful . . . because I foresaw an opportunity for what I was once so fond of and what my health does not now prevent me from indulging in: a duel." He was naturally disappointed, but not as far as Jaloux was concerned, for the critic finally published, in *L'Eclair*, an altogether favorable study of the novel.

In the month that followed the dinner at the Boeuf sur le Toit, Proust's routine was occasionally broken, as before, by visits and excursions, by controversies with the N. R. F., and by negotiations that held out the promise of extra money or more striking publicity. For a while he was very much interested in pushing two favorable articles—Jean Schlumberger's "Une nouvelle 'Comédie humaine,'" which had appeared in *Le Figaro*, and Camille Vettard's "Proust et Einstein," which had appeared in the N. R. F. He arranged echoes or persuaded his publishers to arrange them—often a difficult task since he was dealing with men who, he felt, completely lacked vision. "Up to the present time," he told them, "all the publicity we have had has come from me, in articles by my friends and readers. Now as far as publicity is concerned, when I am not quite so ill as I have been the last two days we must go over the whole matter together. But, without waiting for that, you should immediately buy space in the 'Revue des journaux' of *L'Action française* for an extract of the Schlumberger article (and without showing that the request comes from me). It is quite possible that in the meantime I may get it automatically myself through friends I have there." Still the main thing was to get the space, even if it involved disclosing that he himself was directing the publicity campaign.

Meanwhile he was trying to make up his mind whether or not to sell the manuscript and corrected proofs of *Sodome II*, for which he had been offered 7,000 francs. It was certainly a good offer, perhaps a little too good. He was half inclined to sell but for somewhat less, say 5,000. "But what makes me hesitate," he told a friend, "is that the collections of this person are going to be left to the state. Now it is not very pleasant to think that anyone who wants to (assuming that people are still interested in my books) will be permitted to examine my manuscripts, to compare them with the definitive text, to draw inferences that will always be quite wrong about my way of working, about the evolution of my thought, etc. All this disturbs me a little and I ask myself whether I shouldn't cut down my absurd and pointless expenses by 5 or 7,000 francs instead of committing this posthumous indiscretion."

Further reflection convinced him that he should not be indiscreet and that he should at all costs prevent posterity from prying into his manuscripts. He therefore rejected the offer, and furthermore rejected another offer of 10,000 francs, this one because the prospective purchaser was a man he liked. But instead of cutting down his expenses, he sold another long extract to *Oeuvres libres*. The N. R. F. fulminated again, and Proust fulminated at the N. R. F. which, he now seemed to discover, was sanctioning an English translation with such preposterously inaccurate titles as *Swann's Way* and *Remembrance of Things Past*. "I shall certainly not let *Du Côté de chez Swann* appear under the title you mention," he told his English informant. "I knew nothing about this translation. I should have known about it. But you can't imagine how completely impossible it is for me to take care of anything. Furthermore Gallimard is (he doesn't say where but I know he is in Vendée) and Rivière is in Bordelais. Nevertheless I am going to telegraph them this very day to express my indignation."

II

The routine at home went on into September, and then suddenly —just as Proust hired a typist again and began preparing the copy for *Oeuvres libres*—all his old complaints returned in accentuated forms. His asthma was very bad, worse at times than it had ever been in his whole life. His dizzy spells made walking hazardous; sometimes he could not even get out of bed without falling. His speech was thick and difficult; his eyesight seemed impaired. He was half inclined to think that he was dying, unless perhaps—the idea finally occurred to him—unless perhaps he was being poisoned by carbon monoxide in the room. Investigation established that there were cracks in the chimney, and his doctor seemed to agree that the poisoning was a possibility. But giving up fires was by no means easy for a man who had lived so long in stifling heat.

It was afterwards said that the worse Proust got the more

feverishly he worked, and he certainly wanted to work. His books now seemed to him the one important thing in the world. He was inclined to compare the solicitude he felt for them with that of the fossorial wasp for its eggs. Actually, however, he was not able to do very much, even after doses of adrenalin and caffeine. He put off making the selection for *Oeuvres libres* and he was barely able to get together two short extracts for Rivière (those subsequently published by the N. R. F. as "La Regarder dormir" and "Mes réveils"). Most of the time he rested, as indeed he had to. The few friends he was able to see usually found him lying on his back, with his eyes closed and his hands crossed over his chest. Papers, pens, newspapers, notebooks, and medicines surrounded and even covered him; letters disappeared and got lost somewhere in the tumble of sheets and blankets. Very late at night or in the early hours of the morning he was sometimes able to get dressed, stagger to the elevator, and go out. The fresh air seemed bracing and he was a little more inclined to believe that the chimney was the source of his trouble. Still, when he got home, he could detect no permanent improvement. "I can no longer walk, or speak, or think," he once told his publishers, "and I am never free from pain." At the end of September his doctor told him that he would have to expect a long period of convalescence.

Early in October Proust caught cold after one of his excursions, but Dr. Bize, whom he consulted, was not unduly alarmed. He recommended nothing more than rest and a normal diet. A few days later Proust went out again but this time was obliged to return almost at once. He felt so ill that, instead of going to bed, he stretched out on a couch and lay there until he was thoroughly chilled. Céleste helped treat his asthma and wanted to build a fire but, for obvious reasons, he refused to let her. She noticed that he kept sneezing in an unusual way and that for the time being he said nothing about work. Dr. Bize, who came again, now took a more serious view of the case and repeated his recommendation more urgently. But the invalid was by this time refusing to eat at all and living on beer from the Ritz, cooled in a bucket of ice at his bedside.

By the middle of October he was running a temperature, at least intermittently, and having severe coughing spells. Still in his better moments he was able to look over the proofs of "La Regarder dormir"; in a note to Rivière, taken at dictation by Céleste, he pointed out how much he disliked the way the passage ended. On October 21 he wrote Jaloux about Montesquiou's memoirs, which were obviously still worrying him. "The best thing," he said, "would be to cut out everything [about me], even my name, in case I don't survive the strange complaint I am suffering from at the moment." A few days later he received page proofs of "La Regarder dormir" and was shocked to find that the ending had not been changed. It had to be changed, there could be no doubt about that, and he told Rivière so quite peremptorily. He even wrote out rough directions for the changes he wanted, and then, in one of those moments of cruelty that invalids sometimes have, he went on to accuse Rivière of deceiving him. "I don't trust you any more," he said.

At the end of October he was delirious, but a few days afterwards he was again lucid enough to send off his manuscripts—the extract from *La Prisonnière* to *Oeuvres libres* and the notebooks of the unpublished volumes to the N. R. F. At the same time he wrote friendly and fairly long notes to both Rivière and Gallimard. "The desperate efforts I have put in on *La Prisonnière*," he said to the latter, "(it is done but needs rereading—the best thing would be for you to get the first proofs and I will correct them), these efforts have made it impossible for me, especially in my dreadful condition these days, to do anything with the following volumes. But three days of rest might be enough." When he was shown an acknowledgment from Duvernois, editor of *Oeuvres libres*, he wrote still another note, probably the last to an outsider. "As to the 'novel,'" he said, "since there is nothing left do anything you want with it or throw it into the fire. I am not surprised that my crazy instructions were quite unintelligible. . . . If I have another good hour, I am going to ask my friend Robert de Flers to spare me 'After a long and painful illness courageously borne,' which would in any case be quite untrue because this one has nothing to do with what went before. Anyway I still think I am going to pull through. But in that case, which I prefer all the same, the convalescence I am promised makes me shudder. My dear friend, don't answer me. . . . From now on don't expect anything from me but silence, imitate mine."

In his last days he seems to have made at least intermittent efforts to keep his doctor away, but whether this was clear-sightedness or delirium, whether he knew that he had pneumonia and objected to having his agony prolonged, or whether he was merely expressing a feverish and instinctive desire to get back to his old routine, it would be difficult to say. Once he had a full-scale quarrel with his brother, who wanted to send him to a hospital, and once at least he made Céleste promise that she would not let anyone into the room—anyone, that is, who would try to keep him from working. Still he was reluctant to offend Bize, and so, as a conciliatory gesture, he ordered flowers for him. "Well, Céleste," he said when the flowers had been sent off, "that's another thing settled if ever I come to die." Somber subjects seem to have been recurrent in his conversation. He told Céleste exactly what she was to do if the worst came to the worst (put a rosary in his hands and wire the Abbé Mugnier) and he once said that he would want to die if he thought he would find his mother in another world. When he felt unable to talk, he wrote notes asking Céleste for a few drops of port, or a dish of stewed pears, or an apricot or a peach from the Ritz. "I've just coughed a thousand times or more," he said in one note, "and I have no back or stomach or anything left. It's really incredible. I just have to have very warm sheets and woolen sweaters. Be sure you remember that. All your sheets have a pungent smell and so quite unnecessarily I get coughing fits. I hope you are going to follow my instructions exactly, if not I shall be more than angry."

On November 17 he felt somewhat better and was quite cheerful when he talked with his brother and Céleste. He was sure that the next few days would be the critical ones, and he offered to eat something fairly substantial if Céleste really felt that he should. That night he proposed to work a little and actually dictated what have been described as supplementary notes on the death of Bergotte. After reading them over (or so it would seem, for he made a correction on one of the sheets) he asked

Céleste to see that they were inserted in their proper place.

At six on the morning of November 18 he asked for coffee or milk and seemed annoyed that Céleste was still in the room with him. At ten he asked for beer—Odilon was despatched to the Ritz. After remarking that the beer, like everything else, would probably arrive too late, he suddenly raised one arm and pointed at a figure he seemed to see near the door—a hideous black woman. "Céleste! Céleste," he cried. "She is so fat and so black; she is entirely black! She frightens me." Céleste offered to chase the woman away, but Proust stopped her. "You must not touch her, Céleste," he said. Odilon returned with bottles of beer just as Dr. Proust and Dr. Bize, who had been surreptitiously summoned by Céleste, came in to give the invalid an injection. Proust showed his displeasure by ignoring Bize and warmly thanking Odilon. As the injection was administered, he protested by pinching Céleste's arms and whispering, "Oh, Céleste, why?" Other treatments followed but none seemed to help. "I move you rather a lot, little one," Dr. Proust said as he lifted the dying man on to the pillows; "I hurt you." "Yes, my dear Robert," Proust whispered. He never spoke again. Late in the afternoon he died, quietly, without stirring, his eyes wide open.

That evening the news spread rapidly by telephone and *pneumatique*. Friends were informed by Dr. Proust or Céleste or Hahn, and many of them went to the apartment on the Rue Hamelin. They entered the dismal bedroom and saw by candlelight the thin, pale, bearded face, looking younger than they remembered it, as the face of Madame Proust had looked younger in death many years before. Jaloux noticed greenish shadows about the features, like the shadows that play about corpses in Spanish paintings; Gregh noticed the slight hump on the nose, the one that had worried Proust so much when he was a young man; Lucien Daudet later seemed to notice a smile on the lips, a distinctly happy smile. A younger friend, Porel, slipped on one of the dead man's fingers a treasured memento, the ring that Anatole France had given Madame Réjane on the first night of *Le Lys rouge*. At Dr. Proust's suggestion several painters and photographers were invited to record their impressions of that thin, bearded face.

Bibliographical Note

"LA REGARDER DORMIR" and "Mes réveils," the excerpts from *La Prisonnière* that Proust worked on in his last illness, came out in November, 1922, the very month in which he died. The whole of *La Prisonnière*—advertised as edited by Proust's brother and Jacques Rivière—followed in 1923; *La Fugitive*, or *Albertine disparue* as it was called, in 1925; and *Le Temps retrouvé*, the final novel in the series that makes up *A la Recherche du temps perdu*, in 1927. *Chroniques*, also published in 1927, was a volume of Proust's miscellaneous pieces, many of which had originally appeared in *Le Figaro*. Thus in the five years that followed his death, four books—seven volumes altogether— were added to the list of Proust's works.

A generation later investigation of his papers turned up material for four more volumes: the three volumes of *Jean Santeuil*, published in 1952, and the single volume of *Contre Sainte-Beuve*, published in 1954. It is at least possible that more manuscripts remain to be discovered and that the whole of Proust's work is not yet in print.

The first volume of Proust's letters, those to Louis de Robert, appeared in 1925, and similar volumes have been pouring from the presses ever since. Dozens of correspondents and hundreds of letters are involved; in the course of time Proust may well turn out to have been an even more prolific letter writer than Madame de Sévigné or Horace Walpole. Professor Philip Kolb has already devoted a very substantial volume to the dating of the letters, and more work of the same sort remains to be done.

Books of memoirs and articles containing biographical information about Proust have also come out in considerable numbers. Of the books, the early ones by the Duchesse de Clermont-Tonnerre (*Robert de Montesquiou et Marcel Proust*, 1925), Robert Dreyfus (*Souvenirs sur Marcel Proust*, 1926), and Robert de Billy (*Marcel Proust. Lettres et conversations*, 1930) are still among the best. Of scholarly articles, first place must be given to Robert Vigneron's "Genesis of 'Swann' " (published in French in *La Revue d'histoire de la philosophie*, January 15, 1937, in English in *Partisan Review*, November-December, 1941, and subsequently in *The Partisan Reader*, 1946). There are three biographies—those by Léon Pierre-Quint (1925), Derrick Leon (1940), and André Maurois (1949)—and there are sketches of Proust's life in other books, for example Harold March's *The Two Worlds of Marcel Proust* (1948).

Nearly all of Proust's own work is now available in English but under titles that Proust objected to or would certainly have objected to if he had lived. *A la Recherche du temps perdu* is oddly—for Proust had no idea of alluding to Shakespeare—*Remembrance of Things Past*. *A l'Ombre des jeunes filles en fleurs* is *Within a Budding Grove*, *Sodome et Gomorrhe* is *Cities of the Plain*, and *Albertine disparue*—perhaps the oddest of all because it sounds so very Victorian —is *The Sweet Cheat Gone*. (See Walter De la Mare's poem "The Ghost," in which the final line is "The sweet cheat gone.") Much of the material in *Pastiches et mélanges* and *Chroniques* has been translated in the volumes *Marcel Proust, a Selection from His Miscellaneous Writings* and *Pleasures and Days and Other Writings*.

The biographies of Pierre-Quint and Maurois have appeared in English, and so too have some of the letters, selected and translated by Mina Curtiss. There are even a few volumes of letters translated complete, those to Lauris, to the Bibescos, and to Madame Proust being the most interesting. There is a handbook to the novel, by P. A. Spalding, and there are several books of interpretation and criticism, most of them very much concerned—rather too much, I feel— with Proust's thought. There is even a book about Proust criticism— Douglas W. Alden's *Marcel Proust and His French Critics* (1940).

The student of Proust will thus find a great deal of material in English, but there are many things that, unfortunately, he will not find. First in order of importance is the Pléiade edition of Proust's novel, with variants from the proof sheets and manuscripts (1954), an edition that can really be described as indispensable. Then there are the letters, a great many volumes of them, and finally there is Albert Feuillerat's *Comment Marcel Proust a composé son roman*, still, I think, the most valuable single book on the novel. It is one of the oddities of American publishing that this book, brought out by the Yale University Press in 1934, is still available only in French.

My own account of Proust is based chiefly on his letters, on articles and volumes of memoirs written by his friends, and on contemporary newspapers and magazines. The last of these sources is much the easiest to describe. I have generally used *Le Figaro* for public events (the Dreyfus Case, the Charity Bazaar fire, the World War, etc.) and *Le Figaro* and the Paris edition of *The New York Herald* for society news (parties attended or given by Proust and his friends). I have used other papers for reviews, announcements of books, publicity, etc.

Without attempting anything like a complete bibliography, I can perhaps list some of the books and articles on which I have relied for the different periods of Proust's life.

1871-1890: Early years (Chapters I to II).

Letters to his father and mother (*Correspondance avec sa mère,* 1953), to his grandmother (*Lettres à Mme C[atusse]*, 1946), and to Robert Dreyfus (*Souvenirs sur Marcel Proust* and *Correspondance générale,* Volume IV, 1933). Memoirs by Robert Dreyfus, Daniel Halévy (*Pays parisiens*, 1932), Jeanne Pouquet (*Le Salon de Madame Arman de Caillavet,* 1926).

1891-1906: Years of the early works (Chapters III to X).

Letters to his mother, Robert de Billy (*Marcel Proust. Lettres et conversations*), Antoine Bibesco (*Lettres de Marcel Proust à Bibesco,* 1949), Reynaldo Hahn (1956), Montesquiou (*Correspondance générale,* Volume I, 1930), Marie Nordlinger (*Lettres à une amie,* 1942), Louisa de Mornand (*Correspondance générale,* Volume V, 1935), Madame Emile Straus (*Correspondance générale,* Volume VI, 1936).

Memoirs of Billy, Fernand Gregh (*Hommage à Marcel Proust,* 1927, and *L'Age d'or,* 1947), Lucien Daudet (*Autour de soixante lettres de Marcel Proust,* 1929), Duchesse de Clermont-Tonnerre (*Robert de Montesquiou et Marcel Proust*), Antoine Bibesco (*Cornhill Magazine,* Summer, 1950), Marie Nordlinger-Riefstahl (*London Magazine,* August, 1954).

1907-1914: Years during which A la Recherche du temps perdu was written (Chapters XI to XVI).

Letters to Hahn, Madame Straus, Madame Catusse, Lucien Daudet, Georges de Lauris (*A un ami,* 1948), André Gide (1949), Louis de Robert (*Comment débuta Marcel Proust,* 1925), René Blum (Léon Pierre-Quint, *Comment parut "Du Côté de chez Swann,"* 1930), Jean-Louis Vaudoyer (*Correspondance générale,* Volume IV). Memoirs by Gaston Gallimard and others (*Hommage à Marcel Proust*), Marie Scheikévitch (*Time Past,* 1935), Céline Cottin (interview in *Figaro littéraire*, September 25, 1954), Lauris (*Souvenirs d'une belle époque*, 1948).

1915-1922: Years during which *A la Recherche du temps perdu* was revised and enlarged (Chapters XVII to XXVII).

Letters to Madame Straus, Madame Catusse, Lucien Daudet, René Blum, Gaston Gallimard (*Lettres à la NRF*, 1932), Jacques Rivière (1955), Princesse Soutzo (Paul Morand, *Le Visiteur du soir*, 1949), Sydney Schiff, Paul Souday, Jacques Boulenger, Jacques-Emile Blanche (all collected in *Correspondance générale*, Volume III, 1932), Walter Berry (*Correspondance générale*, Volume V, 1935), Maria de Madrazo (*Bulletin de la société des amis de Marcel Proust*, 1953), Duc de Guiche and Madame Jean Hennessy (Princesse Bibesco, *Le Voyageur voilé*, 1949), Comtesse de Chevigné (Princesse Bibesco, *La Duchesse de Guermantes: Laure de Sade, Comtesse de Chevigné*, 1950).

Memoirs by Paul Morand (*Journal d'un attaché d'ambassade*, 1949), Marie Scheikévitch, André Gide (*Journals*, Volume II, 1948), Henri Bardac (*Carrefour*, April 28, 1948, and *Revue de Paris*, September, 1948, and August, 1949), Jacques Porel (*Fils de Réjane*, 1951), Céleste Albaret (interviews in *London Mercury*, April, 1938, and *Nouvelles littéraires*, November 20, 1952), Emmanuel Berl (*Sylvia*, 1952), Maurice Sachs (*Le Sabbat*, 1946), Harold Nicolson (*Peacemaking, 1919*, 1933).

Chronological Table

1871	July 10	Marcel Proust born.
1873		Brother, Robert Proust, born.
1880		First attack of asthma.
1882		Enters Lycée Condorcet.
1889		*Baccalauréat.*
	November	Enters the army.
1890	January 2	Grandmother, Madame Nathé Weil, dies.
	November	Leaves the army and enters the university.
1892	March-July	First pieces in *Le Banquet.*
	August	Trouville.
1893	April (?)	Meets Montesquiou.
	August-September	Saint-Moritz and Trouville.
	July-December	Pieces in *La Revue blanche.*
	October 10	Degree in Law.
1894	May 30	Montesquiou's party for Delafosse.
1895	March	Degree in Philosophy.
	May 28	*Portraits de peintres* given at Madame Lemaire's.
	June 29	Appointed to the staff of the Mazarine Library.
	July-October	Kreuznach, Dieppe, Beg-Meil.

	December 24	Granted leave from the Mazarine Library.
1896	May 10	Great-uncle, Louis Weil, dies.
	June	*Les Plaisirs et les jours* published.
	June 30	Grandfather, Nathé Weil, dies.
	September	Finishes the first notebook of *Jean Santeuil*.
	October	Fontainebleau.
1897	February 5	Duel with Lorrain.
	May 24	Dinner for Montesquiou, Anatole France, Rod, etc.
1898	January	Gathers signatures for a Revisionist petition.
	July	Mother operated on.
1899	April 24 (?)	Dinner for Montesquiou, Anatole France, Madame de Noailles, etc.
	Autumn	Evian.
1900	January 27	Obituary notice on Ruskin in *La Chronique des arts et de la curiosité*.
	February 13	"Pèlerinages ruskiniens en France" in *Le Figaro*.
	April-August	Articles on Ruskin in *Le Mercure de France* and *La Gazette des beaux-arts*.
	May	Venice and Padua.
	October (?)	Prousts move to 45 Rue de Courcelles.
1901	June 19	Dinner for Anatole France, etc.
1902	October	Belgium and Holland.
1903	February 2	Dr. Robert Proust married.
	February 25	"Un Salon historique," the first of the *salon* articles in *Le Figaro*.
	February-March	Excerpts from the translation of *The Bible of Amiens* in *La Renaissance latine*.
	September	Evian.
	November 26	Father dies.
1904	February (?)	Translation of *The Bible of Amiens* published.

1905	March 6	Tea with music by Hahn and the Comtesse de Guerne.
	March-May	Translation of "Of Kings' Treasuries" in *Les Arts de la vie*.
	June 2	Montesquiou's reading.
	June 15	"Sur la Lecture" in *La Renaissance latine*.
	September	Evian.
	September 26	Mother dies.
	December	Enters Dr. Sollier's nursing home.
1906	January	Leaves the nursing home.
	May	Translation of *Sesame and Lilies* published.
	August-December	Versailles.
	December	Moves in at 102 Boulevard Haussmann.
1907	February 1	"Sentiments filiaux d'un parricide" in *Le Figaro*.
	March 20	"Journées de lecture" in *Le Figaro*.
	July 1	Dinner for Calmette at the Ritz.
	August-September	Cabourg.
	November 19	"Impressions de route en automobile" in *Le Figaro*.
1908	February-March	Parodies on the Lemoine case in *Le Figaro*.
	February	Tells Madame Straus he wants to get started on a long work.
	July-November	Cabourg and Versailles.
	December (?)	Asks for advice about his essay on Sainte-Beuve.
1909	May	Asks Lauris about the name Guermantes.
	August	Tells Madame Straus he has just begun and finished a long book.
1910	Summer	Novel rejected by *Le Figaro*. Bedroom lined with cork.
1911	Summer	Novel being typed.
1912	(?)	Agostinelli takes over the typing.
	March-September	Excerpts from the novel in *Le Figaro*.
	November-December	Novel rejected by the N. R. F. and Fasquelle.

1913	February	Novel rejected by Ollendorff.
	March	Novel accepted by Grasset.
	November 12	Interview in *Le Temps*.
	November 14	*Du Côté de chez Swann* published.
1914	May 30	Agostinelli dies.
	June-July	Excerpts from *Le Côté de Guermantes* in the *N. R. F.*
	August-October (?)	Cabourg.
1915	November	Summarizes the Albertine story in Madame Scheikévitch's copy of *Swann*.
1916	August	Shifts from Grasset to the N. R. F.
1917	March 4	Meets the Princesse Soutzo.
1919	June	Moves to 8 bis Rue Laurent-Pichat. "Légère esquisse du chagrin que cause une séparation et des progrès irréguliers de l'oubli" in *N. R. F.* A *l'Ombre des jeunes filles en fleurs* and *Pastiches et mélanges* published; *Du Côté de chez Swann* reissued.
	October	Moves to 44 Rue Hamelin.
	December 10	A *l'Ombre des jeunes filles en fleurs* wins the Goncourt Prize.
1920	September	Awarded the Legion of Honor.
	September 30	Attends the meeting of the Blumenthal Foundation at which Rivière wins the Blumenthal prize.
	October	*Le Côté de Guermantes I* published.
1921	May	Gide article on Proust in the *N. R. F.* *Le Côté de Guermantes II, Sodome et Gomorrhe I* published. Visits the Vermeer and Ingres exhibitions.
	November	"Jalousie" in *Oeuvres libres*.
	December 11	Montesquiou dies.
1922	May 1	*Sodome et Gomorrhe II* published.
	May 2	Proust's accident with adrenalin.
	November 18	Death.

Index

ABOUT THE AUTHOR

Richard H. Barker, who now teaches at Brooklyn College, was educated at Stanford University and received his Ph. D. at Columbia. A Rhodes Scholar, he read Philosophy, Politics, and Economics at Oxford University. He has previously published books on Colley Cibber and Thomas Middleton. Marcel Proust: A Biography *grew out of Dr. Barker's reading of Proust; he writes: "Trying to work out the chronology of Proust's novel, I began looking over files of* Le Figaro *to check on dates and to learn something about French society in the 1890's and particularly the society that Proust himself frequented. In the course of time I realized that I was preparing myself to write a book on Proust."*